DADA AND SURREALIST FILM

DADA AND SURREALIST FILM

Edited by

Rudolf E. Kuenzli

WILLIS LOCKER & OWENS • NEW YORK

Printed in the United States of America

Published by Willis Locker & Owens
71 Thompson Street, New York, NY 10012

Library of Congress Cataloging-in-Publication Data

Main entry under title:

Dada and Surrealist Film.

   Bibliography: pp. 220–254
   1. Surrealism in motion pictures. 2. Dadaism in
motion pictures. I. Kuenzli, Rudolf Ernst, 1942-
PN 1995.9.S85D34   1987   791.43'09'091   86-27465
ISBN 0-930279-12-3 (alk. paper)
ISBN 0-930279-11-5 (pbk.: alk. paper)

COVER: Film still from René Clair's and Francis Picabia's *Entr'acte*
(1924). The Museum of Modern Art Film Stills Archive.

CONTENTS

Introduction
Rudolf E. Kuenzli

Interest in Dada and Surrealist cinema has been primarily kept alive by experimental filmmakers in America and Europe after 1945. They have found a cinematic vocabulary in these early films as well as useful strategies for their own practice of anti-commercial, art/anti-art cinema. Studies of postwar experimental or underground films therefore include introductory chapters on Dada and Surrealist film, but they necessarily emphasize those aspects that were appropriated by post-war experimental filmmakers.

A related interest in these early films stems from recent developments in film theory. The Surrealist film has become a major field for Lacanian analysis, whereas the playfulness with cinematic codes and the radical questioning of illusionist cinema in Dada films has attracted the attention of deconstructionists.

When we, however, consider the films labeled "Dada" or "Surrealist" in relation to the respective movements, we realize that these connections are highly complex. Most historians of avant-garde cinema regard Hans Richter's and Viking Eggeling's abstract films as "Dada." But in what ways are these films related to Dada? These abstract films, as well as other "Dada" and "Surrealist" films, might be discussed more productively in relation to the quite different and distinct developments of avant-garde cinema in the twenties: film as an extension of painting; film modeled on oneiric activity; the Impressionists and their concept of "photogénie"; and the Russian films.

Cubist, Futurist, Dadaist, and Constructivist painters, obsessed with capturing the sensation of physical movement in their work, saw in film a means of overcoming the static nature of painting through "moving pictures." Léopold Survage's project entitled *Le Rhythme coloré*, which he described in Apollinaire's *Les Soirées de Paris* in 1914, outlines the future direction of abstract art as cinema:

Colored Rhythm is in no way an illustration or an interpretation of a musical work. It is an art in itself, even if it is based on the same psychological facts as music.
On its analogy with music. It is the mode of succession in time which establishes the analogy between sound rhythm in music, and colored rhythm – the fulfillment of which I advocate by cinematographic means. Sound is the element of prime importance in music. . . . The fundamental element of my dynamic art is *colored visual form,* which plays a part analogous to that of sound in music.
This element is determined by three factors:
1. Visual form, to give it its proper term (abstract);
2. Rhythm, that is to say movement and the changes visual form undergoes;
3. Color.[1]

1

With the exception of the third factor, color, Survage's project announces the abstract films of Walther Ruttmann, Viking Eggeling, Hans Richter, and Henri Chomette. His insistence on abstraction and the importance of visual rhythm was realized in Richter's *Rhythmus 21, 23* and *25* (1921–25), and in Eggeling's *Diagonal Symphony* (1924), whose title underlines Survage's emphasis on the analogy with music. This cinema as abstract, kinetic art wanted to be autonomous, without reference to outside reality. Kasimir Malevich, who asked Richter to collaborate on an abstract film, therefore attacked the Russian films of Eisenstein and Vertov for serving ideology:

Art was freed by Cubism from dealing with ideological content, and it began to build up its own character. It had served its ideological master for many centuries; it had cleaned, powdered, colored its cheeks, its lips and made up its eyes. Today, it has refused to do this to the advantage of its own culture. This is the same for the cinema, which, for the moment, is another maid which needs to be liberated and made to understand. As the Cubist painters understood, paintings can exist without imagery, without everyday references, and without obvious ideology. The cinema too should think about its own identity.[2]

The relationship between Richter's and Eggeling's experiments and Dada can only be recognized if we do not ignore the dynamic tension in the Dada movement between destructive and constructive tendencies, which Marcel Janco emphasized in his essay entitled "Dada at Two Speeds."[3] The connection between Dada and Constructivism was very close in Zürich and Berlin. While participating in the "great negative work of destruction," many Dadaists sought at the same time an elementary art, that could serve as a building block for a new culture. Richter's and Eggeling's kinetic experiments attempted to produce nothing less than a universal, elemental pictorial language, a grammar and syntax of contrasting relationships between geometric forms. Their endeavor was thus closely related to Moholy-Nagy's and Klee's investigations of form at the Bauhaus.

Marcel Duchamp's experiments with optics and movement, which he began with his *Nude Descending a Staircase,* can also be considered as an extension of the static nature of painting. From 1920 to 1926, he collaborated with Man Ray on experiments that gave two-dimensional geometric designs on plates or disks the illusion of three-dimensionality through rotary movement. Among these were *Rotary Glass Plates (Precision Optics)* (1920), *Rotary Demisphere (Precision Optics)* (1925), and experiments in stereoscopic cinema. Duchamp's film *Anémic cinéma,* which he produced with the help of Man Ray and Marc Allégret in 1926, can thus be seen as an exploration of visual and verbal multi-dimensionality. Moving disks with geometric spirals regularly alternate in a slow rhythm with disks containing spirally printed puns. The rotating disks with spiral lines produce the effect of three-dimensionality, whereas the spirals of verbal puns, although appearing in motion optically flat, suggest multiple dimensions of verbal signs. The motor which rotates the disks thus transforms the different lines and words into indifference, stability into instability, decidability into indecidability. Duchamp's radical questioning of the certainty and stability of optical vision and language, which serve as the social, "scientific" guarantors of truth, is very central to Dada's critique of cultural myths of "fact" and "reality."

2

Man Ray's first film, ironically titled *Retour à la raison* (1923), is not an extension of painting, but a kinetic extension of his photographic compositions. This film, only five minutes in length, was put together in one night for Tristan Tzara's Soirée du Coeur à barbe, the last Dada manifestation in Paris, where it was shown together with Richter's *Rhythmus 21*. Man Ray made this film partly without a camera by applying his technique of the Rayograph to the film celluloid: "On some strips I sprinkled salt and pepper, like a cook preparing a roast, on other strips I threw pins and thumbtacks at random; then I turned on the white light for a second or two, as I had done for my still Rayographs."[4] Other short sequences deal with objects seemingly selected by chance, but which are related through their slow rotating motions: the turning egg crate, juxtaposed to the turning torso of a woman; the rotating merry-go-round and the turning spiral lampshade. These short sequences resemble films of sculptures. But instead of the camera turning around the object, the object rotates in front of the static camera. In addition to his *Lampshade* (1919), Man Ray included his two-dimensional painting *Dancer/Danger* (1920). Since he could not rotate it, he suggested movement by blowing billowing smoke over it. His own remarks about his filmmaking suggest that he preferred the static medium of photography to film:

All the films I made were improvisations. I did not write scenarios. It was automatic cinema. I worked alone. My intention was to put the photographic compositions that I made into motion. As far as the camera is concerned, it serves me to fix something which I do not want to paint. But it does not interest me to make "beautiful photography" in cinema. Principally, I do not like so much things that move.[5]

Retour à la raison, commissioned by Tzara, expresses through its anarchic arrangement of sequences and strips of Rayographs Tzara's Dada spirit of spontaneity and chance, which were the Dadaists' strategies to disrupt logic and rational order.

Three years after Breton and his Surrealist friends had forcefully broken up Tzara's Paris Dada at the Soirée du Coeur à barbe, Man Ray, with generous financial backing from Arthur Wheeler, attempted to make a Surrealist film in his "ciné-poème" *Emak Bakia:* "I had complied with all the principles of Surrealism: irrationality, automatism, psychological and dramatic sequences without apparent logic, and complete disregard for conventional storytelling."[6] This film is Man Ray's exploration of the camera's potential to transform the familiar world, and thus to create surreality. The opening and closing sequences suggest such an interpretation. The film opens by introducing the apparatus of transformation: a film camera rolling film and Man Ray as cameraman next to it. In the lens we see his eye upside down, since he filmed himself filming by aiming the camera at a mirror. The film ends with the following shots:

Shot of a woman's [Kiki's] face from above as she is lying down. Her eyes have a blank, artificial look.
She gets up, faces the camera, opens her eyes (what we saw before was a pair of eyes painted on the eyelids) and smiles.
She closes her eyes and returns to her former position. As she does so, a superimposition of her face with closed eyes appears upside down. It starts to rotate in the customary distorted fashion until it is the only image left on the screen.[7]

3

The two pairs of eyes (seeing the familiar world vs. "seeing" with eyes closed in dream) suggest the two different kinds of vision: reality and surreality. Throughout the film, familiar images are juxtaposed to and transformed into unfamiliar ones via cinematic manipulation and montage.[8] The film apparatus is thus presented as a means that is superbly capable of transforming the symbolic order into the imaginary. Man Ray was dumbfounded when his Surrealist friends did not greet this film with enthusiasm.[9] They probably considered *Emak Bakia* still too Dada because of Man Ray's too radical, "complete disregard of conventional storytelling," his breaking of cinematic illusion by pointing to the film as a product of the camera, and his use of abstract Rayographs.

Fernand Léger's and Dudley Murphy's *Ballet mécanique* (1924) is, according to Standish Lawder, "the classic example of a fully developed painting aesthetic transposed into film by a modern artist of major significance."[10] Although certain sequences of this film recall Man Ray's films, Léger's carefully calculated choreography of ordinary objects and actions lacks the spontaneity and chance of Man Ray's first film, and his preoccupations with surreality in his second. *Ballet mécanique* puts into motion Léger's aesthetics of his "mechanical period." The special rhythms of his paintings become sequences of precisely controlled rhythms. Everything in *Ballet mécanique* is caught in machine-like, contrasting rhythms, from the slow movement of the girl in the swing to numbers, geometric figures, machine parts, Christmas ornaments, and the washerwoman climbing stairs. Everything dances in this ballet according to calculated, changing tempos. Although Kiki of Montparnasse too opens and closes her eyes in this film, these repeated sequences do not suggest two different visions, as they do in Man Ray's *Emak Bakia*, but are used here as yet another instance of rhythmic movement, similar to her mouth breaking rhythmically into a smile.

The carefully contrasted rhythmic structures of *Ballet mécanique* and its non-narrative sequences have been regarded as a purely formal experiment. But Léger's aim was less to dazzle his viewers than to exasperate them through the repetition of mechanical motion:

In "The Woman Climbing the Stairs," I wanted to *amaze* the audience first, then make them uneasy, and then push the adventure to the point of exasperation. In order to "time" it properly, I got together a group of workers and people in the neighborhood, and I studied the effect that was *produced* on them. In eight hours I learned what I wanted to know. *Nearly all of them* reacted at about the same time. [11]

One month after the first showing of *Ballet mécanique*, Picabia presented his "instantanist" ballet *Relâche*, and during intermission René Clair's film *Entr'acte*, for which Picabia wrote the outline of the sequences. Léger, who attended the presentation, summed up the effect of the ballet and the film as "a lot of kicks in a lot of behinds, sacred or not."[12] Picabia's "Instantanist" movement was directed against Breton's group, especially the First Surrealist Manifesto, which had been published two months earlier.[13] Cinema, according to Picabia, must also become "instantanist"; it "must orient itself toward the spontaneity of invention which will always be more alive than the foolishness of a beautiful photograph."[14] Unlike Léger's fascination with non-narrative mechanical movements of objects, *Entr'acte* consists of loosely connected narrative sequences. The actors are Picabia's friends, who in 1924 were neither in Tzara's nor in Breton's camp: Marcel Duchamp, Man Ray, Eric Satie, and members of the Ballet Suédois. The ballet and film were conceived as a total performance that was meant to attack the viewers' conventions and values. In the Program for the performance Picabia wrote: "I would rather hear them shouting than applauding." At the performance, large signs taunted the audience: "If you are not satisfied, go to hell!" "Whistles are for sale at the door." The ballet opened with a "curtain raiser" in the form of a short film sequence: Picabia's and Satie's cannon shot aimed at the audience. After the first act of the ballet, the actual film *Entr'acte* was shown at intermission.

The film consists of a series of humorous gags: Picabia "hosing down" Duchamp's and Man Ray's game of chess on top of a roof; a dancing ballerina filmed from underneath, only to be revealed as a bearded man; a huntsman shooting an ostrich egg, only to be shot himself; a funeral hearse drawn by a camel, and the chase of the funeral procession after the hearse; and finally the huntsman dressed as magician climbing out of the coffin. These gags were suggested by Picabia, who wrote about the film in the Program:

Entr'acte does not believe in very much, in the pleasure of life perhaps; it believes in the pleasure of inventing, it respects nothing except the desire to *burst out laughing*.[15]

Although these gags are in the film, René Clair playfully explores the full cinematic potential of Picabia's proposed scenes by using the whole inventory of cinematic tricks and techniques: changes in tempo, superimpositions, sudden disappearances and transformations. Through Clair's montage, Picabia's illogical sequence of scenes receives an imagistic continuation. In the first part of the film, the discontinuous episodes of the chess game, the ballerina, the shooting of the ostrich egg are connected through superimposed and interjected lyric images of rooftops and buildings of Paris. The actual film (after the "curtain raiser") begins with a series of eleven different long shots of houses and roofs seen diagonally or completely upside down. The sequence of the chess game is interspersed with different shots of the columns of La Madeleine to the extent that through dissolves and superimpositions they are defamiliarized to the extent that they become a play of geometric forms. Through Clair's playful association the grid of the chessboard is repeated in the cinematographic manipulation of the columns. He even superimposes the chessboard on shots of the Place de la Concorde, thus relating the chess moves to the moving traffic. The shower of water that finishes the chess game leads to the lyrical sequence of the superimposed paper boat floating over the roofs of the city.

The chase scene, which makes up the whole second part of the film, again indicates the differences between Picabia's plans and Clair's film. Picabia's intent to lampoon the social conventions of funerals becomes for Clair a pretext to explore cinematographically movements of all kinds, and via montage to increase the tempo from slow motion to only blurs of movement. The funeral procession, which runs faster and faster after the hearse, is joined by a group of racing cyclists, speeding cars, an airplane, and a racing boat. The accelerated movement is then associated with the feeling of sitting in a roller coaster, which serves as the dominant metaphor for the chase.[16]

Although minimally connecting the illogical episodes, Clair undermines the logic of conventional narrative films through his free play of metaphoric and metonymic associations. At the end of the film, he even reveals cinema directly as an illusion-producing apparatus. The huntsman emerges from the coffin in the guise of a magician who, through the waving of his wand, makes the coffin, the members of the funeral procession, and himself disappear. The word "End" appears on the screen. Suddenly a man in slow motion jumps through the "film screen," thus breaking the illusion of Georges Méliès's magic and Mack Sennett's chase scenes, which Clair quoted in this film. In this sense, *Entr'acte* constantly undermines and explodes not only social conventions, but also the logic and norms of conventional filmmaking.

One month after the opening performance of *Relâche* and *Entr'acte*, Picabia and Clair collaborated on a ballet entitled *Cinésketch*, which indicates the pervasive influence of cinema even on the ballet. The stage was divided into three equal sections, in which actors performed simultaneously. The lightbeam focussed on one section, then cut over to another, thus achieving a rough equivalent of montage in film. "Until the present," Picabia commented, "the cinema has been inspired by the theater. I have tried to do the contrary in bringing to the stage the method and lively rhythms of the cinema."[17]

Hans Richter's film *Filmstudie* (1926), which was first shown in Paris at the Studio des Ursulines together with Man Ray's *Emak Bakia*, explores, similarly to Man Ray's film, but in a much more structured and lyrical rhythm, the cinematic metamorphosis of objects. Suspended heads change into eyes, eyes into moons, moons into peas, peas into rain, rain into waves, and waves into heads. Richter was surprised when his film was called "Surrealist" at its first performance, since he did not even know then what Surrealism was.[18] The film was based on an actual dream, and Richter's *Filmstudie* creates the illusion of a dream sequence, in which images are transformed into other images. His next film, *Vormittagsspuk* (Ghosts Before Breakfast, 1928) recalls the sequence of the flying collars in *Emak Bakia*. Richter describes the film in the following way:

Four bowler hats, some coffeecups and neckties "have enough" (are fed-up) and revolt from 11:50 to 12 A.M. Then they take up their routine again. (Darius Milhaud and Hindemith are actors in the film; the original score was composed by Hindemith, but later destroyed by the Nazis). The chase of the rebellious "Untertanen" (objects are also people) threads the story. It is interrupted by strange interludes of pursuit which exploit the ability of the camera to overcome gravity, to use space and time completely freed from natural laws. The impossible becomes reality and reality, as we know, is only one of the possible forms of the universe.[19]

In *Vormittagsspuk* and his other films of the late twenties—*Inflation* (1927–28), *Rennsymphonie* (1928–29), *Zweigroschenzauber* (1928–29), and *Alles dreht sich, alles bewegt sich* (1929), Richter's aim is to create lyrical, playful "film-poetry," which presents the illogical world of imagination.

6

With the exception of Richter's and Eggeling's films, all other Dada-related films were made in Paris, where a network of ciné-clubs provided possibilities for showing these works. The Berlin Dadaists did not produce any films, although "Dada Monteur" John Heartfield had worked in a film studio in 1917. Instead of films, the Berlin Dadaists developed the collage and photomontage to produce simultaneous, disparate, multiple images, that attempted to catch the dynamics of chaotic movement.[20] Raoul Hausmann even called his photomontages "static films."[21] He titled his first photomontage "Synthetic Cinema of Painting" (1918), and a later one "Dada-Cinema" (1920). George Grosz's and John Heartfield's *Life and Action at Universal City at 12:05 Noon* (1919) clearly relates their montage of film-related photographs to cinematic montage. Photomontage served Berlin Dadaists as a chief means for their political activities. By literally cutting up and rearranging the reality produced by mass media, the Dadaists exposed that reality as illusion. A Berlin Dada film would thus have consisted of a montage of carefully chosen cuttings from existing popular films and newsreels, and thus would have made visible their ideology.

Dada-related films have several characteristics in common: they disrupt the viewers' expectations of a conventional narrative, their belief in film as presenting reality, and their desire to identify with characters in the film. Dada films are radically non-narrative, non-psychological; they are highly self-referential by constantly pointing to the film apparatus as an illusion-producing machine. Through their cinematic defamiliarization of social reality, they attempt to undermine the norms and codes of social conventions, and thus of conventional filmmaking, which has as its goal to reproduce that conventionality.

While the relationship between Dada and film has remained largely unexplored, a series of studies have examined the connection between Surrealism and film. In 1925, Jean Goudal expressed the Surrealists' enthusiasm and hope for film to become *the* ideal means for the realization of surreality, of the marvellous:

The cinema . . . constitutes a conscious hallucination, and utilizes this fusion of dream and consciousness which Surrealism would like to see realized in the literary domain. . . . Not only does the application of Surrealist ideas to the cinema avoid the objection with which you can charge literary Surrealism, but that surreality presents a domain actually indicated to cinema by its very technique. . . . It is time cinéastes saw clearly what profits they may gain in opening up their art to the unexplored regions of the dream. . . . They should lose no time in imbuing their productions with the three essential characteristics of the dream: the *visual*, the *illogical*, the *pervasive*.[23]

Twenty-five years after the publication of Goudal's essay, Breton stated with regret that the Surrealists had only made "parsimonious use" of cinema.[23] Recent commentators on Surrealist film tend to agree with Breton's assessment. For Marguerite Bonnet, "the whole history of Surrealism's relation with cinema is, in reality, that of a great hope betrayed,"[24] and for Alain and Odette Virmaux, it was "a failed convergence."[25] These critics only include two or three films as truly Surrealist: certainly Luis Buñuel's and Salvador Dalí's *Un Chien andalou* (1929) and *L'Age d'or* (1930), and either Man Ray's

L'Étoile de mer (1928) or Antonin Artaud's and Germaine Dulac's *La Coquille et le clergyman* (1928). Critics who have argued for a much richer relationship between Surrealism and film have tended to emphasize the second wave of Surrealism in film after 1945; they point to Surrealist aspects in commercial films, and they emphasize the great impact of cinema on Surrealist writing.[26]

Breton, who had "never known anything more magnetizing" than cinema, made surprisingly few references to film in his writings. In recalling the Surrealists' fascination with film in the twenties, Georges Sadoul wrote: "So intransigent in all domains (even in regard to food and tourism), Surrealism did not, properly speaking, have a cinematic doctrine."[27]

In reading Breton's, Desnos's, and Buñuel's writings on film, we realize that the Surrealists had two quite different notions regarding film and the activities of the Surrealist spectator: popular films demanded an active viewer, whereas truly Surrealist films posited a passive spectator. In his recollection of the days with Jacques Vaché in Nantes during the war, Breton wrote:

I never began by consulting the amusement pages to find out what film might chance to be the best, nor did I find out the time the film was to begin. I agreed wholeheartedly with Jacques Vaché in appreciating nothing so much as dropping into the cinema when whatever was playing was playing, at any point in the show, and leaving at the first hint of boredom – of surfeit – to rush off to another cinema where we behaved in the same way and so on (obviously this practice would be too much of a luxury today). I have never known anything more *magnetizing:* it goes without saying that more often than not we left our seats without even knowing the title of the film which was of no importance to us anyway. On a Sunday several hours sufficed to exhaust all that Nantes could offer us: the important thing is that one came out "charged" for a few days.[28]

The film that Breton saw on a given Sunday was a montage that he himself made of sequences of several films which, probably because of the incongruous juxtapositions, charged him for a few days. Man Ray similarly felt the need to actively transform ordinary films through his device of special movie glasses:

I go to the cinema without choosing the programs, without even looking at the posters. I go into the cinemas which have comfortable seats.... I invented a system of prisms which I glued on my glasses: thus I could see black-and-white films which bored me in color and as abstract images.[29]

The Surrealists used films as material, as sparks for their own oneiric activities. Their favorite films were the very popular serials: *Fantômas, Les Vampires, Les Mystères de New York,* as well as American films by Charlie Chaplin, Mack Sennett, and Buster Keaton. They absolutely rejected the avant-garde films of the Impressionists (Louis Delluc, Marcel L'Herbier, Jean Epstein), who attempted to create a pure cinematic art. The Surrealists liked popular films precisely because they were not part of bourgeois art, but a new anti-art medium. "Modernity," according to Salvador Dalí," does not mean . . . Fritz Lang's *Metropolis,* but a hockey pullover of anonymous English manufacture; it also means comedy film, also anonymous, of the silly nonsense type."[30]

Charged and inspired by viewing films, the Surrealists began to write cinematically. As early as 1917, Soupault wrote "cinematographic poems," in which he used filmic devices (metamorphoses of objects, sudden disappearances, abrupt changes). The fluidity of Breton's and Soupault's *Les Champs magnétiques* (1921) is certainly related to the flowing images in cinema. Even Breton's chief device for achieving surreality through the juxtaposition of unrelated images of objects and ideas ("Beautiful as the chance encounter of a sewing machine and an umbrella on a dissecting table") seems to be derived from filmic montage of images.

Although the Surrealists loved popular films, they seem to have been primarily interested in the cinematic devices. Their own illogical writings and film scenarios could hardly be used as outlines for sequels like *Fantômas*. Their own film scripts and writings on cinema rather called for a new genre of films that would reproduce the world of dreams. In 1923, Robert Desnos wrote:

I should like a film director to take a fancy to this idea. In the morning after a nightmare, let him note exactly all he remembers and let him reconstruct it with exact care. It would no longer be a matter of logic, of classic construction, or of flattering the incomprehension of the public, but of things seen, of a higher reality, since it opens a new domain to poetry and to dreaming.[31]

Of the numerous Surrealist film scenarios, only very few were made into movies. The reason for the small number of films was probably due to the complexity of filmmaking. The members of the Surrealist movement were primarily writers and painters, and not filmmakers. They must have soon realized that making a film and distributing it was more complicated and above all much more expensive than writing and publishing a book. "So long as the movie-maker's capital sets the fashion," wrote Walter Benjamin, "as a rule no other revolutionary merit can be accredited to today's film than the promotion of a revolutionary criticism of traditional concepts of art."[32]

A few Surrealist film scenarios were, however, made into films: Desnos's "L'Etoile de mer," Artaud's "La Coquille et le clergyman," and Dalí's and Buñuel's collaborative scripts. While the viewing of popular films incited the Surrealist spectator to actively transform these "readerly" films into "writerly" ones (Breton's and Vaché's cinema-hopping in Nantes, Man Ray's special glasses), the truly Surrealist films put the viewer in a passive role, since their montage of incongruous sequences aimed at breaking open the spectator's unconscious drives and obsessions. Cinematographic techniques were thus only a means to disrupt the symbolic order, and to let the unconscious erupt. Buñuel therefore violently reacted to critics who aestheticized and thus rendered impotent his *Un Chien andalou:*

A *successful film,* that is what the majority of the people who have seen it think. But what can I do against the devotees of all forms of novelty, even if the novelty outrages their deepest convictions; against a press that has been bribed or is insincere; against the imbecile crowd that found *beautiful* or poetic something which was, basically, but a desperate, passionate call to murder?[33]

In order to rupture the symbolic order, these Surrealist films rely on characters, on narratives, on optically realistic effects which hook the viewer into the world portrayed by the film. Only through the viewer's identification with the familiar world invoked by the film can the film's sequential disruptions of that invoked familiar world have the potential to disrupt the viewer's symbolic order and open up the suppressed unconscious drives and obsessions. Unlike Dada films, Surrealist movies do not use slow motion, they do not present the images produced by the cinematic apparatus as yet another illusion. The cinematic apparatus is used by Surrealist filmmakers as a powerful means to realistically portray the symbolic order, which they then disrupt with shocking, terrifying images.

The difference between Dada and Surrealist films thus lies in their different strategies of defamiliarizing social reality. Surrealist filmmakers largely rely on conventional cinematography (narratives, optical realism, characters) as a means to draw the viewer into the reality produced by the film. The incoherent, non-narrative, illogical nature of Dada films, which constantly defamiliarize the familiar world through cinematic manipulations, never let the viewer enter the world of the film.[34] A distance is thus created between viewer and film from the beginning, which accounts for the viewer not being deeply disturbed by these films.

The essays in the present collection provide important new contributions to the already existing studies of Dada and Surrealist films. Since no general studies of Dada films are available, Thomas Elsaesser's essay on "Dada/ Cinema?" presents the central aspects regarding the relationship between Dada and film. In his essay on "Exploring the Discursive Field of the Surrealist Scenario Text," Richard Abel analyzes Surrealist film scripts within the broader context of writing and film in the twenties. The studies of Peter Christensen on Benjamin Fondane and David Wills on Robert Desnos provide particular analyses of these writers' concepts of film. Linda Williams examines in her essay the different critical approaches that have been used in discussing Surrealist film. The other essays in this collection present new research and challenging analyses of major Dada and Surrealist films of the period between 1924 and 1932.

The "Documents" section contains a photographic reproduction of Robert Desnos's scenario "L'Etoile de mer," which was believed to have been lost, and which is published here for the first time. Inez Hedges transcribed and translated the scenario. Her introduction focuses on the new insight we gain into Robert Desnos's and Man Ray's collaboration on *L'Etoile de mer* through the discovery of this scenario. Our thanks to Janis Ekdahl and Michel Fraenkel for giving their permission to publish Robert Desnos's scenario.

I would like to thank Michael Newton for his generous editorial assistance, Judith Pendleton for her artistic sense, and June Fischer for her excellent typing.

Notes

1. Léopold Survage, "Le Rhythme coloré," *Les Soirées de Paris* 26–27 (July–August 1914): 426–27; quoted from Standish D. Lawder, *The Cubist Cinema* (New York: New York University Press, 1975), 22.

2. Kasimir Malevich, "And They Fashioned Jubilant Faces on the Screen," *A. R. K. Kino* 10 (1925); quoted from Patrick de Haas, "Cinema: The Manipulation of Materials," in *Dada-Constructivism* (London: Annely Juda Fine Arts, 1984), 53–54.

3. Marcel Janco, "Dada at Two Speeds," in Lucy Lippard, ed. *Dadas on Art* (Englewood Cliffs, N.J.: Prentice-Hall, 1971), 36–38.

4. Man Ray, *Self-Portrait* (Boston: Little, Brown, 1963), 260.

5. See "Témoignages," *Surréalisme et cinéma,* ed. Yves Kovacs. Special issue of *Etudes cinématographiques* 38–39 (1965): 43.

6. *Self-Portrait,* 274.

7. Steven Kovács, "Shot Analysis of *Emak Bakia,*" in his *From Enchantment to Rage: The Story of Surrealist Cinema* (London and Toronto: Associated University Presses, 1980), 266.

8. See Mimi White, "Two French Dada Films: *Entr'acte* and *Emak Bakia,*" *Dada/Surrealism* 13 (1984): 42–47.

9. Man Ray probably misunderstood the Surrealists' coolness towards *Emak Bakia,* when he thought that it "was due to my not having first discussed the project with them beforehand . . . . It was not sufficient to call a work Surrealist, as some outsiders had done to gain attention – one had to collaborate closely and obtain a stamp of approval." *Self-Portrait,* 274.

10. *The Cubist Cinema,* 65.

11. Fernand Léger, "Ballet mécanique," in his *Functions of Painting,* trans. Alexandra Anderson, ed. Edward F. Fry (New York: Viking Press, 1965), 51.

12. Fernand Léger, "Vive 'Relâche,'" *Paris-Midi* 17 Dec. 1924: 4.

13. In answer to Breton's manifesto, Picabia wrote: "André Breton is not a revolutionary . . . he is an arriviste . . . he has nothing to say; having no sensitivity, never having lived, this artist is the type of petit bourgeois who loves little collections of paintings. . . ." See "Poissons volants," *L'Ere nouvelle* 24 Nov. 1924: 3; quoted from William Camfield, *Francis Picabia* (Princeton: Princeton University Press, 1979), 208.

14. "Instantanéisme," *Comoedia* 21 Nov. 1924: 4.

15. "Programme de *Relâche,*" in *La Danse* (November 1924); rpt. in Francis Picabia, *Ecrits* (Paris: Belfond, 1978), II, 167.

16. See Steven Kovács' analysis of *Entr'acte* in his *From Enchantment to Rage,* 65–113.

17. Paul Archad, "Picabia m'a dit . . . avant 'Cinésketch' au Théâtre des Champs-Elisées," *Le Siècle* 1 January 1925: 4; quoted from Camfield, *Francis Picabia,* 213.

18. See Hans Richter, "Ma première rencontre avec le surréalisme . . . ," in *Surréalisme et cinéma,* ed. Yves Kovacs, 55–56.

19. Hans Richter, "Dada and Film," in *Dada: Monograph of a Movement,* ed. Willy Verkauf (New York: St. Martin's Press, 1975), 42–43.

20. See Hanne Bergius, "Zur Wahrnehmung und Wahrnehmungskritik im Berliner Dadaismus," *Sprache im technischen Zeitalter* 55 (1975): 234–55; and Anton Kaes, "Verfremdung als Verfahren: Film und Dada," in *Sinn aus Unsinn: Dada International,* ed. W. Paulsen and H. Hermann (Bern: Francke, 1982), 71–83.

21. Raoul Hausmann, "Photomontage," in his *Am Anfang war Dada,* ed. Karl Riha and Günther Kämpf (Giessen: Anabas Verlag, 1980), 50.

22. Jean Goudal, "Surréalisme et cinéma" (1925), transl. in *The Shadow and Its Shadow,* ed. Paul Hammond (London: British Film Institute, 1978), 52–54.

23. André Breton, "Comme dans un bois," *L'Age du cinéma* 4–5 (1951): 26–30; transl. in *The Shadow and Its Shadow*, 42–45.

24. Marguerite Bonnet, "L'Aube du surréalisme et le cinéma: attente et rencontres," in *Surréalisme et cinéma,* ed. Yves Kovacs, 83.

25. Alain and Odette Virmaux, *Les Surréalistes et le cinéma* (Paris: Seghers, 1976), 31.

26. See J. H. Matthews, *Surrealism and Film* (Ann Arbor: University of Michigan Press, 1971), and his *Surrealism and American Feature Film* (Boston: Twayne, 1979); Michael Gould, *Surrealism and Cinema* (Cranbury, N.J.: A. S. Barnes, 1976); and Ado Kyrou, *Le Surréalisme au cinéma* (Paris: Editions Arcanes, 1953).

27. Georges Sadoul, "Souvenirs d'un témoin," in *Surréalisme et cinéma,* ed. Yves Kovacs, 14.

28. André Breton, "Comme dans un bois," in *The Shadow and Its Shadow,* 42–43.

29. Man Ray, "Tous les films que j'ai réalisés . . .," in *Surréalisme et cinéma,* ed. Yves Kovacs, 45.

30. Salvador Dalí, "Poesia de l'útil standardizat" (1928), in *Oui 1. La révolution para noïaque-critique* (Paris: Denoël/Gonthier, 1971), 66.

31. Robert Desnos, "Le Rêve et le cinéma," *Paris-Journal* 27 April 1923; quoted from J. H. Matthews, *Surrealism and Film,* 27.

32. Walter Benjamin, "The Work of Art in the Age of Mechanical Reproduction," in his *Illuminations,* trans. Harry Zohn, ed. Hannah Arendt (New York: Schocken, 1969), 231.

33. *La Révolution surréaliste* 15 Dec. 1929; quoted from J. H. Matthews, *Surrealism and Film,* 91.

34. It is due to this distance, which abstraction or radical defamiliarization creates between films and viewers, that the Surrealists were not enthusiastic about Man Ray's *Emak Bakia,* and that Artaud rejected abstract film as an error, when he stated: "One can only be unmoved by purely geometric lines." ("Cinéma et réalité," *Nouvelle Revue Française* 170 [1927]).

Dada/Cinema?

Thomas Elsaesser

Cinema – An Invention without Origin or Use?

There is something altogether appropriate about the fact, noted by film historians,[1] that the cinema has no origin other than the multiplicity of chemical, technical, optical, and scientific discoveries and devices which made possible the first public showings around 1896. It cautions anyone looking at cinema history not to imbue it with an ontology or to ascribe to its development a particularly stringent logic.

We tend to forget, for instance, how many of the decisive discoveries or applications were, in fact, "byproduct[s] of other more urgent concerns"[2] and the workings of "objective chance." Such is the case of Marey's chronophotography, which its inventor hoped would facilitate medical research into cardiac and vascular diseases. The desire of analyzing movement needs to be distinguished from the ability of reproducing it mechanically. The development of mechanical aids for drawing, for portraiture, and for achieving likeness can be shown to antedate photography and the cinema, but they are clearly crucial to an understanding of the ideology of self-representation which has marked the cinema as a social institution. On the other hand, the will to record, classify, collect, describe, observe, and analyze, which Michel Foucault sees as characteristic of the eighteenth and nineteenth centuries, has left its mark on many of the early uses of photography and the cinema with its tributary inventions benefited from the need for precision instruments to satisfy the scientific rage for order. "Physiology applied to the field of optics"[3] is one way of designating the probing, investigative urge underpinning the cinema, but it does not fully explain why and how the desire for the di-visible became the fascination for the visible. If we owe the cinema to certain advances in the applied technologies – the same, it has been remarked, that produced the sewing machine and the telegraph tape – it is nonetheless true that the desire for the cinema, for the perfect reproduction of appearance and vision, existed well before the machinery of its realization had been assembled.

Dada and the Cinema

The cinema, displaying a flagrant (and ironic) discrepancy between the bricolage of its mechanical, optical, chemical processes on the one hand, and the homogeneity, unity, illusory cohesion of its effects on the other, would seem to be a quintessentially Dada artifact – a contention which conversely might suggest that Dada artifacts are quintessentially nineteenth-century technological fantasies.

The combination Dada/cinema is thus interlaced with the more general history of inventions and apparati, and with the crises provoked in the arts when it became impossible to separate technology from technique or scientific from artistic experiment. The explosive development of new means of representation and reproduction towards the end of the nineteenth century, indicating for the first time that aesthetic effects can be attributed to machine-made objects or images, had profoundly ruptured a traditional relation between art and mimesis. It had also cruelly exposed the delicate relationship between crafted object and art object in respect to labor, skill, and value.

Two aspects are worth singling out. One is to look, especially in the context of Germany and Berlin Dada, at the forms of spectatorship and pleasure that might be associated not so much with watching Dada films but watching films as Dada. The second point concerns the kinds of reflection which the cinema as total apparatus—psychic, economic, erotic—occasioned among the avant-garde and Dadaists in particular, as a model or metaphor for representing the relation of body to social environment, or even for conceptualizing the art-work as event, rather than as object, no longer as products but as circuits of exchange for different energies and intensities, for the different aggregate states matter can be subjected to between substance and sign through an act of transposition, assemblage, division, and intermittence. The cinema, in other words, between photo-montage and meta-mechanics.

Unlike "Surrealism and Cinema," on which one can consult volumes, the subject "Dada and Film" has not entered into the histories of the movement, nor into film history as a distinct entity. Apart from a short, mainly autobiographical essay by Hans Richter in Willy Verkauf's monograph,[4] references to Dada films have until a few years ago only turned up in histories of avant-garde cinema, experimental or abstract film.[5] The focus of these accounts tends to sever the examples from their Dada connections and to annex them as the precursors of a tradition either of graphic or structuralist cinema. Dada films thus appear briefly in the prehistory of the New American Cinema, but the connections seem rather tenuous compared, again, to the profound influence of Surrealism on the American film avant-garde.

The problems of talking about Dada film are twofold. Firstly, the question of attribution and contribution. Should one resist calling *Ballet mécanique* a Dada film, because Léger is usually considered a Cubist? Hans Richter did not think so:

Though Léger was never a Dadaist, his *Ballet mécanique* is 100% Dada.[6]

Do Francis Picabia's disagreements with the Paris Dadaists disqualify *Entr'acte*? We know that the ballet *Relâche*, for which Picabia and René Clair conceived *Entr'acte*, was in part a protest against Breton's takeover of the Surrealist movement.[7] By a reverse logic, should Hans Richter's *Rhythm 21* and *Rhythm 23* be discussed as Dada films because Richter makes a case for Dada art as abstract art? Candidly, he himself admitted:

After I have stated this fact "Dada equals abstract art" I happily wish to insist on the other point, "Dada equals non-abstract art." And this is also true if not truer.[8]

Ambiguity of one form or another surrounds most other potential candidates. Duchamp's *Anémic cinéma* is usually called a Dada film, with which Duchamp would presumably not have quarreled, if he had not baulked at calling it a film at all, preferring to see it as part of his "precision optics."[9] In Man Ray's case, we have *Retour à la raison*, first performed at the famous "Soirée du Coeur à barbe" in July 1923, an occasion which signaled the break-up of Paris Dada. Man Ray considered his subsequent two films *Emak Bakia* and *L'Etoile de mer* to be Surrealist films. Hans Richter calls his own *Film-studie* "rather more surrealist."[10] This only leaves two or three short films by Richter: *Ghosts before Breakfast* and *Two-Penny Magic* as uncontested Dada films.

The second problem is chronology. If one takes a generous view, one can start with 1920, the year Richter and Eggeling applied for facilities and funds to the UFA Film Company in order to carry out work which resulted in *Rhythm 21, Rhythm 23*, and *Diagonal Symphony*. In the same year Duchamp and Man Ray conducted the first and almost lethal experiments with revolving glass discs and 3-D stereotypes, out of which grew *Rotating Demisphere* and *Anémic cinéma*. It is not until 1923 that *Retour à la raison* appears, and in 1924, *Entr'acte. Ballet mécanique* follows in 1925, and in 1926 comes Hans Richter's *Filmstudie*, Man Ray's *Emak Bakia*, and Duchamp's *Anémic cinéma*. Finally, in 1927 Richter completes *Ghosts before Breakfast* and *Two-Penny Magic*, and in 1928 Man Ray's *L'Etoile de mer* is shown. No chronology of Dada stretches that far.

The reasons for the sparse and late appearance of Dada films are in part financial and in part geographical. There was little commercial interest in either Richter's or Eggeling's work, even though it was sponsored by the powerful UFA Studio, which successfully marketed other types of animation film (Walther Ruttmann's or Lotte Reiniger's). *Entr'acte* was specifically commissioned, and Man Ray's films were made with money from a wealthy expatriate, Arthur Wheeler, who had tried to persuade Man Ray at one stage to become a professional film-maker, with his backing. During the 1920s, France was more receptive to experiments in the cinema, not least because the flourishing ciné-club movement gave film-makers an outlet and a form of distribution, however marginal in relation to the commercial cinema.[11] In Germany, by contrast, the artistic avant-gardes were quite hostile to the cinema during most of the 1910s and early 1920s mainly for political reasons: Germany had a very powerful and successful commercial film industry, and only the arrival of the "Russenfilme" sparked off practical interest in an "alternative cinema."[12] There was, in consequence, less of a viable exhibition system for experimental shorts produced outside the film industry.

One of the few times that one can talk of a Dada film soirée occurred in May, 1925, in Berlin, when Eggeling's *Diagonal Symphony*, Richter's *Film is Rhythm* (the two Rhythm films spliced together) Ruttmann's *Opus I, II* and *IV*, Léger's and Murphy's *Ballet mécanique*, Picabia's and Clair's *Entr'acte*, as well as three films by Moholy-Nagy (made at the Bauhaus) were screened together.[13]

More recent literature has in contrast stressed the ways in which Dada techniques or practices were inherently "cinematic." Anton Kaes, in an article on "Verfremdung als Verfahren: Film und Dada,"[14] argues that the cinema suggested to the Dadaists the need to represent "the hectic acceleration of life," and in particular, he compares Hans Richter's work with the "Cinematism" in painting (Balla's famous *Dog on a Leash*), with "Fotodinamismo" and the multiple-exposure studies popular among not only avantgarde photographers in the early teens.[15] But more important for Kaes is the fact that a revolutionary conception of cinema has in common with Dada the principle of montage "because it problematizes the relationship between object of perception and the subject of perception. Montage does not allow for a coherent perspective in which the subject is in control."[16] Kaes quotes Franz Kafka and Thomas Mann to indicate that even the commercial cinema caused an experience of shock to its earliest spectators.

This approach goes beyond the more traditional histories of avant-garde movements, where Dada or Surrealist films are simply searched for examples of techniques already familiar from the literary or visual productions. Kaes can point to a potential area of research, where historical investigations of Dada converge with questions of current film theory, once more interested in the ideas about spectatorship first formulated by Siegfried Kracauer and Walter Benjamin, and recently given a more explicitly psychoanalytical turn.[17]

The Tyranny of the Eye

The general shift from an environment experienced through all the senses to one increasingly dominated by the eye and obeying its control undoubtedly forms part of both the history of the cinema and of Dada. The confusion of active and passive roles under the rule of spectacle is well caught in a poem by George Grosz: "I am like a film-strip and like a child in a thousand luna parks . . . someone is always cranking the handle."[18]

In this sense, the cinema is indeed that "phenomenon par exellence which has to be traced along the minute cracks and fault-lines that run through late Victorian society in Europe."[19] It is the expression of a sensibility excited by motion, by the means of locomotion, relishing dioramas and panoramas, flocking to world fairs, crowding into the Crystal Palace and climbing the Eiffel Tower. The need for physical mobility, spatial displacement, for the bird's eye view and for being driven or carried along precede the cinema at the same time as these pleasures were significantly transformed, realized, and interpreted by the cinema. Their social dimension leads one inevitably to demographic facts: for the cinema is unthinkable without the big cities. Perhaps the best guide through its prehistory is Benjamin's Baudelaire. In order to understand the changes in perception forced upon people living in the cities as well as for intimating the implications of those changes, Benjamin constructed a Baudelaire who serves him as a poetic "precision instrument" to trace those very fault-lines. The poem about wandering the suburbs at daybreak like a fencer thrusting and parrying imaginary blows suggests to Benjamin that Baudelaire reacted to "ennui," the spectre of specular fascination and voyeuristic control, by a new involvement of the body in the very act of writing, modeled on the experience of fighting one's way through crowded streets and public places:

The meaning of the hidden configuration (which reveals the beauty of that stanza to its very depth) probably is this: it is the phantom crowd of the words, the fragments, the beginnings of lines from which the poet, in the deserted streets, wrests the poetic booty.[20]

However fanciful this reading may be to a Baudelaire scholar, Benjamin isolates an important aspect of Dada technique: a reaction to, as well as an exploitation of the tyranny of total vision which invaded the early decades of the century. When characterizing the (to him ambiguous) contribution made by Dada to avant-garde art, in his essay on the "Work of Art in the Age of Mechanical Reproduction," Benjamin sees Dada objects replacing one kind of spectatorship (contemplation) with what he calls "a new tactility":

In the decline of middle-class society, contemplation became a school for asocial behavior; it was countered by distraction as a variant of social conduct . . . . From an alluring appearance . . . the work of art of the Dadaists became an instrument of ballistics. It hit the spectator like a bullet, it happened to him, thus acquiring a tactile quality.[21]

One might compare this negation of contemplation to Duchamp's categorical demand to destroy the "retinal" aspect of painting, and thus to counteract the supremacy of the eye. Whereas the Russian post-revolutionary avant-garde abandoned painting and turned to film and photography, Duchamp and other Dadaists on the whole rejected the cinema, not least because, even in its avant-garde forms, it seemed too close to the synesthesia of the Impressionists and the advocates of the Gesamtkunstwerk. That the difference in political situation between East and West played its part is accurately perceived by Benjamin:

Dadaism . . . sacrificed the market values which are so characteristic of the cinema in favor of higher ambitions. . . . The Dadaists attached much less importance to the sales value of their work than to its uselessness for contemplative immersion. The studied degradation of their material was not the least of their means to achieve this uselessness.[22]

Dadaism in many of its manifestations was reactive, seeking ways of radically short-circuiting the means by which art objects acquire financial, social, and spiritual values. Thus, while from the point of view of the material base, the cinema seemed an art of waste-products, and its conditions of reception were anything but auratic, the very popularity of films meant that the cinema soon represented tremendous financial, and with it, social value. This paradox marked the Dadaists' involvement from the start: the cinema seemed initially anti-contemplative as an entertainment, and at least Benjamin saw in its visual forms an element of tactility; but it soon acquired its own aura: that of glamor and total specular entrancement. It is therefore perhaps not surprising that interest of some Dadaists focused in the first instance on the behavior of the crowds, the character of a happening, and the "degraded" nature of film spectacle, parodying subversively the theater and the concert hall. A certain physicality and body-presence of the first cinema audiences is what might be called the Dada element in film.

"Das Kino"

While few theorists today would be very satisfied with drawing a dividing line between Meliès and Lumière when it comes to establishing an opposition between "realism" and "fiction" or documentary and fantasy, there has recently been a great deal of interest and controversy around the possibility of distinguishing between so-called "primitive cinema" (up to 1917) and "classical narrative cinema" on the basis of different types of spectatorship. Alongside oppositions such as commercial versus avant-garde cinema, illusionist versus materialist film, historians have speculated on the kind of involvement and participation elicited by early cinema. In one of the most interesting formulations, Noel Burch contrasts two kinds of Imaginary underpinning different practices: the "Edisonian" (a fascination with the apparatus of cinema in view of a total simulacrum of life, and the "analytical" one, aiming to break down movement into smaller and smaller particles.[23] Both seem relevant to Dada, whose interest in the cinema was in some sense a nostalgic one, attached to the film performance of the 1910s and the figure of the inventor-bricoleur. What remains problematic about both the generic distinction and the definition of a filmic avant-garde in the context of early cinema is that we still know very little about the actual viewing experience during the period in question.

In a typical program, say in Berlin in 1913 (but surviving in the suburbs well into the early 1920s), non-narrative films would be mixed with sketches and fantasies. The Kaiser (or Hindenburg) would be shown on parade right after a filmed variety number. The items would be introduced, a lecturer would stand at the back of the room or hall and comment sarcastically or pathetically on the action, explain, or provide the kind of epic distance that Brecht, copying from the cinema, tried to create in his theater. There was little sense of "illusionism" or any suspension of disbelief.

Skepticism and sarcasm mingled freely with wonder and amazement. The viewing experience seemed, as it were, embedded in drinking and furtive sex, and if it was "structured," it derived this structure from the ambience of the event as much as from the films. "Das Kino" or "Kintopp" was characterized by its communality of reception on the one hand, and its discontinuous flow on the other. Here is an early testimony of a film-show in Berlin:

The room is darkened. Suddenly the Ganges floats into view, palms, the temple of the Brahmins appears. A silent family drama rages with bon vivants, a masquerade – a gun is pulled. Jealousy inflamed. Mr. Piefke duels headlessly and they show us, step by step, mountaineers climbing the steep, demanding paths. The paths lead down through forests, they twist and climb the threatening cliff. The view into the depths is enlivened by cows and potatoes. And into the darkened room – into my very eye – flutters that, that . . . oh, dreadful! One after the other! Then the arc lamp hissingly announces the end, lights! And we push ourselves into the open . . . horny and yawning.[24]

Van Hoddis's response is to the total environment, of which the film is only one part. The interest in early cinema on the part of today's theorists like Noel Burch resides in the fact that the so-called "codes of representation" have not yet become hierarchized and subjected to certain "laws" whose ideology a later (film-)avant-garde was to deconstruct. This hierarchy is above all one organized around the dominance of the look; it becomes the distinguishing mark of the cinematic watershed between "primitive" and "Griffithian" film-making. To quote from an article by Pascal Bonitzer:

The look in Griffith was not something that had been there since the beginning of the cinema. There was, first of all, the 20 years during which the cinema was content merely to be the object of viewing, recording phenomena and movements and the sights of the world. When today we see these early films . . . we are seeing the varied fruits of a cinematic Eden where the coldness and sophistication of the look had not yet penetrated. . . . A cinema where the only currency was that of gesture, where the viewers' eyes are functioning but not looking. According to Edgar Morin . . . it wasn't until 1915–1920 that the gesticulation typical of actors gave way to a degree of immobility. This is the turning point represented by Griffith. . . . What we have here is a cinematic revolution. With the arrival of montage, the close-up, immobile actors, the look (and its corollary – the banishment of histrionics) an entire façade of the cinema seemed to disappear and be lost forever, in a word, all the excrement of vaudeville. . . . The cinema was innocent and dirty, it was to become obsessional and fetishistic. The obscenity did not disappear . . . it passed into the register of desire.[25]

As Bonitzer goes on to show, it is the look circulating within the fiction that, inducing desire, produces narratives, which are in turn based on subjecting to a more or less rigid logic the articulation of cinematic space and sequence. And as Bonitzer also remarks, it is the German Expressionist cinema which for the first time systematically exploited the look as the cinematic signifier par exellence. The introduction of the look into the film diegesis thus constitutes the end point of a development, the final cornerstone of the edifice of control and containment which has governed the development of mainstream cinema. If I claimed that Dada spectatorship is nostalgic, it is perhaps because the presence or absence of the charged look as the agent and motivator of both continuity and discontinuity, of sequence and cut distinguishes Surrealist interest in *film* (consider the importance of the eye and of point of view in *Un Chien andalou*) from Dada interest in *cinema*.

Not the Film, But the Performance Is Dada

What was Dada in regard to cinema was not a specific film, but the performance, not a specific set of techniques or textual organization, but the spectacle. One might argue that in order for a film to have been Dada it need not be made by a Dadaist, or conversely, that there were no Dada films outside the events in which they figured. "What is a Dada film?" would resolve itself into the question *"When* was a film Dada?" This gives a special place to the screening of *Entr'acte* as part of *Relâche* (as opposed to its cinema première a year later at the Studio des Ursulines), and to the Soirée du Coeur à barbe. At a time when the cinema had become itself a thoroughly respectable (and "institutionalized"} form of entertainment, both film text and viewing context had to combine in order to defamiliarize the occasion, in order to recapture the cinema's "excremental" age of scandalously guilty innocence.

Entr'acte works hard at "deconstructing" what had already become set as the conventions of the feature film and the cinema experience. It mocks the solemnity of state-occasions as they might have been presented in contemporary newsreel. By its satirical look at funerals, parades, and photo features from the world of arts, entertainment and leisure, *Entr'acte* explodes the conventions of the newsreel in forms themselves borrowed from the cinema (American slapstick, the Keystone Cops, for instance), and thus could be considered as being in turn part of a filmic genre – that of parody, were it not for the event for which it was conceived.

Picabia and Satie had wanted the audience to whom *Entr'acte* was shown during the intermission of the ballet *Relâche* to provide their own "musical" accompaniment by the mumbling, scraping, protesting, guffawing and general noise to be expected during an intermission. To their disappointment the spectators remained respectfully in their seats, silent, staring at the screen. The projection failed to ignite into a Dada performance.[26]

This incident, I think, is symptomatic of a problem that made film a less than perfect medium at Dada events. For the conditions of a reception in the cinema – the dark room, the stable rectangle of the screen, the fixed voyeuristic position of the spectator – all counteract not only the sense of provocation, but they also compensate for the absence of a coherent diegesis and for the non-narrative organization in the filmed material. Under normal viewing conditions, that is, in a movie theatre and not as part of a performance aspiring to the condition of the happening, Dada films such as *Entr'acte, Ballet mécanique,* or Hans Richter's works are almost inescapably contained, unified and finally recuperated in a way that the classic examples of Surrealist cinema are less vulnerable to, for reasons which have mainly to do with the fact that Surrealist films so closely mimic the figurative operations of narrative cinema, and compensate for the ruptures of their time-space continuum by a massive investment in the on-screen and off-screen look, which lures the spectator into the play of projection, fetish, and identification described by Bonitzer as typical for illusionist cinema.

"Geist" and "Stoff"

Film technology confers on even the most banal object the aura of erotic presence. The scandal resides in the cinema bypassing aesthetics while at the same time providing a source of aesthetic appeal. It opened an old wound in German literary culture – the debate about "form" and "material" ("Geist" and "Stoff"). The very achievement of classical literature (no less than of Romantic art) had been the suppression of materiality, its total transfiguration into "form." What for some writers categorically excluded the cinema from being art ("in the cinema, the material substance is preserved in its crude factuality, whereas in drama the material is wholly consumed and transformed by form, of which the main agent is language"[27]), was for others the cinema's chief claim to attention: that it could produce emotion of an aesthetic kind out of pure materiality. Thomas Mann recognized the same dilemma when in 1928, after seeing the first film version of his novel *Die Buddenbrooks,* he wrote:

A pair of lovers, both young and beautiful, who in a real garden with billowing grass say goodbye "forever" . . . who could resist, who would not enjoy letting it all pour out. This is pure material, not transformed by anything.[28]

Mann concluded from this that it was pointless to try to apply to cinema the criteria developed by classical aesthetics. Sixteen years earlier, Georg Lukacs had already warned against solving the problem in this fashion:

. . . something new and beautiful has developed in recent times, but instead of taking it as it is, people are attempting to classify it. . . . The cinema is regarded either as an instrument of education or as a cheap substitute for the theater; either didactic or economic. Few people if any remember that something beautiful belongs first and foremost to the realm of beauty and its definition and evaluation is properly a task for aesthetics.

Lukacs, in other words, recognized clearly that the cinema posed a challenge to classical aesthetics which had to be answered, and not as Mann was to suggest, by merely relegating it to the side of "life" as opposed to "art." Lukacs goes on:

The images of the cinema . . . possess a life of a completely different kind [from those on the stage]; in one word, they become – fantastic. But the fantastic is not the opposite to living, it is another aspect of life: life without presence, without fate, without causality, without motivation; a life with which the core of our being will never be identical, nor can it be; and even if it – often – yearns for this kind of life, this yearning is merely after a strange precipice, something a long way off, inwardly distanced. The world of the cinema is a life without background or perspective, without difference of properties or qualities. [The cinema] is a life without measure or order, without being or value, a life without soul, mere surface . . . the individual moments, whose temporal sequence brings about the filmed scenes, are only joined with each other insofar as they follow each other without transition and mediation. There is no causality which could join them, or more precisely, its causality is free from and unimpeded by any notion of content. "Everything is possible": this is the credo of the cinema, and because its technique expresses at every moment the absolute (even if only empirical) reality of this moment, "virtuality" no longer functions as a category opposed to "reality": both categories become equivalent, identical. Everything is true and real, everything is equally true and real; this is what a sequence of images in the cinema teaches us.[29]

What Lukacs here analyzes with a certain lugubrious melancholy is nothing other than what Raoul Hausmann or Kurt Schwitters celebrate: "Everything is true and real, everything is equally true and real." The fundamental Dada paradox, namely that the real is the material, but that this irreducible materiality has no reality other than as a sign or a representation, finds its implicit resolution, if Luckacs is right, in the cinema – except in a cinema equated philosophically if not empirically with life itself. It is in this theoretical impasse that Dadaists remained caught when thinking about the cinema, and it gives some justification to Benjamin's assertion that the Dadaists' attitude to the new technologies of visual reproduction and imaging was retrograde, but necessarily so, given their radical aspirations:

The history of every art form shows critical epochs in which a certain art form aspires to effects which could be fully obtained only with a changed technical standard, that is to say, in a new art form. The extravagances and crudities of art which thus appear . . . actually arise from the nucleus of its richest historical energies . . . : Dadaism attempted to create by pictorial – and literary – means the effects which the public today seeks in the cinema.[30]

From Benjamin's perspective and vantage point this estimation of Dada technique as anachronistic in relation to a revolutionizing technology seems at least strategically plausible. But it may also (perhaps deliberately) misread Dada activities and their main thrust. The Berlin Dadaists, for instance, were finally only interested in two kinds of cultural objects: live performance and the newspaper, prototypes of an interventionist use of the mass-media. In both cases, by utilizing already existing forms and formats, maximum effect could be achieved through a minimum of effort – a reversal of bourgeois value-creation which the labor-intensive and time-consuming process of filmmaking does not exemplify particularly well. The principle of the ready-made (the spectacular ratio of effort to effect of an upturned urinal labeled "Fountain" and exhibited in a gallery) was generally of cardinal importance to the Dadaists, not only because it suited the movement's libidinal economy (the excremental against the obsessional): it demonstrated Dada's anti-mimetic concept of realism (preferring material literalism over metaphoric constructions of the materials of art), while at the same time undercutting the traditional equation of skill, effort or inspiration with art, value, status and morality. Wieland Herzfelde wrote:

The tasks [of painting] have been taken over by photography and film, and they solve them infinitely more perfectly than painting ever could. . . . [Since their invention] all art movements can be characterized as having, despite their differences, a common tendency to emancipate themselves from reality. Dada is the reaction to all these attempts at disavowing the factual, which has been the driving force of impressionists, expressionists, cubists and even futurists (in that they refused to capitulate to film); however, the Dadaist doesn't try to compete with the camera, or to breathe soul into it (as did the impressionists) by giving the worst lens – the human eye – priority, or (like the expressionists) turn the apparatus round and simply depict the world inside their own bosom.
The Dadaists say: Whereas once inordinate amounts of time, love and exertion were expended on the depiction of a body, a flower, a hat, the shadow cast by a figure, etc., today all we have to do is take a pair of scissors and cut whatever we need out of the paintings, the photographic reproductions of these things; if the objects are small, we don't even need the representations, but take the objects themselves, e.g. pocket knives, ash trays, books, etc. – things which in the museums of old art are wonderfully painted, but only painted.[31]

This passage from Wieland Herzfelde's "Zur Einführung in die Erste Internationale Dada Messe" seems to illustrate Benjamin's point even as it tries to embrace the cinema, only to reject film as not material enough. Herzfelde, despite his bold polemics, does not fully rise to the challenge of the problem already posed by Lukacs: how does the apparently unmediated reality conveyed by the photographic image constitute itself as a sign?

In practice, Dada products were often far from subscribing to Herzfelde's naive literalism of taking the objects themselves and putting them on display. The typical Dada artifact, the photomontage, indicated that the materials were not primary materials, but already formed by mechanical processes, which meant that what in one context constitutes the end-product is treated by Dada as raw material. Likewise, the point about Duchamp's ready-mades is that a semantic transformation has taken place, and not only a transgression of space, status, and use. The shift from end to means in the case of Duchamp especially is always doubled by what might be called a process of semiotization, where an object of little or no value is transformed not into a value but into an (ironic) signifier of value. Raoul Hausmann, in looking back at Berlin Dada, makes a similar point:

Anti-art withdraws from things and materials their utility, but also their concrete and civil meaning; it reverses classical values and makes them half-abstract. However, this process was only partially understood and only by some of the Dadaists.[32]

Hausmann's notion of "half-abstract" would be worth following up further, if one wanted to situate more precisely the Dadaists' use of images and the critical status of photographic or filmic illusionism in the early practice of photomontage.[33] From the vantage point of an interest in non-linguistic sign systems and visual sign production, the work of Grosz, Hausmann, and Heartfield has yet to be fully explored, because—and here Benjamin is undoubtedly right—Dada "anti-art" contributed less to the overturning of contemporary value systems than it participated in the transformation of a perceptual apparatus which the cinema changed so drastically and rapidly that it seemed to put the intellectual avant-gardes on the defensive.

Meta-Mechanics and the Perceptual Apparatus

The pre-history of the cinema, as mentioned earlier, comprises two quite distinct strands: that of the spaces and places where the new mass-public gathered for entertainment—fairgrounds, traveling circuses, vaudeville and nickelodeons—, and that of the optical or scientific toys, such as the zoetrope or the phenakistoscope, where images—painted, printed, or photographed— deceived the eye into perceiving movement and continuity where there was merely intermittence. If the Dadaists took an interest in the phenomenon of the masses eroticized by cinematic spectacles, they were equally alert to the fact that here was a machine organized in a peculiarly contradictory way: the cinematic apparatus is devised to function so as to disguise the actual movement *of* the image (passing through the projector gate) in order to create a nonexistent movement *in* the image. Energy in the cinema appears not as in productive machines, to transmit, transfer, or transform movement, but in order to nullify, disguise, and revalue movement: mechanics has become the metamechanics of imaginary motion. This gives the cinema, in terms of its apparatus, the status not of an optical toy, but rather, it makes it available as a philosophical toy, a machine transforming the useful energy of cogs and transmission belts into a useless energy of illusionist simulation. It is this aspect of the cinema—the devaluation of matter through its perfect reproduction, as in the photograph, but coupled with the transformation of mechanical movement from one aggregate state to another—which is explored and elaborated in Duchamp's *Anémic cinéma*. The film grew out of lengthy and dangerous experimentations with glass discs on which geometrical segments and lines were painted in such a way as to produce particular illusionist effects when put in revolving motion.

The rotoreliefs by themselves were illusionist devices, where motorization created a sense of depth and of spatial extension, a movement from inward to outward and vice versa. As such, Duchamp's work is comparable to that of Richter and Eggeling, only that *Anémic cinéma* plays with more overtly anthropomorphic sensations of heaving or breathing, and thus focuses on the eroticizing effect of animating the inaminate by a cunning arrangement of geometrical lines. But what decisively distinguishes Duchamp's film from other work is that the painted discs are intercut with other discs on which a series of ingeniously punning sentences are inscribed, whose semantics and syntactics exploit the mirror effect of syllabic division ("L'aspirant habite Javel, et moi, j'avais l'habite en spirale"). The two types of discs taken together create contrasts between flatness and depth, between negative and positive space, between reading and illusion, between literal and metaphoric.[34] Furthermore, the puns themselves, which are almost all erotic, interact by a sort of metaphoric contagion with the shapes and movements of the discs, to create the impression of seeing male and female protruberances in endless motion, whose consummation is frustrated through the intervention of the machine, a typically Duchamp topos.

Indeed it is not simply the intervention of one machine, but rather the synchronization of two machines: the recording camera and the revolving motor that spins the discs—two circular motions, distinct from each other, synchronized and dephased to produce endlessly closed circuits. Useless energy has been transformed into semiotic energy, via punning and mirroring effects, and the film—referring the spectator to the apparatus that makes its effect possible—reveals itself as peculiarly auto-erotic. The cinema-machine has become a bachelor-machine.[35]

Manipulating Materials of Expression or Reproduction

The insertion of art into the sphere of technological, capitalist modes of production becomes, according to Benjamin, the only position from which a critique of that mode of production is possible. In this respect, the idea of cinema, viewed from the perspective of its particular apparatus, could serve as a sort of model for the representation of the relation between body and matter, "Geist" and "Stoff," which goes beyond the disavowal of Thomas Mann as well as the polemical-sadistic materialism of the Berlin Dadaists.

When Hausmann compares the soul of the Berlin bourgeois to a "libretto machine with a reprogrammable morality disc,"[36] the metaphor brutally substitutes the spiritual connotations of soul with the image of a gramophone. Hausmann's *Tatlin at Home* or Grosz's *The Engineer Heartfield,* on the other hand, depict precision machines carefully inserted in the place of brains and heart respectively. Clearly there is a difference, both actual and intended, between these two uses, and it highlights the ambiguity of the machine metaphor in much Dada work, poised between futurist machines, which were, invariably, mimetic representations of machines in the conventional media of bourgeois art (oil paint, bronze, etc.), and constructivist machines which were, in a fundamental sense, real machines.

In Picabia's *Portrait of Marie Laurencin,* however, the machine parts neither propose a likeness, nor a polemical statement. The work suggests a coalescence of heterogeneous attributes whose perfection, harmony, or subtle interaction is signaled by machine elements. Similarly, in Man Ray's famous *Dancer/Danger,* the cogs are interlocking so tightly that, as a machine, it cannot function. The picture needs a dancer, a human element with the precision and dexterity of a machine, to make the mechanism turn. But it also remains blocked as long as it is viewed as the representation of a real machine. Only when we notice and thereby activate the energy of the pun (doubled by the fact that it works in two languages) does the cog of the letter G "make the connection": the Dada machine is not so much a metaphoric machine, as it is a metonymic machine which solicits the imaginary participation by an act of dis-placement, requiring the viewer to look and think in several dimensions at once. Secondly, as the examples from Duchamp, Man Ray, and Picabia make apparent, Dada machines are word machines; they explicitly semiotize the relations that exist between the parts.

Dada practice, like the cinematic apparatus, redefines the relation of part to whole, the relation of part to part. It is the cut, the montage principle that makes the energy in the system visible and active. However, unlike the cinematic apparatus, where heterogeneity at the level of the material components and technologies becomes "retinal" and fantasmatic, Dada machines, whether drawn on paper or printed, enacted in front of a public or built out of glass and wire, use the contradictions and frictions in the system to remain non-mimetic. A Duchamp ready-made invites both tactile and conceptual viewing, but never contemplative attention. The bicycle wheel mounted on a stool is only complete as a "work" when it arouses the desire to make it revolve, and it apparently was installed in a place where, to Duchamp's quiet satisfaction, no-one passed without at least attempting to give it a furtive spin.

Where the Dada machine thus differs from the cinematic apparatus is that at the level of the representations it remains intentionally anti-psychological. The obsessional, projective-introjective functions of the cinema contrast with Duchamp's lifelong exploration of natural processes, of mechanics and optics in search of material supports for the play of ideas which are anti-intentional and non-expressive, but articulate themselves as traces of a presence figured in metonymies. Duchamp's representational systems and constructs – even those which most obviously parody the cinema by figuring it as "nature morte," such as *Etant donnés* – eschew the kinds of closure and homogeneity which typify the developments of film form.

Thus, the complex combination of mechanics, optics, chemistry and time-lag which makes cinematic reproduction possible was an invention very much in the Dada spirit, for the Dada object always manipulates the materials of technical reproduction (and not those of expression). The few Dada experiments in film pushed in this direction, as did Dada interest in spectatorship, since it recognized the cinema as a machine not only in view of the recording/screening apparatus of camera, film-strip and projector, but also as a social machine, in which the spectator had a programmed place, physically, physiologically and economically.

Yet that which made cinema so powerful a social institution – its ability to simulate in its *textual* effects the psychic apparatus as a desiring machine (the cinema as the most efficient simulacrum of the psychic apparatus when mapped onto the perceptual system, as has consistently happened since Freud – by and large ran counter to Dada: it was the Surrealists who saw in filmic processes a way of representing the relation of psychoanalysis to matter, mediated through rhetoric and figuration.[37] If, as Benjamin suggested, there is something anachronistic about Dada and cinema, the difference between Dada and Surrealism in this respect parallels and repeats the development of the cinema generally: the first focus of attraction for a paying public was the machinery itself, its novelty, its intricacy, its basic effects. Only subsequently was this fascination displaced to the stories, the stars, the spectacular and the specular. Recent film theory, however, seems to indicate that interest in the apparatus has staged its own return.[38] Perhaps the contradictions and frictions of Dada/cinema may yet become productive.

Notes

1. Eric Rhode, *A History of the Cinema* (Harmondsworth, 1978), 3–29.

2. Ibid., 15.

3. Ibid., 5.

4. Willy Verkauf, ed., *Dada: Monographie einer Bewegung* (Teufen, 1957), 66.

5. See, for instance, Stephen Dwoskin, *Film Is . . .* (London, 1975), or Sheldon Renan, *An Introduction to the American Underground Film* (New York, 1967). Perhaps the best study of European avant-garde cinema as part of a tradition of non-narrative, noncommercial cinema is David Curtis, *Experimental Cinema* (New York, 1971).

6. Verkauf, 68.

7. Mimi White, "Two French Dada Films: *Entr'acte* and *Emak Bakia,*" *Dada/ Surrealism* 13(1984): 37.

8. Verkauf, 68.

9. "I would regret it if anyone saw in this . . . anything other than 'optics.'" M. Duchamp, *Marchand du Sel,* ed. Michel Sanouillet (Paris, 1958), 185.

10. Quoted in Curtis, 36.

11. White, 37.

12. Toni Stooss, "Erobert den Film! oder 'Prometheus' gegen 'Ufa' & Co.," in *Wem gehört die Welt* (NGBK Berlin, 1977), 482–524.

13. This Dada film screening may have occurred to commemorate Eggeling, who died that month.

14. Anton Kaes, "Verfremdung als Verfahren: Film und Dada," in W. Paulsen, ed., *Sinn aus Unsinn – Dada International* (Berne, 1982), 72–73.

15. See for instance Pontus Hulten, ed., *Futurismo e Futurismi* (Milan, 1986), 479–480.

16. Kaes, 73.

17. See the forthcoming issue of *New German Critique* on "Early German Film Theory."

18. Quoted in Hanne Bergius, "Zur Wahrnehmung und Wahrnehmungskritik im Berliner Dadaismus," *Sprache im Technischen Zeitalter* 55 (June–Sept., 1975):244.

19. Rhode, p. 24.

20. Walter Benjamin, *Illuminations*, trans. Harry Zohn (New York, 1969), 165.

21. Ibid., 238.

22. Ibid., 237.

23. Noel Burch, *To the Distant Observer* (London, 1979), 61–67.

24. Jakob van Hoddis, "Variété," *Der Sturm* 47 (1911):374.

25. Pascal Bonitzer, "It's Only a Movie," *Framework* (England) 14:23.

26. Richter, 198.

27. Moritz Heimann, "Der Kinomatographen-Unfug," in *Kino-Debatte*, ed. Anton Kaes (Tübingen, 1978), 37.

28. Thomas Mann, "Über den Film," in *Kino-Debatte*, 165.

29. Georg Lukacs, "Gedanken zu einer Aesthetik des Kinos," in *Kino-Debatte*, 113–115.

30. Benjamin, 237.

31. Wieland Herzfelde, "Zur Einführung in die Erste Internationale Dada-Messe," in *Dada Berlin*, ed. Karl Riha and Hanne Bergius (Stuttgart, 1977), 117–118.

32. Raoul Hausmann, "Dada empört sich, regt sich und stirbt in Berlin," in *Dada Berlin*, 10–11.

33. See Bergius, 242–44.

34. "Glyphes et graphes s'engendrent indéfiniment du même mouvement, dans un espace en quelque sorte sans réalité, espace tropologique du jeu de mots, espace illusoire de l'éffet optique." Jean Clair, *Marcel Duchamp. Catalogue raisonné* (Paris, 1977), 119.

35. See G. Deleuze and F. Guattari: "A genuine consummation is achieved by the new machine, a pleasure that can rightly be called auto-erotic, or rather automatic: the nuptial celebration of a new alliance . . . as though the eroticism of the machine liberated other unlimited forces." *Anti-Oedipus, Capitalism and Schizophrenia* (Minneapolis, 1983), 18.

36. Raoul Hausmann, "Pamphlet gegen die Weimarische Lebensauffassung," in *Dada Berlin*, 50.

37. See, for instance, Linda Williams, *Figures of Desire: A Theory and Analysis of Surrealist Film* (Urbana, 1981).

38. Among the recent literature on the "Cinematic Apparatus," one could single out Jean Louis Baudry, *L'Effet Cinéma* (Paris, 1979), S. Heath, T. de Lauretis, eds., *The Cinematic Apparatus* (London, 1979), and Constance Penley, "Feminism, Film Theory, and the Bachelor Machines," *m/f* 10 (1985).

Bridging Purism and Surrealism: The Origins and Production of Fernand Léger's *Ballet Mécanique*

Judi Freeman

Completed and first presented publicly in late September 1924, Fernand Léger's film *Ballet Mécanique* was created at the moment when the artist's painted output shifted from the exploration of diverse images of machine age life to the study of relatively abstract, closeup views of objects. In a sense his painted work stood at the crossroads between Purism and Surrealism, two endeavors seemingly without overlap but in fact – and this is certainly evident from Léger's particular position between them – possessing considerable interconnections. His films, like his other collaborative, non-easel painting projects, generally have been considered apart from the dialogue about the traditional fine arts in the early twentieth century.[1] When critically examined, however, it is clear that his films and other activities are integrally tied to these movements as well. Curiously, although *Ballet Mécanique*, along with Viking Eggeling's *Symphonie diagonale* (1921), Marcel Duchamp's *Anémic Cinéma* (1926), and Man Ray's *Emak Bakia* (1926–27), most often are presented together in series devoted to Dada and Surrealist films or to avant-garde cinema, *Ballet Mécanique* always seems to be uncomfortably situated in this context.

The peculiar nature of *Ballet Mécanique*, both in the context of Léger's career and within a notion of Dada and Surrealist film, is testimony to its significance within Léger's *oeuvre* as well as to the particular contributions of Léger's collaborators. The film was of such importance to the artist that in the final years of his career, he planned to remake it, in collaboration with Henri Langlois, in a version to be called *Ballet des couleurs*.[2] It is worthwhile, then, to reconstruct the genesis and development of the *Ballet Mécanique* project and to resolve how Léger made the film and how it fits into the painting he produced in the 1920s.[3]

Among the earliest French avant-garde artists to recognize the potential of cinema within the fine arts, Léger enthusiastically embraced the medium in numerous writings. As an active member of Ricciotto Canudo's Club des amis du septième art (Club of the friends of the 7th art), he attended regular screenings and dinners with directors, film editors, and other *réalisateurs* in the burgeoning French film industry. Clearly, though, Léger did not possess sufficient technical know-how to realize a film. But by 1923, when he embarked on the making of *Ballet Mécanique*, he had amassed considerable ex-

28

perience of the filmmaking industry. His first hands-on participation was in the making of Abel Gance's *La Roue* (*The Wheel*), in 1922. Although Gance's film was highly narrative, it contained notable passages of rapid montage that led later to his more sophisticated use of this technique in *Napoléon* (1927). In his admiring essay devoted to these montage sequences, Léger highlighted the portion of the film where the "machine becomes *the leading character, the leading actor"*:

This new element is presented to us through an infinite variety of methods, from every aspect: close-ups, fixed or moving mechanical fragments, projected at a heightened speed that approaches the state of simultaneity and that crushes and eliminates the human object, reduces its interest, pulverizes it . . . The plastic event is no less there because of it, it's nowhere else; it is planned, fitted in with care, appropriate, and seems to me to be laden with implications in itself and for the future.

The advent of this film is additionally interesting in that it is going to determine a place in the plastic order for an art that has until now remained almost completely descriptive, sentimental, and documentary. The fragmentation of the object, the intrinsic plastic value of the object, its pictorial equivalence, have long been the domain of the modern arts. With *The Wheel* Abel Gance has elevated the art of film to the plane of the plastic arts.[4]

Not only was Léger present at the film's debut at the Gaumont-Palace in Paris in December 1922, but he also witnessed the film's shooting in Nice and the French Alps. Léger joined his old friend, the poet Blaise Cendrars, who at this time served as Gance's key assistant and troubleshooter on the film, involved with every aspect of the production – from arranging for props to paying bills.[5] Also present was Jean Epstein, then a young writer on film and the arts in Lyon, who was observing portions of the shooting.[6] Léger discussed his impressions of the film and his general ideas on cinema's potential with Gance, who, in turn, encouraged him and commissioned him to write on the film as part of the carefully orchestrated publicity campaign surrounding *La Roue*'s release in December 1922 (Fig. 1).[7] Following the film's première, Léger supplied Gance with his view of the audience's response to the film, telling the director that the "simultaneous passage" was the most successful but that other parts of the film had considerable problems.[8]

   It is interesting to note how Léger initially asked Gance to describe him in the biographical note to be attached to Léger's promotional article on the film which appeared in *Comoedia*:

Fernand Léger is the modern French painter that first considered the *mechanical element* as a possible plastic element; he has incorporated the concept of *equivalence* into numerous pictures. Abel Gance has asked him to offer his view of the plastic value of his film *La Roue*.[9]

Léger's paintings of 1922 were not devoted to mechanical elements seen in close-up. In 1918–19 Léger had produced several canvases on themes of mechanical elements or disks but his paintings of 1922 and 1923 continued themes begun in 1920 – women, still lives of ordinary household objects situated in an interior, figures at work in the city or country – with equiva-

29

Figure 1

lences established between seemingly unrelated forms. For the artist, the link between his earlier works and his current pursuits was the exploration of plastic values. *Ballet Mécanique* served as an opportunity to test his ideas on these values in another medium by selecting aspects of that medium that permitted their expression.

The actual making of *Ballet Mécanique* is complicated by several conflicting accounts. Léger is known to have collaborated with four Americans resident in Europe: aspiring cameraman Dudley Murphy, fledgling composer George Antheil, the poet Ezra Pound, and the artist-photographer Man Ray. Their precise contributions to the film, however, are clouded by the contradictions present in their individual written accounts. Dudley Murphy, for example, recounted his perceptions of how the film was made:

One day, when I was visiting Ezra Pound and talking about my work, he told me that a friend of his, Ferdinand [sic] Leger, wanted to make a movie. Also George Anteil [sic], the young protege of Stravinsky would like to make a movie. So he brought the three of us together and we decided to make one. I had met an attractive American divorcee who had a beautiful house in Paris and who was intrigued with me, Gladys Barbour. I told her of my plans and she lent me the money to buy a movie camera.

The tools of a film-maker can be very simple. It is really a camera and film. So, having the camera, we only needed film, so Leger and I financed our film equally with the understanding that he would have the European rights of the finished film and I would have the American rights. We talked over ideas and I set out with my camera and the film, executing the ideas we had talked over and photographing things that stimulated my imagination around Paris. The premise on which we decided to make the film was based on a belief that surprise of image and rhythm would make a pure film without drawing on any of the other arts, such as writing, acting, painting. In other words, we were going to make a pure film. Our project was called *Ballet Mécanique.*

I saw an old washerwoman climbing a flight of stone stairs. When she reached the top, she was tired and made a futile gesture. The scene in itself was banal, but by printing it 20 times and connecting the end of the scene with the beginning of her climb, it expressed the futility of life because she never got there. This scene in the editing followed a very intricate piece of shiny machinery, somehow correlated in movement and rhythm to that of hers.

Another scene showed a tremendous piston, brilliant and shiny, plunging up and down in a very phallic movement. This was followed by the bulging stomach of Katherine [Hawley, Murphy's wife], who was now pregnant.

I was intrigued to do something with the artificial legs that exhibit silk stockings and decided to do a stop motion dance with these legs around a clock. In bringing the legs to the studio, I drove through Paris in an open cab, with a leg over each shoulder, screaming.[10]

Dudley Murphy began his film career at Metro-Goldwyn-Mayer (MGM) in the late 1910s under the tutelage of eminent Hollywood art director Cedric Gibbons. From there, he moved into art directing positions at assorted Hollywood studios. He made several poetically inspired films, starring his first and second wives, and attempted to distribute them commercially. With the help of an investor he then formed in the early 1920s a company called "Visual Symphonies," the goal of which was to identify a method to establish a frame-by-frame correspondence with a musical composition.[11] The first film to emerge from these efforts was *Danse macabre,* a dance film choreographed to and therefore necessarily performed with Saint-Saens's music. *Ballet Mécanique* followed two years later; by this time, Murphy had accumulated considerable experience in shooting and editing film. More-over, he considered the film to be an extension of his "visual symphonies."[12]

Murphy's account helps to explain how Léger, an artist without specific technical expertise in cinema, actually made a film. Yet the story of the project's origins conflicts with the account of another contributor, Man Ray:

> One day a tall young man appeared with his beautiful blond wife, and introduced himself as a cameraman from Hollywood. . . . Dudley Murphy said some very flat-tering things about my work and suggested that we do a film together. He had all the professional material, he said; with my ideas and his technique something new could be produced. We became quite friendly, spent a few days together discussing subject matter – I insisted on my Dada approach if we were to work together, to which he readily agreed . . . We took some walks together, I bringing my little camera and shooting a few scenes without any attempt at careful choice of people or setting, emphasizing the idea of improvisation. For the more tricky effects we planned indoors, Dudley set up an old Pathé camera on its tripod, the kind used in the comic shorts of the day. He showed me some complicated lenses that could deform and multiply images, which we'd use for portraits and close-ups. The camera remained standing in my studio for a few days, which annoyed me, as I never like to have my instruments in view . . . When Dudley appeared again, he announced that he was ready to go to work and would I purchase the film. I was surprised, thinking this was included with his technical equipment – that I was to supply the ideas only. He packed up his camera, took it over to the painter Léger's studio, explaining that he himself had no money and that the painter had agreed to finance the film. I made no objection, was glad to see the black box go, and relieved that I hadn't gotten in-volved in a co-operative enterprise. And that is how Dudley realized the *Ballet Méca-nique,* which had a certain success, with Léger's name.[13]

The goal of the Dadaists, according to Man Ray, was to "try the spectators' patience."[14] And clearly that concept was incorporated into the final form of the film in the repetition of the washerwoman climbing the stairs and in the fracturing of repeated forms, such as that of his mistress's, Kiki of Montpar-nasse's, face toward the end of the film.[15]

Man Ray's description curiously is not corroborated in the other accounts of the making of *Ballet Mécanique.* While the film clearly bears the imprint of Léger's predominantly machine aesthetic in the first half of the 1920s, it also contains Man Ray's distinctive treatment of people in his photographs and other films. It is worth noting that in 1926, when Man Ray embarked on the making of *Emak Bakia,* he envisioned the film in terms similar to Léger's stated intentions for *Ballet Mécanique:*

> A series of fragments, a ciné-poem with a certain optical sequence make up a whole that still remains a fragment. Just as one can much better appreciate the abstract beauty in a fragment of a classical work than in its entirety, so this film tries to in-dicate the essentials in its contemporary cinematography.[16]

Man Ray's involvement with *Ballet Mécanique,* nevertheless, was restricted to the shooting of imagery in the earliest phases of the project.

Ezra Pound's role in the film's production was also limited, in this case to the introduction of the various makers of the film to one another. In a letter of July 1923 to his parents, Pound noted, "Dudley Murphy, whom I met in Venice in 1908, he being then eleven; turned up a few days ago . . . he is trying to make cinema into art."[17] By September, he stated "We [Pound and George Antheil] have a new Léger 'projet' waiting to be framed."[18] In November, Murphy wrote "I have practically completed the film with Ezra Pound and it looks quite interesting . . . it is quite abstract – no people – only interesting forms."[19] It is clear by January 1924 that the three collaborators, Pound, Murphy, and Léger, were at work on the film; "Also work on vorticist film – experiment interesting, but probably Murphy hasn't brain enough to finish the job in my absence or without pushing."[20]

Pound had very much become, in the early 1920s, the key sponsor of aspiring composer Antheil.[21] While Pound himself was deeply interested in music and was in fact composing his own compositions and operas, he encouraged Antheil to embark on a performing tour of Europe, with Pound's mistress, pianist Olga Rudge. In 1923, Antheil gave a Paris concert with music so deliberately audacious that it provoked a major riot in Paris's Théâtre des Champs-Elysées; the riot was caused intentionally and was filmed for use in Marcel L'Herbier's 1923 film *L'Inhumaine*. The notoriety Antheil gained from this performance emboldened the composer to propose publicly a new project. Whether Léger's and Murphy's project predates this and whether it was Ezra Pound who encouraged Antheil to join in is unclear, given the lack of reliability characteristic in much of Antheil's writings; nevertheless, it is Antheil's account of *Ballet Mécanique*'s origins that further confuses the issue of who made what and when:

[In October 1923] I announced to the press that I was working on a new piece, to be called "Ballet Mécanique." I said that I also sought a motion-picture accompaniment to this piece. The newspapers and art magazines seemed only too happy to publish this request, which interested a young American cameraman, Dudley Murphy. He had really been flushed by Ezra Pound, who convinced him.

Murphy said he would make the movie, providing the French painter Fernand Léger consented to collaborate. Léger did.[22]

Antheil's composition, which was scored for machines, bells, anvils, automobile horns, player pianos, and percussion and was converted into three Pleyela piano rolls, was not completed, however, until the autumn of 1925.[23] Léger was eager to get it, writing to Antheil in April 1924, "Where is your composition, *Ballet Mécanique*? Let me know what is available to listen to . . ."[24] To Léger's dismay, the score was not completed by September 1924, when Léger first screened the film publicly at the Internationale Ausstellung für Theatertechnik organized by Frederick Kiesler. Léger was so confident that Antheil's music would be finished and successfully merged with the film that the title card on the print screened in Vienna referred to the synchronized score. Its first known performance was, like most of its subsequent performances, independent of the film's screening; by this time, several different prints of the film were already in distribution. Léger's reaction to the music was, according to Antheil, wildly enthusiastic:

. . . I hear that Léger has been simply crazy since he heard the Ballet Mécanique several days ago. He heard it for the first time, for I've been very busy with my opera and couldn't go to him. So we arranged a performance of the music several days ago, and after it was over he simply embraced me. Léger expected a great deal, but he said it was beyond his expectations and that it was as right as right can be.[25]

Figure 2

In several letters to both Antheil and Ezra Pound, Léger refers to an additional collaborator on *Ballet Mécanique,* Charles Delacommune.[26] Delacommune's company, Synchro-Ciné, is credited by the use of its logo, at the end of The Museum of Modern Art's print of the film, which Léger gave to the museum in 1935. It is clear that Léger and Murphy knew and worked with Delacommune at the time of the film's making in 1923–24 because Léger acknowledged his role in his article on the film published in *Little Review* in 1924.[27] At the time, Delacommune founded a company called Synchronisme cinématique (known as Synchro-Ciné after 1928), which served as an umbrella organization for Delacommune's research into synchronization. One of the first films he "synchronized," through the use of punched musical scores aligned to sprocket holes in nitrate films, was Murphy's *La Valse de Mephisto.* Murphy continued to employ him on *Ballet Mécanique,* paying him 300 francs on January 18, 1924 for his services on the film,[28] and Léger entrusted the distribution of his prints to him in the late twenties and early thirties.

Léger was so engrossed in Delacommune's method of synchronization, which Delacommune had patented in 1922 and 1923, as well as the "cinépupitre," the mechanical apparatus he invented, that he sketched the machinery to be used on back of notes made in relation to *Ballet Mécanique* (Fig. 2).[29] On the front of these pages, Léger made specific notes on ideas he

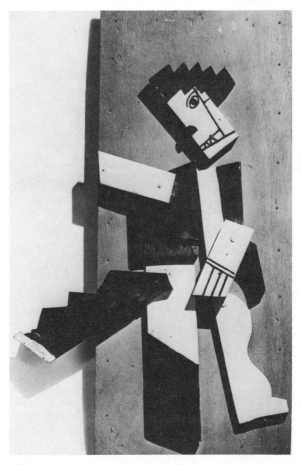

Figure 3

had, perhaps with Murphy and/or the other collaborators, on the film's imagery.[30] He proposed dividing the screen into nine equal sections, an idea that anticipated Gance's use of this device in the opening sequences of his 1927 film *Napoléon*. He envisioned figures engulfed by mechanical objects, integrated into an array of constructed objects, typewriters, pendulums. The alternation of black on white and white on black was to be explored. Advertising images were to be used frequently. Above all, contrasts were intended to reign, a way of suggesting equivalences through the use of quick-fire juxtaposition.

In addition to individual images Léger suggested for inclusion in the film, he also fused a previously unrealized film project into *Ballet Mécanique.* The painter was a passionate fan of the work of Charlie Chaplin, having been first introduced to Chaplin's films during the First World War by the poet Guillaume Apollinaire.[31] Léger was fascinated by Chaplin's control over his audience and, by extension, the potential of cinema to affect and manipulate

35

Figure 4

audience response.[32] He illustrated an edition of Ivan Goll's book, *Die Cha-plinade* (1920) and shortly thereafter began work on a scenario for an animated film, *Charlot Cubiste*. Léger's scenario was extremely detailed, chronicling every moment in a day in the life in Paris of Charlot, who was constructed as a marionette in relief (Fig. 3). At least five lengthy drafts of the scenario were penned by Léger; however, the film appears never to have been made, probably due to the lack of financial backing.[33]

Léger made use of the marionette and the idea of a disintegrating/reconstituted Charlot at the begining and end of *Ballet Mécanique*. He is almost always juxtaposed in his jerky choreography with the repetitive movements of the woman (Katherine Hawley Murphy) seen at the beginning of the film on the swing and seen later sniffing flowers in a garden (Fig. 4). But between Léger's involvement with his *Charlot Cubiste* project and the undertaking of *Ballet Mécanique*, his work on another film, this time for filmmaker Marcel L'Herbier, intervened and redirected Léger's attention toward the potential of mechanical imagery in his films. For L'Herbier's 1923 *L'Inhumaine*, Léger created the sets for the film's climactic laboratory scene (Fig. 5). Machinery in this silent film suggested, presumably with the help of a live orchestral accompaniment, whirring, buzzing, clanging, and pumping, thereby enhancing the sensory experience for the viewer. Léger incorporated the lessons from that film into the images he chose for *Ballet Mécanique*: swinging Christmas ornaments and saucepan covers (Fig. 6), incessantly pumping pistons, whirling gelatin molds, gyrating pieces of corrugated sheet metal. It

36

Figure 5

appears that Léger instructed Murphy to shoot many of these images, along with other images Murphy already had shot with Man Ray or, in several instances, chosen with Pound or on his own; many of the refracted and frac-

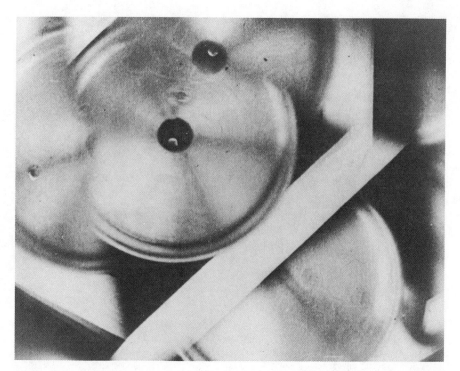

Figure 6

tured images, such as Kiki's face (Fig. 7), the owl, or the corrugated sheet metal resulted from Pound's ideas on film inspired by his experience with the vortographs of Alvin Langdon Coburn and from Man Ray's rayogram experiments.[34]

When the actual fusion of the images into a final film took place, however, it was Léger's evolving vision that dominated that of Pound, Man Ray, and Murphy. While his machine aesthetic dominated much of the imagery finally selected when Léger and Murphy sat down at the editing table, the rapid montage that Léger had learned by watching Abel Gance dominated his editing style. He reflected later that the "editing gave me a lot of trouble. There are long sequences of repeated movements that had to be cut. I had to watch the smallest details very carefully because of the repetition of images." The minute and extensive frame by frame cutting that occurred is visible on the nitrate print of the first known version of the film, premiered at the Internationale Ausstellung für Theatertechnik in Vienna and preserved by Frederick Kiesler.[35]

Léger declared:

The particular interest of the film is centered upon the importance which we give to the 'fixed image,' to its arithmetical, automatic projection, slowed down or accelerated – additional, likeness.

No scenario – Reactions of rhythmic images, that is all.

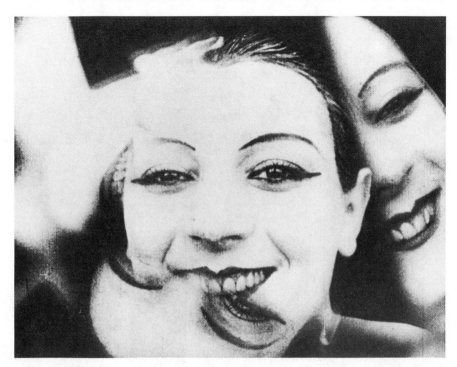

Figure 7

Two coefficients of interest upon which the film is constructed:
The variation of the speeds of projection:
The rhythm of these speeds.
. . .

We persist up to the point when the eye and spirit of the spectator will no longer accept. We drain out of it every bit of its value as a spectacle up to the moment when it becomes insupportable.[36]

Léger's fascination with the mechanical aspects of movement were coupled with his curiosity about the audience's response to it. His description of the editing of the washerwoman climbing the stairs, also recalled by Murphy, underscores his desire to challenge the spectator:

. . . in "The Woman Climbing the Stairs," I wanted to *amaze* the audience first, then make them uneasy, and then push the adventure to the point of exasperation. In order to "time" it properly, I got together a group of workers and people in the neighborhood, and I studied the effect that was *produced* on them. In eight hours I learned what I wanted to know. *Nearly all of them reacted at about the same time.*[37]

The wish to challenge the spectator and to juxtapose images, speeds, and rhythms in order to establish equivalences characterize Léger's approach to his painting. In his work, he sought to apply a "law of plastic contrasts," one that allowed him to combine different forms: flat vs. modeled surfaces, fig-

Figure 8

ures vs. flat building façades, volumes of smoke vs. active architectural surfaces, pure, flat vs. gray, modulated tones.[38] Léger believed we "live in a
state of frequent contrasts" and that the role of art was to be of its time.[39] He
also aspired to "conquer his public":

We live surrounded by beautiful objects that are slowly being revealed and perceived
by man; they are occupying an increasingly important place around us, in our interior
and exterior life.

Figure 9

Cultivate this possibility, release it, direct it, extend its consequences.[40]

Increasingly, however, the imagery which Léger chose to present to his public changed. Whereas in 1923 Léger's absorption was with observed life in the machine-dominated modern era in paintings such as *Le grand rémorqueur*, by 1924 he returned to more abstract *Eléments mécaniques* (Fig. 8), a theme he had previously pursued in the late 1910s. The imagery became the machine, then the machine closeup, then the closeup of everyday life. By

41

1926, Léger had immersed himself almost completely in making drawings and paintings of closeup imagery (Fig. 9).

What intervened was *Ballet Mécanique.* The effect of a hat alternating with legs, with ornaments, with shoes, triangles, alternating with circles, a pearl necklace alternating with the words "un collier des perles," single zeros alternating with multiple zeros – all of these opened up new avenues of exploration for Léger. By narrowing his vision, he could focus on the varied meanings and associations of objects. In painting, his intentions approached those of René Magritte and Max Ernst. Certainly Léger had not become a Surrealist; indeed he went to great pains to distance himself from the group. He had not completely abandoned Purism either, still portraying objects from daily life that belonged to the machine age as much of his imagery. But *Ballet Mécanique,* as a collaborative product by artists from various media, allowed Léger to see the potential of his ideas in another medium, as well as helped to redirect the values he endeavored to explore in his own favored medium of painting.

Notes

1. This is the case in the most recent major monographs devoted to Léger: Christopher Green, *Léger and the Avant-Garde* (New Haven and London: Yale University Press, 1976), and Peter de Francia, *Fernand Léger* (New Haven and London: Yale University Press, 1984).

2. Georges Sadoul referred to the film in an article written after Léger's death in 1955; see Georges Sadoul, "Fernand Léger ou la cinéplastique," *Cinéma* 59.35 (April 1959:81), and *Bulletin de l'ACA* 4 (January–February 1959): 7.

All known footage for *Ballet de couleurs* belonged to Nadia Léger until her death in 1982 and presumably is part of the Léger estate. Nadia Léger and Georges Bauquier were collaborating with Mary Meerson, formerly of the Cinémathèque française, Paris, to complete this film, left unfinished at Léger's death, and present it in the early 1980s. To my knowledge, the film has never been publicly screened. Mary Meerson, in conversation with the author, Paris, November 1982 and Jean Mitry, in conversation with the author, Neuilly, April 1983.

3. In this context I will not address the relationship of *Ballet Mécanique* and contemporary theorists' writings on film. In doing so, I have concluded that this context does not help to illuminate the making and meaning of the film and therefore disagree with Richard Brender, who, in a recent article devoted to Léger's cinema, assessed the film by evaluating it against these theorists' expectations. See Richard Brender, "Functions of Film: Léger's Cinema on Paper and on Cellulose, 1913–25," *Cinema Journal* 24.1 (Fall 1984): 41–63.

4. Fernand Léger, "A Critical Essay on the Plastic Quality of Abel Gance's Film *The Wheel,"* *Comoedia* (1922), translated in Fernand Léger, *Functions of Painting*, translated by Alexandra Anderson, edited by Edward F. Fry (New York: Viking Press, 1965), pp. 20–21.

5. See the extensive correspondence from Blaise Cendrars to Abel Gance on a variety of topics related to the making of *La Roue* (Abel Gance archives, Centre national de cinématographie, Paris, and the Abel Gance papers, Cinémathèque française, Paris).

6. Léger already knew Epstein, having published his "La couleur dans la vie (Fragment d'une étude sur les valeurs plastiques nouvelles)" in Epstein's journal *Promenoir* 5 (1921): 66–67.

7. Gance commissioned articles from Jean Epstein, Blaise Cendrars, Jacques Thévenet, and Léger for various newspapers. See Abel Gance, "Définitif La Roue," unpublished manuscript, 1 p. (Abel Gance papers, Cinémathèque française, Paris).

8. Letter from Fernand Léger to Abel Gance, 11 November 1922 (Abel Gance papers, Cinémathèque française, Paris).

9. *Ibid.*

10. Dudley Murphy, "Murphy by Murphy," unpublished autobiographical manuscript, January 1966 (Erin Murphy O'Hara, Malibu, California). The image of Katherine's bulging pregnant stomach is not present in any of the known versions of *Ballet Mécanique*. However, according to Dudley Murphy's son, the filmmaker Michael Murphy, Murphy possessed a print, one he carried with him from Paris to the United States in 1926 and screened in New York theatres in that year, which contained this and other nude, particularly suggestive images. It appears that all extant copies, which appear to have been distributed only by Léger and as early as 1924, had these passages deleted. Interview with Michael Murphy and the author, Malibu, August 1982.

11. "'Visual Symphonies' Find Recognition; New Short Subjects Replace Prologues," *Moving Picture World* (January 28, 1922): 387.

12. Letter from Dudley Murphy to Herman Dudley Murphy, July 20, 1924 (Poco Murphy, Sea Cliff, New York).

13. Man Ray, *Self Portrait* (New York: McGraw-Hill Book Company, 1963), pp. 266–267. It is worth noting that Man Ray claimed Léger financed the film, while Dudley Murphy asserted that Ezra Pound did; see letter from Dudley Murphy to Herman Dudley Murphy, November 19, 1923 (Poco Murphy, Sea Cliff, New York).

14. *Ibid.*, p. 260.

15. Man Ray in fact published and signed a number of these images as independent prints; see, for example, *Kiki of Montparnasse* (1924), in: *Man Ray, Photographe* (Paris: Musée national d'art moderne, Centre national d'art et de culture Georges Pompidou, 1982), p. 104, pl. 107. Other images are currently preserved in glass negatives in the Man Ray studio in Paris.

16. Frank Stauffacher, *Art in Cinema* (San Francisco: San Francisco Museum of Art, 1947), p. 53.

17. Letter from Ezra Pound to his parents, July 1923 (Ezra Pound Archives, Beinecke Rare Book and Manuscript Library, Yale University, New Haven, Connecticut).

18. Letter from Ezra Pound to his parents, 12 September 1923 (Ezra Pound Archives, Beinecke Rare Book and Manuscript Library, Yale University, New Haven, Connecticut).

19. Letter from Dudley Murphy to Carlene Murphy Samoileff, November 16, 1923 (Poco Murphy, Sea Cliff, New York).

20. Letter from Ezra Pound to his parents, 29 January 1924 (Ezra Pound Archives, Beinecke Rare Book and Manuscript Library, Yale University, New Haven, Connecticut). I am grateful to Archibald Henderson III for suggesting that I consult these letters.

21. On the relationship between Antheil and Pound and especially on Pound's interest in music, see Archibald Henderson III, "Pound and Music: The Paris and Early Rapallo Years," Ph.D. dissertation, University of California at Los Angeles, 1983.

22. George Antheil, *Bad Boy of Music* (New York: Garden City, New York: Double-day, Doran and Company, Inc., 1945), pp. 134–135.

23. The three piano rolls, recorded in Paris in 1925, are currently in the collection of the Archives of the History of Art, Getty Center for the History of Art and Humanities, Santa Monica, California.

24. Letter from Léger to George Antheil, dated April 1924 (Ezra Pound Archives, Beinecke Rare Book and Manuscript Library, Yale University, New Haven, Connecticut).

25. Letter to Ezra Pound from George Antheil, n.d. (1925), (Ezra Pound Archives, Beinecke Rare Book and Manuscript Library, Yale University, New Haven, Connecticut).

26. See, for example, letters from Léger to Ezra Pound, dated 22 April, 23 November, and 14 December 1932 (Ezra Pound Archives, Beinecke Rare Book and Manuscript Library, Yale University, New Haven, Connecticut), and Léger to George Antheil, February 5, 1933 (George Antheil Archives, El Cerrito, California).

27. Fernand Léger, "Film by Fernand Léger and Dudley Murphy, Musical Synchronism by George Antheil," *Little Review* (Autumn-Winter 1924–1925):44.

28. Katherine Hawley Murphy's datebook for 1924 (Poco Murphy, Sea Cliff, New York), page for January 18, documents this payment.

29. These notes were first published by Standish D. Lawder in his pioneering study, *The Cubist Cinema* (New York: New York University Press, 1975). Pierre Alechinsky purchased the notes on the advice of film historian Lotte Eisner, who recognized that they were notes for Léger's film. Previously they were in the possession of Robert Hessens, the Belgian filmmaker, who was making a short film on Léger analogous (in Léger's view) to personal manuscripts and notes in preparation; see letter from Léger to Robert Hessens, n.d. (1950s), (Pierre Alechinsky, Bougival, France).

30. Murphy's own notes list white gloved hands moving in black spaces, nude bodies writhing in blackness, water falling through a triangle, a wheel approaching the camera, and numerous stunts. Whether these were Murphy's or Léger's ideas is unclear; the pronounced contrasts among the images listed suggest that these were mainly Léger's thoughts. Dudley Murphy, "Page of notes," Unpublished MS., 1 p. (Poco Murphy, Sea Cliff, New York).

31. Léger was so taken by Chaplin that he devoted an admiring article to him, describing his first impressions of the filmmaker/actor; see Léger, "Charlot Cubiste," unpublished MS., 7 pp. (Fernand Léger Archives, formerly Musée national Fernand Léger, Biot) and Léger, "Temoignage," *Les Chroniques du Jour* (special issue devoted to Chaplin) 73 (December 15–31, 1926).

Léger also referred to Chaplin's "mechanical" possibilities in his "L'avenir du cinéma," Unpublished MS., n.d. (1923), 1 p. (Fernand Léger Archives, formerly Musée national Fernand Léger, Biot).

32. Léger considered both Chaplin and Buster Keaton's work to have this ability; see Léger, "Sur le cinéma," Unpublished MS., 1 p. (Fernand Léger Archives, formerly Musée national Fernand Léger, Biot.

33. For the five scenario manuscripts, see the unpublished documents in the Fernand Léger Archives, formerly Musée national Fernand Léger, Biot.

Léger alluded to his difficulties in obtaining this backing in his letter to Jean Epstein, March 2, 1923 (Marie Epstein, Paris).

34. See Lawder, p. 140, 142.

35. This print, found in 1976 by Lillian Kiesler, the artist's widow, is presently in the collection of Anthology Film Archives, New York. Its condition and important provenance and screening history makes it the definitive version of the film, to be used in evaluating the film's relationship to its score. All published studies of *Ballet Mécanique* to date have been based on the Museum of Modern Art's print of the film, given by Léger to the museum at the time of his retrospective in 1935. A considerable amount of material has been edited out of MOMA's version.

36. Fernand Léger, "Film by Fernand Léger and Dudley Murphy, Musical Synchronism by George Antheil," *Little Review* (Autumn–Winter 1924–25): 42–44.

37. Fernand Léger, "Ballet Mécanique," (listed as c. 1924, but most certainly not written before 1926), printed in: Fernand Léger, *Functions of Painting,* p. 51.

38. Fernand Léger, "Notes on the Mechanical Element," 1923, published in *Functions of Painting,* p. 29.

39. *Ibid.,* p. 30.

40. Fernand Léger, "The Spectacle: Light, Color, Moving Image, Object-Spectacle," *Bulletin de l'Effort Moderne,* 1924, reprinted in: *Functions of Painting,* p. 44–45.

List of Illustrations

Anemic Vision in Duchamp: Cinema as Readymade

Dalia Judovitz

> Today's film does not lack Surrealist fantasy, but optics.
>
> Raoul Hausmann

Marcel Duchamp's experimental film *Anémic Cinéma* (1924–26), filmed in collaboration with Man Ray, is generally regarded by film critics as an early instance of abstract film representing a series of verbal puns.[1] The anagrammatic play of the title *Anémic* and *Cinéma*, as well as its content, a series of spirals intercalated by nine alliterative verbal puns, have helped foster this impression. This literal and literary interpretation of the abstract character of the film fails, however, to account for its particular visual graphic character. Although critics recognize that Duchamp's film is not strictly cinematic, since it represents an effort to find "kinetic solutions to pictorial problems," this insight has not radically affected its actual interpretation.[2] Moreover, the film's historical context, its emergence in the anti-aesthetic context of the Dada period and Duchamp's own efforts to experiment, expand and eventually break with painting, has not been taken sufficiently into consideration.

Anémic Cinéma, as I shall show, problematizes the abstract character of the filmic image, since Duchamp already rejected the formal language of abstraction in painting by 1913 with production of the readymades and his optical and kinetic experiments. The film is neither cinematic in terms that the early avant-gardes sought to define it from a Romantic perspective by highlighting its synthetic character and estheticizing cinema as a total art (Riccioto Canudo's "seventh art"), nor is the film the expression of the photogene of the "image," of its abstract and formal character, of what is "specifically cinematic" as set up by the French Impressionist vanguard of Germaine Dulac, Jean Epstein, and Louis Delluc in the 1920s.[3] Rather, through the strategic juxtaposition of visual and discursive elements, *Anémic Cinéma* challenges the definition of both traditional and abstract cinematic image by questioning its visual esthetic status.

Duchamp's *Anémic Cinéma* will be considered as a critique of the cinematic image as object of visual sensation. Rather like the readymade, which is doubly constituted through the interplay of an object and its title, *Anémic Cinéma* will not be examined purely as a film, since it cannot be read either purely visually, or discursively as the mere visual presentation of a series of verbal puns. Instead, *Anémic Cinéma* will be interpreted as an instance of Duchamp's passage from a critique of the pictorial image to a more general critique of the esthetic vision as constitutive of the character of an art object.

The readymades anticipate Duchamp's cinematic project insofar as they represent the de-estheticization of the art object by both its phenomeno-logical and discursive reduction. The readymade is the culmination of Duchamp's critique of esthetic vision by seeking to transform it, to under-mine its optical verisimilitude by its reinscription through verbal and cognitive activity. The visual experience of a readymade is one of in-difference and anesthesia since the object has been selected on purpose be-cause of its lack of "esthetic emotion," as a defense against the "look." The readymade is thus an expression of both "visual indifference" and the total absence of consideration of good and bad taste.[5] The readymade engages the viewer/spectator in a new dynamic, one where the object is not defined by its visual presence as an esthetic object, since the readymade is often a commonplace object (a bicycle wheel, comb, snow shovel, urinal, etc.). Duchamp's intervention thus consists not in its artisanal production but rather in its selection and display. The *Bicycle Wheel* (1913) is displayed with the fork upside down, screwed to a kitchen stool. The *Bottle Dryer* (1914), like the *Hat Rack* (1917), is hung from the ceiling, whereas the coat rack, called *Trap* (1917), is nailed to the floor instead of the wall, its usual place. This decontextualization of the object's functional place draws attention to the creation of its artistic meaning by the choice of the setting and position ascribed to the object. The readymade is thus not merely an art object on display, but one which displays the constitution of the art object as value and meaning.

Duchamp's selection and display of the readymade also involves the nam-ing of the object, since the readymade becomes a work of art by virtue of Duchamp's performance, his declaration that it is such. Thus the title of the readymade inscribes the object into a temporal and linguistic dimension. Duchamp explains: "That sentence, instead of describing the object like a title, was meant to carry the mind of the spectator towards other regions, more verbal."[6] In his later readymades like the coat rack entitled *Trap* (1917), Duchamp explores this possibility of opening up through punning the referential character of the readymade. *Trap* (*Trébuchet*) is an instance not only of physical displacement, but also logical displacement, since, as Arturo Schwarz notes, the word itself is a pun on the phonetically identical chess term *trébucher*, the French word meaning "to stumble over."[7] The punning character of the title of such readymades as *Fresh Widow* (1920), a pun on French window, destabilizes the identity of the title as a linguistic referent and frame of the object.

These titles are the expression of Duchamp's verbal and poetic concerns with language, his conception of words as entities separate from meaning. He also thought about words in visual terms as "photographic details of large-sized objects." Schwarz observes, referring to his conversations with Duchamp, that Duchamp was motivated by the desire "to transfer the sig-nificance of language from words into signs, into a visual expression of the word, similar to the ideograms of the Chinese language."[8] Thus Duchamp's

47

act of nomination of the readymade is not a gesture of closure, that of en-closing the visual referent by a discursive one. For the title of the ready-made as a pun is the interplay of linguistic, visual and phonetic elements, that is to say, the destruction and disseminition of its objective character. Thus the readymade, like its title, is both more and less an object. Its mean-ing and existence as an object are created through the act of nomination, its title. But the title actually fragments the object by its own visual and objec-tive character as signifying material.

The readymade thus emerges as a conceptual operation on vision and dis-course, rather than as an art object, or even common object. The mutual contextualization of the visual and discursive elements draws attention to the fact that esthetic representation is less about objects proper, defined by phenomenological properties, than about conceptual operations in visual and discursive contexts. The readymade is a combination of visual and ver-bal signs, a three-dimensional emblem whose visual and discursive compo-nents are juxtaposed against each other like words within a language. This conflation of visual and discursive material produces the spiraling effect of irresolution and indifference, anesthetizing the viewer to both a purely visual or discursive experience.

Duchamp's anemic film, like his readymades, is marked by an indiffer-ence to esthetics. He explains in a 1961 interview:

As for recognizing a motivating idea: no. Indifference. Indifference to taste, taste in the sense of photographic reproduction, a taste in the sense of wellmade materials. The common factor is indifference.[9]

This indifference to esthetics is not merely a criticism of the retinal, sensa-tional character of painting or of film. Rather, in a more radical sense, Duchamp's attitude of indifference reflects his rejection of the logical op-positions that underline the very notion of difference. He explains: "For me there is something else in addition to *yes, no* and *indifferent*—that is, for in-stance, *the absence of investigations of that type.*"[10] Indifference thus comes to mean an activity and an operation upon objects and contexts marked by the oppositional difference of vision and discourse. In an even more radical sense, Duchamp also rejects the difference made by vision, insofar as vision is equated metaphysically with knowledge, sexuality and power. Duchamp moves away both in painting and cinema from an "eros of vision" to "eros c'est la vie" corresponding to his signature *Rrose Sélavy*. Paintings such as *Nude Descending a Staircase No. 2* (1912), *The Bride Stripped Bare by Her Bachelors, Even* (The Large Glass) (1915–23), challenge the metaphorical equation of sexuality and vision through a mechanical and thematic render-ing of the erotic subject. In *Anémic Cinéma* Duchamp pursues the tradi-tional interrogation of the sexual difference as the expression of the struc-tures of vision, as the retinal euphoria that constitutes the desire of the spectator.

A more precise analysis of the relation of *Anémic Cinéma* to *Nude Descend-ing a Staircase* highlights Duchamp's rejection even on the pictorial level of the equation of vision and eroticism. Its provocative character can best be understood when we consider both its rejection by the Salon des Indépendants in 1912 and the public furor occasioned by its exhibition at the New York Armory Show in 1913 where the public was divided between outrage and laughter.[11] Duchamp explains that the scandal of the painting was provoked as much by the painting as by its title:

> What contributed to the interest provoked by that canvas was its title. One just doesn't do a nude woman coming down the stairs, that's ridiculous. It doesn't seem ridiculous now, because it's been talked about so much, but when it was new, it seemed scandalous. *A nude should be respected.*[12] (Emphasis added)

Nude . . . No. 2 thus presents a clash of literal and visual expectations that are the expression of the history and conventions of painting. The scandal involves the destruction of the traditional subject of painting. The nude female body has been a subject of desire from the Renaissance to the late nineteenth century when it is finally put into question by painters such as Manet, who in paintings such as *Olympia* confront the inscription of the desiring look of the spectator.[13] The *Nude . . . No. 2* reduces the subject of both painting and desire to the status of a series of fractured volumes and virtual violence.

The picture presents the viewer with a kind of "vertigo of delay," to use Paz's term, rather than a vertigo of acceleration.[14] Duchamp's interest in kinetics is here conceptual: the movement in the painting is produced through the decomposition of the graphic. The staggered motion of the "nude" demonstrates an analysis of movement rather than the futurist seduction with the dynamics of movement.[15] The kinetic character of the nude is not merely thematization of movement as a pictorial fact, but rather, as Duchamp claims, in the decomposition of forms.

> Painted, as it is, in severe wood colors, the anatomical nude does not exist, or at least cannot be seen, since I discarded completely the naturalistic appearance of a nude, keeping only the abstract lines of some twenty different static positions in the successive action of descending.[16]

The renunciation of the visual erotic character of the nude in favor of its twenty positions in the successive act of descent reflects Duchamp's radical critique of painting through a chronophotographic freeze frame technique.[17] What is at issue here is more than a challenge of the pictorial medium through cinema – a certain ideological interpretation of pictorial vision as retinal, the cognition of communication and pleasure. Duchamp explains his anti-retinal bias in terms of his effort to expand and return to the original meaning of painting not as visual/erotic stimulation but as a conceptual intervention, one that puts the painter on the same level with the philosopher. He explains:

> Since Courbet, it's been believed that painting is addressed to the retina. That was everyone's error. The retinal shudder! Before, painting had other functions: it could be religious, philosophical, moral. If I had the chance to take an antiretinal attitude, it unfortunately hasn't changed much; our whole century is completely retinal, except for the Surrealists, who tried to go outside it somewhat. And still, they didn't go so far![18]

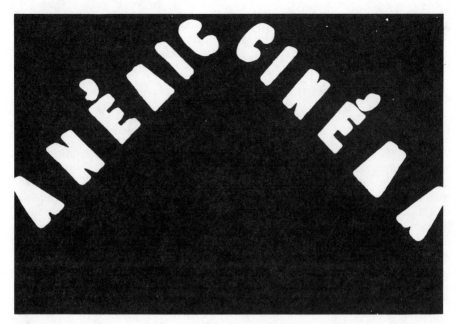

Figure 1

Consequently, Duchamp's critique of retinal vision does not imply the mere equation of cinema with painting, but rather the displacement of both media, insofar as *Nude . . . No. 2* can be considered a cinematic painting and *Anémic Cinéma* a pictorial film. Like the painting that portrays the nude as an "anti-machine" (to use Octavio Paz's evocative terminology), *Anémic Cinéma* will be considered as an anemic machine, whose kinetic character is produced through the visual literalization of graphic and discursive elements.

Anémic Cinéma (1924–26) emerges out of the kinetic and optical experiments that Duchamp conducted with Man Ray.[19] Duchamp's experiments with rotoreliefs, which he called "kinetic paintings," were assembled and filmed in *Anémic Cinéma.* They were mounted and rotated on a wheel, recalling another readymade. Thus the referent and material basis or support of *Anémic Cinéma* are themselves a combination of different readymades – the juxtaposition of optical graphic research and the readymade. The literal overlay of these two constitutive elements defines the graphic and kinetic structure of the movie. Rather than functioning as a transparent medium reflecting some external reality, the referent of the film is the visual character of esthetic perception. The opacity of the cinematic medium is doubly thematized in the film through its graphic and phonetic character. Like the readymade *Fresh Widow* (French window whose black leather panes suggest a night sky), *Anémic Cinéma* perversely plays with the transparency of the filmic medium in order to draw our attention to its material opacity. The film, like the French window, becomes an anagrammatic object of undecidable character, alternating between its visual sense and its literal meaning.

50

The presentation of the title is the only linear moment of this "round" film (Fig. 1). The two words in the title, *Anémic* and *Cinéma,* are presented as diagonal mirrors suggesting an infinite perspective whose vanishing point opens up towards the spectator. The perspectivism of traditional painting is here turned absurdly towards the viewer, since the effect of depth constituted by the later movement of the spiral opens up three-dimensionally and protrudes into the space of the spectator. The vanishing point (which Viator called subject) is no longer constituted within the confines of the pictorial space, but rather within the conceptual space of fourth-dimensional illusion. The viewer is thus excluded from representation in the picture (as a *ratio* or mathematical entity within the frame), nor is s/he allowed to constitute a stable subjectivity.

The film's effort to destabilize the traditional spectator position from the beginning with the title is pursued throughout the film not only graphically by the spiraling rotoreliefs, but also linguistically, since some of the disks have alliterative puns written upon them. In order to read the words on the rotoreliefs, the spectator is compelled to move physically. Thus, rather than producing a mere graphic inscription, Duchamp modifies the body of the viewer to move, forcing it to adapt to the projection of the image as if it were itself a screen. Interestingly enough, the rotary disk, rather than acting as a screen, mimics the shape of the eye. This illusion is reinforced by the fact that the rotoreliefs alternate by moving in opposite directions and by the fact that a flickering light constantly interferes with the legibility of the verbal puns, creating the effect of natural blinking. The eye of the viewer is thus represented figuratively, at once the site and the screen of vision literally materialized before the eyes of the spectator.

This transition between Duchamp's perspectival concerns and his critique of retinal vision as thematized in the film by the eye (both screen and object of projection) is elaborated in his notes on perspective. Duchamp claims: *"Physically* – the eye is the sense of the perspective. Because of this, *perspectivity resembles a color,* which, like color, is also not controllable by touching it.[20]

In the passage from the title or mise-en-scène of perspective, Duchamp posits the eye as both the raison d'être of perspective (its site of meaning), and also as a cognitive device that can create an optical illusion which simulates sensation, as if depth were a color. Duchamp explains, regarding the difference between third- and fourth-dimensional perspective as follows: "The vanishing point of lines corresponds to a vanishing line of planes in Perspective."[21] The problem of perspective in three-dimensional space and Duchamp's research into four-dimensional space is graphically figured in *Anémic Cinéma.* It can also be seen in Duchamp's original design for the projection of the film on a specially treated screen of translucent glass with silver mirror backing. The light would penetrate the screen before being reflected back to the viewer, producing a sense of depth and infinite dimension or recession. The rotoreliefs in movement stage an object of perception – the virtual space of the film (its fourth dimension) – at the same time that they simulate the subjective position, imitating the eye of the viewer. Through the problem of perspective, the film thus graphically enacts the

51

Figure 2

poetic transition between subject and object through the agglutination of their shared element, the eye serving as generator of both cognitive meaning and perception.

The spiraling movement of the rotoreliefs intensifies the hypnotic character of the moving image in *Anémic Cinéma,* since it establishes a movement within the frame which defies the linear movement of the film (Figs. 2 and 3). At the same time, the spiraling images abolish the naturalistic three-dimensional perspectival space by inaugurating a fourth dimension, or, as Clair called it, a "conceptual space" of optical and linguistic games. The graphic alliteration and collapse of language of the rotoreliefs amplifies the effect of this "fourth dimension," or conceptual space, which emerges as the dual effect of both optical and linguistic plays. The film thus puts into question the premises involved in our phenomenological assumptions regarding space. The film produces a new conceptual space whose character is neither purely visual nor discursive. Retinal vision is bracketed by poetic puns which threaten to transform themselves in turn into visual analogues.

Earlier, I suggested that the creation of this new conceptual space also corresponds to the character of eroticism espoused by Duchamp. From the most obvious graphic perspective, the spiraling movement of the rotoreliefs suggests an in-and-out movement, a literal allusion to the sexual act. This decomposition and mechanization of sexuality, however, cannot be reduced to a particular gender.[23] Whereas the projective movement of the spirals might literally suggest a breast, it soon becomes clear that such effects function merely as visual puns. The movement of the rotoreliefs in concentric circles also suggests a male or "malic" function — that of looking like a dart board, re-

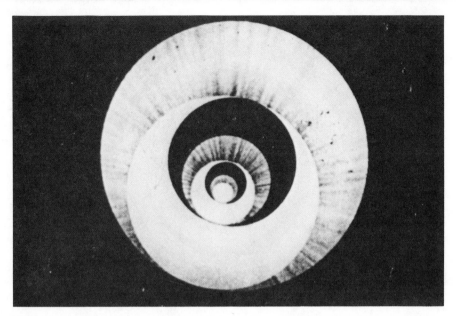

Figure 3

calling Duchamp's *Object-Dard* (Dart-Object; 1951), a pun on the French slang word for penis (Figs. 4 and 5).

The male and female functions are thus simultaneously inscribed into the conceptual space of the viewer, acting as visual puns whose meaning cannot be decided, and whose indifference threatens the viewer with its androgynous, transitional, and partial eroticism. *Anémic Cinéma* pursues the project of the anagrammatic displacement of sexuality that Duchamp inaugurates with his adoption of a new signature that closes the film – Rrose Sélavy. This new name signature/identity, accompanied by its visual analogue – Man Ray's photograph of Duchamp, echoes the question that the film itself raises about sexual difference and the identity of the film. The spiraling rotoreliefs present travesties of sexuality in such a way as to redefine the meaning of identity in general. The anagrammatic play between the spiral/dart board, female/male and the literary and phonetic elements sets the cinema into motion as a transitional object, as a readymade, a pun whose undecidable character informs its erotic character.

Visual indifferentiation produced by the self-referential rotoreliefs is also echoed on the phonetic level. The spiral movement of the rotoreliefs leads to the aspiration not only of image but also of sound or breath. The similarity of sounds and letters – their alliterative character – further diffuses any differential relations. The viewer cannot escape but must endow these verbal puns with a subjective inflection producing an endless train of associations. This can be seen in lines such as *"l'Aspirant habite javel et moi j'avais l'habite en spirale,"* *"Esquivons les ecchymoses des esquimeaux aux mots esquis,"* or *"Avez-vous déjà mis la moële de l'épée dans le poêle de l'aimée?"* or *"Inceste ou passion de famille à coups trop tirés"* (Fig. 6).

53

Figure 4

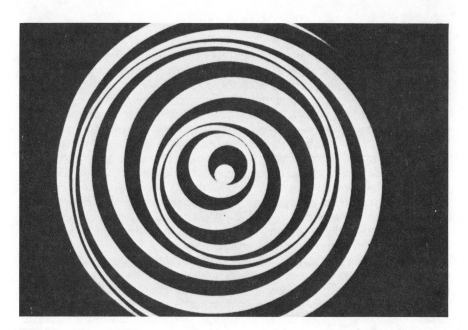

Figure 5

54

Figure 6

As Katrina Martin has eloquently shown, these verbal puns set into motion a series of mirroring consonants that play out on a vertical and horizontal axis.[24] This consonance is not purely linear but also graphic, and it is tied to the disruption of all legibility by the spiraling movement of the image. The erotic elements that Katrina Martin attempts to isolate in her article are reduced in the film to an undifferentiated sexuality that cannot be classified according to gender. Her suggestion that Duchamp is trying to attain through the ambivalence of the visual and linguistic motion the "representation of a double sexual identity, or even the realization of androgyny which would be absolute union and perfection," seems to me to diminish the character of Duchamp's erotic play in *Anémic Cinéma*.[25]

The eroticism of *Anémic Cinéma* cannot simply be reduced to a traditional interpretation of sexuality in terms of sexual difference. Duchamp does not — to use Martin's terms — "seek to master and control fleeting orgasm, and through his innovative mechanics project this split second of ecstasy into eternity."[26] Rather, Duchamp in *Anémic Cinéma* despecifies the erotic meaning of language, producing an undifferentiated erotic referent which cannot be located, viewed or possessed. The erotic here emerges merely as a kind of relay, a moment of consonance, alliteration, a spiral exploded through its obverse, the movement of aspiration as respiration. It suffices to remember that Duchamp describes his own artistic activity as nil, as not making a difference: "each breath is a work which is inscribed nowhere, which is neither visual nor cerebral."[27]

The transitional eros of *Anémic Cinéma* stages, in relation to the viewer, a new kind of subjectivity, that of the unconscious. But this unconscious is not personal, it is no more Duchamp's than the spectator's. It has been noted that two people watching the film at the same time would not perceive it in the same way.[28] This observation, however, is less the affirmation of optical differences between viewers, or a statement about their difference of imagination, than the affirmation of the otherness of the unconscious as symbolic play. This unconscious is ex-centric in character, never itself in the sense of a proper identity, but always other, spiralling anagrammatically between the film and the viewer, undecidably image, discourse or simply, a breath. The repetitive movement of the spirals and their alliterative complicity mark the insistence and persistence of eros not as a sign, but rather as signifying chain, as language. Within this chain there is no message but only the movement of signs marking the redundancy and also fluidity of both the male and the female positions. Subjectivity in *Anémic Cinéma* is reduced to this circuit and relay of signifiers in motion, that is *eros, c'est la vie* or *Rrose Sélavy*, Duchamp's travestied identity and signature to the film. Like a readymade, "a pun in three-dimensional projection," *Anémic Cinéma* affirms the transitional status of both art and eros, a rendezvous whose ostensibly indifferent character attests to the necessarily erotic character of art.

Notes

1. Cf. David Curtis, *Experimental Cinema* (New York: Universe Books, 1971); Jean Mitry, *Le Cinéma expérimental* (Paris: Seghers, 1974); Malcom Le Grice, *Abstract Film and Beyond* (Cambridge: MIT Press, 1977); and more specifically Katrina Martin, "Marcel Duchamp's Anémic-Cinéma," *Studio International* 189/973 (Jan.–Feb. 1975): 53–60.

2. A number of critics such as Le Grice and also Peter Wollen ("The Two Avant-Gardes," *Studio International* 190/978 [Nov.–Dec. 1975]) base their conclusions about the film on Barbara Rose's interpretation in "Kinetic Solutions to Pictorial Problems: The Films of Man Ray and Moholy-Nagy," *Artforum* (Sept. 1971): 68–73.

3. For a discussion of the history of the early film avant-gardes and the question of cinematic specificity, see Ian Christie, "French Avant-garde Film in the Twenties: From 'Specificity' to Surrealism," *Film as Film* (London: Arts Council, 1979), 37–45.

4. Marcel Duchamp, *Duchamp du Signe: Ecrits,* ed. M. Sanouillet (Paris: Flammarion, 1975), p. 49.

5. Pierre Cabanne, *Dialogues with Marcel Duchamp,* trans. Ron Padgett (New York: Viking, 1971), p. 48.

6. Cited by Hans Richter in *Dada Art and Anti-Art* (New York and Toronto: Oxford University Press, 1978), p. 89.

7. Arturo Schwarz, *Marcel Duchamp* (New York: Abrams, 1975), p. xxviii.

8. Schwarz, pp. xxvii–viii.

9. Otto Hahn, interviewer, "Passport No. G255300," *Art and Artists* (July 1966):10.

10. "Une Lettre de Marcel Duchamp," *Medium* (Paris, New York, Jan. 1955), p. 33; cited by Schwarz, p. xxxi.

11. For a historical assessment of Duchamp's impact in America, see Milton W. Brown, *The Story of the Armory Show* (New York: The Joseph Hirshhorn Foundation, 1963).

12. Cabanne, p. 44.

13. For a history of the female nude as object of male spectatorship and desire, see John Berger, *Ways of Seeing* (London: Penguin Books, 1972), pp. 45–64.

14. Octavio Paz, *Marcel Duchamp: Appearance Stripped Bare,* trans. R. Phillips and D. Gardner (New York: The Viking Press, 1978), p. 2.

15. See Duchamp's own qualification of abstraction in the *Nude* as more cubist than futurist in Sanouillet, p. 223. He claims not to have known the futurist works at the time (Cabanne, p. 28).

16. Sanouillet, p. 222.

17. See Duchamp's discussion of chronophotography and the cinematic influence on the *Nude* in Cabanne, p. 34.

18. Cabanne, p. 43.

19. See Schwarz's discussion of Duchamp's optical experiments, beginning with his stereoscopic slides that create three-dimensional effects through two-dimensional means, in Buenos Aires (1918), to the experiment with 3-D film based on anaglyphic process, and his construction of the first optical machine, *Rotary Glass Plates* (Precision Optics; 1920).

20. Sanouillet, p. 123.

21. Sanouillet, p. 128.

22. For his discussion of *Anémic Cinéma,* see *Le Surréalisme au cinéma* (Paris: Editions Arcanes, 1953), pp. 182–3.

23. Toby Mussman interprets the film as the metaphorization of female sexuality in "Anemic cinema," *Art and Artists* (July 1966), pp. 50–1.

24. Martin, pp. 54–5, 60.

25. Martin, p. 60.

26. Martin, p. 60.

27. Cabanne, p. 72.

28. Cf. Mussman's comments on *Anémic Cinéma,* pp. 49–51.

Exploring the Discursive Field of the Surrealist Film Scenario Text

Richard Abel

For us and us alone, the Lumière brothers invented the cinema. There we were at home. Its darkness was like that of our bedrooms before we went to sleep. The screen, we thought, might be the equal of our dreams.

Robert Desnos[1]

For us the cinema was an extraordinary discovery, and it coincided with our earliest formulations of surrealism. [. . .] we thought film a marvelous mode of expression for the dream state. [. . .] I myself believed it was possible to transpose surrealism to the screen because I considered the cinema a marvelous instrument through which one could achieve a form of surrealist poetry.

Philippe Soupault[2]

But the poets of that period were not satisfied with enjoying the (often involuntary) poetry of silent films; they themselves wrote scenarios, most of them unfilmable – oneiric confessions projected onto an imaginary screen.

Georges Neveux[3]

So let's kick off the era of unfilmable scenarios.

Benjamin Fondane[4]

In the twenties and thirties, French writers, many of them Surrealists, wrote a good number of film scenarios and published them as literary texts. Most of these hybrid textual forms appeared within a ten-year period straddling the late silent and early sound cinema, bounded approximately by the special issues of *Les Cahiers du mois* (1925) and *Les Cahiers jaunes* (1933), which were devoted exclusively to scenarios, including several by Robert Desnos.[5] Only a few of these texts, as is well known, were actually filmed – e.g., Antonin Artaud's "La Coquille et le clergyman" (by Germaine Dulac, 1928) and Luis Buñuel and Salvadore Dali's "Un Chien andalou" (1929). Critics and historians have focused attention, with good reason, on these published texts – situating them within the general aesthetic framework of Surrealism, considering specific ones in the context of a certain writer's oeuvre, analyzing several individually as unique compositional forms.[6] The quoted remarks by Desnos, Soupault, Neveux, and Fondane constitute a concise outline of the usual answer to the question of why the Surrealists bothered to write and publish film scenarios. But what were the broader cultural practices which constituted for these scenario texts a "horizon of utterance"? Specifically, what discursive practices attached to the production and exhibition of actual films – especially in the newspapers and weekly or monthly film magazines – may have provided an incentive for them? What literary publishing ventures may have offered models of composition? And what conditions within the French film industry may have given these writers some hope of actually "transposing surrealism to the screen"? In attempting to address these questions and explore the discursive field within which the Surrealist film scenario texts emerged, this essay turns to the years during and just after the Great War, especially to the period of 1917–1923.

Guillaume Apollinaire's famous speech at the avant-garde Théâtre de Vieux-Colombier, on 26 November 1917, can serve as a convenient point of departure.[7] As a theoretical statement, "L'Esprit nouveau et les poètes" moved in two contradictory directions at once. One carried it within range of the "classical renaissance" tendency in French art which, having gained impetus from the war, was beginning to curb and reverse the radical aesthetic of the pre-war period – signaling the return, in art, of patriotism, classical common sense, and moderation.[8] The other, however, extended Apollinaire's earlier advocacy of an art of experimentation, which could produce original combinations out of everyday materials and provoke "*surprise* [...] *the greatest source of what is new.*" Here the cinema, as "the popular art *par excellence,*" represented a unique opportunity.

> We should not be astonished if, with only the means they have now at their disposal, [the poets] set themselves to preparing this new art (vaster than the plain art of words) in which, like conductors of an orchestra of unbelievable scope, they will have at their disposition the entire world, its noises and its appearances, the thought and language of man, song, dance, all the arts and all the artifices [. . .] with which to compose the visible and unfolded book of the future.[9]

At the time, these words succinctly summed up the hopes of a generation of young French writers who had discovered the cinema during the war in Paris – e.g., Blaise Cendrars (editor of Editions de la Sirène), Pierre Reverdy (editor of *Nord-Sud*), Pierre Albert-Birot (editor of *SIC*), Philippe Soupault, Louis Aragon, André Breton – and among whom Apollinaire was a central figure of inspiration.[10] But were there grounds for these writers to take Apollinaire's prophetic call seriously?

Before the war, the French cinema, much like its American counterpart, relied on writers both inside and outside the industry to supply story ideas and scenarios for its films.[11] Popular novelists such as Pierre Decourcelle and Michel Carré wrote scores of scenarios for S.C.A.G.L. and Pathé-Frères, and, in the case of Carré, even directed several films. Established theater directors such as Camille de Morlhon formed film production companies, in alliance with Pathé, and directed their own original scenarios. Virtual unknowns such as Henri Fescourt and René Le Somptier used their initial scriptwriting skills to become fulltime directors at Gaumont, while others such as Abel Gance and Robert Boudrioz sold story ideas and original scenarios to S.C.A.G.L., Pathé, Gaumont, Eclair, and Film d'Art, at the same time continuing to chart careers in the theater or in journalism. As the industry turned to adaptations of novels and plays in order to satisfy the demands of the increasingly popular feature-length film format, which became standardized between 1912 and 1917, the acquisition of original scenarios declined to some extent. But young writers could still break into filmmaking during the war by writing their own scenarios – witness the initial efforts of Jacques de Baroncelli, Jacques Feyder, Marcel L'Herbier, and, of course, Gance. What this suggests is that the French film industry was hardly closed to writers at the time that Apollinaire's words were galvanizing his audience.

For various reasons, however, the industry proved unconducive to the kind of work Apollinaire had in mind. The production and distribution sectors of the industry were in a state of retreat before the "invasion" of American films; technical facilities were woefully outdated; industry leaders such as Charles Pathé were calling for scenarios appropriate for American audiences; fewer and fewer original scenarios were being filmed.[12] The writers accepted into the industry, consequently, were not drawn from the avant-garde, especially those who were seeking to annex a popular art form such as the cinema to an aesthetic project intent on breaking radically with past literary conventions and with renewing or even revolutionizing textual forms. Apollinaire's own experience was instructive. In collaboration with André Billy, writes Alan Virmaux, he had just finished an original scenario, La Bréhatine, whose melodramatic storyline catered to the recent fad in France for "Breton" films.[13] The scenario involves a novelist writing a serial about the tragic love affair of a country girl – the scenes alternate between Paris (written by Apollinaire) and Brittany (written by Billy) – and a real country girl who recognizes herself in the serial and commits suicide. The alternating scenes employ quite different styles and modes of narration – Apollinaire includes a minimum of dialogue, terse images, abrupt ellipses, interpolated shots – which may have disconcerted potential film producers.[14] For, although it was sold to the film exhibiter and financier, Serge Sandberg, La Bréhatine remained unfilmed, as well as unpublished.[15] Soupault and Albert-Birot experienced similar disappointments. Cendrars, who actually worked closely with Abel Gance on two landmark French films – J'ACCUSE (1919) and LA ROUE (1922–1923) – also found his own way blocked; as did the "Unanimist" writer, Jules Romains, whom Cendrars had persuaded to try his hand at scenario writing. In each case, these writers were deflected from the prospect of seeing their scenarios become films and instead turned to what Alain and Odette Virmaux have called the "bastard genre" of the ciné-roman and the scenario or script as literary text.[16] Here two different publishing practices already current on the margins of the French film industry helped determine the final form of their writings.

One practice involved the publication of "films racontés" which began to appear in conjunction with the new exhibition format of film serials early in the war.[17] The first of these "films racontés" seems to have been Pierre Decourcelle's version of the famous Pearl White serial, LES MYSTÈRES DE NEW YORK (1915–1916), which Pathé imported as a compilation of three Louis Gasnier serials originally produced by its American counterpart, Pathé-Exchange, in partnership with William Randolph Hearst. Decourcelle's serialization of LES MYSTÈRES DE NEW YORK was published weekly in the Paris mass daily Le Matin, beginning on 27 November 1915, each chapter coming one week in advance of the film's twenty-two weekly episodes.[18] Both film and serialization proved immensely popular, and there followed a flood of parallel film/print texts. Soon most of the Paris newspapers were printing weekly installments of either French or American film serials – e.g., *Le Petit Parisien* (the largest Paris daily) published Arthur Bernède's advance copy of Louis Feuillade's JUDEX (12 January to 30 March 1917) and LA NOUVELLE MISSION DE JUDEX (11 January to 29 March 1918), while *Le Journal* (the third largest daily after *Le Matin*) offered Maurice Leblanc's adaptation of another Pathé import, Ruth Roland's LE CERCLE ROUGE.[19] The practice became so profitable that popular book publishers began planning series of "films racontés" in multiple and, later, single volumes. La Renaissance du livre, for instance, launched its "Romans-Cinémas" with Decourcelle's *Les Mystères de New York* (1917), quickly followed by Marc Mario's *Les Exploits d'Elaine*, Marcel Allain's *Le Courrier de Washington*, Bernède's *Judex*, Leblanc's *Le Cercle rouge*, and a host of others.[20] Other series or collections included: Jules Tallandier's "Cinéma-Bibliothèque," beginning in 1917; Arthème Fayard's "Les Grands Films" beginning in 1918; and J. Ferenczi's "Le Roman complet" also built up around Feuillade's popular serials, beginning with LES DEUX GAMINES in 1921.[21] By 1922, the French reading and film-going public could support several weekly film magazines devoted largely or even exclusively to all kinds of "films racontés" and not only serials – *Ciné-Miroir* (published by *Le Petit Parisien*), *Mon Ciné*, and *Le Film complet*.[22] Finally, a number of "limited edition" romans-cinémas were even aimed at a more elite audience: Philippe Hériat's novelization of L'Herbier's EL DORADO (La Lampe merveilleuse, 1921) and Ricciotto Canudo's version of Gance's LA ROUE (J. Ferenczi, 1923).[23]

A second publishing practice, no less important though much less widespread, appeared in a limited number of film journals toward the end of the war. Here Louis Delluc, the young editor and chief film critic of *Le Film*, seems to have played a crucial role. Shortly after Apollinaire's speech at the Vieux-Colombier, Delluc broached a singular indea in his "Notes pour moi" column: the publication of actual scenarios.

Now that we are getting respectable scenarios – much as happened in music not long ago – let's publish them. Let's print them just as they were written. And I predict that they will be read with delight. [. . .] One piece of advice: print such texts without any sort of illustration.[24]

The immediate impetus for these words was the release of Mercanton and Hervil's LE TORRENT (1917), which he felt conventionalized Marcel L'Herbier's quite lyrical and highly symbolic original scenario. A little over one month later, in *Le Film*, Delluc tentatively introduced the first example of such a scenario, Soupault's short cinematic poem, "Indifférence," with a note reiterating Apollinaire's call for young poets to write and direct for the cinema.[25] Then, more boldly, he launched a series of longer scenarios in the magazine, selecting the original work of writers and writer-directors whom he considered the advance-guard of a renewal of the French cinema. L'Herbier's scenario for BOUCLETTE (which was released in November, 1918) led off the series in April, 1918, followed by Gance's initial draft of J'ACCUSE, for which shooting had just begun, and Georges Lacroix's HAINE (which was previewed one week later, in June, 1918).[26]

61

Although this initial scenario series was soon discontinued, when Delluc and Henri Diamant-Berger (the publisher of *Le Film*) increasingly turned their attention toward actual film production, at least one significant variation on this venture cropped up in the new industry journal, *Filma*. One year after the initial release of J'ACCUSE, and as a further sign of its considerable impact in France, *Filma* published the full découpage or continuity script of Gance's film – including shot numbers, camera set ups, framing and editing devices, intertitles, and frame illustrations.

665. American shot. Jean lets in all the people who are pressing at the door [of François and Edith's house]. He is absolutely lucid: "I am the one who invited you, come in, all of you . . ."
666. American shot. The great hall is filled with mothers in mourning, widows and war orphans, old men, youngsters. Only the hearth fire lights the room. [. . .]
667. Reverse angle shot. – Near the hearth. – The flames of the roaring fire illuminate the figures in front of it. All these poor anxious people, whether well or ill, are seated in a circle or are clustered in the depths of the room.
668. Close up of Jean. With the air of a clairvoyant, he draws everyone's attention to himself.
669. Close up of Edith, disconcerted, but not daring to question Jean.
Slow iris out.
670. Iris in on a wing of the hospital.
(Take a negative image of Ecce Homo)
671. Close up. A doctor speaks to a guard:
Screen: "Have you found Jean Diaz, the escapee from the asylum?"
End of shot: "No," says the guard. . . .
Slow iris out.
672. Iris in on the interior of François' house. All the listeners are gathered around Jean.
673. Close up of Jean. He speaks with passionate conviction:
Screen: "That evening I was on sentry duty on the battlefield. All of your cherished dead were there, all your cherished dead . . . every one of them . . ."
End of shot: *Fade out*[27]

Although this découpage format saw only limited use throughout the rest of the decade, it nonetheless provided an alternative model to that of the more popular "film raconté" for the new kind of literary text which was then emerging.

The first unfilmed scenario texts to appear in the context of these two publishing practices – e.g., Cendrars' "La Fin du monde filmée par l'ange N.-D." (1919), Albert-Birot's "2 × 2 = 1" (1919), Romains' "Donogoo-Tonka ou les miracles de la science" (1919) – represent both an extension of the one practice and its radical reorientation through the influence of the other.[28] In one sense, these texts tend to look like "films racontés" rather than detailed découpages. Cendrars' and Romains' scenarios, for instance, divide their fantastic adventures into short omniscient scenes, involve a good deal of movement through space and time (without resorting to framing or editing devices), and exhibit a prose style marked by clipped sentences or phrases.

God the father gets into his luxurious automobile.

We see the straight and rectilinear new quarters of the GRIGRI COMMUNION TRUST Co. Ltd., whose huge neon sign is ablaze in the twilight. It's evening. Thousands of employees are leaving their offices. Bustling crowds. Indescribable comings and goings. Eddies. Congestions. An infinite variety of costumes. Monks, priests, popes, seminarians, clergymen, missionaries, catechumens have been put in charge of the offices in which lovely young nuns are typists.[29]

The form of these scenario texts was probably due not only to the sheer volume of "films racontés" in the newspaper kiosks and bookshops in Paris but also to the young writers' obvious interest in and use of popular literature. The "films racontés," after all, constituted a new form of the popular "roman-feuilleton" which had dominated French fiction since the 1830s, when publishers such as Gervais Chapentier and Gustave Barba as well as new papers such as *La Presse* and *Le Siècle* began printing cheap serial editions of novels by Paul de Kock, Alexandre Dumas, and Eugène Sue.[30] And many of the authors then currently writing both scenarios and "films racontés" – e.g., Decourcelle, Bernède, Allain – were among the most prominent exponents of the "roman-feuilleton" tradition. Before the war, Apollinaire had already evidenced a strong interest in such popular fiction, and particularly its conjunction with the cinema, in the pages of his arts magazine, *Les Soirées de Paris* (1912–1914). There he and his associates (including Cendrars) celebrated the policier serials – specifically, the Pierre Souvestre-Marcel Allain novels and Louis Feuillade's five film adaptations (1913–1914), which detailed the exploits of the arch-criminal Fantômas, and in honor of whom they even formed a special "Société des amis de Fantômas."[31] The "films racontés" within this "roman-feuilleton" tradition thus provided an apt resource for the subject, fantastic action, and stylistic format of these early scenario texts or ciné-romans.

However, there was one important difference between the two. People usually read the "film raconté" before going to the cinema, or shortly thereafter, and thus used it as either a prior text or a proscriptive framework for perceiving, understanding, and recalling any one film, specifically as a story. As Alain Virmaux suggests, the "film raconté" may have performed a crucial function in conventionalizing and standardizing the discursive possibilities of the early French narrative cinema.

At first the public was baffled by the rapid succession of images [in the cinema]; they came up against a precipitate rhythm for which they were unprepared, and they tended to resist this uninterrupted wave of signs and sought a way of securing a hold over their elusive unfolding. To the mind disconcerted, manhandled, and tossed head over heels by this headlong rush, the printed text, read and reread calmly and at leisure, immediately seemed the best possible kind of harness. It served to immobilize what always eluded them, escaping all control and slipping through their fingers. In a civilization governed by speech and ruled over many centuries by the conventions of print, such a response was perfectly natural and predictable. The written text allowed for the secure reining in of the intractable image.[32]

Inextricably bound up with a particular film text, the "film raconté" tended to subdue and stabilize the film's sequence of images and close off its meaning.

By contrast, much like the scenarios published in *Le Film,* the scenario texts of Cendrars, Albert-Birot, and Romains sought to import the "elusive, head-long rush" of film discourse into verbal language and thus generate an imaginary flow of images whose specific representation would vary according to the reader and whose meaning would remain more open. In a sense, then, these texts constituted an attempt to recover and redeploy what these writers most admired in the cinema—first in the French and American serials, then in the Mack Sennett and Charlie Chaplin comedies, and even in the older trick films—the transformation of the ordinary and everyday through surprising juxtapositions and marvelous metamorphoses. Blocked from using their texts as blueprints to produce actual films (Pathé apparently rejected an initial draft of Cendrars' scenario),[33] the writers turned them into a new textual form of *play.* If, as creators, they could not gain access to the new popular art of the cinema, at least they would use it to "revolutionize" the forms and conventions of literature itself.

A different form of ciné-roman appeared shortly after this first series of scenario texts, a form that eschewed the model of the "film raconté" for that of the découpage. Here the key text was another Cendrars scenario, "La Perle fièvreuse," published in the literary review, *Signaux de France et la Belgique* (1921–1922).[34] Apparently Cendrars wrote this scenario originally for the Rinascimento Studio in Italy (under a contract secured through his previous production work with Gance), but it too was never filmed. The subject was no less difficult and wide-ranging than that of *La Fin du monde,* for it involved "a spoof on current detective fiction, with Fantômas, Nick Carter, Arsène Lupin, Gustave Le Rouge, Conan Doyle, Maurice Leblanc (author of the Arsène Lupin stories), and Rouletabille (hero of a series by Gaston Leroux) as a kind of Keystone cops trying to solve the disappearance of two women."[35] Yet in format, "La Perle fièvreuse" closely followed the notational system established by the découpage of Gance's "J'Accuse," published just one year before in *Filma.* It was divided into approximately 850 shots and included very detailed technical notations on framing and editing.

1. Iris in slowly on a small statue of Shiva dancing. Hold; then pan slowly over to the maid Co-Thaô, standing in a simple black dress. Hold; then track-dolly (in the same direction as the pan) until the camera reaches the door, which opens.

2. Now dolly through the doorway toward the meeting of the Hindu dancer Rougha and Miss Ethel Berkshire, who enters with an armful of flowers.

3. Close shot of Miss Ethel, surprised and delighted, brightly lit, a little in front of the door.

4. Close shot of Rougha, slightly severe, smiling mysteriously, in the shadow of the door.

5. Long shot of [room] I, taken from the doorway (similar to [shot] 2 [reverse direction]). The two young women enter the room. Rougha drops her cloak to reveal a dazzling dance costume. The young women sit down on some low cushions, after having disposed of the flowers; Ethel is very amused, Rougha keeps smiling mysteriously and signals to the maid who exits (very quickly).

6. American shot. The young women chat, particularly Miss Ethel, who is a little excited.

7. All at once she lets out a cry as she draws her feet up and looks at the floor in fright.
8. Quick tilt down in the direction of Miss Ethel's look; we see three porcupines pass by.
9. Close shot of Miss Ethel – who bursts out laughing – (several images).
10. Close shot of Rougha who smiles slightly more – (several images).
11. American shot of the two young women chatting as in [shot] 6.[36]

Addressed to an audience outside the film industry (in contrast to "J'Accuse"), in Alain Virmaux's words, this text challenged the reader with

a deliberately flat language, technicalized to the extreme, stripped of any verbal magic, [a language] which reflected – in a way that was slightly provocative – the canons of the most up-to-date as well as the most overtly commercial film productions.[37]

Although one could hardly agree that Cendrars's opening lines here are devoid of "verbal magic," the publication of "La Perle fièvreuse" certainly did give a technical document or blueprint the independent status of a literary text.

The assumption that sophisticated or even ordinary French readers could accept and comprehend such a printed text shortly thereafter provided the basis, in part, for Delluc's decision to publish four of his own scenarios (although previously filmed, none had come close to being popular or profitable) in *Drames du cinéma* (Le Monde nouveau, 1923).[38] The four scenarios are divided into individual shots (ranging from 150 to 425 shots each), but Delluc deliberately eschews the technical notations which mark Cendrars and Gance's scripts and opts instead for the clipped, elliptical language of Cendrars and Romains' earlier scenarios.

1. Pierre alone, in his rooms. Beside a reading lamp. Dressing gown. Book or evening paper. Cigar. Quiet.
2. The table next to which he is seated.
3. A woman's photo. It's Suzie. Young, elegant, well dressed. Nearby, a letter.
4. Pierre's hand. Neatly manicured. Three or four rings in exquisite taste.
5. The hand moves toward the letter: it picks up the photo.
6. Pierre looks at the photo, smiling. He is pleased thinking of Suzie. A physical rather than romatic pleasure.
7. The hand places the photo back on the table and picks up the letter. In order to make reading it more easy, the other hand puts down the cigar . . .
8. . . . in a glass and copper ashtray on the opposite corner of the table.
9. In his armchair, Pierre opens the letter. The scent emanating from it makes him smile.[39]

Here a further assumption seems to determine this choice, an assumption that reverses the priority of verbal language over the film image – as in the "film raconté." For Delluc assumes (perhaps questionably) that the conventions of film discourse are sufficiently known and understood so that, even if unmentioned, they now shape, if not "harness," the unfolding of each "shot" or descriptive phrase and its duration in the reader's imagination. "It is his imagination, aided by his intelligence [or knowledge of film conventions]," he insists, "that will evoke the images according to the intended distance, the intended scale or dimension, and the intended movement."[40] Delluc's scenario texts thus constitute an intriguing synthesis of the "film raconté," the scenario, and the découpage – a synthesis in which the conventions of film discourse could function as a given of the common cultural horizon or ground.

By the middle and late 1920s, then, a broad spectrum of publishing practices in France formed a material context for the Surrealist scenario texts. The "films racontés" format flourished in the magazine market, in cheap weeklies such as *Mon-Ciné, Ciné-Miroir*, and *Le Film complet* as well as in special deluxe publications such as *La Petite Illustration* (seventeen numbers between 1925 and 1931).[41] In the book market, it encompassed a wide range of series from the most popular – the "Cinéma-Bibliothèque" series of Jules Tallandier – to the most prestigious – the "Cinéma-romanesque" series of Gallimard, launched in 1928.[42] Original scenarios or ciné-romans cropped up everywhere – e.g., the special issue of *Les Cahiers du mois* (1925), Gallimard's "Cinario" series (1925–1927), Henri Barbusse's *Force* (Flammarion, 1926), Alfred Marchard's *Le Clown et sa chimère* (La Renaissance du livre, 1927), Henry Poulaille's *Le Train fou* (Grasset, 1928), Pierre Chenal's *Drames sur celluloid* (Les Perspectives, 1929), the special issue of *Le Rouge et le noir* (1928).[43] Detailed découpage excerpts from the work of Jean Epstein, Germaine Dulac, and others were featured in Jean Dréville's deluxe monthly, *Cinégraphie* (1927–1928);[44] and at least two full-length découpage texts saw publication, both attributed to Gance – *Napoléon vu par Abel Gance* (Plon, 1927) and *La roue, scénario original arrangé par Jean Arroy* (Tallandier, 1930).

Given the context of this spectrum, the Surrealist scenario texts of the late 1920s and early 1930s hardly constituted the anomalous, autonomous objects they are too often still taken for. Some such as Francis Picabia's *La Loi d'accommodation chez borgnes* (1928), Georges Ribemont-Dessaignes' "Le huitième jour de la semaine" (1930), and even Artaud's "La Révolte du boucher" (1930) employed a format similar to that established ten years before by Cendrars, Romains, and Albert-Birot.[45] Most, however, used a synthetic format modelled on that which Delluc had developed for his *Drames du cinéma*. In a 1927 note, which reciprocated the critic's generosity toward the young Dada-Surrealists in the pages of *Le Film*, Desnos acknowledged the impact of Delluc's work: "for the first time in France we witnessed an actual cinematically-created film based on a genuine scenario."[46] Desnos' own earliest published scenario, "Minuit à quatorze heures," followed that model closely:

15. The lover tries to free his fishing line which is tangled in the reeds.

16. He leans out over the bridge parapet. Leans out further and falls.

17. Rippling circles on the water.

18. On a nearby hilltop, a peasant has seen the fall. He runs off.

19. The two other characters [his mistress and a young man who have gone for a surreptitious stroll] come out on the bridge. They call for their companion. Lean out over the parapet: rippling circles on the water.

20. The sun. The two strollers become dizzy. White circles dance around them.
21. The fishing line drifts downstream.
22. The peasant runs up. Explanations.
23. Rippling circles on the water.
24. A skiff. Probings with a gaffe.
25. The shoreline downstream. The body of a drowned man at the foot of a tree.
26. Evening. The woman and the young man stand pensive at a window.
27. The setting sun a round ball.
28. Kisses.
29. Their eyes in close shots. The pupils wide.
30. Night. The lamp is lit. A circle of light on the ceiling. A circle outlined by the lampshade on the floor.[47]

Desnos himself continued to use this format in his later scenarios; and his example, along with Artaud's "La Coquille et le clergyman" (1927), inspired others as well—e.g., Fondane's *Trois scénarii* (1928), Georges Neveux's "L'Amazon des cimetières" (1930).[48]

Fondane's 1928 call for an "era of unfilmable scenarios," consequently, came not at the beginning but at the height of the French publication of such texts. And the change over to sound films or "talkies" in 1929–1930, which severely restricted independent film production in France, merely confirmed that most of these scenarios would remain "unfilmable."[49] Despite their small number and the characteristics they indeed shared with the deluge of "films racontés," ciné-romans, and découpages at the time, the Surrealist scenario texts did, of course, have a unique significance. After all, they constituted an important front in the Surrealist project to revolutionize perception and representation, as it informed both cultural and socio-economic practices. The cinema seemed to offer a means of producing a discourse analogous to that of the dreamwork or unconscious processes so crucial to the Surrealists, whether on actual cinema screens or on an imaginary screen constructed by the scenario text. Even here, however, they were responding to the groundwork and fertile visions of their predecessors, and not only those of Apollinaire. The earliest and perhaps best description of the cinema as a dream scene came from Jules Romains, in 1911:

The group dream now begins. They sleep; their eyes no longer see. They are no longer conscious of their bodies. Instead there are only passing images, a gliding and rustling of dreams. They no longer realize they are in a large square chamber, immobile, in parallel rows as in a plowed field. A haze of visions which resemble life hovers before them. Things have a different appearance than they do outside. They have changed color, outline, and gesture. Creatures seem gigantic and move as if in a hurry. What controls their rhythm is not ordinary time, which occupies most people when they are not dreaming. Here they are quick, capricious, drunken, constantly skipping about, sometimes they attempt enormous leaps when least expected. Their actions have no logical order. Causes produce strange effects like golden eggs.[50]

The Surrealists simply wanted to make sure those golden eggs kept coming.

Notes

1. Robert Desnos, "FANTOMAS, LES VAMPIRES, LES MYSTÈRES DE NEW YORK," *Le Soir* (27 February 1927). All translations are my own unless otherwise indicated.

2. Jean-Marie Mabire, "Entretien avec Philippe Soupault," *Etudes cinématographiques* 38–39 (Spring 1965): 29.

3. Georges Neveux, "De JUDEX à L'ETOILE DE MER," *Etudes cinématographiques* 38–39 (Spring 1965): 47.

4. Benjamin Fondane, "2 × 2," *Trois Scénarii* (Paris: Robert Bazc, 1928), [n.p.].

5. Robert Desnos, "Minuit à quatorze heures," *Les Cahiers du mois* 12 (1925) – reprinted in Desnos, *Cinéma* (Paris: Gallimard, 1966), 21–28. Robert Desnos, "Y a des punaises dans le roti de porc," *Les Cahiers jaunes* 4 (1933): 46–50.

6. See, for instance, Marie-Claire Dumas," Un Scénario exemplaire de Robert Desnos," *Etudes cinématographiques* 38–39 (Spring 1965): 135–139. J. H. Matthews, *Surrealism and Film* (Ann Arbor: University of Michigan Press, 1971), 51–76. Alain et Odette Virmaux, *Les Surréalistes et le cinéma* (Paris: Seghers, 1976), 64–75. Steven Kovács, *From Enchantment to Rage: The Story of Surrealist Cinema* (Cranbury: Associated University Presses, 1980), 59–61, 157–176.

7. Apollinaire's essay was published a year later, shortly after his death, in *Mercure de France* 491 (1 décembre 1918): 385–396.

8. See, for instance, Kenneth Eric Silver, *Esprit de Corps: The Great War and French Art, 1914–1924* (Ann Arbor: UMI Press, 1981).

9. This translation is by Roger Shattuck, from *Selected Writings of Guillaume Apollinaire*, ed. Shattuck (New York: New Directions, 1971), 228.

10. See, for instance, André Billy, *L'Epoque contemporaine, 1905–1930* (Paris: Jules Tallendier, 1956), 174; Michel Décaudin, "Les Poètes découvrent le cinéma (1914–1918)," *Etudes cinématographiques* 38–39 (Spring 1965): 78; Philippe Soupault, *Ecrits sur le cinéma, 1918–1931*, ed. Odette and Alain Virmaux (Paris: Plon, 1979), 24; Kovács, *From Enchantment to Rage*, 23–27.

11. See, for instance, Yhcam, "La Cinématographie," *Ciné-Journal*, 192 (27 April 1912): 25–26. Information on scenario attributions can be found in the pages of *Ciné-Journal* (1908–1914) and *Pathé-Journal* (1911–1914) as well as in Jean Mitry, *Filmographie universelle*, tomes XXIII and XXIV (Bois d'Arcy: CNC, 1981). For an excellent analysis of the early American cinema's practice of using scenarios written by short story writers, see Kristin Thompson, "From Primitive to Classical," in David Bordwell, Janet Staiger, and Thompson, *The Classical Hollywood Cinema: Film Style and Mode of Production to 1960* (New York: Columbia University Press, 1985), 165–166.

12. For a fuller analysis of French film industry conditions at the end of the war, see Abel, *French Cinema: The First Wave, 1915–1929* (Princeton: Princeton University Press, 1984), 7–14. Delluc noted, for instance, that, of the winning entries submitted to the scenario contests organized by *Cinéa* and *Bonsoir* in 1922–1923, not one had been taken up for filming by the French production companies – Delluc, "Prologue," *Drames du cinéma* (Paris: Le Monde nouveau, 1923), i.

13. Alain Virmaux, "*La Bréhatine* et le cinéma: Apollinaire en quête d'un langage neuf," *Archives des lettres modernes* 126 (1971): 106–108. See also André Billy et Guillaume Apollinaire, "*Le Bréhatine,*" *Archives des lettres modernes* 126 (1971): 75–96. Soupault and Breton collaborated similarly on a prose text which Breton would later

consider the earliest Surrealist work, *Les Champs magnétiques* (Paris: Au sans pareil, 1920), excerpts of which first appeared in their magazine, *Littérature*, in 1919.

14. Virmaux, *"La Bréhatine* et le cinéma," 110–111.

15. Virmaux, *"La Bréhatine* et le cinéma," 98, 116.

16. Alain et Odette Virmaux, *Le Ciné-roman: un genre nouveau* (Paris: Edilig, 1983), 13.

17. For a summary analysis of the development of the French film serial format, see Abel, *French Cinema: The First Wave, 1915–1929,* 71–85.

18. Pathé-Frères ads in *Ciné-Journal* 322 (15 octobre 1915), and 327 (20 novembre 1915). See also Georges Dureau, "Genre nouveau," *Ciné-Journal* 323 (22 octobre 1915): 3–4.

19. René Jeanne et Charles Ford, *Le Cinéma et la presse, 1895–1960* (Paris: Armand Colin, 1961), 164–165. Francis Lacassin, *Louis Feuillade* (Paris: Seghers, 1964), 193. Claude Bellanger, Jacques Godechot, Pierre Guiral, et Fernand Terrou, *Histoire générale de la presse française,* Tome III: De 1871 à 1940 (Paris: Presses universitaires de France, 1972), 430–431.

20. Christian Bosséno, "Le Cinéma et la presse (II)," *La Revue du cinéma: image et son* 342 (septembre 1979): 94–95.

21. Lacassin, *Louis Feuillade,* 194–195. Some of this information generously was provided by Emmanuelle Toulet, an assistant curator at the Bibliothèque de l'Arsenal in Paris.

22. Bosséno, "Le Cinéma et la presse (II)," 96–97.

23. Hériat wrote under the pseudonym of Raymond Payelle and eventually was elected to the Académie Goncourt.

24. Louis Delluc, "Notes pour moi," *Le Film* 94 (décembre 1917): 14. This essay is reprinted in Delluc, *Cinéma et cie* (Paris: Grasset, 1919), 98–99.

25. Philippe Soupault, "Indifférence," *Le Film* 101 (18 février 1918): 18–19. Soupault's poem had first appeared in *SIC* 25 (janvier 1918): 4. Delluc's connections with the circle of young Dada-Surrealists was such that he also published Louis Aragon's first poem, "Charlot sentimental," in *Le Film* 105 (18 mars 1918): 11, as well as his famous essay, "Du Décor," *Le Film* 131 (16 septembre 1918): 8–10.

26. Marcel L'Herbier, "Bouclette," *Le Film* 106–107 (2 avril 1918): 75–94. Anon., "Présentations," *Le Film* 138–139 (11 novembre 1918): 18–19. Abel Gance, "J'Accuse," *Le Film* 108–109 (15 avril 1918): 10–12, 16, 18–20, 21–22. Georges Lacroix, "Haine," *Le Film* 117 (10 juin 1918): 15, 18–24, 28. Anon., "Présentations," *Le Film* 118 (17 juin 1918): 13.

27. Abel Gance, "J'ACCUSE (découpage)," *Filma* 67 (mai 1920) – reprinted in Virmaux, *Le Ciné-roman,* 130.

28. Blaise Cendrars, *La Fin du monde filmée par l'ange N.-D.* Composition en couleurs par Fernand Léger (Paris: Editions de la sirène, 1919). Pierre Albert-Birot, "2×2=1," *SIC* 49–50 (15–30 octobre 1919): 389–392. Jules Romains, "Donogoo-Tonka ou les miracles de la science," *Nouvelle Revue française* 74 (novembre 1919): 821–869, and 75 (décembre 1919): 1016–1063. Fragments of Cendrars' scenario had appeared earlier in *La Caravane* (octobre 1916) and in *Mercure de France* 491 (1 décembre 1918): 419–430. Romains' scenario was also published in book form by the *Nouvelle Revue française* in 1920. A related German literary text published shortly after those of Cendrars, Romains, and Albert-Birot was Ivan Goll's *Die Chaplinade, eine Kinodichtung* (Dresden: Rudolf Kaemmerer Verlag, 1920), translated into French in *La Vie des let-*

tres et des arts (juillet 1921). Canudo also published a serial "roman visuel," *L'Autre Aile,* in *Le Figaro* (1921), as well as "Schahrazade, la fille de la cité, graphique de poème visuel," in *Le Figaro* (19 juillet 1921). L'AUTRE AILE was released as a Henri Andréani film in 1924 and published in one volume by Eugène Fasquelle the same year.

29. Cendrars, *La Fin du monde filmée par l'ange N.-D.,* 18. For a brief analysis of Cendrars' scenario, see Abel, "American Film and the French Literary Avant-Garde, 1914-1924," *Contemporary Literature* 17 (Winter, 1976): 93-94, as well as Monique Chefdor, *Blaise Cendrars* (Boston: Twayne, 1980), 69-71. For a brief analysis of Romains' "Donogoo-Tonka," see Denis Boak, *Jules Romains* (Boston: Twayne, 1974), 71-74.

30. Yves Olivier-Marin, *Histoire du roman populaire en France, de 1840 à 1980* (Paris: Albin Michel, 1980), 27-29, 43-45.

31. For a brief analysis of Apollinaire's interest in the cinema as expressed in *Les Soirées de Paris,* see Virmaux, *"Le Bréhatine* et le cinéma," 105-106; Abel, "The Contribution of the French Literary Avant-Garde to Film Theory and Criticism, 1907-1924," *Cinema Journal* 14 (Spring, 1975): 21-22; and Abel, "American Film and the French Literary Avant-Garde, 1914-1924," 87-88.

32. Alain et Odette Virmaux, *Le Ciné-roman,* 17.

33. Alain et Odette Virmaux, *Le Ciné-roman,* 29. *Littérature* announced the appearance of a Louis Aragon film or scenario entitled "La Main chaude" in both its May and June issues, in 1920; but no such text was ever published or filmed. Several of Soupault's "cinematic poems" apparently were filmed by Walter Ruttmann in Germany in 1922, but no prints seem to have survived.

34. Blaise Cendrars, "La Perle fièvreuse," *Signaux de France et la Belgique* 7 (1 novembre 1921): 345-352; 9 (1 janvier 1922): 476-491; 10 (1 février 1922): 530-544; 11-12 (mars-juin 1922): 606-666. *Signaux de France et de Belgique* was a monthly literary review edited by André Salmon (in Paris) and Franz Hellens (in Brussels).

35. Jay Bochner, *Blaise Cendrars: Discovery and Re-creation* (Toronto: University of Toronto Press, 1978), 65-66. Several films "spoofing detective fiction" actually preceded or immediately followed Cendrars' scenario – e.g., Jacques Feyder's LE PIED QUI ENTREINT (1916), Alexandre Volkoff's LA MAISON DU MYSTERE (1922-1923), and Ivan Mosjoukine's LE BRASIER ARDENT (1923). Cendrars's title, "La Perle fièvreuse," may well have been a take off on Gustave Le Rouge's *La Tour fièvreuse* (La Maison du livre moderne, 1913). Shortly after this script was published, he assembled phrases from another Le Rouge serial novel, *Le Mysterieux Docteur Cornélius,* into the "assemblage" poems of *Kodak* (1924) – see the Exposition catalogue, *1913* (Paris: Société des Amis de la Bibliothèque nationale, 1983), 66.

36. Blaise Cendrars, "La Perle fièvreuse," *Signaux de France et de Belgique,* 7 (1 novembre 1921), 345-346.

37. Alain et Odette Virmaux, *Le Ciné-roman,* 30.

38. The four scenarios were for LA FÊTE ESPAGNOLE (filmed by Germaine Dulac, 1920), LE SILENCE (1920), FIÈVRE (1921), and LA FEMME DE NULLE PART (1922). An extract from LA FEMME DE NULLE PART also appeared in *Cinémagazine* 3 (6 juillet 1923): 17-19.

39. Louis Delluc, "Le Silence," *Drames du cinéma,* 19-20. Delluc himself used lines 201 to 205 from "Fièvre" as an example of his style, in the "Prologue" to these collected scenarios. For a brief analysis of Delluc's LE SILENCE, see Abel, *French Cinema: The First Wave, 1915-1929,* 314-315.

40. Louis Delluc, "Prologue," *Drames du cinéma,* v.

70

41. For the complete list of *La Petite Illustration* issues, see Bosséno, "Le Cinéma et la presse (II)," 96-97.

42. Virmaux, *Le Ciné-roman,* 35-37.

43. Virmaux, *Le Ciné-roman,* 33-34, 36-39.

44. See, for instance, Germaine Dulac, "LA FOLIE DES VAILLANTS (fragments)," *Cinégraphie* 1 (15 septembre 1927):9-10; Jean Epstein, "SIX ET DEMI X ONZE (UN KODAK)," *Cinégraphie* 2 (15 octobre 1927): 33-35; Henri Chomette, "LE CHAUF-FEUR DE MADEMOISELLE," *Cinégraphie* 4 (15 décembre 1927): 65-67.

45. Francis Picabia, *La Loi d'accommodation chez borgnes* (Paris: Th. Briant, 1928). Georges Ribemont-Dessaignes, "Le huitième jour de la semaine," *La Revue du cinéma* 7 (1 février 1930): 13-27. Antonin Artaud, "La Révolte du boucher," *Nouvelle Revue française* 201 (1 juin 1930) – translated by Victor Corti in Alain Virmaux, "Artaud and Film," *Tulane Drama Review* 11 (Fall, 1966): 180-185. For a brief analysis of Picabia's scenario, see Kovács, *From Enchantment to Rage,* 96. For an analysis of Artaud's scenario, see Matthews, *Surrealism and Film,* 64-66, and Kovács, *From Enchantment to Rage,* 174-176.

46. Robert Desnos, "Louis Delluc (1927)," *Cinéma* (Paris: Gallimard, 1966), 196.

47. Desnos, "Minuit à quatorze heures," 22.

48. Georges Neveux, "L'Amazon des cimetières," *La Revue du cinéma* 6 (1 janvier 1930): 48-54.

49. For a summary analysis of the change over to sound film in France, see Abel, *French Cinema: The First Wave, 1915-1929,* 59-65, 272-73.

50. Jules Romains, "La Foule au cinématographe," *Puissances de Paris* (Paris: Eugène Figuière et cie, 1911), 120.

Benjamin Fondane's
"Scenarii intournables"
Peter Christensen

In 1928 Benjamin Fondane published his *Trois Scenarii—Ciné-poèmes* in Brussels through Esprit Nouveau. These scenarios were not reprinted until they appeared in 1984 along with five essays on film in an edition, *Ecrits pour le cinéma*, edited by Michel Carassou, the chief instigator of the Fondane revival.[1] These scenarios, "Paupières mûres," "Barre fixe," and "Mtasipol," have not yet found their way into a history of Dada/Surrealist film practice and theory. This essay will try to correct this situation by providing a background to the scenarios, an analysis of them, and a comparison of them with other avant-garde films and scenarios of the 1920s.

The best introduction to Fondane's career as a poet and existentialist philosopher is still John Kenneth Hyde's *Benjamin Fondane: A Presentation of His Life and Work* (1971). However, Hyde does not consider Fondane's scenarios or essays on cinema.[2] Michel Carassou's introduction to *Ecrits pour le cinéma* is too brief to analyze the content of the scenarios, but he points out why Fondane was attracted to silent films:

> Because he had lost all confidence in words, Fondane was able to get excited about silent films. Totally freed from language, and thus from rational discourse, and from the norms and limits which it engenders, the cinema seemed to him like a new form of knowledge, more authentic even than poetry. It offered a chance to arrive at another conception of the human—at something lived which no longer allowed itself to be in contradiction with thought.[3]

Fondane's own six-page preface, "2×2," to the scenarios also does not discuss the filmscripts themselves, only the rationale behind them. Fondane, who began as a symbolist poet, writing in his native Roumanian, wanted his scenarios to be read only, not filmed. Near the close of "2×2," he writes:

> Let us therefore inaugurate the era of unfilmable scenarios. A little of the amazing beauty of a foetus can be found there. Let us say at once that these scenarios written to be read will be suddenly drowned by literature (note the trace of acid in my cine-poems), the true scenario being by nature very difficult to read and impossible to write. But then why deliberately hold on to this nothingness? Because a part of myself which poetry represses, in order to be able to pose its own agonizing questions, has just found in the cinema an all-purpose amplifier. (E 19–20).

It seems as if the hope that Fondane, as a young man, originally had in poetry was first transferred to the provocations of Dadaism and Surrealism and then to film. His later move to existential philosophy in the *Faux Traité d'Esthétique* (1938), was furthered by the death of silent film, as well as by the approaching death of Surrealism as it degenerated into a codified means of gaining knowledge and avoiding encounters with the real ("le réel").

In "Présentation de films purs" (the first of four theoretical essays on the cinema), delivered in Argentina in 1929 before a film screening for Vittoria Ocampo's circle, we see Fondane's messianic hope in a nebulous new world instigated by the avant-garde.

To the attentive eye, the modern spirit, including Dada and Surrealism, is characterized not as a destructor but as an "agent provocateur," obliging European civilization to produce at an accelerated rate the acts of suicide necessary to make place finally for something else. (E 64).

In a striking analogy, Fondane states that Dada was to cubism what the Terror was to the States-General or what the October Revolution was to the February Revolution. The nihilistic and catastrophic element of Dada is apparent in the idea of films which cannot be filmed; they do not harden into works of art, but exist as events in the reader's mind. For Fondane, the pure film ("film pur"), a term not specifically defined by him, was "an individual operation of beginning from scratch, of analysis, of transformation – an episode of struggle" (E 62). The sound film, Fondane thought, had no element of contestation about it. In his 1930 essay, "Du muet au parlant: Grandeur et décadence du cinéma," Fondane insists that the sound film is dangerous because it purports to give access to the real, whereas it only opens up on a false reality (E 81).

Fondane's attraction to the film was primarily due to its movement. In "Le Cinéma dans l'impasse" (1931) he writes:

The cinema is an art of movement – the only one perhaps which seriously mocks space, all the while borrowing from space the elements of its magic and enhancing its prestige. Dialogue forces this nomad to stabilize itself. In so far as it approaches theatre, it becomes a servant of space, a bad servant. (E 90).

Although Fondane goes on to denounce the hold that dialogue was having on film, he was not against the theatre as such, for he himself wrote three plays in the course of his career.

In his last cinema essay, "Cinema 33," written for the special film issue of *Cahiers jaunes,* No. 4, 1933, Fondane compares his own despair at the death of silent film with that of two celebrated contemporaries:

I regret that today, spirits as different but equally clairvoyant and honest as Salvador Dalí and Antonin Artaud, in their hatred for current cinema, agree on reproaching it for the only things which it has preserved of film as film, the only things which keep it being film and not something else. Dalí reproaches it for movement, that is, for its mode of being, and Artaud is critical of its images for being a copy of reality, that is, for seeming to be. These arguments have to be taken as welcome reactions, but excessive ones. (E 104).

Fondane continues by saying that Artaud hoped to find in the Theater of Cruelty the lost path of the cinema. By 1933, Fondane had once again turned to poetry (rather than theater as did Artaud), having completed and published *Ulysse* (written 1929-1933). He did have a chance to work on two films, *Rapt* (1934), as a scenarist to Kirsanov in the adaptation of Ramuz's novel; and *Tararira* (1936), an absurdist experimental film which he made in Argentina, but which is now lost.

The four theoretical essays on the cinema show Fondane's sympathy for Dadaism through his valorization of movement and love of absurdity. They do not criticize Surrealism, but neither are they polemics for the movement. Elsewhere we can find sharp criticism of Surrealism: (1) in the short articles collected by Carassou for the appendix of the recent edition of *Faux Traité d'Esthétique;* (2) in *Rimbaud le voyou* (1933, but written c. 1930), with its attack on misinformed Surrealist appropriations of Rimbaud; and (3) in *Faux Traité* itself (1938). Another group of articles, contributed to *Cahiers de l'Etoile* in 1929-1930, and apparently neither reprinted nor analyzed by critics, offer some further reflections on film which Fondane does not make elsewhere.

In the essay, "Brancusi," in praise of his fellow countryman, we sense that Fondane fears that the film medium may not come up to the level of his own expectations of valorizing the arbitrary side of life:

To achieve apparent order, clarity, and intelligibility is not the difficulty for the great artist – as if order for us were not the most natural thing that is, the siamese twin of all mental activity. No, the artist's wager is to save, in spite of order, a certain arbitrariness; to give free rein to profound obscurity, and to make seem unintelligible that which is too unintelligible. It's not difficult to show us how to eat gracefully a roasted chicken; this is quite intelligible. But it is quite something else to eat an old shoe sole with muddy nails in the same elegant fashion, as Chaplin does in *The Gold Rush.* That's where the automatism of a rule strives to make manifest a whole level of basic absurdity, the only province of human lyricism. But let us never think that the intention of the artist is to create art. Brancusi believes such an idea less than anyone else.[4]

For Fondane order is only apparent. The profound natural state is the arbitrary and the absurd. Those artists who can enable us to see the unintelligibility of life behind its apparent orderings are Fondane's heroes. The constant transformation of objects in his screenplays is an attempt to capture this sense of disorder.

Fondane had begun his artistic career with an idealist appreciation of the art object, an attitude he broke with totally. In "Réflexions sur le spectacle" we see another of Fondane's objections to the cult of art: its ignorance of the presence of creativity in human endeavors outside the realm of canonized art:

The characteristic of our time (Is it for this that civilization feels itself in danger?) is to have understood how small and paltry the role of art is next to other activities to which it has refused the name of "creations." Our age has pointed out the marvelous which is everywhere to some extent – in a match box or in an electric carpet sweeper. It has elevated the form of a car or airplane to the great honors of architecture and clearly pushed aside the idea of a theatrical event ("spectacle") as we have previously conceived it. From now on a meeting, a parade, an exit from the subway, and a shop window, are as much a part of theatre as a play or vaudeville performance. Now that cinema has threatened to replace it, the theatre itself seeks new laws, and sports have furnished some of their own. It is a significant fact that today's chronicle of theatrical events is equally attentive to a boxing match, a tennis match, a play, a film, and the miraculous tightrope walk. The technique of risk and the effect of surprise are well worth the technique of formal production and the effect of harmony.[5]

Stressing the elements of risk and surprise, Fondane says that Breton's convulsive beauty will have to be achieved while art is in the process of being formed, not after it is finished and dead as an art object. The sensibility of the "spectacle" is opposed to the cult of art objects because "spectacle" stresses movement. For a long time, art has been a reconstitution of movement rather than movement itself. By extension, we can say that the unspooling of the unfilmable film in the mind avoids this mediating process of reconstitution.

Fondane had little sympathy with the bourgeois art of 1930. In his review of Marc Ickovic's *La Littérature à la lumière du matérialisme historique,* he sees no cause to feel that Eisenstein's *Battleship Potemkin* offers much in the way of visible revolt, since it adopts traditional bourgeois forms for its proletarian message. Although this may be a simplification of Eisenstein's filmmaking practice, it does indicate Fondane's belief that revolt would have to develop the new artistic forms to go with it.

Is a book written according to the givens of the bourgeois novel, a book by Gorky or Barbusse, proletarian because it serves the proletarian cause through its apparent ideological evaluations? Is *Battleship Potemkin* a film representative of a new culture, or is it (and here must I give pain to Léon Moussinac?) a film which is indistinguishable from European-American films except for its subject matter (and even here *Germinal* came first) and its exceptional success? Truly, the gap is smaller between *Battleship Potemkin* and a European film than between a European film and an American film.[6]

Fondane's desire for revolutionary art forms rather than old art forms expressing revolutionary messages, reflects debates on art in the aftermath of the Russian Revolution and anticipates the Narboni/Comolli statement in *Cahiers du Cinéma* in the wake of May 1968.

In *Trois Scenarii* it is the Surrealist revolt which is questioned and found wanting. This critique is made through the fate which overtakes each of Fondane's male protagonists. In "Paupières mûres," "l'amour fou" leads the hero to fall pathetically to his death from Notre Dame. "Barre fixe" ends with the protagonist accommodating himself to bourgeois existence after a useless experience of Surrealist social anarchy. In "Mtasipol" the man's dream foreshadows his own symbolic suicide and does not lead to any privileged state of being. The scenarios are double-edged, for they use Surrealist elements to ask questions about the validity of the movement at a time (1926–28) when such prominent figures as Soupault, Artaud, Vitrac, and Desnos were being excluded from the ranks through Breton's autocratic actions. In addition to my analysis, a Freudian or archetypal explanation of the scenarios is always possible. However, we should remember that Fondane reproached Surrealism for traveling through dreams and the unconscious with Freud's work as a Baedecker.

In "Paupières mûres," "l'amour fou" leads the protagonist to death. A young man works in a bar, where he, as well as five customers, is smitten by a

75

woman. He follows her, as do the other men, into the street. Although he is in Paris, he pursues her by gondola, arriving at Notre Dame. From the balustrade, he sees "une femme" (shot 10), who may or may not be the object of his desire ("la femme"). Nevertheless, he gives her his love (perhaps because he cannot see from so high up, perhaps because he is fickle). We find him literally with his heart in his hand (129) and with an edelweiss in his heart (128). In the woman's hand, he turns into a monkey, phonograph, begonia blossom, and a glass jar with red fish. Eventually, he becomes a snake which she has to kill. The young man, in anguish, once again is on the balustrade of Notre Dame. He falls off, dies, and is surrounded by billiard balls from the bar where he worked (cf. Picabia's interest in the motion of billiard balls). Someone takes out a wallet from his limp body, throws away the photo of the woman and tears up a letter (a love letter from her?). The stranger slides the wallet into the pocket of a passer-by whom he asks for a cigarette. In the last shot, we are treated to a close-up of the "fantastic head" of the author, done by Man Ray. Illuminated by a cigarette lighter, he may or may not be one of the men in the final scene.

It appears as if Fondane is presiding over the loss of love. Not only does the young man lose the woman, but, in addition, the two documents of this love are destroyed as well. Perhaps the person who destroys them is a robber who finds no money upon the dead man. This motif would link him to the opening shots of the film, where an animate street lamp witnessed a brawl, which may have been an attempted robbery, for the scene ends with the hand of a person rummaging through another's pocket. The lack of causation for many actions allows the reader to mentally project a film for himself/ herself in which images will fill in some, but not all, of these gaps.

There are many playful Dadaist incongruities in "Paupières mûres," more so than in the other two scenarios. Included are images of a woman's knee with an eye in it (25), neon lights announcing a ball (cf. Man Ray's "Chaque soir à Magic City" and the flashing lights in *Emak Bakia*) (28), and an applauding mannequin (22). There are trick shots of the young man looking at himself in a bar window and seeing the woman's legs on his body; the woman's detachable head, which forms a still-life with a half-empty glass, saucer, and tip; the woman's head made out of wood; and men marching while dressed in their tables. In the bar, at one point, the woman appears as a drowned person, and later her face is placed in superimposition on the woman in the street whom the man sees from Notre Dame. Colliding balls, a ballet of Browning rifles, and the use of Notre Dame as an observation point, all suggest that the reader will take cues from the scenario to fashion his own creative film. Elaborate, beautiful, and arty descriptions of movement and images are avoided.

The scenario's title is suggestive, but has no fixed significance. The words "Paupières mûres" do not recur after the title. Should we imagine the women and mannequins with these ripe eyelids, indicating the desirability of the female body? On the other hand, is the young man's eye ripe for loving? Or are our eyes ripe for watching this film about desire? Each suggestion seems possible.

Although pacing is left to each reader, the abbreviated style of rendering the images suggests that these images should be connected by a chain of rapid movement. Here are the transformations the man undergoes for the woman:

136   she puts him in her hand, looks at him: he becomes by turns
137   a marmoset
138   which she caresses
139   a phonograph
140   whose crank she turns
141   a begonia blossom
142   which she puts into her buttonhole
143   the young man looks at her, smiles with happiness
144   he becomes a glass jar in which red fish are swimming
145. the begonia blossom becomes a mouse (E 28).

All of the man's transformations to please the woman turn out to be futile. She treats him like a pet when he is a marmoset. He becomes an object of manipulation when he is a phonograph. As a begonia, he serves as an object to adorn her. Later (156) when he becomes a serpent, she disembowels him, showing herself to be more dangerous than he. The man's face expresses anguish (153), but there is no indication that he is capable of having a real relationship with the woman.

When the hero drops to his death from Notre Dame, the shot is followed by that of a billiard ball falling to earth (162), thus recalling the initial encounter of the man and the woman. We are also given a shot (164) of a bas-relief of those who go to hell among the devils, taken from the façade of Notre Dame. The torment of the dead man has also taken him to a kind of hell. Maurice Nadeau points out that for the Surrealists, the true revolution was the victory of desire.[7] As an essayist, Fondane went on to criticize Surrealism as a movement which led men to madness, chaos, and suicide, while offering few compensations.[8] In "Paupières mûres" this later position is anticipated.

In "Barre fixe" the protagonist's torment is more metaphysical and less personal. A young man in a wall poster steps down and becomes a real person. He suddenly shoots the only customer in the store which he has entered (30). Here Breton's statement about firing into a crowd as a Surrealist act is used, acted out, and shown to lead nowhere. A price of 100,000 francs is put on the protagonist's head, and he tries to commit suicide three times, but fails in every instance. At the Jardin des Plantes, he shoots a monkey. Then he becomes upset when he sees a woman walking nearby. He chases her into a cage with a whip and gives her a long kiss. He follows her home to bed, but a fiasco results. Again in the street, he meets a bald man and follows him. He ends up in front of the poster he had left, and he has to decide whether to become a part of it again or to continue to flee from arrest in the everyday world. He flips a coin and decides to live, taking up a job in some office or factory in which there is a time punch. The last shots read:

165   seen from the back he has his ticket punched by a time clock
166   he kisses a hand for a long time
167   it is the hairy hand, then the arm, the black robe of the parish priest

168   on the steps of a church
169   the young man with the statue of Voltaire
170   with the statue of Voltaire dressed as a bride (E 38).

Fondane's hero is tricked by the rhetoric of the French Revolution. In the opening shot there is a wall on which we see the slogan, "Liberté, Egalité, Fraternité." The words play on the wall (1), and it is when the young man, still in the poster on the wall, sees a worker reading the word "Liberté" in a newspaper, that he takes up living. Unfortunately, there are limits to liberty, and he ultimately seeks to be part of a collective, symbolized by the shot of an anthill (162). He does not have to resist the world of business firms — "la Glé d'Assurances Générales, The Insurance, L'Assiguratrice Italiana, Winterthur, Yorkshire, Graham" (164).

The term "barre fixe" has two connotatons. As a bar (gymnastic apparatus) it is the locus of feats of strength, agility, and balance, as well as a place which can be privileged as "spectacle." The hero is unsuccessful in mastering the "barre fixe" of life. Forced to perform against his will, he tries to throw himself off the bar. "Barre fixe" as a fixed barrier also suggests a no-exit situation, a variation of the "huis clos" later made famous by Sartre. The barrier is the idea of liberty, in three conflated forms — a deep seated-human desire, the promise of the French Revolution, and the anarchic ideal of Breton.

In "Barre fixe" it may appear as if the man is looking for death. He throws himself into the Seine, shoots himself, and jumps off the Eiffel Tower. Yet the specific situation involving the poster indicates that re-entering it is the real death (not the traditional forms of suicide), and that is what he ultimately flees. His decision to remain alive is, however, a choice for minimal existence. Both religion and philosophy are in cahoots to engineer his resignation from seeking freedom.

In "Barre fixe" Fondane does not suggest that society should stop repressing man's natural desires. No image of a possible authentic life is held up to be admired. The killing of the customer in the store is not condemned for being immoral. It is put on display as a useless act, leading the protagonist in despair to the opposite point of the spectrum — the desire for respectability as the bride of Voltaire. The scenario's ending is pessimistic, but satirical, rather than conservative. Voltaire is a villain because Voltaire believed in knowledge. For Fondane, knowledge usually bars the way between man and existence, and the Surrealists, in his view, also offered up this barrier of knowledge.

"Mtasipol" (dedicated to Georges Ribemont-Desaignes, who alone may have known the significance of the strange title, perhaps an anagram) resembles both "Paupières mûres" and "Barre fixe" in that it contains elements of an unhappy love story. Just as love and anarchic revolt are shown in the other scenarios to be inadequate forms of behavior, here we see that the dream state is not a privileged one. Instead it is a nightmare. In the dream which opens "Mtasipol" a man is dancing with a woman at a bar in a cafe. She shows him a calling card of Dr. Ixe. The man fires a pistol in the air to attract her attention, but she falls down wounded. A black musician starts to hit him with one of her shoes. Then we find that he is in bed, where his own arm is swinging at an alarm clock. Awake, he realizes that one arm is twice as long as the other, and he goes to see Dr. Ixe, where his arm grows twice as long again. It eventually has seven fingers and is put in a jar of alcohol. Suddenly, the scene shifts to the man's office, where a female client comes up to him and becomes more and more beautiful. She slaps him, and he chases her into the street. However, he becomes older and older, and four women come between them, one at a time. Finally, all five women appear before him on the order of the brothel madam, who has the black man's head. The first woman is the dancer, who brings the jar with the seven-fingered hand in it. Once again the scene changes. The man, now old, uses his revolver to force a younger passer-by to take his beard, skull, and umbrella. Then he looks at a mirror and finds that he himself has the black man's head. He fires at the mirror and falls. Thus the premonitory nature of the dream leads not to a better life, but to either death or symbolic death. The last shot shows us some roosters on some night tables, symbols of defeated desire which cast doubt on the value of the Surrealists' worship of love.

Although the scenario is basically the story of a man's pursuit of a woman and then of his attempt to catch up with the various women he encounters in the street, we do not see the love interest resolved. When the dancer gives him the jar with the seven-fingered hand, they embrace, but immediately the protagonist is out on a deserted street. Perhaps he finds that the romantic affair cannot work because he is too old and life has passed him by:

163   the old man in a deserted street
164   he is on the lookout at the corner of the road revolver pointed
165   a young man passes
166   at gunpoint he raises his arms
167   the old man hands him his beard his skull his umbrella orders him to leave
168   head of the old man on the body of the man who leaves
169   the old man begins to run into the night (blurred)
170   he stops in front of a mirror
171   in the mirror the head of the black man winking an eye
172   he takes out a revolver from his pocket and fires at the mirror
173   in the mirror we see him fall
174   several roosters – in lap dissolve – on several night tables (E 46–47).

The scenario shows a man who awakens from one nightmare by clutching an alarm clock, only to face a nightmarish life which leads to death. The dream is connected to "reality" by means of the accidentally wounded (murdered?) dancer and by the doctor's calling card. The doctor had written "life in jeopardy" (48) as his diagnosis when he saw the seven fingers. Thus it is not surprising that once the seven fingers show up again, death follows soon after. The dancer has her revenge. Wounded in the dream, she comes back to lead him to his death.

The women in the scenario are associated with Medusa (81, 108, 139). But unlike the Medusa of myth, they do not turn men to stone, but, in pursuing them, the man loses his youth. All of the women seem to reflect the man's castration anxiety. At the brothel, the first two women show him his first two younger heads in a mirror. The third, almost like Salome, carries his head in on a platter. The man appears to be powerless because he projects his own emotions onto the women. That is why he is constantly confronted with a mirror, in this case, a symbol of narcissism. If he symbolically dies by shooting at the mirror rather than at himself, the scenario suggests that by losing the image of his identity, he can no longer function. The mirror here suggests a visible wholeness which is only an illusion, a concept which the psychic splitting in the dream reinforces. On the other hand, if the man actually dies because he shoots at the mirror, the scenario is more in line with the death of Dorian Gray in Oscar Wilde's novel. Thus we have a fantastic tale in which man's essence is located outside of himself. The dream is useless in providing literary inspiration, or even avoiding death, for it blends so wholly with "daily" experience, infected with the kind of absurdity it is. With life itself separated from reason, dream has no privileged status.

The uniqueness of Fondane's scenarios can best be seen by looking at them with reference to Dada film, Surrealist film, other unfilmed Surrealist screenplays, and the avant-garde narrative cinema in France. Fondane knew the two major Dada films, *Entr'acte* and *Emak Bakia*. There is no reference in his essays on film, however, to either Duchamp's *Anémic Cinéma* or Léger's *Ballet mécanique*. Fondane wrote a review of Clair's film for *Integral* in 1925, and he refers to *Emak Bakia* in his essay "2×2."

Did Fondane know of the Surrealist films of 1927–1928 when he wrote his scenarios? "Paupières mûres" suggests that he might have been in contact with Man Ray (creator of two illustrations for *Trois Scenarii*), who was filming *L'Etoile de mer*. It is a matter of speculation whether Fondane saw Artaud's *La Coquille et le clergyman* either in late 1927 or early 1928. Obviously, *Trois Scenarii* antedates the Buñuel/Dalí films.

Fondane's first essay on the cinema was apparently his review of *Entr'acte*. He praises it as a film in which the camera plays the hero. It is a work which puts to shame the consciously artful and artificial film, *The Cabinet of Dr. Caligari*. However, Fondane also believes that the liberty suggested by Clair's approach to film must add up to something. He declares:

I hope that René Clair may become the Rimbaud of the cinema, but on one condition – that he learn in time that technique is not only liberty without shame but also a well understood servitude. A new technique doesn't yet make a beautiful film, a new subject matter even less. What is needed is a technique put at the service of a subject matter, which does not give up language. We need neither novelty nor technique, but the work. (E 53).

Fondane's screenplays recall *Entr'acte* through their use of playful images and sudden transitions. Although *Entr'acte* was less startlingly scandalous than some other Dada creations, as Mimi White shows, the film questions typical narrative structures and asks whether they are natural or necessary. After all, she writes, "why . . . should one expect a film to proceed according to an a priori notion of logic and continuity when it is, after all, merely a construction, an assembly of images?"[9] Despite the fact that Fondane's three scenarios also violate typical expectatons of continuity, in 1928 (four years later) his techniques could no longer have had the same effect. Fondane's interest is not directed toward issues of film vision and representation. In each scenario, he has a protagonist who comes to an unhappy end. His goal is to say something about man's existence in the world.

It is through his protagonists that Fondane makes his strongest links to the interior dramas of *L'Etoile de mer* and *La Coquille et le clergyman.* Despite its starfish, "Paupières mûres" does not depict woman as an embodiment of violent force. It shows "l'amour fou" leading to the protagonist's death, not to the metaphorical violation of the woman as in Man Ray's film. In *L'Etoile de mer* the woman manifests a far greater eroticism. She is beautiful like flowers of glass, flesh, and fire. At various times she holds a knife and a spear. She is actually having a relationship with the hero and initially seems ready for a sexual encounter. *L'Etoile de mer* clearly presents the starfish and the woman as enigmas to be understood. In "Paupières mûres" the woman is not having an affair with the protagonist. She is noticed in the bar/restaurant by him and five other men. She gives all the men the cold shoulder, and she forcefully discourages the men who try to pick her up. Whereas Man Ray shows us the violence and ambiguities that permeate most relationships, Fondane presents us with an obsession which leads to a pathetic ending– death by falling.

La Coquille et le clergyman is closer in spirit to "Paupières mûres," since the woman in Artaud's film scenario is not a femme fatale. The clergyman needs to reach a state of inner unity before he has any hope of winning her love. She continually eludes him, as happens with the corresponding characters in "Paupières mûres." Nevertheless, Artaud, unlike Fondane, does not suggest that there is anything wrong with the pursuit of the woman in itself. If the officer/priest is really another side of the clergyman's personality, then we can assume that the woman is someone he really knows. We have enough published information to interpret Artaud's film scenario autobiographically (e.g., his love for Génica Athanasiou), but so far we can not do so with Fondane's scenario.

Fondane championed the Buñuel/Dalí films which appeared after his own scenarios. He even presented *Un Chien andalou* to Vittoria Ocampo's friends in Argentina in 1929. However, his essays on the cinema contain only the most fleeting references to these famous collaborative efforts. Since the Buñuel/Dalí films defend the primacy of desire, we must suspect that Fondane's enthusiasm for them is to be found elsewhere, probably in three areas: (a) in the appreciation of absurdity and employment of absurd chronological frameworks, (b) in the attack on the bourgeois world and its attendant hypocrisies, and (c) in the satires on Christianity.

Since Fondane's three scenarios were not filmed, it may be possible that he was influenced by some other unfilmed Surrealist scenarios. Two of the most important of these are Robert Desnos's "Minuit à quatorze heures," which appeared in the special issue of *Cahiers du mois* in 1925, and Georges Ribemont-Dessaignes' "The Eighth Day of the Week," published in English in Nos. 19–20 of *transition* in 1930. I have found no references to these screenplays in Fondane's writings, but Desnos's scenario was readily available in print, and Fondane carried on a correspondence with Ribemont-Dessaignes, to whom he dedicated "Mtasipol." If Desnos and Ribemont-Dessaignes published their screenplays with no thoughts of having them filmed, they would be more closely associated with Fondane's work in this genre.

"Minuit à quatorze heures" is a notable scenario because it uses filmic possibilities to suggest mental states. A woman betrays her lover with a younger man while her lover is out fishing. He falls from a parapet and dies. Although the woman and her new boyfriend are not responsible for the lover's death, they have guilty feelings because of the way they betrayed him. Their life together is destroyed by a huge, mysterious ball which terrorizes their house. Eventually house, inhabitants, and ball are swallowed up and replaced by a funnel. All signs of death, adultery, and guilt are gone. Desnos uses numbered shots (a system which Delluc also used) as a frame for his actions. This is the same method Fondane employs, and his scenario is about the same length as Desnos's.

It is the images, rather than the system of shot breakdowns, which connect "The Eighth Day of the Week" to Fondane's scenarios. The visit to the doctor's office, female mannequins, a woman lying on a billiard table, and a man who shoots himself in a mirror are all closely related to images in Fondane's work. Ribemont-Dessaignes' scenario tells the adventure of Sadie, a femme fatale who has several admirers. In the end, she is murdered by a hunchback who crushes her head. The use of the femme fatale and the violent ending recall *L'Etoile de mer* more than "Paupières mûres."

The reader of Richard Abel's *French Cinema: The First Wave, 1915-1929* has a chance to compare Fondane's scenarios with many seldom-shown films of the period – particularly experimental narrative films not in the Dada/Surrealist orbit. One such film, not mentioned by Fondane, is Ivan Mosjoukine's *Le Brasier ardent* (1923). Abel finds the film an outrageous parody of "l'amour fou."[10] A woman has a nightmare about a demonic and powerful Detective Z, which is a type of compensation for an unsatisfactory relationship with her husband. Although in the end, Detective Z turns out to be a timid man devoted to his mother, the woman becomes paired with him, offering a maternal form of love, while her husband happily goes off to his new-found freedom. Fondane's "Mtasipol" also begins with a nightmare in which the dreamer wakes up in an agitated position representing a graphic match with the dream action. In each case, the nightmare is an obvious sexual fantasy which introduces the themes of the non-dream action. In "Mtasipol" the hero meets up with Dr. Ixe (cf. Detective Z), who cannot cure him of "causeless maladies" (human existence in general). The woman lost to the hero in the dream is also lost in daily life. Despite the similarities in the treatment of the nightmare, it is obvious that Mosjoukine's film arrives at a happy ending, whereas Fondane's scenario ends in either death or symbolic death. Since Fondane had close connections with Russian émigrés both through Leon Shestov and the *Cahiers de l'Etoile* circle, it would not be surprising if he had seen *Le Brasier ardent* and other Albatros films.

Fondane arrived in Paris in 1923, the year of Mosjoukine's film. According to Michel Carassou he soon got to know fellow Roumanians Tzara and Veronca.[11] They put him in touch with former Dadaists rather than with the members of Breton's Surrealist group, which was then being organized. During the next five years, until the *Trois Scenarii,* Fondane wrote very little and seems to have abandoned creative writing (poetry and plays). Thus the questioning of film itself in the scenarios is not surprising for a person reassessing the function of art in his own life after a period of crisis. Here the Dadaist connection overlaps with his own tentative rededication to a life of artistic endeavor.

The unfilmable scenarios were written to create a provisory state of the spirit which memory would consume with the act of reading, as Fondane says in "2×2" (E 21). Here we see him trying to overcome the problem pointed out by Thomas Elsaesser, namely, that "the fixed nature of film texts and production circumstances seems to be at odds with the Dada emphasis on performance and active provocation."[12] Fondane rejects the fixed nature of film texts. He writes:

One no longer writes in order to keep oneself in countenance. One publishes nothing except to question the audience and throw doubt before as many men as possible without hope of finding the rest of mankind. (E 20).

Thus Fondane's scenarios should be seen in the Dadaist tradition of returning to a zero state and beginning anew. *Entr'acte* and *Emak Bakia* raised the issues of logic/continuity and vision/representation, respectively. *Trois Scenarii* makes a fitting close to the Dada era of metaphysical questioning. Even the film is gone.

In five short articles published in *Integral* in 1927–1928, we can trace Fondane's attitudes towards Surrealism, as it was reaching an internal crisis. In "Louis Aragon ou le Paysan de Paris," he declares that Surrealism created an aesthetic doctrine which was only that of second-degree Dada (FT 126). After Dada had brought man back to the beginning ("fait table rase") and used Cartesian doubt to conceive of only nothing ("le néant"), Surrealism posited the dream as a category which allows for the existence of a nebula in distant space, that is, a hope for the doubters (FT 126). Fondane is suspicious of this consolation. His sympathies are with those who do not need such hopes.

Fondane's very brief appreciation of Paul Eluard's *Capitale de la douleur* (March 1927) does not criticize Surrealism, but one month later in "Les Surréalistes et la Révolution" he points out that Surrealism and Communism are movements logically at odds with one another, an issue which Breton was hedging on. He stresses his distaste of Communism, a totalizing system of order, and advocates the irrational in life, which might ultimately crush Surrealism.

In the June–July 1927 issue, Fondane underlines his desire to accelerate conditions devouring the century. For him it is not the time to create masterpieces. This is the essay of the *Integral* group closest in tone to "2 × 2." "Pierre Reverdy" (April 1928), perhaps contemporaneous with the writing of *Trois Scenarii,* praises poetry as a postulate of the identity of the poet with the universe (FT 144) and finds it preferable to the poem, or art object. This idea can be linked to the valorization of the film unspooling in a person's mind while reading the written scenario.

Also in 1928, Fondane participated in the Discontinuité group with Arthur Adamov and Claude Sernet. He was friendly with René Daumal and Roger Victor Leconte, members of Le Grand Jeu. In 1930 Fondane was so hostile to Breton that they ended up in a physical scuffle. Two years later he refused to sign the petition on behalf of Aragon in the wake of the controversy surrounding Aragon's "Front rouge."

With the publication of two essays on Leon Shestov (some of whose work he had already read in Roumania) in 1929, Fondane turned more and more to a form of existentialism to confront the agony of individual human existence. He also returned to the writing of poetry at about the same time. He continued on these two courses until his death in a concentration camp in 1944, in his forty-sixth year.

It is too simple to say that Fondane left Dada and Surrealism behind him, for his poetry and his lost film, Tararira, are indebted to these movements. However, in 1938 in the *Faux Traité d'Esthétique* he expressed his most revealing criticism of Surrealism. It contains the following passage:

It's starting with the Surrealists that poetry makes an effort to be a type of knowledge, makes sacrifices to morality and politics, in short, wishes to be something. It's among the Surrealists that for the first time poetry tries to establish its structures; puts a stop to the transcendant and an embargo on dreams; sets up connections with the social, moral, and political spheres; determines what it considers sin; and promulgates a system of immediate sanctions against "intellectual bloodstains." Poetry finally becomes *something*. (FT 46–47).

Having become "something," poetry then can be put to the service of the revolution and then to the service of the proletarian revolution. The liberty postulated by the movement turns out to be a mirage, a conclusion already apparent in "Barre fixe," an unfilmable film, a resistance to the notion of poetry becoming "something."

Notes

1. Benjamin Fondane, *Ecrits pour le cinéma: le muet et le parlant,* ed. Michel Carssou (Paris: Plasma, 1984). All subsequent references to Fondane's essays and scenarios in this edition are marked by E in the essay.

2. John Kenneth Hyde, *Benjamin Fondane: A Presentation of His Life and Work* (Geneva: Droz, 1971).

3. Michel Carassou, "Préface: Benjamin Fondane et le cinéma." in Benjamin Fondane, *Ecrits sur le cinéma,* pp. 7–11. See p. 10.

4. Benjamin Fondane, "Brancusi," *Cahiers de l'Etoile* 2 (1929): 708–25. See p. 710.

5. Benjamin Fondane, "Réflexions sur le spectacle," *Cahiers de l'Etoile* 2 (1929): 256–67. See p. 260.

6. Benjamin Fondane, "Review of Marc Ickovicz's *La Littérature à la lumière du matérialisme historique," Cahiers de l'Etoile* 2 (1929): 616–21. See p. 618.

7. Maurice Nadeau, *Histoire du surréalisme* (Paris: Seuil, 1972).

8. Benjamin Fondane, *Faux Traité d'esthétique: Essai sur la crise de réalité* (Paris: Plasma, 1980), p. 74.

9. Mimi White, "Two French Dada Films: *Entr'acte* and *Emak Bakia," Dada/Surrealism* 13 (1984):37–47. See p. 42.

10. Richard Abel, *French Cinema: The First Wave, 1915–1929* (Princeton: Princeton Univ. Press, 1984), pp. 367–73.

11. Michel Carassou, Radio Program on France-Culture, February 1986.

12. White, p. 37.

I would like to thank Hela Michot-Dietrich for helping me translate Fondane's writings, Richard Abel for suggesting ways to improve an earlier version of this essay, and Dudley Andrew for calling my attention to some recent material on Fondane.

SLIT SCREEN
David Wills

It took fifty-odd years until the Surrealists' naive intuitions concerning possible resemblances between a film and a dream were productively developed by the work of Christian Metz.[1] And it took about as long before Eisenstein's tentative conclusions concerning the language of cinema were, thanks to research undertaken by Marie-Claire Ropars-Wuilleumier, transformed into a theory of "writing."[2] Few Surrealist writers were as interested in cinema as Robert Desnos, author of articles of criticism and scenarios published in the volume *Cinema*,[3] as well as other texts edited by Marie-Claire Dumas in *Nouvelles Hébrides et autres textes 1922–1930*.[4] Few were those who, in my opinion, elaborated a notion of writing as pertinent to the contemporary context as that evidenced in the wide variety of texts produced by Desnos.

In this article I should like to refer principally to two of those texts in order to discuss a particularly interesting intersection between cinema and Surrealism, on the one hand as those domains connect with dream and the unconscious, and on the other as they connect with writing. I intend from the outset to inscribe upon what follows the signs which mark all of Desnos' Surrealist writings, those of rupture and fragmentation.

The idea of rupture occurs first of all with respect to original sense, the possibility of there being any originary sense, for the word in Desnos begins in play. The paradigm for poetic usage in his texts is the homonym, which, like paronomasia or the spoonerism, defers the establishment of a singular sense, and always refers elsewhere. In the so-called Surrealist image, this rupture is conveyed by an absence within normal linguistic articulation. The sign (say, "umbrella") which is completely incongruous with its neighboring element in the syntagm (say "sewing-machine"), but to which it is nevertheless compared, parodies any absolute concept of difference. The difference which structures the linguistic sign always includes an absence of sense, just as difference as a play between the same and the other represents a *decadence* of the referential function of language.

When language is as systematically *decentralized* as it is in Desnos' poems, there is inevitably a risk of loss, or by extension, of death. Thus one of the major themes in his writing is that of the shipwreck, writing as the casting of words upon the waves, the text as flotsam, and elsewhere, the text as murderous:

The inkwell-periscope lies in wait for me round the corner
my pen-holder retires into its shell
The sheet of paper unfurls its great white wings
Before long these talons

86

will gouge out my eyes
I will see only fire my body (*du feu mon corps*)
my dead body.[5]

If a sheet of paper can figure as a wing, that is because the possibility of apotheosis never excludes the threat of a fall:

By yesterday's post you will telegraph
that we really did die with the swallows.
Postman sad postman a coffin under your arm
go take my letter of flowers with the strength of her wings
(*ma lettre aux fleurs à tour d'elle*).[6]

As it happens, Desnos' death, in combination with a desire on the part of criticism to accord to his work its plenitude, has meant the publication of several volumes of such wreckage, the flotsam and remainders of his creative activity. They say that he would have wanted them to be published had he stayed alive (at least he is supposed to have had such a project at one time, although he later deferred it). I am therefore tempted to conclude that these texts were destined for an even more radical and random dissemination than actually occurred, that being the risk and invitation of any text. In any case, among this flotsam and jetsam exist certain projects for films, as well as the manuscript entitled *Pénalités de l'enfer ou Nouvelles Hébrides*,[7] towards the end of which one goes to the cinema.

Before undertaking to discuss these texts, I wish to point out a possibility which I do not think has been sufficiently exploited in Marie-Claire Ropars' discussion of writing and cinema, for all the detail of her analysis. If montage, especially that developed by Eisenstein, "by putting the accent on the tension between the fragments, prevents all possibility of bringing those fragments back within a progressively more aligned sense,"[8] it is just as true that any *piecing together* of film, even the most reticent, or that which respects a Bazinian prescription for *mise-en-scène,* or that which "forbids" montage, nonetheless implies an intervention at the level of the cinematic signifier which deprives it of all possibility of originary coherence. In order to make a film, one must cut, stick, and discard images. As a result of those operations, and of the work which is produced, there are always remainders, traces, and in a much more explicit and material way than in the case of spoken or written language. This irremediable fact has been taken up by few film-makers, and it is the work of Marguerite Duras that stands out as a notable exception.[9] There is nothing more manifest than the marks of a writing which breaks so radically with its origin, which reveals that origin as being always already written, such as is made explicit in the materiality of cinematic production, in its grafting of traces and remainders.

* * * * *

Towards the end of *Pénalités de l'enfer ou Nouvelles Hébrides,* the first-person narrator who calls himself Robert Desnos, goes to the cinema, after first visiting the Trocadéro aquarium and the Musée Grevin:

Quite disgusted by this event, I sought a safe place to rest. The Trocadéro aquarium seemed to be to my liking. I entered . . . I reached the Musée Grévin . . . I stopped in front of a cinema. Beautiful faces were smiling on the posters. I entered. (*NH*, 99–100)

At the aquarium the narrator discovers Vitrac dead in the arms of someone called Suzanne. She is biting the belly of his corpse and red fish and eels come out. When the narrator invites her to love him she is transformed into a flowering water lily which he puts in his buttonhole. He goes away "with Suzanne's perfume and Suzanne herself on [his] clothes" (*NH*, 99). At the wax museum he finds the statues of M. and Mme. Breton, which are revealed to be their corpses "covered with a thin layer of wax. . . . When one pushes Breton's belly, a mechanism says: 'What you just did is a mean trick.'" (*NH*, 99). It's just like the movies, you will say, but we are not yet there. It's just like a dream, you will say, and it is evident that certain word-plays like "to wear a perfume" relate here to the rebus-effect of dream in the way that they depend on linguistic short-circuits like metaphor and metonymy, which in turn relate to condensation and displacement. You might also say that these scenes are almost primal. For the moment I wish only to stress the importance of the scopic or visual, the mention of death, and the particular progression of systems of representation. The aquarium relies on flesh and blood, fish framed within a system of transparence; the wax museum (in this peculiar case) on corpses framed by another opaque and artificial skin; the cinema on the play of light on a screen:

On the blank screen, a luminous disk was projected without any images of people or landscapes. The assembly of empty seats attentively followed some magnificent spectacle invisible to me.

Furious, I wanted to see from closer up. I climbed towards the screen. I was blinded by the light from the projector lamp and saw in the screen two holes large enough to allow a man to pass through. I put my head through one of them. (*NH*, 100)

The screen is here presented as a "carte blanche," "*blanc-seing*" as a poem from *L'Aumonyme*[10] has it, that is to say as a form of coherence which is nevertheless fashioned by writing, by the ideas of the frame and the trace. Such ideas will become more and more important within the chain of signification to the extent that they provoke a rupture in the system of representation.

The cinema scene strikes this reader in the way it suggests the principal stages of psychoanalytic research into the cinematic signifier and the cinema as apparatus. As Metz has shown concerning correspondences between the cinema and the (Lacanian) mirror, what counts here is the appearance of an "intersection which is at one and the same time so direct and so out-of-sync"[11] between this fictional text (or dream-text if you wish), and a certain evolution of cinematic theory. The significant discrepancy concerns the notion of the other, and it is the absence of the other, or rather the radical absence which the other represents, which displaces this representational scene.

Metz has explained to what extent the experience of the spectator of a film differs from the experience of the mirror developed by Lacan:

The spectator is absent from the screen; contrary to the child in front of the mirror, he cannot identify with himself as object, but only with those objects of which he is not one. The screen, in this sense, is not a mirror.[12]

The spectator who has experienced the mirror stage can constitute a world of objects "without having to recognize himself there with them."[13] Now, in the case of the text by Desnos, the spectator is deprived to the point of lacking even this world of objects; he is obliged to constitute such a world from a blank surface of representation. The Desnosian spectator, having lived through not only the mirror stage but also the experience of cinema, finds himself lured by a world of objects which doesn't at all correspond to his desire. This cinema with a screen which is void of objects refers thus to the mirror stage, but in a disturbing way. Such disquiet had already been expressed in the previous "scopic" scenes, at the aquarium and at the wax museum, where the other existed in strange modes half-present half-absent, somewhere between a continuous and a distinct object vis-à-vis the spectator.

The text in question here also defines a radicalization of the normal cinematic experience in the case of relations between spectators. Whereas it is true that "the audience for a film projection does not, as in the theatre, form a real 'public,'" but rather "a sum of individuals who, in spite of appearances, resemble much more the scattered set of readers of a novel,"[14] the narrator of this film experience is even more isolated and uneasy in that role. Faced with an assembly of empty seats that follow the spectacle which remains invisible to him, the narrator is like the child abandoned by the mother before having acceded to the realm of the symbolic, before experiencing the mirror stage. By the same token, an important manifestation of the other does remain to determine the response of the spectator, and this in turn evokes a third type of identification discussed by psychoanalytic theory.

That other is the camera. All the more absent since there are no images, the structure of the camera being filled entirely by the projector. It is in this sense that our scene also evokes the anguish of an unresolved primary identification. The light projected on the screen does not give here the illusory reassurance of a fetish, that is to say that it only provides the fetish as an illusion, more flimsy than ever, as a lure and as a threat. On the other hand, one can point to a strong reinforcement of monocular perspective, such that the attention of the spectator cannot fail to be concentrated on a vanishing point which seems to disappear through the other side of the screen. Furthermore, the other side of the screen, that which is behind it, appears as the sole *hors-champ*. In the event the spectator allows himself to be lead towards this vanishing point in such a way as to suggest that the ideological regime of the apparatus determines only one response, given his incapacity to confront the structures of absence of the symbolic, that response implies a regression to a purely linear and teleological arrangement of the scopic experience. Here then, suture would be synonymous with incision, to the extent that the spectator and the apparatus are *projected* along a single implacable axis. The light of the projection illumines nothing but a void, and the spectator, furious at being abused by his own desire, finds his escape assured only through an expression of violence which represses all detours, namely the renting of the veil that is the screen.

The text does not clearly explain whether the luminous disk covers the major part of the screen or if it is concentrated on a central point, whether, in terms of the metapsychology of the spectator, it amounts to a reinforcement or cancelling of the keyhole effect. However, whether the spectator's response is a rectification or a repetition is not the issue. The result is the same: scopic displeasure, the experience of the cinema as a "bad object," leads to a rupture. And one thing is sure: once it is reduced to a play of light on a screen, cinema no longer poses the problem of representation at the same level at which debate concerning the impression of reality is normally carried out. As it reveals itself to be *pure* representation void of any relation to a visible reality composed of objects, the cinematic apparatus is reduced to the terms employed by Jean-Louis Baudry, to being "a simulation of a state of the subject, of a subject position, and a subject-effect;"[15] to the "gamble of desire in action . . . that is to say at one and the same time the desire to attain the archaic forms of satisfaction which in fact structure all desire, and the subjects' desire to put on stage and to represent that which recalls the functioning of desire itself."[16]

Confronted with that which is only desire, traversed by desire and all the absence it implies, the spectator attempts to live the lure of an unmediated libidinal operation, along a straight line with no separation between desire and object. It is Baudry who has also pointed out the extent to which such a lure inhabits the cinematic apparatus, as "an effect of regression, the reiteration of a stage of development during which representation and perception were not yet differentiated, and the desire to regain that state and the mode of satisfaction attached to it."[17] That is in fact the undertaking of our spectator, who, after successive experiences which provided a combination of perceptual and representational effects (aquarium), and a representational scene in which the effect of representation could easily be recognized as transparence (wax museum), now finds himself before a pure representation which only represents nothing more than his own desire. He therefore seeks to destroy the scene of representation, to disavow this perversion of perception whereby that perception is required to deal with so many absences. And so he passes to the other side of the screen:

I put my head through one of them. A panorama of the city was spread out before my eyes. Aragon and Breton had their bellies impaled on two cathedral spires.
I understood that they also had wanted to see what was happening behind the screen and the great beauty of their suicide was revealed to me. (NH, 100)

You will be even more tempted to say it's just like the movies. On the other hand, everything about the scene suggests that we are no longer in that place. The slit screen is now a window from which the spectator has regained his position of privileged observer. Representation is no longer at issue, even if fantasy seems to have taken over.

The scene which begins in the cinema now rejoins the two preceding scenes. All three put into play perception and representation, introduce other characters, and finally reimpose the idea of death. But in the third scene death is neither a simple event nor a condition, but the realization of desire. I am lead to wonder whether the representation of desire that the cinematic apparatus puts into play does not in fact occlude the extent to which the structure of absence which is so clearly identified in it, in fact stands in for death; that is to say the extent to which all desire is desire for death. The advantage of the cinematic scene in its direct and out-of-sync relations with the mirror stage resides in the way in which it provides a topography for structures of absence, as if by means of a series of metonymic effects. The result is perhaps that it obscures the metaphoric play of absence as figure of death; just as sub-mobility has to be a figure for the immobility of death.

If one concurs with Roland Barthes (from "Rhétorique de l'image" to *La Chambre claire*[18]), the structure of death, which exists so clearly in the photograph, would be obscured by the movement of images in film:

... in Photography, something *was placed* in front of the little hole and remained there for ever ... but in the cinema, something *passed* in front of the same little hole: the pose is rendered insignificant and denied by the consecutive series of images ... .[19]

Would it then be, in Baudry's terms, yet another "subject-effect" to insist upon the importance of movement in the cinema, for such movement has after all, along with perspective or the arrangement of objects in space, been held to be the *sine qua non* of the cinema's impression of reality? In other words, not only does narrative-representative cinema, the paradigm for all cinema, put into play a libidinal mechanism within which perception and representation need not be differentiated, but it even manages to obscure the effect of discontinuity that in fact defines perception. Now, as our text demonstrates, the role of death in the play of desire is revealed on the blank screen; it is manifested in the desire to "see from closer up," to "see what was happening behind the screen"; it is the desire to enter the scene of representation. Given that the principal difference between mirror scene and cinema is the lack of a representation of the spectator, to want to appear there would be a suicidal desire. It would mean the death of cinema since one would no longer be a spectator; but it would also mean living the primal scene on the plane of its differential effect, as it were on the surface of the mirror, there where one cannot avoid being struck with the full force of the idea that what the symbolic displaces above all else, is the sense of death:

Thus when we wish to reach within the subject that which exists before the series of games played by the spoken word, and that which is prerequisite to the birth of symbols, we find it in death, wherein the existence of the subject finds everything it means.[20]

We may well have identified here that which feeds the desire of those who love cinema enough to want to intervene in it more actively than the average spectator, and the way in which cinematic analysis itself enters into the libidinal mechanism. To read a film in the active sense, to see in a film a dynamic process, constitutes a gamble which is far from extra-cinematic, and by no means foreign to desire.

* * * * *

I have suggested that the notion of rupture works in another way in the cinematic apparatus, namely in the syntagmatic chain constituted by traces of writing, the latter terms being understood in the sense Derrida gives to them. Contrary to the preceding scenes, the cinema in the episode from *Nouvelles Hébrides* under discussion is characterized by silence. The dialogue between the narrator and Suzanne which takes place at the aquarium, is followed by Breton's *epigram* at the Musée Grevin. On the other hand, in the cinema the scene of representation is presented simply by a luminous disk projected onto the screen, that is to say as a blank screen articulated by whiteness. This serves to underline the importance of the screen in cinema, the whole series of effects concerning it which one tends to overlook, which cinema itself may well conceal. For in practice, the screen, fundamental frame and support for cinematic mediation, only exists as it were once it is covered by the image. Before that its whiteness remains in the dark, behind a curtain or deprived of light until the play of light that is film comes and effaces it. However, in the case before us, where ordinary colors or black and white are replaced by plain whiteness, the play of light effaces not only the screen as frame necessary to its operation, but it effaces at the same time its own constitution as a system of luminous differences. The disk projected on the screen could after all be a rapidly revolving image of all the primary colors.

It may well be said then that the forms of punctuation in use in the cinema are designed to perpetuate this occlusion of the screen, of the cinematic frame. The fade and the dissolve always prevent the screen from being perceived in its blankness. Moreover, as psychoanalytic research has noted,[21] the cinema as a room takes advantage of the theatrical model in order to have the screen function as a window rather than as a solid and obvious fourth wall. The screen is noted for its diaphanous effect, and when the curtain is opened it reveals yet another veil, as if ready to give way in turn to the real which supposedly exists behind it. If a form of stage is still in use, this does not serve the needs of optics, since projection would be possible on any part of a fourth wall; it seems rather to serve as a form of that paradoxical desire to venerate what is about to be disavowed. Whether this amounts then to a form of fetishization or to a material manifestation of *différance*, the function of the cinematic screen seems comparable to the hymen as discussed by Derrida.[22]

In *Nouvelles Hébrides,* the differential play of whiteness institutes and inscribes a whole series of traces within the cinematic apparatus. Similarly its apparent silence speaks volumes concerning the visibility of this absence of words. The narrator believes himself to be excluded from a system of coherence which unites the other spectators with some "magnificent spectacle." But the audience occupies empty places, it is therefore a void which speaks to him of its place within the claimed system of coherence, affirming the manner in which absence *attends* presence. The same thing occurs with the screen where the narrator believes that the distance separating him from the empty image is alone responsible for the spacing effect which actually structures representation. He is persuaded that this distance can be bridged and original presence retrieved. What he finds on the screen – blindingly obvious – is the way in which the structure of *différance* plays even within the scene of representation. In trying himself to consecrate a new presence, he is obliged, as I have said, to enter into the differential play.

I have so far taken advantage of the narrative progression of *Nouvelles Hébrides* in order to advance a teleological analysis of the representative scene as it falls victim to effects of rupture. However, I noted earlier, that this notion of rupture often operated in Desnos' texts in conjunction with those of scattering, of dissemination, and of fragmentation of writing and its support, the blank page. In the text in question, once the narrator crosses through the screen he enters the domain of death, indicated not only by the suicides of Breton and Aragon, but also a little further on by a whole cemetery populated predominantly by writers. Page 102 of the text is blank except for the words, in capitals: "Here is the cemetery of the passengers of the Sémillante lost with all hands on the reefs of the Sanguinaire Islands"; and the following page arranges the tombs in regular rows, with a "Here lies . . ." in each case (except in the case of Desnos for whom the verb is in the future tense, and in the case of a list of poets known to be dear to him – Rimbaud, Ducasse, Jarry, Apollinaire, Baudelaire, etc. – who lie in a common grave).

The dialogue from the aquarium, the museum epigram, the noisy silence of the cinema, all find their echo in this series of simple epitaphs. However, instead of continuing discussion of that text, I wish to follow through the ideas of fragmentation and rupture in another text by Desnos which concerns the cinema, namely a fragment of a scenario dating from 1928, also published in the collection *Nouvelles Hébrides et autres textes*, a project for a film entitled *La Part des lionnes*.

The scene interests me on several counts: its place within the scenario as a whole; its representing the intersection of poetic with filmic writing; and finally, the way in which it points towards a theory of writing applicable to cinema. It is to be taken first of all as the climax to the narrative:

124) André and the fourth woman
125) Kiss
126) André takes her by the hand and leads her away
127) A vacant lot
128) André goes away
129) The fourth woman alone
130) She remains motionless
131) André continues on his way
132) The woman leaning against the bust of a naked woman
133) The dagger on the ground
134) André raises the dagger
135) André alone on a deserted path
136) The fourth woman stretched out on the ground with the dagger stuck between her shoulders
137) The four women of the film together in a field. (*NH*, 484)

Let me note as a parenthesis that this episode also poses the more general question of the functioning of transgression in Surrealist writing, that is to say the extent to which Surrealism, by means of its systematic transgressions on the ideological as well as the poetic level, managed to either subvert or simply reinforce the esthetic and ideological principles it sought to overturn.[23]

As far as the narrative structure of the scenario goes, it should be pointed out that the four women mentioned here are all involved in relations with André which follow a more or less linear progression. The following model is established: meeting, sexual encounter, rupture, separation. The sequence cited seems therefore to repeat the same progression, at least until shot 131. The fourth woman has in fact appeared in the scenario without any explicit textual justification, whereas the others meet André in an official context, even if by chance. It would seem that the fourth woman's presence is justified solely by the thematic and narrative structure that the text has established, according to the threefold repetition of an internal logic, thanks to a type of textual economy. Moreover, a series of displacements of textual elements from earlier on in the narrative operates in conjunction with the condensation I have just mentioned. First, in the sequence cited it is the fourth woman who seems to be the victim of André's violence, although the logic of the narrative up till now would have had him kill the first woman, Ilsa. Secondly, the dagger which figures in this extract was found on a chair in Ilsa's room in the previous scene. And finally, the fourth woman is here characterized by an immobility that was before the mark of André.

The sequence is difficult to analyze since it represents the point of intersection between Surrealist and cinematic writing. It is well known that the Surrealist image consists of the juxtaposition of two incongruous elements without their being between those elements the metaphoric relation of more traditional poetry, even if a relation is suggested on an altogether different, even metaphysic, level. Such a technique invites two possible explanations: either an exaggeration of the paradigmatic choice available to metaphoric comparison, to the extent that the principle of similarity no longer governs that operation—this would seem to be the intention of the Surrealists who saw the explicit incongruity resolved or sanctioned in the idea of the "marvellous"; or else an affirmation of syntagmatic priority, always judiciously exploited in poetry through rhythm, rhyme, and figurative usage in general, but more obviously relevant to the language of film, language without a grammar. I do not mean by this that the Surrealist image does not obey syntax, but that there is interference in the normal articulation of the syntagmatic and paradigmatic functions. Sense is not after all established on a single plane, but through this very articulation of two planes, creating a strange type of tension at the base of language.

To return to the Surrealist image. Its effect of disturbing standard operations of sense derives from the terms chosen for the comparison (an umbrella and a sewing-machine, for example, in the Lautréamont paradigm), which as a result lose their automatic referential status. The Surrealist image is in fact always tautological; its referent is necessarily language since all reference to the conceptual referent is blocked or undermined by the nonsense that such a reference would imply, given the presence of the second incongruous term. In language, an umbrella can easily meet a sewing-machine, it could well be beautiful; but on a dissecting table seen as conceptual reality, their coexistence poses problems.

Paradoxically there is then a close resemblance between the cinematic image and the terms of the Surrealist image: neither has much interest in referring to that which it represents. In the first case the relation is "too" analogical, in the second it is impaired by a non-sense. However, in both cases that relation takes on great importance on the ideological level. In calling the relation between cinematic image and its referent "analogical," one is relying on a sense or a reference which such an image always presupposes, namely its reference to the ideology of realism. In calling the relation between the two terms of a Surrealist image "metaphorical," one is reinforcing the sense of Surrealist metaphysics.

In his essay on metaphor and metonymy, Christian Metz maintains a strict line of demarcation between syntagmatic and paradigmatic relations operating at the level of discourse (either filmic or poetic), and metaphors and metonymies which always relate to the referent (either "real" or diegetic):

. . . every film (every discourse) is a vast syntagmatic chain . . . Metaphor and metonymy, on the contrary . . . operate on similarities and contiguities which are perceived or understood between the *referents* which the figure involves.[24]

But in this fragment of a scenario, sense fails to operate normally both with respect to the "real" referent and also with respect to the diegetic referent. Surrealist precepts claim that their image provides a discursive contiguity which is a putative referential similarity, even if that relation is neither "perceived" nor "understood." For example, the vacant lot of shot 127 of *La Part des lionnes* functions at the discursive level as the site of the act of lovemaking between André and the fourth woman; but it should also be compared with the image of flames that has often been seen in film in the place of explicitly sexual shots. Surrealism substitutes the idea of a void for the ardour expressed by traditional metaphor. Hence the example could easily be read as conforming to one of Metz's categories.[25] But that classification becomes more difficult as the sequence continues and one cannot say whether shots 132–137 are supposed to belong to the diegesis, or whether they represent autonomous shots which should be explained in terms of their rhetorical function.

Nevertheless, it would be erroneous to claim that sense is lost on the referential level in this series of "filmed" (Surrealist) images. It would be more correct to say the signifier refers back to itself in one case (that of the "real" referent), and that it fragments in the other (that of the narrative). Language (words or images) continues to function, but it functions by breaking down, because the space which allows its referential operation, as well as the rupture which constitutes its syntagmatic interlinking, are here interiorized. Taken at its word, the Surrealist image always makes the same reference: between the two elements of this figure there is inevitably a relation of rupture and absence; before becoming a problematic similarity, the contiguity of its elements should be understood as expressing this notion of rupture. In the sequence I cited one can identify an acceleration and a condensation (in the literal sense) of effects of rupture which are enunciated as much through the syntagmatic chain as through the ever more explicit filmic images of emptiness, of separation, and of death.

Operations such as the fragmentation of the narrative, the juxtaposition of images which no longer find their explanation in metaphoric or metonymic operations, or in the logical progression of the diegesis, render explicit the discontinuity which in fact constitutes cinema. Marie-Claire Ropars has clearly demonstrated this in the case of Eisensteinian montage: the rupture inscribed there defines cinematic language as writing. By virtue of the confusion it maintains between paradigmatic and syntagmatic operations, my example of Surrealism in transition between poetry and film allows us to identify the same effect of rupture between the cinematic image and its "real" referent. The analogical relation between cinematic image and real referent, a relation which is so vaunted by the partisans of idealism, is shown to hide a tautological underside. For this supposed reconciling of the image in a relationship of presence with its referent in no way annuls the spacing which constitutes every sign; its effect is to interiorize the relay of signification such that the image becomes subverted from inside by its own difference. The paradigmatic "poverty" of the cinematic image cannot prevent such a structure of absence from being installed on the vertical plane; and as this meeting between Surrealist and cinematic images has shown, the effects of rupture produced on the syntagmatic plane of a Surrealist film, and which are intrinsic to, although obscured from, every film which consists of a series of discontinuous images, act in concert with the above-mentioned tautological effect of the paradigmatic plane, itself obscured by the ideology of realism. As the Surrealist image demonstrates, as every word-play implies, the sign can only function by assuming that absence, that rupture, that spacing. If the image is to be compared with a neologism from the point of view of its paradigmatic function, it continues all the same to put language into play, and to be marked by all that is implied by such play.

The critical moment of the process of fragmentation taking place in *La Part des lionnes* occurs in shot 136. The following shot begins an attempt at reintegration which continues to the end of the film (shot 157). Absolute rupture is here expressed by the violence of murder, a murder which, for the purposes of this discussion, I would read more in terms of death and the violence of structures of absence than murder. Death and absence relate to each other both metaphorically and metonymically. Death, already seen in Desnos' poems in close relation with writing, as the other side of the screen in *Nouvelles Hébrides,* reappears here as *inscription* – a tattoo on the woman's body – inscription of rupture within cinematic signification, *impression* of a structure which identifies the effects of writing within that form of signification, and which *underlines* its differential function. According to Derrida, this differential and supplementary function is a fact not only of the image, but of the imagination itself, and hence of every scene of representation:

The image can only re-present and add the representation to the represented to the extent that the presence of the represented already overlaps itself in the world, to the extent that life refers back to itself as if referring to its own lack, to its own request for a supplement. The presence of the represented is constituted thanks to the addition to itself of this nothing that the image is, the announcement of its dispossession in its own representation and in its death.[26]

The representational play that is the cinema cannot escape this supplementary structure neither in an attempt to efface its syntagmatic differences such as those undertaken by narrative, nor in the notion of a privileged relationship between representation and represented governing the paradigmatic plane. On the contrary, the more the image resembles and approaches its referent, the more it reveals its pure supplementarity. If it only reproduces, it may as well disappear; by remaining very close it demonstrates its own excessiveness.

My aim here has been to follow certain threads or traces of writing of the cinema as system of traces, fragments and ruptures, such as they show up in two texts destined to be forgotten within the Surrealist corpus. The weave of such threads would be nothing other than a theory of writing which is only just beginning to find its place in cinematic studies.

Notes

The French version of this esssy ("Un Ecran déchiré") appears simultaneously in *Hors cadre* 4 ("L'Image, L'Imaginaire," Presses Universitaires de Vincennes, 1986). Certain of the ideas are developed in a different context in an article entitled "Theories of Spectacle/Spectacle of Theory" to appear in *Iconics* (Tokyo, 1986).

1. *Le Signifiant imaginaire* (Paris: Union générale d'éditions, 1977). By metonymic effect I include in the current represented by Metz, the work of Jean-Louis Baudry (see *Communications* 23, 1975), and in another context that of Jean-Pierre Oudart (see *Cahiers du cinéma* 211, 212: 228–230).

2. *Le Texte divisé*, (Paris: Presses Universitaires de France, 1981). M. C. Ropars' research is to a great extent inspired by that of Derrida.

3. Edited and annotated by André Tchernia (Paris: Gallimard, 1966).

4. (Paris: Gallimard, 1978). Henceforth cited as *NH*.

5. "Porte du second infini," in *C'est les bottes de 7 lieues*, reprinted in *Destinée arbitraire* (Paris: Gallimard, 1975), 50. All translations from French texts are my own.

6. "Les Gorges froides," ibid., 57.

7. *NH*, 23–104.

8. *Le Texte divisé*, 40.

9. One could mention the cry of Lol V. Stein as the excess around which a whole series of texts is constructed, but in such a way that the cry can never be considered as originating center. Similarly, the films *India Song, Son nom de Venise dans Calcutta désert, Agatha,* and *L'Homme l'Atlantique,* which involve repetitions of certain textual elements, or construction of a new film based on the remainders of a previous one, are texts which work to exploit rather than obscure the discontinuities which constitute them.

Structurally speaking, a film which consisted of a single shot (e.g. Warhol's *Empire*) would still amount to a "cutting" process with respect to the unexposed film, still a differential process albeit of another kind.

10. *Corps et biens* (Paris: Gallimard, 1968), 59.

11. *Le Signifiant imaginaire,* 70.

12. Ibid., 68.

13. Ibid., 66.

14. Ibid., 89.

15. "Le Dispositif," *Communications* 23 (1975): 72.

16. Ibid., 68.

17. Ibid., 70.

18. "Rhétorique de l'image," *Communications* 4 (1964); *La Chambre claire* (Paris: Editions de l'étoile, Gallimard, Seuil, 1980).

19. *La Chambre claire,* 123. Barthes' emphasis.

20. J. Lacan, *Ecrits* (Paris: Seuil, 1966), I, 205.

21. *Le Signifiant imaginaire,* 89.

22. "La Double séance," in *La Dissémination* (Paris: Seuil, 1972), 199–317.

23. Jean-Louis Houdebine, "Le 'concept' d'écriture automatique : sa signification et sa fonction dans le discours idéologique d'André Breton," *La Nouvelle critique,* no. 39bis (1970); and from another point of view Xavière Gauthier, *Surréalisme et sexualité* (Paris: Gallimard, 1971).

24. *Le Signifiant imaginaire,* 221, 222.

25. Ibid., 227–229.

26. J. Derrida, *De la grammatologie* (Paris: Minuit, 1967), 261.

Constellated Visions:
Robert Desnos's and Man Ray's
L'Etoile de Mer

Inez Hedges

Of all the artists in the Dada and Surrealist movements who tried their hand at cinematography, Man Ray must surely be the most reluctant filmmaker. Arriving in Paris on Bastille Day in 1921, he was introduced to the Dadaists by Marcel Duchamp. It was Tristan Tzara who became responsible for Man Ray's first film, as Man Ray relates in his autobiography:

One Wednesday morning, Tzara appeared with a printed announcement of an important Dada manifestation to be held the following night in the Michel Theater. On the program my name figured as the producer of a Dada film, part of the program entitled *Le Coeur à barbe*.[1]

The five-minute film Man Ray produced in twenty-four hours, *Le Retour à la raison,* is an important document of an artist learning new ways of producing images at the same time as the audience is asked to learn to "read" them; the strategy of the artist was basically to produce kineticized versions of his earlier work. These included animated Rayographs (obtained by sprinkling salt, thumbtacks, and nails on strips of celluloid and then exposing them to light), and a kinetic version of his "Dancer/Danger" painting to which smoke was added to produce the illusion of motion. The nocturnal city is presented in terms of a brightly lit revolving merry-go-round, a fact that foregrounds cinema's own status as "writing motion in lights" (*kinematographein* and *photo-graphein*). At the same time, the artist's inclusion of filmed sequences of moiré patterns on a nude, a moving image version of a photographic project that was to become a recurrent theme in his work, accentuates the idea of the celluloid as skin, since the equivalent French word "pellicule," comes from the Latin word for "little skin."

Retour à la raison is a near perfect example of artistic "bricolage," an experimental outgrowth of Man Ray's other artistic activities brought before the public in all the immediacy of improvisation. In addition, it exhibits many typical qualities of Dadaist work, including the use of mixed media, the placing of the human body on an equal footing with objects in the turn away from representation, and the affirmation of nothingness as a compositional theme (the film includes a photograph of the 1924 Man Ray "poem" consisting only of black ink marks representing the length of words). The idea that materials assembled by chance will bear a resemblance to the creator is enacted by a spiraling rolled manuscript followed by the signature "Man Ray Noir" written across two frames; earlier, "Man Ray à tirer 5 fois" appears written across five frames. Because the images were written across the negative, they appear backwards in the film. Finally, the work is typically Dadaist in that it was produced for public performance, "to try the spectators' patience," as Man Ray says.[2]

Man Ray's next film was financed by Arthur Wheeler, a retired American stockbroker, and again he had to be talked into the project. Although made in 1926 after Dada had been supplanted by Surrealism, *Emak Bakia* is a more extended version of the first Dada film.

In this second film Man Ray expands the metafilmic elements. The representation of the nighttime city is now expanded to include revolving neon messages, a "writing in lights" that anticipates the artist's 1931 composition, "La Ville." For the rest of the cinematic apparatus, the artist assembled a series of props—deforming mirrors, an electric turntable, an assortment of crystals, and lamps—which were used to foreground the motion of cinema and the lenses of photography. In *Emak Bakia,* Man Ray celebrates cinema as *machine célibataire,* or machine that, producing nothing, is "pure invention."[3] As such, he includes references to protocinematic toys such as zootrope by photographing whirling objects and hallways in deforming mirrors. The deformation of the film's title and credit sequence by these stratagems announces that these are major concerns of the film. There is a sequence of a man jumping against a background diagram of his successive body positions that recalls the early motion studies developed by Etienne Jules Marey. Thus, despite Dada's proclaimed break with the past, the films exhibit forms of intertextuality which ally artistic production with the technology of a cinema seen as modern and progressive.

Second only to the machine theme is the theme of vision, actively foregrounded by the first shot of the film, in which an eye is shown in reverse against the lens. According to Mimi White, this image links up with the later images of women looking directly at the camera (the spectator) to make the issue of vision and perception a central theme.[4] Man Ray carried the idea of the "camera eye" to the furthest possible extent in *Emak Bakia,* filming underwater fish "au milieu du bassin de Neptune" as an illuminated news message promised earlier.

At the end of *Emak Bakia,* the film's only intertitle announces a mock explanation, "La raison de cette extravagance" (the reason for this extravagance). In this final section, a man gets out of a car and enters a building in what is the only use of a conventional match on action modeled from the narrative cinema. But the "story" never gets any further; narrative dissolves again in the abstract study of the shapes of men's collars wheeling about in screen space. This sequence has been described by critics as yet another trick played on the viewer, who is led to believe that there will be an explanation to all the material that has come before. I think, instead, that the sequence looks ahead to the theme of the voyage that becomes important in Man Ray's next film, *L'Etoile de mer,* a film which portrays a Surrealist, as opposed to a Dadaist, sensibility.

L'Etoile de mer is the only film Man Ray volunteered to make and finance himself; the last one, *Le Mystère du château du dé*, was financed by the Vicomte de Noailles. *L'Etoile de mer* was based on a poem or scenario by Robert Desnos, which, unknown to previous commentators on the film, has been in the collection of the Museum of Modern Art since 1972.[5]

In *L'Etoile de mer*, the theme of the voyage into the unknown becomes a focus and metaphor for the experience of love; the voyage becomes associated with the mystic quest which in Surrealism was couched in overtly alchemical terms. As so often in Surrealism, the "woman" comes to stand for a complex set of cultural associations which underscore the driving sexual metaphor of androgyny in Surrealist theory, that is to say the ideal union of the male and female personality in the single artist. The Surrealist quest must not be seen as the search for an ideal "other," or as yet another instance of the idealization of "woman," but rather as the (admittedly narcissistic) goal of incorporating the womanly into one's male persona. Salvador Dalí's concept of "paranoia-criticism" and his paraphrase of Breton's dictum — "beauty must be edible, or not at all" — is but the most extreme instance of the Surrealists' desire to incorporate, rather than to admire, the feminine.

In accordance with the quest theme of the film, the woman's body becomes narrativized, rather than fragmented as in the earlier, more Dadaist films. It has become, in a word, the "obscure object of desire." Throughout the film protagonist's search for the woman, familiar tokens of the occult appear: the tower and star of the tarot; the elements of air, fire, water, and earth. The "mer" of the title is the dangerous sea on which the alchemist sets out, searching for the unification of elements, represented as male and female. The starfish is the androgynous symbol that lies at the end of that search; enclosed in glass, the alchemists's vessel, it is a combination of the feminine elements of earth and water (as fish), and the masculine air and fire (as star). With its five points, it resembles the hermaphrodite that stands at the end of the alchemical operation.

Much has been made, in previous commentary on *L'Etoile de mer*, of a scene of leave-taking which takes place early in the film. In this scene, a young man follows a young woman up to her apartment, where she proceeds to take off her clothes in the most matter-of-fact manner. The man remains seated on the bed while she undresses. Lying down on the bed, she adjusts herself comfortably. As he gets up, she stretches out her hand to bid him goodbye. Kissing it, he takes his leave, as the word "Adieu" appears scrawled across the screen. I think it interesting that most commentators have sought a psychological motivation for the man's departure without considering the larger philosophical background of Surrealism. Thus P. Adams Sitney writes that an intertitle appearing previously, when the couple was walking outside — "Les dents de femmes sont des objets si charmants qu'on ne devrait les voir qu'en rêve ou à l'instant de l'amour" (women's teeth are such charming objects that one should only see them in dreams or at the moment of love) — explains that the man leaves because he is afraid of sex.[6] Lauren Rabinovitz also subscribes to the view that the reference to teeth refers to the "castrating nature of woman's active sexuality."[7] Alan Thiher compounds the threat of the woman's teeth ("a primordial expression of man's fear of female sexuality") by reminding us that the poet's exit lines ("si belle! Cybèle?") are a reminder of the "Phrygian Aphrodite, an erotic deity associated with castration rites."[8] Steven Kovacs describes the scene as "the man walking out at a moment of great anticipation by the woman,"[9] while Norman Gambill states that "the man does not accept the woman's obvious offer."[10]

In fact there is very little evidence for attributing psychological motivations to the characters. For one thing, neither the man nor the woman show the slightest erotic interest in one another; the woman pulls her clothes off in a most unseductive manner, almost as though she were about to pose as a model. In fact she *is* posing—for the camera, and Man Ray uses a gelatin filter on the lens to accentuate the abstract visual quality of the image (and also to please the censors, he claimed). The man sits at the foot of the bed without even looking at her. He seems to be waiting politely for her to get comfortable so he can take his leave.

The humor of the scene (noted by Adou Kyrou and Steven Kovacs)[11] comes from the clash between the spectator's willingness to read eroticism into the scene where there is none. The musical notations of the manuscript show that the passage was originally scored for a tango in order to heighten this expectation. The voyeurism of the spectator is also humorously frustrated by the filmmaker's use of the gelatin filter which effaces both the woman's nudity and the man's facial expression. It is impossible to say, in addition, whose "Adieu" is handwritten across the screen: every viewer is left to decide for him or herself whether this is the man, the woman, or the narrator "speaking."

Rather than attempting a psychological reading of the film, I would like to propose one that identifies the woman as the *soror mystica* of alchemy, whose relationship to the man resembles that of the poet and Nadja in Breton's Surrealist novel, *Nadja*. The poet's quest in *L'Etoile de mer* then becomes a mystical quest similar to the theme of the voyage in Breton's work. The humor of the film (as evidenced in the scene when the man departs after the woman has undressed) can be seen as part of its narcissistic structure, as the man uses the woman in order to attain an inner, spiritual goal. This view is consistent with Freud's view of humor who speaks of it as the "exaltation of the ego, to which the humorous displacement bears witness, and of which the translation would no doubt be: 'I am too big (grossartig) to be distressed by these things.'"[12]

In the reading I am now proposing, many of the film's mysterious elements are explained. The star is associated with the seventeenth card of the Tarot, which represents one of the final stages of the alchemist's spiritual journey. Breton specifically linked this arcanum to love in his novel *Arcane 17*; in addition, in his discussion of alchemy, Jung links the starfish to the myth of psychic regeneration.[13]

Interestingly, the manuscript from the archives of the Museum of Modern Art in New York lends additional credence to this interpretation. In the first place, it contains notations in the hand of Man Ray for accompanying music to the film which do not correspond to the vague references to "popular music" in the artist's autobiography. Instead, the music constitutes a parallel "argument" to the film that explains many of its images. Finally, the changes in the order of sequences and the subtitles added later underscore the alchemical theme.[14]

The intertitles that are later additions to the film are as follows:

1. "Les dents des femmes sont des objets si charmants qu'on ne devrait les voir qu'en rêve ou à l'instant de l'amour"

2. "Si belle! Cybèle?"

3. "Nous sommes à jamais perdus dans le désert de l'éternèbre"

4. "Il faut battre les morts quand ils sont froids"

5. "Et si tu trouves sur cette terre une femme à l'amour sincère . . ."

6. "Le soleil, un pied à l'étrier, niche un rossignol dans un voile de crêpe"

(Translation: 1) Women's teeth are such charming objects that one should only see them in dreams or at the moment of love 2) So beautiful! Cybele? 3) We are forever lost in the desert of the eternitenebrous [a portmanteau word made up of "eternity" and "tenebrous"] 4) You have to strike the dead when they are cold 5) "And if you find on this earth a woman who loves sincerely" 6) The sun, one foot in the stirrups, nests a nightingale in a veil of crêpe.)

If all the above lines are by Desnos, they do not appear to belong to a single poem but to call up associations with different stages of his work or to replay many of the dominant poetic discourses of the period. We can recognize the style of Surrealist "écriture automatique" (6) and Surrealist games of overturning popular expressions (4). The sentence, "le soleil, un pied à l'étrier, niche un rossignol dans un voile de crêpe" also has multiple semantic associations with the alchemical symbolism I have already touched upon. The image of the vigorous, rising, phallic sun is counterbalanced by the feminine "voile de crêpe" (crepe veil) which appears to be a death image (it calls up associations with widowhood) associated with the setting sun (crépuscule, from crêpe). The "rossignol" associates the elixir, often represented as a bird, with the red color of the alchemical rubedo (in Italian, "rosso,"), which comes after the death of the couple following the *coniunctio*.

Of the lines more directly connected to other poems by Desnos, there are puns of the "Rrose Sélavy type" (2), and the association between love, mystery, and darkness (3), as in the poem "Ténèbres! O ténèbres" (Darkness! O darkness) which figures in the collection *Les Ténèbres* dating from 1927. This collection also contains a poem, "Chant du ciel," (Song of the Sky) in which many of the elements appearing in the film—a boat, the fire, a flower, etc.—combine to sing the woman's praise: "elle est belle, elle est belle" (She is beautiful). More importantly, the starfish in glass and its relation to the poet's inspiration recalls "Si tu savais" (If you knew), a poem included in the 1926 collection *A la mystérieuse*: "Loin de moi, une étoile filante choit dans la bouteille nocturne du poète. Il met vivement le bouchon et dès lors il guette l'étoile enclose dans le verre, il guette les constellations qui naissent sur les parois, loin de moi, tu es loin de moi."[15] As Desnos was not in Paris while the film was made (the last shot in which he walks off with the woman was filmed before his departure), it is likely that Man Ray added other material from Desnos's oeuvre and from the Surrealist environ-

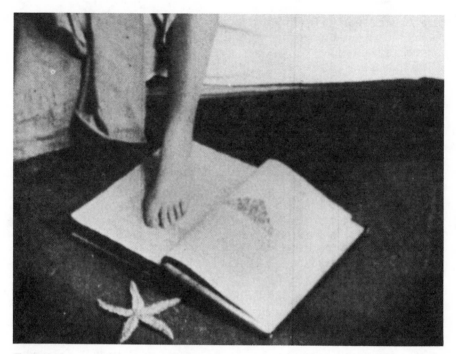

Figure 1

ment in which he was working in order to complete the film.

One of the most interesting aspects of the manuscript is a set of musical notations in Man Ray's hand which establish a musical "argument" to parallel the visual one. The music "frames" the narrative with the song "Plaisir d'amour ne dure qu'un instant / chagrin d'amour dure toute la vie." In between come other songs ("O sole mio," and a "carmagnole," or rondeau popular during France's reign of terror), the "Last Tango," the Blue Danube Waltz, and an aria by Bach. Each one of these pieces has semantic associations that add to an understanding of the film. The tango suggests the possibility of an erotic encounter that is avoided;[16] the Blue Danube Waltz and the well-known Italian song metaphorically associate the man's love for the woman with the theme of the voyage, as mentioned previously. The association is accentuated by the silence which accompanies the shot of the departing vessel in XIII. It is the woman's independence (and not her teeth) that threaten the man's quest, as the manuscript version plainly shows; the Phrygian costume, which was described as a "symbol of liberty" by Man Ray,[17] is accompanied by a rondeau popular during the French revolution (XIV–XV). But gradually the Italian song returns to drown out the woman's rebellion, gaining final ascendancy in the shot of the woman with her foot on a book and the starfish beside it (XVI). The Bach aria then begins and continues until the final shot of the man alone with his starfish (XXXIII).

The transitional shot before the beginning of the aria is crucial to understanding the occult imagery of the film, for the book the woman

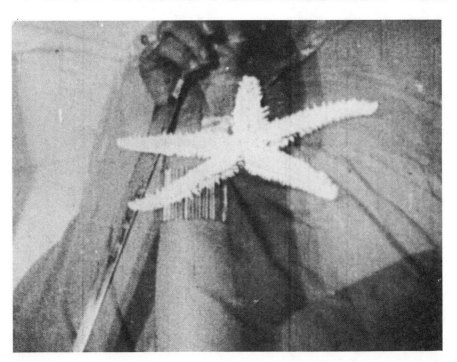

Figure 2

touches with her foot has all the appearance of being an alchemical text; moreover the disposition of the foot, the book and the starfish reproduce a faithful image of alchemical iconography (Figure 1). In Man Ray's and Desnos's film, the woman becomes the path to the starfish, which is the symbol of the man's Surrealist quest; thus at the end of the film he can accept her loss ("qu'elle était belle," how beautiful she was) because he has found the "étoile" ("qu'elle est belle," how beautiful she is). Like Breton's *Nadja,* the woman is means to an end, a stage of apprenticeship for the vampiristic artist who ends up by incorporating her narcissistically and hence has no further need for her. It is he, rather than she, who really has the dangerous teeth.[18] Toward the end of the film, the nude woman reappears, this time with the intertitle "vous ne révez [sic] pas" (you are not dreaming). Within the film's overall structure, this intertitle matches the first ("Women's teeth are such charming objects that one should only see them in dreams or at the instant of love), since it marks the transition back to the road where the woman and man first walk together. If the preceding film has been a dream fantasy, the point is that it is now time for the poet to turn to his true work. The handwriting and the wrong accent on "révez" strongly suggest that this addition is by Man Ray.

I have said before that the film switches the order of some of the shots as given in the manuscript. One of these changes brings the film even closer to *Nadja,* because it associates the woman with madness. In the film version, the scene of the woman climbing the stairs with a knife (XXI) is imme-

Figure 3

diately followed by the shot of the prison (which once functioned as an insane asylum), La Santé (XXIV).[19]

The second major change involves the shot of the woman in Phrygian costume (XV), which is moved to a place toward the end of the film (following XXVIII). By this move, the woman's resistance is not overcome in the early stages as described above, but remains to thwart the man. By this time, he has already practically declared her insane, so that her assertion of liberty leaves him all the more free to sublimate his desire in the starfish. We should note, in passing, the shots that come between La Santé and the Phrygian costume and which recast the woman's image in terms of the elements of alchemy (earth, air, water and fire). This sequence is immediately preceded by the superimposition of the starfish over the woman who climbs the stairs with the knife in her hand (Figure 2). I think the shot marks her entry into the allegory of alchemical transformation: the sundering of elements by the sword is frequently used in the iconography to represent the first stage, or *dissolutio;* after which the divided elements are recombined to create the androgyne. The still-life of the red wine bottle, banana peel and starfish (XXVII), which would have interrupted this sequence, is moved to a place where it can underscore the rising importance of the starfish over and against the woman, in a sequence of three shots ending in the turning point described earlier (XVII, XXVII and XVI). In the penultimate shot of the film, the glass through which the woman is filmed shatters (Man Ray added the comment, "explosion," to this sequence). The

106

breaking of the glass recalls a line of Breton's and Paul Eluard's quoted in the *Dictionnaire abrégé du surréalisme:* "VERRE: La grande question serait d'obtenir que lorsqu'un être a trompé un autre être, il soit incapable de prendre à la main un verre qui ne se brise pas aussitôt."[20] The glass breaking thus underscores another reason for transcending the woman, who has been found incapable of "sincere love," as one of the intertitles suggests.

Glass objects figure heavily in alchemical symbolism and iconography as glass was the preferred representation of the alchemical vessel. The repeated references to glass ("si les fleurs étaient en verre," and "belle comme une fleur de verre") are visually repeated in the shot of the glass door which opens and closes the film, the jar which contains the starfish, and the multiple screen effect in one shot which displays a dozen rotating or moving glass objects (Figure 3). Antonin Artaud used a comparable profusion of glass vessels in his film *La Coquille et le clergyman* (filmed by Germaine Dulac). The intertitle, "Il faut battre les morts quand ils sont froids" (a variation on the popular saying, "Il faut battre le fer quand il est chaud," strike the iron while it is hot) recalls the fact that the middle stage of alchemy was represented as the death of the couple (the *mortificatio*) which eventually led to the resurrection.[21]

On the basis of the manuscript and the marked difference between *L'Etoile de mer* and Man Ray's other films, it seems likely that it was Desnos's poem which originally suggested the alchemical allegory to Man Ray. This would indicate that Desnos's role in the film is much greater than has hitherto been supposed. If any aspect of the film may be ascribed exclusively to Man Ray, it is the opposition between abstraction and allegorical narrative that threatens to pull the film in opposite directions. The progress of the story is continually threatened by stasis, by shots that appear as experiments in animating still photographs, and that recall his earlier films. This is true not only of the shots filmed with a gelatin filter, but the shots of newspapers blowing across the street (see sequence VIII of the manuscript), the multiple split screen of rotating glass objects (Figure 3), the perspectives taken from a passing train (sequences XI–XII in the manuscript) and many others in which diegetic time comes to a standstill. If, as I have suggested, the woman is more narrativized in this film, this is not true of the other objects, whose photographic abstraction points toward the ultimate assimilation of narrative and life into the permanence of art.[22] In the finished film, this is reinforced by the inclusion, in the first and last shots, of an opening and closing circular window. Finally, if Man Ray's film style is not totally integrated with Desnos's allegory, this is what one might expect from a "coproduction" of two artists of such magnitude.

Man Ray's last film, *Le Mystère du château du dé,* was commissioned by the Vicomte de Noailles. The film more or less abandons the alchemical theme, and returns to the abstract study of shapes and moving forms, despite a rudimentary story line. There is, however, one alchemical element: Man Ray celebrates the triumph of the androgynous society in the "piscinéma" (read "piscine," "cinéma," and "pisces"; swimming pool, cinema, and fish) where men and women cavort together without sexual overtones. In alchemy, the *soror mystica,* or female soulmate of the alchemist is most

107

often represented as Melusina, the mythical mermaid. Breton refers to the Melusina myth both in connection with Nadja and with Elisa in *Arcane 17*. In this last film, the "bassin de Neptune" of *Emak Bakia* has become the alchemical soup. But otherwise, perhaps because of the absence of Desnos as collaborator, one can find few Surrealist elements.

Notes

1. Man Ray, *Self Portrait* (Boston: Little, Brown and Co., 1963), 260.

2. Ibid., 260.

3. Louis Aragon, "L'Ombre de l'invention," *La Révolution surréaliste* 1 (December 1924), 24–25.

4. Mimi White, "Two French Dada Films: *Entr'acte* and *Emak Bakia*," *Dada/Surrealism* 13 (1984), 37–47.

5. For accounts of the genesis of *L'Etoile de mer*, see Man Ray's *Self Portrait*, op. cit., 276–278, and the account by Desnos quoted in Arturo Schwarz, *Man Ray: The Rigour of Imagination* (New York: Rizzoli, 1977), 297. The most important passages are reproduced in my comments on the manuscript, included in the "Documents" section.

6. P. Adams Sitney, "Image and Title in Avant-Garde Cinema," *October* 11 (Winter 1979), 108.

7. Lauren Rabinovitz, "Independent Journeyman: Man Ray, Dada and Surrealist Filmmaker," *Southwest Review* 64 (1979), 371.

8. Alan Thiher, *The Cinematic Muse: Critical Studies in the History of French Cinema* (Columbia: University of Missouri Press, 1979), 40.

9. Steven Kovacs, *From Enchantment to Rage. The Story of Surrealist Cinema* (London and Toronto: Associated University Presses, 1980), 136.

10. Norman Gambill, "The Movies of Man Ray," in *Man Ray: Photographs and Objects* (Birmingham: Birmingham Museum of Art, 1980), 35.

11. Adou Kyrou, *Le Surréalisme au cinéma* (Paris: Editions Arcanes, 1953), 181; Kovacs, 136.

12. Sigmund Freud, *The Standard Edition of the Complete Psychological Works, Vol. 8*, trans. and ed. James Strachey (New York. W. W. Norton, 1963), 234.

13. Carl Gustav Jung, "The Fish in Alchemy," in *Aion: Researches into the Phenomenology of the Self*, trans. R.F.C. Hull (Princeton, New Jersey: Princeton University Press, 1959), 126–137.

14. A complete shot-by-shot breakdown of the film may be found in Kovacs, 268–275.

15. Translation: "Far from me, a shooting star falls in the poet's nocturnal bottle. He quickly corks it and ever after he spies on the star enclosed in the glass, he spies on the constellations that are shining forth from the walls, far from me, you are far from me." Robert Desnos, *Corps et biens* (Paris: Gallimard, 1953), 96.

16. I am grateful to Miriam Hansen for pointing out to me that in 1921, Rudolf Valentino's *Four Horsemen of the Apocalypse* had established the tango as the dance that was the highest expression of romantic passion.

17. Man Ray, 276.

18. I am grateful to both Mary Ann Caws and Susan Rubin Suleiman for opening up the question of feminism and Surrealism. See Mary Ann Caws, "Ladies Shot and Painted: Female Embodiment in Surrealist Art" in Susan Suleiman, ed. *The Female Body in Western Culture: Contemporary Perspectives* (Cambridge: Harvard University Press, 1986); and Susan Suleiman, "Women, Madness, and Narrative," in Shlomith Rimmon-Kenan, ed. *Discourse in Literature, the Arts, Psychoanalysis* (forthcoming). I would also like to thank Susan Suleiman for making many helpful suggestions for the revision of this article.

19. Even though in Man Ray's time La Santé had become a prison, I feel that his choice of this particular institution was bound up with its history as a place of confinement, not only for criminals, but also for the insane: "Founded in the 13th Century by Marguerite de Provence (widow of Louis IX) as an overflow hospital for the Hôtel-Dieu, [La Santé] was later used as an annexe of the prison Bicêtre, and like Bicêtre, had many lunatics among its inmates. In the mid-19th Century it became a prison mainly for offenders serving short sentences." Joyce M. H. Reid, *The Concise Oxford Dictionary of French Literature* (Oxford: Clarendon Press, 1976), 574.

20. Translation: "The point of everything would be to obtain that when one person has betrayed another, that person would be unable to pick up a glass without its immediately breaking." Louis Aragon et al., *Dictionnaire abrégé du surréalisme* (Paris: Galerie Beaux-Arts, 1938), 29.

21. For an explanation of some of these points, see Inez Hedges, *Languages of Revolt: Dada and Surrealist Literature and Film* (Durham, N.C.: Duke University Press, 1983), 3–33.

22. In addition to making many helpful suggestions for the revision of this article, Rudolf Kuenzli has suggested a fascinating reading for these oppositions which I reproduce here: "Some shots look like impressionist paintings due to the use of the gelatin filter. It is as though Man Ray is playing off filtered shots (works of art, transformed reality) with unfiltered shots (reality). This might work with an overall bipolar structure used in the film: reality (transience)/art (permanence). There is a polarity of immutability (flowers of glass, art, books, dead seastar) and mutability (woman, reality, seastar alive – "après tout"). It thus seems to be a voyage, an alchemical trip from mutability to immutability. The flowers of glass recall Novalis and Baudelaire's *paradis artificiel.*"

The Image and the Spark:
Dulac and Artaud Reviewed

Sandy Flitterman-Lewis

Within recent years, several articles and books in English have reconsidered the famous and famously misunderstood "bagarre coquille," that debate around *The Seashell and the Clergyman* between its director, Germaine
Dulac, and the creator of its scenario, Antonin Artaud.[1] The details of the
dispute are well-known: As the film was being projected on its opening
night (February 9, 1928) at the Studio des Ursulines, a commotion among
the audience erupted, involving nasty epithets launched at both the film
and Dulac herself. Several known Surrealists figured in the riot, some protesting the film, some protesting Dulac, and some, in fact, protesting Artaud.[2] What remains murky, or at least incompletely theorized, however, is
the extent to which the disagreement surrounding *Seashell* represents two
fundamentally conflicting aesthetic theories, and with them divergent notions of the peculiar articulation of the cinema and unconscious desire. To
reconsider the debate in terms of the cinematic apparatus, the mechanisms
of the dream, and the spectator is to get to the heart of all discourse on the
cinema in the twenties: that much-discussed "essence" which concerned not
only a filmmaker like Dulac, but the social visionary in Artaud who raged
against the very foundations of representation itself.

To be sure, Artaud's selection of Dulac as the person capable of transforming his written text into cinematic images was not arbitrary: both the
poet and the filmmaker had long been preoccupied with questions of a
visual language. What specific properties of the visual enabled a kind of
spectatorial engagement more direct, more profound, and more authentic
than that evoked by the verbal, theatrical, or novelistic text? How did the
cinematic image, in particular, work on its affinities with the deeper psychic mechanisms of the human unconscious? And what was it about the
spontaneous and almost despotic qualities of the visual image which made
its access to the circulation of desire more immediate? From this single set
of kindred questions, varied aesthetic theories emerged, and it is these
which gave way to the impossible rupture expressed in the riot at the film's
inaugural screening. For Dulac, whose Symbolist antecedents led her to regard the cinematic image as the site of a fusion, the film was conceived as a
condensation of associations whose gradual accretion of meaning allowed
the story to proceed, image by image, in a chain of metaphors. In direct contrast to this fluid sliding of images, Artaud's conception was based on the
Surrealist principles of displacement and dissociative juxtaposition, empha-

sizing instead the film's liberating assault on the continuity system of traditional narrative. In Artaud's version, then, a series of disruptive relations, intended to produce the Surrealistic spark, emphasized the metonymic structure of the film's images in clashing relations of contiguity. The riot over the screening of *The Seashell and the Clergyman* can thus be read in terms of a conflict between the expressive euphoria which Dulac found in the moving visual image and the psychic directness which Artaud sought in the cinematic text.

The highly problematic discussion of the relations between film and dream which preoccupied both the scenarist of the film and its director will provide us with one point of entry into the aesthetic debate I want to trace. A press release situated the film's project even before its actual projection:

A dream on the screen – The most recent psychological research has established that the dream, far from being a formless and chaotic mass of images, always tends to organize itself according to precisely defined rules, and thus has its own – affective and symbolic – logic. Consequently, someone else's dream (if we were able to see it) would be capable of moving us as effectively as any other spectacle, by addressing not our logic and our intellectual comprehension, but this obscure and unconscious sensibility which elaborates our own dreams for us. Such is the bold attempt of poet Antonin Artaud, who has proposed a scenario made of a dream: *The Seashell and the Clergyman.* Mme Germaine Dulac has just finished making this film . . . and we can expect that [she] has surpassed herself in this effort of the avant-garde. It concerns a dream which is not enclosed in any kind of story and which each spectator will have to understand, or better, experience uniquely according to the resources of his own personal sensibility.[3]

The above text's immediate emphasis on the viewer's *experience,* with its implication that every individual might have direct affective access to the film via the unconscious, illuminates a crucial point of exchange between film and dream. For as each poet and filmmaker grappled with that Surrealist "stumbling block"[4] of the similiarities of film and dream, the arguments continually came to rest on that peculiar semi-hypnotic state which characterized both film-viewer and dreamer alike. The anonymous publicist of this text, in fact, goes even further, asserting that the internal coherence of the proposed film's images will find its complement in each individual's psyche, enabling a powerful unconscious impact on the spectator to take place. In this context, both film and dream are understood as fantasmatic productions – films mobilize those same primary processes as the dream-work – and each depends on the participation of its "spectator" in the construction of its meanings. The "subject," whether dreamer of an unconscious discourse or viewer of a cinematic text, is thus the central point in the argument regarding the confluence of film and dream.

From this perspective, then, once we acknowledge a basic similarity in the thinking of Dulac and Artaud, it will become clear that the latter's dissatisfaction with the film has been greatly misunderstood. In fact, although Artaud published several articles in 1927 and 1928 protesting certain portions of the film and clarifying his theoretical positions, he never actually requested that his name be removed from the film's credits. As late as 1932, in a letter to his editor Jean Paulhan, he claimed *Seashell*'s superiority of conception, its absolute refusal to compromise, and its innovative status: ". . . [C]riticism, if there still is such a thing, must recognize the hereditary derivation of all these films [Surrealist films, specifically Buñuel's *L'Age d'or* and Cocteau's *Blood of a Poet*], and say that they ALL come from *The Seashell and the Clergyman*, except of course, for the *spirit*, which has escaped them all. . . . *Seashell* was certainly the first film of the genre [Surrealist film], and its precursor."[5]

Still, Artaud's anger and dissatisfaction–which has survived in virtually every discussion of the film–is a fact which must be dealt with. It appears that Artaud moved from an initial feeling of enthusiasm about the project, through growing resentment at his exclusion from actual production of the film and anger upon its release, to eventual disillusionment with the cinema itself. Artaud's letters to Dulac trace this growing rift and substantiate the idea that he was more disturbed by his inability to participate in the filming than by any distortions of his artistic intentions. The idea for the scenario apparently originated with a dream of Yvonne Allendy, a close friend of Artaud's,[6] though the scenario itself has little in common with it. Nevertheless, it was she who first proposed that Dulac film Artaud's scenario.

Although Artaud had arranged to take a leave from acting in Dreyer's *La Passion de Jeanne d'Arc* in order to work on *Seashell*, circumstances (there is some debate as to whether these were intended by Dulac or not) forced production of the two films to coincide. Nonetheless, in a letter to Dulac, Artaud emphatically denied newspaper accounts that he wanted to interfere in the film's production: "I have not the slightest pretention of collaborating with you. That would be a stupid pretention."[7] The extreme politeness which characterizes his earlier letters to Dulac is everywhere evident. His next letters show an increasing interest in the production of the film, in the guise of further clarification of his original conceptions. Finally, after a silence of two-and-a-half months, Artaud's last available letter to Dulac[8] complains that he knows nothing of the film's progress and vehemently protests an explanatory preface to the film:

. . . I am not very favorable toward the idea of a written preamble. I think the film is self-sufficient. . . . It is a film of pure images. And the meaning must emerge from the very impact [*rayonnement*] of these images themselves. There is no hidden significance of a psychological, metaphysical, or even human[istic] kind.[9]

Dulac's preface was removed, but Artaud's letter clearly indicates, in its emphasis on the conflicting *relationship* between images over the visual manipulation of the image itself, the way in which the debate was to become solidified. Artaud's concern with the direct, unmediated impact of the cinema denies the traditional separation between an image and its meaning. For him, meaning was not some stable, coherent entity to be *disengaged* from its visual sign, but was, rather, the result of productive relations between images themselves, and between text and viewer. Thus while the film was being shot, Artaud began to envision certain types of shots, cinematic renderings of exactly how this directness might be achieved. The problematic issue of transcription–from verbal text to visual image–inherent in any film project, thus became the basis for his dissatisfaction with the film itself. Any attempt on Dulac's part to clarify the meaning of the images (or their association), either by assigning a structure of dream logic, by proposing a discursive preface, or even, in some cases, by interpreting in order to achieve a cinematic equivalent, was seen as a distortion of the original and direct impulse of the images *as they were conceived* by Artaud.

The very labeling of the film as a "dream" was at the crux of the disagreement between Artaud and Dulac. At first Artaud had tolerated this interpretation when his article entitled "Le cinéma et l'abstraction"[10] (published just prior to his viewing of the film) was introduced by Yvonne Allendy's short preface describing "un scénario fait d'un seul rêve."[11] But after Dulac had announced a screening of the film in *Comoedia* (November 3, 1927) under the rubric of "Rêve d'Antonin Artaud, composition visuelle de Germaine Dulac" – a credit said to appear also at the beginning of the film – Artaud's violent protests in published letters and articles achieved the substitution of the more conventional "Scénario d'Antonin Artaud, Réalisation de Germaine Dulac" on the film's credits. The denial became complete when Artaud's own introduction to the publication of the scenario in *La Nouvelle Revue Française* stated explicitly: "This scenario is not the reproduction of a dream and it should not be considered as such."[12]

But we are wrong to interpret this statement as a rejection of the unconscious logic of dreams themselves. The emphasis, rather, should be placed on the negation of the word "reproduction," for it is that word which separates the *thing* (dream-object) from the operations of the text. For if, in fact, we accept the film as the mere "reproduction" of a dream, we imply that the dream itself is a fixed, finite entity – a pre-existent object which is simply translated into visual terms. As Linda Williams cogently maintains, "[U]nconscious desire, if it is to be present in film in the way in which it is present in dreams, cannot also be 'represented' there as a subject: it must be perceived, as the unconscious desires of dreams are perceived, through the transgression of a more familiar discourse."[13] In other words, just as the unconscious can only make itself known to us in jokes, slips of the tongue, lapses – those gaps in our conscious rational discourse which reveal desire at work – so must a film work at those marginal interstices of traditional representation in order to more fully approximate the unconscious. It is in this sense that we must understand Artaud's disclaimer.

For Dulac, *Seashell* marked a necessary step in her development toward a pure cinema free from the narrative constraints of literary or theatrical commercial models. Her experiments with musical structuring and poetic effects can be seen as efforts to contest or subvert the illusionist properties of a cinema founded in the naturalistic reproduction of the real. While Dulac's earlier films, culminating in the psychological explorations of *The Smiling Madame Beudet* (1924), focus on character development through the cinematic expression of interior states of mind, her subsequent films deal increasingly with the visual properties of the image and the plastics of montage. Yet even when dealing with aspects of characterization in the narrative film, Dulac was always aware of the hidden depths of the human psyche which the cinema was capable of exploring. She felt that traditional cinema was too literary because, following in the footsteps of its predecessor, the novel, it developed its action entirely through a succession of dramatic situations. For Dulac, the cinema was most consistent with its expressive and aesthetic potential when it was able to "develop emotively through the image alone."

... The cinema can certainly tell a story, but one mustn't forget that the story is nothing. The story is a surface. The seventh art, the art of the screen, is the palpable rendering of the depth which extends beneath this surface: the musical ineffable [*l'insaisissable musical*]. . . . Visual impact is ephemeral, it's an impact you receive which suggests a thousand thoughts. An impact analogous to that provoked by musical harmonies.[14]

Artaud, in calling for a purely visual cinema in which images were "self-engendered" and governed by "a powerful inner necessity of their own,"[15] appears to theorize a cinema consistent with these aims. In his preface to the publication of the scenario for *Seashell* he elaborated his conception of what the cinema should be:

There has yet to be a film of purely visual situations whose dramatic action springs from a shock designed for the eyes, a shock founded, so to speak, on the very substance of the gaze [*le regard*], and not on psychological circumlocutions which are essentially discursive and thus merely visual translations of a verbal text. It is not a question of finding in visual language an equivalent of written language, for this would only amount to a bad translation, but rather of becoming oblivious to the very essence of [verbal] language [16] transporting the action to a plane where all translation would become useless – where the action itself would operate almost intuitively on the brain.[17]

This passage has strong resonances with Dulac's formulation of a cinematic "musique de l'oeil," one entirely organized by the rhythms and movements of images. For Dulac, the cinema's power to captivate the spectator is profoundly linked to a notion of the ungraspable, something beyond the distortions of rational discourse.

Music, which generates this sort of 'beyond' of human feelings, which records the multiplicity of our feelings, works with sounds in movement just as we work with images in movement. This helps us understand the visual idea, the artistic development of a new form of sensibility. . . . As in all art, it is not the exterior fact (even) which truly interests us, but the emanation from within, a certain movement of things and people, seen across a state of feeling.[18]

This principle, that the visual properties of the image itself dictate the "narrative" flow, is central to Dulac's conception of cinematic structure, from her earlier, more traditional films, to her later abstract cinematic poems. For her a sequence of images is organized according to an internal logic based on plastic relations and harmonies evoked by the visual image, and this strikes a powerful emotional chord in the viewer.

Similar as these passages might appear, however, they are subtended by fundamental differences of aesthetic aim. Artaud's (conceptual) allegiance to Surrealism required a degree of violence in the work of art powerful enough to achieve that psychic directness of the Freudian dream-work (remember that Freud referred to the dream as the "royal road" to the unconscious). Dulac, on the other hand, based her theories on a Symbolist aesthetic of fusion and synthesis, a formulation which lies in direct contrast to the significant quotient of aggression in Surrealist film. Her emphasis is highly emotional: words like "sensibility" and "state of feeling" are not merely descriptive, but resound through her texts in constantly evocative verbal flights. In these terms, Dulac's interest in the cinema's capacity to "develop emotively through the image alone" sharply contradicts Artaud's "shock designed for the eyes," for where the former subscribes to an art of suggestion, the latter calls for the elimination of subtleties in the name of intuitive action on the brain. To Artaud's claim that there is "no hidden significance" in the images of his film, Dulac proposes a world of immanent meaning, synaesthesia, and Baudelairean correspondences.

As is well known, Surrealist cinema aimed at liberating the unconscious of its spectator, evoking the marvelous through the creation of the unexpected, the incongruous, and the enigmatic in works of "convulsive beauty." Conceived as a liberating assault on all traditional institutions and values, Surrealist art used structures of aggression to engage a reordering of perceptions of the viewer, and with that the subsequent questioning of established systems of meaning. The process of dissociation is critical to this notion of art, for it works to create an unexpected *spark* by bringing together two disparate realities. In the Surrealist image, this conjunction produces a transformation in both the relations between elements within the image and the relations between the text and its viewer. This transformation was seen as necessary to the spirit of freedom and revolt which would lead to new perceptions of the world and thus to the social and moral liberation of humanity.

The Symbolist poets, on the other hand, were more interested in the creation of atmospheres and states of mind through the poetic evocation of effects. Their reliance on the associative power of words and images led them to emphasize harmony rather than disruption. An art of suggestion, Symbolist poetry attempted to approximate the effects of music, as in Mallarmé's famous dictum: "Describe not the thing, but the effect it produces." In this, one can trace a fairly direct line to the experiments of *cinéma pur*, that avant-garde movement which avoided referential content altogether. Rather than valorizing the absolute exhiliaration of the Surrealists' *l'amour fou* (mad love), Symbolist poetry exulted in its ineffable musical harmonies, preferring the creation of mood and sensation to the generation of revolutionary and passionate shocks.

These contradictory aesthetics imply different conceptions of the spectator/subject of the cinema. At first glance, Artaud's emphasis on a cinema of "purely visual situations," incapable of verbal translation, and his reliance on "intuitive" powers of vision, seem to have analogues in Dulac's writing. Yet his material insistence on the optic "shock," a physiological spark "founded on the very substance of the gaze," brings a much more violent emphasis to this notion of visual composition. Artaud sought a means of communication which would bypass the rational distortions of verbal language, a mode whose emphasis on the body could reveal those truths hidden by the abstraction of language. That he found the cinema, because of the concreteness of its images and the immediacy of its appeal, a medium well-suited to this is suggested in undeniably physical terms in much of his writing. The following passage has, ironically, become almost a cliché, so completely and concisely does it express Artaud's desire for the cinema to move him beyond representation.

The cinema is a remarkable stimulant. It acts directly on the grey matter of the brain. . . . Above all, the cinema has the virtue of an innocuous and direct poison, a subcutaneous injection of morphine. That is why a film's subject cannot be inferior to its active capability [*pouvoir d'action*] – and must partake of the marvelous.[19]

The corporeality of his language, the emphasis on stimulation of the brain, his repeated references to the plague, to bodily trauma, etc., all imply a much more brutally visceral aesthetic than Dulac's theory of suggestion. This is because Artaud saw in the cinema the possibility to create a new, concrete, physical language of representation, a language which would move the spectator in some fundamentally disorienting way, and, in Guy Scarpetta's words, reveal "all the biological-pulsing reality repressed by symbolization."[20] Artaud's comments on the Marx Brothers are especially illuminating in this vein, for it is here that he links the cinema's peculiar power of fascination with its visceral immediacy:

And the triumph of all this [Marx Brothers' intoxicating magic] is in the kind of exaltation, both visual and auditory, that all these events acquire among the shadows, in their intensity of vibration, and in the kind of powerful anxiety which their total effect ultimately projects into the mind.[21]

In this there is a deep contradiction with Dulac's own more romantic and lyrical search for a visual equivalent of music which would inspire directly. Her musical conception of the film as a "symphonic poem" involved an almost abstract and melodic organization of images where "feelings burst forth not in facts, or in acts, but in visual sonorities. Imperceptibly, narrative storytelling and the actor's performance would lose their isolated value in favor of a broad orchestration of shots, rhythms, framings, angles, lighting, proportions, contrasts and harmonies of the images.[22] Constantly she returns to the evocative power of the cinematic image, the harmonious emotional qualities of rhythm and movement – for her the essence of cinema – whose power to project the viewer into a superior emotional state is unequalled. She invokes fluid rhythms and harmonizing light in the creation of imagery that is "stripped of all meaning that is too human, in order to aspire more successfully toward abstraction and give more space to feelings and to dreams: total cinema."[23]

It can be seen from this that, for Dulac, the spectator was conceived as a sensory/emotional entity which could be affected by plastic forms and movement. This, however, is a somewhat static concept of the spectator, one which rejects dynamism in the meaning-production process in favor of a certainty regarding specific effects. Less interested in provocation than in evocation, Dulac experimented with cinematic technique in the creation of a visual totality [*le cinéma intégral*] which would embrace the spectator in something like a collective euphoria. Assault and revulsion as impetus to action were thus replaced by harmony and rhythm as impulse to feeling in her formulation of the spectator's role.

These contrasting notions of spectatorship can find further clarification in a distinction made by Jacques B. Brunius in his *En marge du cinéma français*. In all of the films which Brunius considers authentic works of the cinematic avant-garde (and he includes *Seashell* among them), a sense of poetry as a means of liberating the unconscious, of appealing directly to the most fundamental desires of the spectator, is profoundly connected to the cinematic devices employed. Thus technique is linked to an entire ethos of liberation, rather than being a simple manifestation of artistic virtuosity. Brunius sees two principle tendencies informing the work of true avant-garde filmmakers: 1) They seek to "represent aspects of the external world and actions in their ordinary appearance, within a poetic context, freeing them from all rational logic;" and 2) they attempt to "create new forms, either by filming people and objects from an unexpected angle or in a new light, or by deforming them, sometimes creating abstract forms."[24] These two tendencies, often combined in a single film, provide some indication of the specific technical manifestation of the Surrealist process of dissociation. The important point here is the emphasis placed on the *liberation* (of unconscious forces, of the irrational, of the absurd) involved in filming things in a new way. For Brunius, as well as for others who criticized the filmmakers of the first avant-garde (Gance, Delluc, L'Herbier, Epstein, and for the most part Dulac) for mere stylistic effects, the linchpin of Surrealist filmmaking was found in this capacity to transform the relationship between spectator and screen. Impressionist filmmaking, with its Symbolist interest in achieving effects, left that relationship basically unmodified.

These contrasting notions of spectatorship might be better understood if we could take a closer look at that problematic notion of the "dream on the screen." For although both Dulac and Artaud subscribed, to some extent, to the film-dream analogy, each had a different conception of what this involved. In positing a literal spectator "watching" a dream, Dulac conceived of *Seashell* as the representation of "dream-like" images, a chaos of associations which would in some sense represent the irrational flow of dream images. On the other hand, Artaud wanted to create the impact of the dream instead of simply reproducing its irrationality. For him, then, the representation of a "dream-*state*," in which the spectator's involvement was one of active participation, was the primary aim of his scenario.

Where Artaud postulated the cinema's power to effect "a total reversal of values, a complete overthrow of optics, perspective, and logic,"[25] Dulac maintained the importance of the cinema's capacity "to express, through rhythms and suggestive harmonies, feelings which we have all more or less experienced."[26] She thus transformed the immediate and direct impact which Artaud sought into an enveloping, expressive force. For Artaud, the dream was a powerful manifestation of the inner spirit, the concretization of those "dark truths of the mind,"[27] the materialization of our "occult life" abounding with "secrets stirring in the deepest parts of consciousness."[28] He saw the film as an attempt to recreate the impact of the dream *as it is being dreamed*:

117

[*The Seashell and the Clergyman* attempts] to find, in the occult birth and wanderings of feeling and thought, the deep reasons, the active and veiled impulses of our so-called lucid acts[.] [This] scenario can resemble, can be related to *the mechanism of a dream* without actually being a dream itself. [It seeks to] restore the pure work of thought.[29]

Thus the impulse behind the scenario was the direct force of the dream experience itself, rather than the waking, secondarized transcription of its flow of images. And yet, while Artaud wanted to recreate the *experience* of the dream for the spectator – with an apparatus peculiarly suited to these requirements – Dulac was more concerned with rendering a dream-like effect, an *impression* of incoherence rather than the power of something deeply felt. Artaud was one of the first to understand something of the cinema's uncanny ability to have an immediate psychic impact on the spectator; Dulac, perhaps lacking this precise inflection of the cinematic apparatus in her thinking, simply tried to reproduce the surface irrationality of the dream. Thus images are used for their isolated evocative value in the film (and the representation of dream *content* that this implies), while Artaud's scenario, concentrating on the *structure* of the dream, intended emphasis to be placed on the *connections* between the images and sequences (and the violation of cinematic continuity that this necessitates).

The distinction can become further clarified if we look at Jean Goudal's strikingly original and prescient essay, "Surréalisme et cinéma," written in 1925.[30] Without recourse to the semiotic vocabulary of film theory, Goudal nevertheless describes the cinematic apparatus in terms of the effect created on the spectator. Fundamental to both the theory of the cinematic apparatus and of Surrealist cinema as well is an understanding of the production processes of the psyche and of the liberating forces of desire. Starting from the premise that Surrealism is fundamentally interested in the unconscious activity of the mind (in its search for a reality superior to that of ordinary life), Goudal demonstrates that, because of its specific properties, the cinema is the ideal technical equivalent of Surrealist aspirations. For Goudal there are two inherent difficulties in the Surrealist aesthetic (as it applies to poetry and painting): 1) If there is an irreducible division between dream and reality, how is it possible to gain access to the unconscious without obviating consciousness altogether? And 2) How can the anti-logical ambitions of Surrealism be achieved without renouncing the power to communicate altogether? Goudal asserts that these problems disappear as soon as the Surrealist theories are applied to the cinema.

The first problem is solved by the cinema's production of a "conscious hallucination" which achieves precisely that fusion of dream and consciousness desired by the Surrealists.

The objection regarding method [the difficulty of joining consciousness and the unconscious on the same plane] is not valid for the cinema, whose spectacle constitutes precisely this: *a conscious hallucination.* Let's go into a movie theater where the perforated celluloid whirs in the darkness. From the moment we enter, our gaze is guided by the luminous shaft toward the screen where, for two hours, it will remain fixed. Life on the street outside no longer exists. Our daily concerns fade away; our neighbors disappear. Our body itself undergoes a sort of temporary depersonalization

118

which robs it of the sense of its own existence. We are nothing more than two eyes riveted to ten meters of white screen.[31]

Yet the cinema can duplicate several important factors of the dream process without entirely overwhelming the consciousness of the spectator. There is something *artificial* about the moving images which allows the spectator to maintain both the belief in their reality and the knowledge of their illusion, "leaving us a confused consciousness of our personality while permitting us to evoke, if necessary, those things available to our memory."[32] This basic duality of the film-viewer's experience (the conditions of the dream combined with the wakefulness of consciousness) enable the forces of the unconscious to work while consciousness itself is maintained, thus avoiding the problems posed by the first objection.

The second problem is answered by the cinema's capacity to produce meaning through a succession of images which create their own sense, totally independent of the logical constructs of verbal language. To illustrate how the cinema can repudiate logic without giving up meaning, Goudal has recourse to a poetic image from Philippe Soupault, one used by Breton in the *First Surrealist Manifesto* to illustrate the degree of arbitrariness best suited to the Surrealist image: "Une église se dressait, éclatante comme une cloche" (A church stood [rose], dazzling [ringing loudly] like a bell). The verbal comparison of the two systems forces a logical association between them which the visual image *produces* automatically.

And if the two images succeed each other with the desired rapidity, the logical mechanism which tries to link the two objects in some way or other will not have time to be set in motion. All one will experience is the almost simultaneous vision of two objects, exactly the cerebral process, that is to say, that suggested this comparison to the author.[33]

In this the cinema uncannily approximates the associative processes of the mind, while being able to avoid the rational structures of symbolization.

This peculiar quality to bypass rational, discursive logic, to profoundly touch us—le rêve est pénétrant," in Goudal's terms—which the cinema shares with the dream—brings us back to Artaud and Dulac. For it is perhaps here that we may gain a bit of insight into the particular problem faced by Dulac as she tried to film Artaud's scenario. Artaud felt the cinema had arrived at a particularly auspicious time: "the precise moment when language, outworn, is losing its power to symbolize."[34] During the shooting of *Seashell,* he wrote:

I have always distinguished in cinema a virtue specific to the secret movement and matter of images themselves. There is in cinema something unforeseen and mysterious which one doesn't find in the other arts. It is certain that every image, even the driest and most banal, becomes transformed when on the screen. The smallest detail, the most insignificant object takes on a life and a meaning belonging to it alone—and this is independent of the significative value of the images themselves, the thought they translate, the symbol they constitute. . . . There is also a sort of physical intoxication which the rotation of images communicates directly to the brain. The mind is affected outside of all representation [*L'ésprit s'émeut hors de toute représentation.*] This sort of virtual power of the images finds hitherto unutilized possibilities in the very depths of the mind.[35]

119

The important thing to note here is Artaud's intuitive sense of the cinematic apparatus as a mechanism which confers upon the film image the ability to signify non-referentially. Not a simple recording—or even reproducing—device, the film apparatus isolates objects out of their habitual context, and giving them to us with a "singular force," enable their representations to take on a life of their own, generating new meanings, meanings apart from conventional signifying systems or symbolization. Artaud wanted his films to illustrate, or better, actualize this power, and thus he conceived scenarios of sudden, unforeseen, and unexpected sequences of images. The element of surprise, that cornerstone of Surrealist aesthetic theory, was thus to be the mainspring of his films, the instrument by which the power of this cinematic transformation manifested itself. The problem arose, however, when the attempt was made to put Artaud's descriptive words into actual cinematic images, for this implied a separation between word and image as two distinct signifying entities. The "physical intoxication" that Artaud sought to evoke by repeated metamorphoses of the visual could not be achieved, for it was, in a sense, betrayed by the word's firm anchoring in referential meaning. For our purposes, a specific example from his scenario for *Seashell* can serve as illustration.

At one point Artaud describes a series of hallucinatory images as they presumably flow before the eyes of the dreaming clergyman. More importantly, he attempts to make the spectator *experience* the visual transformations as they circulate in the dream-space of the film. He writes lyrically, poetically:

And one sees the clergyman's head in close-up, lying down, breathing. From the very depths of his parted lips, from between his eyelashes stream glistening vapors which gather in a corner of the screen, forming a city-scene or extremely luminous landscapes. The head finally disappears entirely and houses, landscapes, cities pursue each other, tangling and disentangling, forming a sort of astonishing firmament [*firmament inouï*] of celestial lagoons, grottoes of incandescent stalactites, and under these grottoes, between these mists, in the midst of these lagoons one sees the ship's silhouette pass back and forth, black on the white background of the cities, white on these fantasmatic settings [*décors de vision*] which suddenly turn black.[36]

In order to convey this highly visual poetry through cinematic means, Dulac was forced to resort to technical ruses. Her fidelity to the scenario itself compelled her to concentrate on the *content* of the images rather than on the *process* of montage itself, a process which actualizes the *transforming* power at the base of the Surrealist juxtaposition. What Goudal's example of the Surrealist image reveals is the cinema's fundamental capacity to *produce* the spark required, where language must rely on verbal associations ("dazzling *like* a bell"). Artaud's apprehension of this power is at the source of his imagery in the scenario, but because the scenario was not really conceived *cinematically*, that power is never released.

Thus to render the passage just cited, Dulac uses miniatures, phosphorescent paint, exaggerated lighting effects, and an array of technical devices (fades, dissolves, superimpositions, split screens, multiple images). In twelve shots which are quite beautiful and technically advanced for their time, she comes as close to visually reproducing the scenario as it is possible to do when lacking what was crucial for Artaud – an understanding of the operations of the apparatus. Images of the clergyman's head at the bottom of the frame, billowing vapor, a little circular mountain village which sparkles as it grows larger in each dissolving image, superimpositions of rippling water and clouds, shimmering diaphanous material, an illuminated ship superimposed on glittering stalactites – all of these appear in succession. But as long as the *content* of these shots serves as the basis for their organization – which it does – the "life of its own" that Artaud attributes to the cinematic image can never take shape. In fact, Dulac comes much closer to achieving this kind of cinematic poetry with her later films where, for example, the permutations and transformations which occur from shot to shot emerge from the images themselves and their formal resonances, creating their own rhythm of signification beyond referentiality. Here, in order for Dulac to have succeeded, she would have had to allow a process of dissociation *in the editing* to occur, destroying the internal reality of the film such that a *break* between the referential function of the image and its representation, between coherent relations of time and space, and between the logical development of narrative sequencing might have been forced.

To return to my initial argument, by way of a conclusion, the conflicting aesthetics of Surrealism and Symbolism lie at the center of the debate between Artaud and Dulac regarding their film. In 1935 Breton wrote: "Marx said, 'Transform the world;' Rimbaud said 'Change life;' these two mottoes are for us one and the same."[37] Artaud, in following the Surrealist impulse combining Rimbaud's appeal with Marx's demand, saw art at the forefront of a move to liberate society. He saw the cinema as an agency of this transformation; cinematic technique was intended to generate a new conception of the world. Dulac, on the other hand, as an inheritor of the Symbolist tradition, sought a synaesthetic experience for her viewers, a change in their *perception* of life which, nonetheless, could always remain on the aesthetic level. Thus for Artaud, a concern with the social inscription of art made the concern with cinematic language move beyond the individual experience, and thus required a more disturbing, more powerful, and more unsettling conception of the cinema.

For Artaud, the cinema was not simply a new and more effective way to tell stories, or even to move the spectator emotionally, but rather a place in which new associations of images, new ideas would emerge from the *collision* of forms, objects, and movements. He sought to tear the cinema away from its status as reflection, reproduction, and representation, and in so doing, to render it capable of signifying the unrepresentable – the fantasmatic world of hallucinations, metamorphoses, and desires. Thus in "Cinema and Abstraction" he would write:

The Seashell and the Clergyman does not tell a story, but develops a series of states of mind, just as one thought derives from another, without needing to reproduce a logical sequence of events. From the clash of objects and gestures, true psychic situations are derived, and from these, rational thinking, trapped, can only seek a subtle escape.[38]

Since, for Artaud, the cinema could provoke a violent reordering of perceptions, not only in the aesthetic experience, but in all of social activity as well, he saw *Seashell* as opening the way to that "total reversal of values" which would come, not from mere technical tricks and the interplay of forms, but from a "profound renewal of the [very] material of the images, toward an authentic liberation, not of the random sort, but linked in a specific way to all the dark forces of thought."[39]

Dulac's evocative harmonies are something of the opposite in intent. In 1927, the same year that she made *Seashell,* Dulac also made *L'Invitation au voyage* which, as the title indicates, is freely inspired from Baudelaire's poem. She conceived the spirit of the two films so closely, in fact, that she intended to show fragments of *Seashell* along with her completed film (*L'Invitation*) at the Salon d'Automne on November 23, 1927. Only the debate about the preface mentioned above ("Rêve d'Antonin Artaud, Réalisé cinégraphiquement par Germaine Dulac") prevented that, requiring the substitution of Kuleshov's *Dura Lex* instead.[40]

One of the exemplary texts of the Symbolist aesthetics of suggestiveness and evasion, Baudelaire's *L'Invitation au voyage* is composed of words used for their evocative qualities; far beyond the simple referential content of the images is an underlying stratum of suggestions and hidden meanings. This is one of Baudelaire's most melodic poems; in it, his research into the science of rhythms and harmonic effects evokes a seductive atmosphere of calm beauty and provides exactly what the title suggests – an invitation to escape. And yet, the poem's incantatory, langorous, and sensuous tones achieve not the description of a particular locale, but the creation of a *desire* for escape.

As some critics point out,[41] the film ostensibly aspires to a visual adaptation of the lines:

Mon enfant, ma soeur,   [My child, my sister,
Songe à la douceur,   Dream of the gentleness
D'aller vivre ensemble.   Of going off to live together.]

but its inspiration could just as well have come from the prose poem of the same name. In each, there is a profound desire to escape to a sensuous elsewhere, and it is this which Dulac uses for her starting point. However, in fact, Dulac's film always maintains its status as a narrative film, using the poetic references only as evidence for the suggestive atmosphere she hopes to create around the armature of the story. A married woman meets a sailor in a smoky bistro, dances with him, and wants to go away with him; he notices that she is married, and she returns guiltily to her home. This narrative pretext allowed Dulac to further her experiments in the creation of a subjective cinema, for she used images of blurred sails, pounding surf and clouds to convey the sense of lyrical transport that the desire for the sailor was to invoke. This type of exploration was fundamental to Dulac's ideal cinema of "pure sensation":

The visual symphony which I dream of creating someday . . . will use fewer characters; it will go further in terms of the play of light, the clash or the union of objects and fleeting expressions. It will escape all literary logic in order to work, as a musician does, only with feelings.[42]

It has been suggested that Baudelaire saw poetry itself as a kind of "invitation to voyage." It seems possible that Dulac, given her theories of cinematic and musical evocation, saw this film as a similar invitation to the spectator – an invitation to participate vicariously in the flights of fantasy and dream as she conceived them, especially if one considers her emphasis on the quality of emotional transport ascribed to both cinema and music.

From this example we can gain some further insight into the *Seashell* rift, for it is possible that in the word "songe" [dream], Dulac found the connection between both projects she was working on. Yet, as I have tried to show, it is perhaps too literal an interpretation of this word which led to her disagreements with Artaud. For, as I have maintained, Artaud's conception of the unconscious and its products involved a radical break with traditional notions of representation and thought. "Briser le langage pour toucher la vie" ["To break through language in order to touch life"][43] was his call; the cinema possessed a degree of psychic directness powerful enough to allow it to bypass language altogether. For him, *Seashell* was to be a shining example of that "visual cinema in which even psychology is devoured by acts," one which could "give this psychology a much more vital and active form."[44] And once this cinema's "psychic ingredient" could attain that deeper reality more commensurate with the darkest desires of the unconscious, feeble approximations like the theater could be relegated to the "memory closet"[45] and left far behind.

On the other hand, Dulac does not *suspect* language in the same way. Ever the believer in the cinema's powers of expression and its capacity to move, Dulac somehow allowed her construction of musical harmonies to remain curiously on the surface of consciousness. To Artaud's violent collisions of images – the French word "heurt" is translated as "collision"; the emphasis on the force of impact is apparent in its synonyms ("choquer" – "to shock," "cogner" – "to hammer") and in its definition ("faire brutalement en contact" – "brutal contact") – Dulac develops a "series of states of mind." Throughout her writing on abstraction, references to the importance of emotion, sensation, and feeling at the basis of all formal concerns abound.

Yes, lines, volumes, surfaces, light, envisioned in their constant metamorphoses, are capable of taking hold of us by their rhythms if we know how to organize them in a construction capable of responding to the needs of our imagination and our feelings. . . .[46]

Dulac's writing is grounded in a belief in the evocative power of the visual image, combining the directness of a film which works primarily through the visual unfolding of its successive shots (as the formal experiments of "pure cinema" could do), with the emotive power of a film which engages the audience psychologically (as the popular commercial films proved capable of doing). For Dulac, *Seashell* provided the opportunity for such expressive interiority, while allowing her to avoid the novelistic constraints of plot and character altogether. The film was a generalized dream-consciousness, and she was the orchestrator of its visions.

Artaud's was perhaps an impossible project – the systematic undermining of the concept of representation in Western culture. Dulac's faith in the image and its endless powers to evoke is certainly more positive, and more within the realm of possibility. Still, whether we read it as a chaotic tangle of associations, or as a profound new language of the unconscious, it is undeniable that *The Seashell and the Clergyman* is an extremely powerful and energetic first document of Surrealist cinema, thanks to the efforts of *both* Germaine Dulac and Antonin Artaud.

Notes

1. Books include Steven Kovacs, *From Enchantment to Rage* (London and Toronto: Associated University Presses, 1980); Linda Williams, *Figures of Desire: A Theory and Analysis of Surrealist Film* (Urbana: University of Illinois Press, 1981); Inez Hedges, *Languages of Revolt: Dada and Surrealist Literature and Film* (Durham N.C.: Duke University Press, 1983), and Richard Abel, *French Cinema: The First Wave, 1915–1929* (Princeton: Princeton University Press, 1984). For articles, see Naomi Greene, "Artaud and Film: A Reconsideration," *Cinema Journal* 23:4, Summer 1984, and my own "Theorizing 'The Feminine': Woman as the Figure of Desire in *The Seashell and the Clergyman,*" *Wide Angle* 6:3, 1984. The present article is part of a more detailed chapter from my book, *To Desire Differently: Feminism and the French Cinema* forthcoming from the University of Illinois Press.

2. The story of the incident, recounted in numerous texts on Surrealism and the cinema, is available only through eyewitness accounts which are contradictory. A loud exchange interrupted the projection of the film: "Who made this film?" "Madame Germaine Dulac." "What is Mme Dulac?" "She is a cow." A journalist who was present claims that Artaud led the disruption; others say that Artaud was not there. However, certain Surrealists (including Robert Desnos and Louis Aragon) participated in the riot, yelling obscenities and throwing objects at the screen. Armand Tallier, director of the theater, demanded an apology and got insults instead; in the ensuing scuffle, some mirrors were broken as the troublemakers were ushered out of the theater. The incident was described in *Le Charivari,* 18 février 1928, and reprinted in *Les oeuvres complètes d'Antonin Artaud* (Paris: Eds. Gallimard, 1978), Vol. III, pp. 326–27. Further references to this volume will be noted as *OC;* it is this volume which contains all of Artaud's film scenarios, letters, and texts concerning the cinema. The edition date is important, as each edition of *OC* contains new material and different pagination. A number of Artaud's scenarios and texts on the cinema, translated into English, can be found in *Tulane Drama Review* 11:1, (Fall 1966), pp. 166–85, as well as in the Susan Sontag anthology, *Antonin Artuad: Selected Writings* (NY: Farrar, Straus, and Giroux, 1976). All translations in the present article are my own.

3. Anonymous, "Un rêve à l'écran," *Cinégraphie* 2, 15 octobre, 1927, p. 32. This appears to be a press release announcing the opening of the film at the end of October, a screening which in fact never took place. There is reason to believe that this text (or portions of it) were written by Yvonne Allendy, Artaud's close personal friend (and, ironically, the same person who was instrumental in the subsequent attacks on Dulac for having "distorted" the scenario by, among other things, calling it a "dream"). "Once the initial agreement with Germaine Dulac was reached, Yvonne Allendy increased communiqués to the press announcing the film; she continued to do so during the film's shooting, and once it was completed, in the weeks preceding its opening. The accent was always placed on the film's uniqueness in being *made of a single dream.* In the beginning of October 1927, Yvonne Allendy wrote an advance

publicity release (we do not know if it was ever published and are working from drafts [provided by Colette Allendy]) which carried the same assertion and whose prospective titles (A Dream-Scenario, A Dream in the Cinema, A Dream on the Screen) are sufficiently characteristic." Editors, *OC*:327.

4. Alain and Odette Virmaux, *Les Surréalistes et le cinéma* (Paris: Eds. Seghers, 1976), p. 25.

5. Letter to Jean Paulhan, 22 January 1932, *OC*:257, 259.

6. *OC*:328 (notes).

7. Letter to Germaine Dulac, c. 19 May 1927, *OC*:120.

8. While doing research on the Artaud-Dulac collaboration, the Virmaux came across an envelope containing Artaud's letters to Dulac. Although there was an indication that Artaud had written seven letters, the last one, in which Artaud was said to have "expressed his opinion of the completed film," is missing. *OC*:363.

9. Letter to Germaine Dulac, 25 September 1927, *OC*:128.

10. Antonin Artaud, "Le cinéma et l'abstraction," *Le Monde Illustré* No. 3645, 29 octobre 1927, *OC*:68–9.

11. *OC*:338 (notes).

12. Artaud, "Cinéma et réalité," *La Nouvelle Revue Française,* No. 170, 1 novembre 1927. Artaud had wanted to clarify his position about the scenario in relation to Dulac's film, and proposed an article to Jean Paulhan, stating, "I have something to defend, and an article could help me defend my film without attacking anyone, in order to more clearly determine my position in relation to this film." (Letter to Jean Paulhan, 29 August 1927, *OC*:127). "Cinéma et réalité" was suggested for the October issue of *La NRF,* but actually appeared in November, functioning as an introduction to the scenario.

13. Linda Williams, *op. cit.*, p. 28.

14. Germaine Dulac, "La musique du silence," *Cinégraphie* 5, 15 janvier 1928, p. 78. The identical statement appears in Dulac's "Films visuels et anti-visuels," in *Le Rouge et le Noir,* juillet 1928, anthologized in Pierre L'Herminier, ed. *L'Art du Cinéma* (Paris: Seghers, 1960), p. 71. I discuss Dulac's work in great detail in my book, covering both her filmmaking and the massive number of theoretical writings she produced. Dulac was highly productive and extremely articulate, and there is a large body of her critical writings available in French. Excerpts of "Films visuels et anti-visuels," translated by Robert Lamberton, can be found in P. Adams Sitney, ed., *The Avant-Garde Film* (New York: NYU Press, 1978), pp. 31–35.

15. Artaud, "Cinéma et réalité," *OC*:19.

16. The text reads "faire oublier l'essence même du langage . . ." in the 1978 edition of *OC*. The published article, which apparently had been copy-edited by Jean Paulhan, had read "faire *p*ublier l'essence . . ." (the difference between "oublier" [to forget] and "publier" [to publish]). The editors of *OC*, however, basing their decision on documents found in the Jean Paulhan archive since their previous edition, have re-established the original manuscript text, as stated in their note 10, p. 332. Because Artaud's handwritten manuscript has only recently been found, the incorrect *NRF* version of the text has been the source of all English translations, including Helen R. Weaver (in the Sontag anthology), Victor Corti (in *TDR*), and Stuart Gilbert, who generally translate the phrase in terms such as ". . . *revealing* the very essence of language . . ." etc. It seems ironic, and eminently interesting, that a single mistaken phoneme could provide such radically contradictory meanings, making one of Artaud's most famous and oft-cited statements say the exact *opposite* of what he meant.

17. Artaud, "Cinéma et réalité," OC:19.

18. Dulac, "L'essence du cinéma, l'idée visuelle," *Les Cahiers du Mois* 16/17, 1925, pp. 64-5. An alternative translation of this article can be found in the Sitney anthology, by Stuart Lamberton.

19. Artaud, "Réponse à une enquête," OC:64.

20. Guy Scarpetta, "La dialectique change de matière," in *Artaud* (Paris: UGE 10/18, 1973), p. 272; cited by Greene, *art. cit.*, p. 30.

21. Artaud, "The Marx Brothers," in *Le Théâtre et son double* (Paris: Eds. Gallimard, 1964), p. 212. Another translation is found in the English version of *The Theater and its Double* (NY: Grove Press, 1958), p. 144.

22. Dulac, "Le cinéma d'avant-garde," in Henri Fescourt, ed., *Le Cinéma des origines à nos jours* (Paris: Eds. du Cygne, 1932), p. 360. Lamberton's translations of portions of this article are in the Sitney anthology, pp. 43-48. A similar, but less precise statement can be found in Dulac's "Les esthétiques. Les entraves. La cinégraphie intégrale," in *L'Art cinématographique*, Vol. 2 (Paris: Alcan, 1927), reprinted in French as *The Literature of the Cinema* (NY: Arno Press, 1970), where Dulac simply refers to "the study of images and their juxtaposition."

23. Dulac, "Du sentiment à la ligne," in *Germaine Dulac Présente: Schémas* (Paris: Imprimateur Gutenberg, février 1927), p. 30-31. Dulac's most ambitious writing project, this journal, conceived and edited by Dulac, only appeared once. A photocopy of the entire issue can be found at the library of the Anthology Film Archives, courtesy of Wendy Dozoretz.

24. Jacques B. Brunius, *En marge du cinéma français* (Paris: Arcanes, Coll. Ombres Blanches, 1954), p. 93.

25. Artaud, "Réponse," OC:63.

26. Dulac, "Du mouvement, des harmonies, et du rhythme: A la symphonie visuelle," p. 6, Chapter VIII of an unpublished manuscript of texts collected by Marie-Anne Colson-Malleville, Dulac's close personal friend and assistant from the time of Dulac's divorce in 1920.

27. Artaud, "Cinéma et réalité," OC:19.

28. Artaud, "Sorcellerie et cinéma," written at the time of the shooting of *Seashell*, this article does not appear to have been published until 1949, when it appeared in the catalogue of the Festival du Film Maudit, Biarritz, 29 July-5 August 1949, OC:66.

29. Artaud, "La coquille et le clergyman," *Cahiers de Belgique* No. 8, octobre 1928, OC:71.

30. Jean Goudal, "Surréalisme et cinéma," *Revue Hebdomadaire* 34, No. 8, 21 février, 1925, pp. 343-357; reprinted in its entirety in Alain and Odette Virmaux, *op. cit.*, pp. 305-317, from which the present article takes its quotes. Goudal's article is translated into English in *The Shadow and its Shadow (Surrealist Writings on Cinema)*, edited and introduced by Paul Hammond (London: British Film Institute, 1978), pp. 49-56.

31. Goudal, p. 308.

32. *Ibid.*, p. 310-11.

33. *Ibid.*, p. 311.

34. Artaud, "Sorcellerie," OC:66.

35. *Ibid.*, OC:65-66.

36. Artaud, "La coquille et le clergyman," OC:23-4.

37. André Breton, *Position politique du surréalisme* (Paris: 1935), p. 97.

38. Artaud, "Cinéma et abstraction," *OC*:68.

39. Artaud, "Distinction entre avant-garde de fond et de forme," *OC*:70.

40. *OC*:325–6 (notes).

41. Richard Abel, *op. cit.*, p. 413, and Charles Ford, *Germaine Dulac* (Paris: Anthologie du Cinema 32, janvier 1968), p. 34.

42. Dulac, Colson-Malleville text, Chapter XIV, p. 6.

43. Artaud, *Le Théâtre et son double*, p. 17; English version, p. 113.

44. Artaud, "Cinéma et réalité," *OC*:19.

45. Artaud, "Réponse," *OC*:64.

46. Dulac, "Du mouvement, des harmonies, et du rhythme: A la symphonie visuelle," *op. cit.* (Colson-Malleville text), p. 6.

Dalí and *Un Chien andalou:* The Nature of a Collaboration

Haim Finkelstein

Studies of collaborations often amount to little more than considerations of paternity and motif hunting. *Un Chien andalou* has had its share of this treatment, to which Dalí and Buñuel have themselves contributed by assigning certain motifs to themselves as well as to one another. Critical works devoted to Buñuel usually underplay Dalí's role in the film or ascribe to Buñuel all the positive values of the film, while Dalí is held responsible for anything in the film which is not good (Aranda, 60). One does not have to be a Dalí apologist to view this collaboration along different lines; Buñuel's letters of the time, which are cited in Aranda's critical biography, tell a different story altogether. I intend to consider this collaboration as a process that reaches its apogee in the period of the writing of the script, when Dalí and Buñuel were "more united than ever," to cite one of Buñuel's letters (Aranda, 58). It should be pointed out that I place greater emphasis in the present study on Dalí's contribution, and on the way *Un Chien andalou* continued to affect his subsequent activities (the paintings of 1929). Needless to say, the film has generally been viewed from the Buñuelian perspective, especially in terms foreshadowing his future development. While not dismissing the idea of a Buñuelian continuity, I aim to show the Buñuel of the *Un Chien andalou* period as an intellectual and creative close partner of Dalí in a collaboration that went beyond its nominal objective of shooting a film in Paris and Le Havre in March 1929.

For Buñuel, who decided on a film career in 1925, wrote film criticism in 1927–8 and worked for two years as an assistant to Jean Epstein, the road to *Un Chien andalou* appears more clear-cut than Dalí's own. Yet Dalí was not just a painter who happened to collaborate with a friend on a film scenario; he had been giving serious consideration to film ever since his earliest published writings. In "Sant Sebastià," his first piece to be published in *L'Amic de les Arts,* the Catalan arts and letters journal, Dalí listed film among the "simple facts motivating new lyrical states" (*Oui* 1, 16–17)[1] associated with modernity and popular culture, together with sports cars and gin cocktails. His notion of film forms one facet of the anti-art campaign he began waging when he joined the *L'Amic de les Arts* group. In his essay "Poesia de l'útil standardizat" (Poetry of the Standardized Utility, March 1928) Dalí asserts that "Modernity does not mean canvases painted by Sonia Delaunay, nor Fritz Lang's *Metropolis,* but a hockey pullover of anonymous English manufacture; it also means comedy film, also anonymous, of the silly nonsense type" (66).

The crucial distinction is between art-film and anti-artistic film, as clearly posited in the title of his most extensive treatment of the subject, "Film-arte, film-antiartistico" (*La Gaceta Literaria,* December 1927), an article dedicated to Luis Buñuel. Dalí's views in this essay and in subsequent writings are fully in agreement with those expressed by Buñuel in a series of critical essays published in the course of 1927–28 in *La Gaceta Literaria* and *Cahiers d'Art*. Both criticize Fritz Lang's *Metropolis*: Buñuel for the irritating triviality of its anecdotal or human element and its stylized and theatrical acting (Aranda, 266– 67), and Dalí for its "theatricality of history painting" (41). Both contrast *Metropolis* with, to use Buñuel's terms, the primitive directness and the authentically cinematic intuition of popular American cinema, the film comedies in particular. There are also some very profound differences between the two. True enough, Buñuel may refer ironically to the "dismal 'taste for art'" which blinds people to the true essence of cinema, yet his anti-art stance with regard to film is not as extreme as Dalí's. Going beyond Buñuel in his dismissal of literature as an element alien to film, Dalí calls for the suppression of "anecdote" altogether. By "anecdote" he means psychological complexity and unexpected turns in the plot; he counters those with primary and standardized emotions, and the monotony of constant action and signs, like the car chase or the villain's moustache. The real poetry of film lies in the "villain's mask, his movements, his manner of dressing, the hand knocking at the door . . ." (40). Buñuel can still respond to Lang's "striking visualizations" and "captivating symphony of movement," and even to some of the crowd scenes, although those on the whole appear to gratify a decorative need (Aranda, 267). Dalí mocks Lang's Dantesque mise-en-scène: infinite perspective and gigantic buildings are not grander than a sugar cube seen on the screen. Art film, he maintains, indulges its maker's grandiose visions, fruits of his imagination. The anti-art film shows us the "new poetic emotions derived from the most humble and instantaneous facts that could not have been imagined or anticipated before film . . ." (42).

The "unlimited fantasy that is born of the things themselves" appears in Dalí's vision to supersede the human dimension, the psychologically motivated human action. More closely associated than Dalí with film making of the more traditional kind, Buñuel can still maintain that "cinedrama, well realized, fully achieved, is more novel, more extraordinary than a film of the so-called 'visual symphony' class" (Aranda, 269), the latter referring to films such as Cavalcanti's *Rien que les heures* which Buñuel greatly admired. Drama, yes, but without melodrama, without sentimentality; Buñuel abhors the melodramatic gestures or the variety of expressions indulged in by Emile Jannings and his school, preferring Menjou's trivial gestures and ghosts of expression glimpsed under his moustache, or Buster Keaton's monochord expression, which he associated with the vitality and lack of cultural tradition of the American school (Aranda, 273; Kyrou 93–5). In the March 1929 issue of *L'Amic de les Arts* Dalí, likewise, extols Harry Langdon as being one of the "purest flowers of cinema" in his "involuntary life, like a water drop," his unconscious movements, like those of small animals, "his total lack of will" (108–9). Next to this "elementary life," in Dalí's view, even Keaton is a mystic, not to mention Chaplin with his transcendental sentimentalism.

These were probably Buñuel's views as well. The winter of 1928–9 was the time of Dalí and Buñuel's greatest intimacy. They thought so much alike in many respects that it would be quite impossible at times to establish precedence. Thus an interview with Buñuel by Dalí published in the same issue as the Langdon essay clearly bears the imprint of both Dalí and Buñuel, and appears to be a collaborative effort in its loaded questions and fully anticipated answers regarding Langdon, Keaton and Chaplin. We should bear in mind that this interview corresponds in time to their collaboration on the script of *Un Chien andalou* and thus is important not only for the attitude it expresses regarding film comedians (which certainly bears upon the film too, as will be made clear further on), but also for the questions it raises concerning Buñuel and Dalí's Surrealist affiliations, as well as the Surrealist orientation of their film venture. It should be noted that there is an almost total lack of reference to Surrealist film in Buñuel and Dalí's other critical or theoretical film texts. It is only in their put-down of art films and the avant-garde, and in their acclaim for the American film industry, and for film comedies in particular, that they seem to conform to views held by the Surrealists and found in numerous publications since the early Dada days.[2] Now, one of the obviously tendentious questions in this interview refers to the "pure Surrealist film" in terms of a "succession of Surrealist images" and "oneiric scenarios." Stating briefly that this is the only kind of film to which they could advantageously aspire, Buñuel can only add that this film too adapts itself to art ideas. In other words, even a succession of Surrealist images can fall into the art or avant-garde trap. This might very well be an oblique reference to the 1928 "Scandale des Ursulines" and to *La Coquille et le clergyman,* Dulac's film adaptation of a script by Artaud. The gist of this quarrel between Dulac and Artaud as reported then, to which Buñuel and Dalí could not have remained oblivious, had to do with Artaud's objection to the characterization of his scenario as a "dream" and his contention, whether justified or not, that the emphasis on technical feats or tricks, while enhancing the aesthetic form and oneiric interpretation of the script, had also detracted from its revolutionary power. They certainly could have read Artaud's text "Cinéma et réalité," which accompanied the script published in *La Nouvelle Revue Française* (December 1927), in which he stated that the "scenario is not the reproduction of a dream and should not be considered as such. I would not seek to excuse its apparent incoherence by the easy evasion of dreams" (Artaud, 24).

Although in the months preceding the filming of *Un Chien andalou* Buñuel expressed growing sympathy for the aims of Surrealism, his writings do not reveal any adherence to a specific Surrealist film technique or form. In conceding that "pure Surrealist film" is the only thing one can aspire to, Buñuel may have been thinking along the lines proposed by Jean Goudal in 1925 concerning the intrinsically oneiric character of film (Virmaux, 312). Thus it comes as no surprise to find out that shortly before beginning his collaboration with Dalí, Buñuel contemplated making a "newspaper" film with Ramón Gómez de la Serna in which news items were to be dramatized and the process of newspaper production documented (Aranda, 59). Such a venture would not have been necessarily out of tune with Buñuel's conception of film. While Dalí's scathing remarks concerning this idea, as expressed in his future autobiography (*The Secret Life of Salvador Dalí*, 205) should be placed in their proper perspective, it is nevertheless quite obvious that such a conception at that time was quite alien to his own vision.

To recapitulate some of my earlier remarks, Dalí's totally non-dramatic conception consists of two basic directions. One relies on the standardization and constant signs of the American commercial cinema; the other partakes of the fantasy inherent in the simple recording of the facts and objects of the external world. His view of Harry Langdon combines the two since he responds to him in terms of the non-human qualities and "elementary life" of a drop of water or a bean plant. Dalí's ideas regarding film and photography were closely related in the course of 1928 to his growing preoccupation with the idea of surreality. In "Realidad y Sobrerrealidad" (October 1928) Dalí followed Breton's expression of reality and surreality as being mutually contained in one another. Aiding in this osmosis between reality and surreality is photography which, through the photographed facts and their infinite associations, offers a constant revision of reality. Dalí insists indeed on the data or "givens" of reality as the basis for any intimations of surreality (88). Hence his reservations regarding abstract film as practiced by Léger and Man Ray (43). Associated with this idea is the notion of the "documentary," an "anti-artistic trend" defined by Dalí as the scrupulously accurate minute documentation of the data of the external world that may be accomplished in film, photography or literature (103). What Dalí still quite tentatively suggests and, to some extent, explores is a theory of reality based on the discovery of patterns of meaning which synchronize the most diverse phenomena in a coherent system of thought, thus compelling the objective world to obey the reality of the mind. In short, this is an embryonic form of Dalí's future Paranoia-Criticism. Referring briefly in a newspaper report from Paris in early May to the presentation at the Ursulines of "Luis Buñuel's *Un Chien andalou*," Dalí announced the forthcoming production of a documentary film about Cadaqués and its coast which would record everything "from the toenail of the fisherman to the crests of the rocks of Cape Creus, passing through the quivering of the grass and the different kinds of underwater algae" (145). This film idea was never realized; viewed, however, against his earlier film essays and his current preoccupation with the "documentary," it clearly indicates where his film interests truly lay. His lackadaisical reference to *Un Chien andalou* is also quite telling. Of course, he may have been biding his time, waiting to see how the film would be received in Paris before claiming paternity. I believe, however, that Dalí at the time was still not fully aware of the implication the film held for his future work (the point will be raised again later on). I contend, indeed, that Dalí in these months was not fully committed to making the kind of film *Un Chien andalou* turned out to be; nor, for that matter, was Buñuel, as the affair of the "newspaper" film makes clear.

For Buñuel, a committed film maker who was ready to undertake almost any film project, and Dalí, whose views of film are quite removed from any considerations of practical realization, *Un Chien andalou* was the common ground on which they both met. They were close enough, in many other respects, to forgo these differences and launch themselves on a course which was by no means inimical to their natural inclinations. It remains to be asked what made them choose this particular course. Here *La Coquille et le clergyman* might be brought up again. Buñuel and Dalí could not have remained oblivious to the script published about a year before. What may have inspired them, though, were not so much Artaud's images and situations, as argued by Alain and Odette Virmaux (48), but primarily the revelation of the inexhaustible possibilities offered by film of escaping from the constraints of logic and of revealing the irrational underside of reality. What is even more important, however, is the marked difference between *Coquille*, film or script, and *Un Chien andalou*. It is necessary to indicate in this respect that, Artaud's protestations notwithstanding, not only the film but the script too dictate the utilization of devices or tricks that cinematically at least account for all the irrational transformations and bizarre appearances and disappearances. There is no sense of dislocation or discontinuity; everything is fully resolved by the miracle of cinema. Thus the priest lifting the officer and swinging him up in the confessional is miraculously transported, by the darkening of the screen, to a mountain top (Artaud 26); vapors emerging from the clergyman's eyes and mouth form a town scene (29). The devices utilized to perform these miracles satisfy our need to be reassured, at least on the level of the "sorcellerie" which cinema makes possible. In *Un Chien andalou* on the other hand, dislocations and disruptions of space and of narrative continuity are matter-of-factly and naturally presented as if requiring no further validation. Artaud's character responds with fear to the sudden reappearance of a woman who had disappeared a moment before (27). Dalí and Buñuel emphasize in their script the young woman's lack of surprise as she turns around and sees the absent cyclist – whose frills, box and collar she has just arranged on the bed – standing in another corner of the room (Buñuel, 86). Later, pulling hard at the door in which the cyclist's hand has been caught, the woman turns away to look at the room which proves to be the same room she had escaped from not a moment ago (Buñuel, 89). These are just a few instances of the film's overall design of subverting the conventions of traditional narrative cinema; of utilizing the conventions of montage against the grain of traditional filmic continuity. Titles indicating time, that appear to establish narrative continuity by suggesting links between the different sequences (eight years later; about three in the morning; sixteen years before), betray the spectator's expectations, thus disrupting the illusion of a coherent narrative form. Those disruptions and betrayals are characterized by the unassuming way, the deadpan manner, in which they come about. This subversive attitude is further enhanced by the parody directed at familiar film conventions associated with the silent movie melodrama. This point has been fully treated by J. H. Matthews (86). The script conveys a full measure of the passionate gestures and exaggerated expressions characterizing film melodrama: the young woman kisses the cyclist "passionately on the lips"; the man "now looking like the villain in a melodrama" stares at the woman "lustfully with rolling eyes" (Buñuel, 86–88). Buñuel, as his writings reveal, is fully aware of the inadvertent comic potential inherent in the melodramatic style of acting. The tango which in the original screening accompanied the stylized chase across the room is a further indication of their parodistic intention. The parodying of silent film conventions is spelled out in the script even in the small detail concerning the bell made out of two hands shaking a cocktail shaker which, according to the script, replaces the silent film convention of showing the actual electric bell ringing (Buñuel, 89). Parody is not limited, however, to the conventions of film; the ludicrous procession of 'burdens,' cork, melon, two priests, pianos and carcasses of donkeys is a malicious caricature of a religious procession. The humorous deflation of seriousness in the film is indicative of a wholly irreverent mood which permeated the making of the film from its early script stages. "The title of my present book is *The Andalusian Dog,* which made Dalí and me piss with laughter when we thought of it," wrote Buñuel to a friend around the time he and Dalí were working on the script (Aranda, 59). Much of this mood was passed to the film together with the title.

In Dalí and Buñuel's poems and poetic prose of the preceding years we discern much of what has been presented above as distinguishing *Un Chien andalou* from *La Coquille et le clergyman* and characterizing its overall conception. Furthermore, it is in their writings that Dalí and Buñuel exhibit their mental affinity. This does not imply a complete identity, although the similarities are many and quite striking at times, but rather a mutual reinforcement and interdependence. My argument does not rest on the similarity of motifs. Beyond iconographic considerations which, indeed, would also reveal some very significant differences, their writings disclose a common core of poetic and narrative forms and textual procedures. This does not preclude some differences in this respect as well; those indeed also prove significant in delineating their respective contributions to the film.

Dalí's texts establish a narrative frame. They often refer to some conventional form, only to undermine it by introducing textual incongruities that defy the reader's attempt to perceive a consistent narrative structure. At times the referential frame is clearly indicated, as in one of the "Dues Proses" (November 1927) entitled "Nadal a Brusselles: Conte Antic" (Christmas in Brussels: Ancient Tale). The piece utilizes some of the trappings of the "ancient" or, rather, Gothic tale (an uninhabited tower, a dark chamber, gruesome murder) to narrate a bizarre story that moves off in unexpected directions through an associative structure involving images of animals and strange metamorphoses: "It was an enormous cow . . . no, it was a telephonist . . . no, it was a bear that begged in the Jewish quarter . . ." [ellipses are in the original]. The expression of disjointedness undermining narrative continuity is also accomplished formally through the use of truncated syntax and a montage of images: "The forest. The hare, the fox, the sea urchin. The ox and the cow, the stable" (36). This procedure is even more forcefully employed in the companion prose piece, "La Meva Amiga I La Platja" (My Girl Friend and the Beach). A conventional narrative structure implying spatial and temporal continuity through indications of setting and temporal sequence (Right this minute; One morning; Today) is undermined by the frenzied and hallucinatory quality of the actions and images:

Right at this moment, on the beach, the printed letters of the daily newspaper are eating a torpid and putrefied ass, clean as mica. . . . [ellipsis is mine]

My friend is stretched with her extremities tenderly sectioned, full of flies and small aluminum helices. . . .

One morning I painted with ripolin a newborn baby which I left to dry on the tennis court. . . . (34–5)

The juggling with what in this prose piece are only spurts of narrative, becomes the underlying formal principle of a poetic prose piece which sets out to be a "story" entitled "Peix perseguit per un raïm" (Fish pursued by a bunch of grapes, September 1928). Here again we experience a discrepancy between a conventional frame, with an exposition of setting and characters engaged in a series of exciting events (car chases, robbers) and a wholly indeterminate narrative space and temporal structure. The opening lines evoke a table-top situation with the fish and the bunch of grapes (referred to as "small things") as protagonists. The scene unexpectedly shifts to the beach where a combination of stones, drying cork, feathers and other incongruous elements evokes the bunch of grapes (similarly to the way the box, tie and frills evoke the cyclist in *Un Chien andalou*). The scene shifts again to a poker game with a bejewelled baroness in the course of which the fish is pursued by the bunch of grapes, both undergoing strange metamorphoses. The ensuing car chase takes place simultaneously on the micro and macro level, with robbers in cars, and later horses and sledges, rushing along a road which is made of "an 8 hole reed-pipe." The chase, formally evoked by the mad rush of images and the breathless syntax, comes to an end as the narrator addresses an elusive female "you" who finally throws a silvery evening gown that turns into a vast sea hiding them from their enemies. The pace changes again to a legato rhythm evoking the mood of a sunny afternoon and the text ends with the wholly inconsequential statement: "I have a pretty photo of New York" (83). The text alludes to several popular film and literary genres, adventure, society romance, cops and robbers. It may more specifically refer to Mack Sennett's films, "les insolites Sennet," as Dalí refers to them (*Babaouo*, 19), and perhaps even to *Entr'acte*, to which Dalí responds more favorably than he does to other avant-garde films because its ideas parallel tendencies found in the American comedy film (*Babaouo*, 16). Indeed, Dalí's syntactical "fast motion" and the absurd turns the action takes are quite similar to the method employed by *Entr'acte*.[3] Note should be again taken of the deadpan manner in which Dalí narrates the most outrageous non-sequiturs and unexpected narrative switches, and his matter-of-fact acceptance of irrational content.

This tension between a firm anecdotal line and irrational content that undermines the causal chain announced by such a structure is also typical of Buñuel's poetic writings. "The Comfortable Watchword of St. Huesca," an outrageously anarchic text that, one suspects, was never intended for publication, is a "picaresque" tale of the adventures or, rather, misadventures of a lump of roast meat. Here too a spatial and temporal pattern established by a series of conventional designators (two hours afterwards; meanwhile; exactly one meter from the base of the cypress, etc.) is undermined by the lack of causal continuity and the utter absurdity of the narrated events:

The lump of meat has started on a rapid career. In a bend of the road two peasants of Aragon grow upon his ears. In the next bend is a split cypress which stops in front of the meat (Aranda, 257).

For both Dalí and Buñuel humor is a function of the absurdities and non-sequiturs introduced into the text. In Buñuel's case, though, humor is often generated by the relentless pace of savage absurdities, as in the above passage or in the well-known "Letter to José Bello" (1928).[4] Dalí's humor, serving as a parodistic device, deflates any attempt at seriousness. Thus, for instance, in his poem "Una pluma" (April 1929), a serious and almost nostalgic look at his childhood landscapes is deflated by the last line:

But the clouds, the foam, the smooth rocks
are nothing but an ancient and known landscape
where I lived my adolescence
my lips, my eyes, lost among the pebbles
my hair imitating the gestures of the stones
viewed solely
by a vigilant olive
joyous
like a violent kick in the ass (123).

The joy implied by the deflationary action described in the last line in-forms much of Dalí and Buñuel's writing, perhaps Dalí's more so since the violence inherent in Buñuel's texts often leaves little scope for true gaiety of any kind. This takes us on to our next subject of investigation, but first I would like to re-emphasize my argument so far by summarizing the pre-ceding line of investigation. I claim then that the narrative procedures em-ployed by Dalí and Buñuel in the texts discussed clearly parallel those found in *Un Chien andalou*. These consist of the disruption of causal continuity and coherent narrative form; betrayal of expectations formed by the utilization of conventional narrative contexts through the irrational content found in the individual sections of the narrative; parody of popular art forms. The world of the film and the world of the texts is one in which incongruities and absurdities are taken in stride.

These parallels do not necessarily imply a similarity of themes or iconog-raphy. *Un Chien andalou* obviously is quite removed from the narrative substance of these texts, the actions, settings or characters. But there are also some significant points of contact between texts and film which I will ex-plore now. It is also in this substance that the distinctions between Dalí's and Buñuel's writings are most glaringly manifested. Let us consider a typical Buñuelian scene ("St. Huesca"): "Suddenly an immense crowd, attracted by the sun, springs from the earth, a million million little tailors of which the tallest is less than a millimetre tall. Some jump a metre in the air, others persecute a lost peasant woman. . . . Half an hour later the road is only an enormous marsh; each tailor dissolves into a drop of urine, dishevelled, sob-bing . . ." (Aranda, 257). This vision has its counterparts in Dalí's writing in images such as that of an "endless number of bread crumbs, each with its small minute hand" (94) or the grasshopper "composed of more than 1,000,000,000 very small sword fish; if one breathes on it, all the sword fish disperse in the air, and left is only an old and very thin furry fountain-pen" (101). As these examples illustrate, the difference between Dalí and Buñuel is not so much in the structure of their vision as in its tone. Dalí appears to amuse himself with these irrational speculations; Buñuel's images, even the most incongruous ones, embody a sense of violence and cruelty, and are often derisively anti-religious, even blasphemous, in their mixing of eroticism with sacred symbols. Thus the chaotic melting of the tailors is accompanied by "echoes of organs, of prayers, of hymns from far-off cathedrals," and later the lump of roast meat is trampled on by "five hundred consecrated hosts, with their members erect. . . ." A special target of derision are the priests or "maristas," as the letter to Pepin Bello referred to above amply illustrates. These elements give Buñuel's writing its sense of direction and drive, and form its spiritual and emotive landscape. Even the most anarchic texts and poems have a firm foundation of eroticism, religion and violence. In "Bacanal" (*La Gaceta Literaria,* No. 50, January 1929), for instance, images of food and eating combine with frenzied pictures of suffering and martyrdom associated with St. Bartholomew who is envisioned as a devil and a faun, and whose corpse is eaten by ants of gold.

Dalí relies on an iconography which is less directed or systematic, but it is by no means fully fortuitous. His is a world of "small things" ("Poema de les cosetes" is indeed the title of one of his 1928 poems), of things viewed on a table-top in a manner evoking the fantasy inherent in the change of scale made possible by film. The world of "small things" is one intimately related to Dalí's own person and to his immediate environment. It consists of ants, hairs (at times perceived singly), parts of the human anatomy; there are also things found on the beach, where Dalí has spent his summers, such as fish, fish spine, sea urchins, snails, seashells, cork, stones of varied colors and shapes. These "small things" are presented in his poetry as "facts" rather than as terms of metaphoric associations. These sequences of stated facts comprise a cinematic movement of rapidly shifting images that are formally connected one to the other by certain operations in the text: Repetitions, statements of identity, statements of sequentiality.

With the sun a small cornet is born to me of a handful of more than a thousand
  photographs of dry matters.
With the sun, near an empty and damp place, sing six blobs of spittle and a
  small snoring sardine.
With the sun, there is a small milk upright above the anus of a snail.
With the sun two small toothless sharks are born to me beneath my arm (100).

These chains of images, when analyzed, might disclose certain conceptual, verbal or visual associations. Often those associations will altogether elude analysis, as illustrated in the following long subtitle of the poem "Una Pluma": "A feather, which is not a feather but a tiny herb, representing a small sea horse, my gums on the hill and at the same time a beautiful spring-time landscape" (121).

Buñuel's intransigence requires a greater communicability. He often resorts to the use of religiously codified symbols combined with metaphor associations which enhance their inherent violence and, at times, erotic undertone. In "Redentora" (*La Gaceta Literaria,* No. 50, January 1929) two sets of notions and qualities are played off one against the other: A. convent, monk, red mastiff, blood, red butcher; and B. corn, spring light, sister, white, dove of peace, white silence. The host, the Eucharistic sacrifice, brings together the two sets of values and one suspects that there is a certain irony involved here concerning this tool of redemption. "Olor de Santidad" (*La Gaceta Literaria,* No. 51, February 1929) comprises a chain of metaphors and other figures intended to convey something akin to the moment of death. There is a vertiginous fall down a chute and one is "converted into one of those screws that the stars hurl in a million turns a second," feeling finally a hand or a wing light gently on the forehead while an eternal voice says "you can die." Death is reached as a sexual climax and, obviously, Buñuel cannot be taken at face value; the two texts offer an ironic commentary on the nature of redemption and on religious expectations directed at death. The nature of Buñuelian irony has direct bearing on certain metaphors in the film, often ascribed to Dalí, that have been repeatedly criticized for being facile or too obvious. Such is, for instance, the image of the man who is ordered to stretch out his arms in the shape of a cross and has a book placed in each, the books turning later into revolvers. The "burden" scene too is generally interpreted along quite simplistic lines. Those should be viewed as being at least double-edged in their ironic concurrence with the spectator's craving for meaning.

Much of the preceding analysis of Dalí's poetic imagery, as well as forthcoming observations regarding the imagery in his paintings, may also be pertinent to consideration of the metaphorical activity in the film. I am referring in particular to the eye-slicing sequence as well as to those following it in the first few minutes of the film: the bicycle rider with his feminine frills and striped box; the evocation of the cyclist by the woman through the arrangements of these objects on the bed; the close-up of a hand full of ants crawling out of a hole, followed by the hairs in the armpit of a woman, a sea urchin, the head of a woman seen from above, the severed hand. In recent years these images have received a great deal of attention from semioticians concerned with the nature of film imagery. It has been argued that the initial eye-mutilation metaphor, followed by a combination of male and female signs in a pattern of assertion and denial of the presence of the phallus (fetish objects; concave and convex forms, etc.) should be seen as an imitation of a discourse of the unconscious involving the fear of castration (Williams). A related view, similarly postulating castration anxiety, sees these metaphors in terms of symbolic equivalence to the genitals that is related to Freud's notions of displacement and condensation. The work of displacement transfers interest from the genitals to the eye and to other elements in this dream text; the condensation entails the placing of the male and female symbols in a single ambivalent signifier (Oswald, 118–19). The crucial distinction between verbal metaphors and film metaphors notwithstanding, a marked formal kinship between Dalí's sequences of rapidly shifting images, dealt with before, and the figural activity of the film may be discerned. It should be stressed that this is a largely formal kinship. The film, in spite of all the metaphorical activity seemingly intruding on its main narrative strand, is still

137

continuously marked by the presence of its human protagonists. Dalí's "small things" often lack a true human dimension; seldom do they combine meaningfully with images pertaining to the human figure. An isolated line such as, "One of my friend's breasts is a calm sea urchin, the other a buzzing swarm" (80), does not offer scope enough for an evolution of meaning within a larger symbolic context. Even the more extensively evoked girl friend on the beach (34–6) remains quite incorporeal and lacks a real sense of erotic presence; consequently, we may not be truly shocked by the horrible mutilations her body is subjected to. Indeed, in view of Dalí's later development, it is quite disconcerting to realize how tame his writings are compared to Buñuel's. Only his canvases of 1927–28 – exhibiting his "small things" alongside blobs, clod-like shapes and some obvious visual references to male and female genitalia – hint at Dalí's sexual preoccupations in these years.

An article he wrote around that time, ". . . L'alliberament dels dits . . ." (The liberation of fingers, March 1929), is Dalí's only attempt prior to his Surrealist period to air his views regarding the nature of symbols. Dalí relates how his childhood fascination with grasshoppers turned to extreme loathing after he caught by hand a fish that looked like a grasshopper. This story is strung together with another one involving an ignorant fellow whom Dalí befriended during his short military service, who had once a remarkable vision of a flying phallus, totally unaware of the existence of this motif, Dalí adds, in ancient civilizations. Dalí associates this motif with another one, the fingers in isolation, which preoccupied him at the time and which he introduced in many of his 1928 works. Reflecting Dalí's growing interest in psychoanalysis, the article seems to allude to the Freudian notion of displacement. The horror of grasshoppers is related to the formal similarity of grasshopper and fish in this childhood experience, and points to a repressed content that is also associated by Dalí with an archetypal image of a flying phallus and with his own predilection for fingers in isolation. Dalí refers to the method employed in this article as "the anti-artistic, faithful and objective annotation of the world of facts" (111) and considers it more pertinent to his aspirations than the tools of defunct poetry (elsewhere he rejects specifically the poetic metaphor). Dalí clearly applies Freudian symbol formation to his own work, although he is reluctant in this essay to follow its conclusions through with regard to his own experiences and disclose the latent meaning of this fear of grasshoppers. He is less inhibited in his paintings which abound in mutilated anatomies, severed hands, truncated female bodies as well as phallic fingers and concave forms suggesting female genitalia. In his painting *Unsatiated Desires,* for instance, an 'androgyne' hand combines male and female signs, one finger protruding and phallic and two others forming a vulva-like shape. Yet the sexuality of such a painting is too dependent on obvious sexual signs to be truly shocking; like the poetic texts it lacks an authentic sense of its human reality. Only in paintings that are more anthropomorphically motivated such as *Bather* and *Beigneuse* [sic] of 1928 with their almost obscene distortions do we sense Dalí's horrible fascination and fear regarding human sexuality. These works, however, rely for their effect on the perception of certain formal qualities as obscene or repulsive rather than on symbolic equivalences based on Freudian dream formation. Elements in the 1928 paintings that could have served as symbols fail to do so because of the lack of a consistent connotative system based on the recurrence of motifs. In the months preceding the work on *Un Chien andalou* Dalí is still seeking the means of communicating on the level of symbols.

In the light of what we have seen so far of Buñuel's writing and Dalí's writing and painting we may define in gross outline their respective contributions to *Un Chien andalou*. To schematize and simplify what is a far more involved relationship, I would suggest the following observations. Both Dalí and Buñuel share equally in the film's parodistic sub-text and its underlying psychological concerns. Buñuel is largely responsible for the overall narrative framework and for the script's, as well as the film's, cinematic character. Dalí contributed to the figural activity of the film as well as to some of its narrative procedures. The film also marks a significant stage in the formulation and consolidation of their aesthetics. Compared to Buñuel's narrative texts with their nightmarish quality, violence, blatant sexuality and anti-clericalism, the film functions much more subtly as a dream text through the manipulation of certain motifs as fetishes, metaphors or symbols. The film is certainly more focused than those texts in its intimate indoor quality and its surface articulation as a continuous narrative comprising a psychological drama involving quite commonplace human protagonists. In his written texts, in particular those not intended for publication, Buñuel no doubt felt free to indulge his wildest and most anarchic whims. To the script and film he brought, however, the more disciplined craftsmanship of a dedicated and relatively experienced film maker. It was around that time that Buñuel wrote an essay on "découpage," or the shooting script stage, describing it as the crucial operation in which the "script or group of written visual ideas abandons literature and becomes cinema" (Ilie, 449).

With all his considerable contribution to the film, Dalí still lacked the discipline and experience necessary to make, alone, this leap from literature into cinema advocated by Buñuel. Yet once he had collaborated on it with Buñuel, *Un Chien andalou* proved to be a significant landmark in his development as an artist. Dalí's development as a painter in the course of 1928 is marked by an increasing adherence to the spirit of Surrealism and to the formal solutions offered by artists such as Ernst, Miró, Arp and Masson. Thus he experimented with an organic language consisting of the biomorphic forms of Arp and Miró and the spectral bird and animal forms populating Ernst's canvases. To these Dalí added his own iconographic contribution of big thumbs and phallic fingers. Late in 1928 he came close to abstraction, especially in works based on Arp's open-ended morphology. It should be noted that in 1928 Dalí hardly refers to his own paintings in his writing, satisfied to apply his surrealist rhetoric to the work of others. Thus, while observing in Miro's work the existence of an osmosis between reality and surreality with an "unlimited scope of mystery" (79), he seems to be arguing much more persuasively for the attainment of this osmosis by means of photography, film and the documentary in all its forms. Indeed, the relative neglect of painting in general in his 1928 and early 1929 writings may hint at his growing disenchantment with painting altogether. His poems and poetic texts, their motifs and iconography closely related to the paintings, hint with their spurts of shifting images and metamorphoses at possibilities that seem to surpass those of painting. It seems as if Dalí is trying in these texts to animate his plastic work, and enlarge its scope of possibilities by verbal means. Some paintings reveal an attempt to approach the multifariousness of the texts or even the chain of images achieved by film, as Dawn Ades notes (56) with regard to *Senicitas* (1928). This painting, with its scattered images – floating fingers, genitalia, skeletons of ghostly donkeys and birds, Miroesque forms and severed limbs – forms a catalogue of motifs of his 1927–8 works. In its multiple details, unfocused composition and indeterminate spatial definition it presents a close analogy to the equally unfocused listing and cataloguing in the poems. I have already commented in some detail on the lack of an authentic sense of the human dimension in these works and the scant and largely immaterial presence of the human figure.

Dalí's paintings of the months following the work on *Un Chien andalou* and its first public showing reveal a radically different approach. Beginning with his painting *The First Days of Spring*, probably painted in the spring of 1929, Dalí's work exhibits a more consistent spatial definition conveying a sensation of deep space by means derived from De Chirico's methods. Those consist of a flat and quite featureless vista extending to the horizon on which are situated objects and human figures, some of which are foregrounded while others appear as diminutive shapes closer to the horizon line. An extensive use is also made of frames, boxes and other framing devices for the purpose of depicting scenes within scenes, thus allowing the merging of different spatial and contextual elements. The Oedipal dramas enacted in this setting are heavily laden with quite explicit symbolic representations, some carried over from the earlier works (severed heads and hands, ants, fingers, fish and other phallic symbols). There are also new ones like the lion (representing desire), bearded men (the Father), abnormally large hands (masturbation). Some of these symbols, like the grasshopper, are personal obsessions of Dalí's. The 'discourse' of these paintings, combining human action with symbolic representation, utilizing all kinds of framing devices and provoking a virtual perceptual "movement" between its constituent elements, presents a remarkable analogy to the discourse of the film. Like the film it utilizes chains of metaphoric associations based at times on formal similarities (similarly to the methods employed in his paranoiac-critical activity). Works such as *The Dismal Game* or *The Illuminated Pleasures* present sequences of action that may be placed in a pseudo-temporal framework.

I do not claim that it was only *Un Chien andalou* that brought about those changes. His paintings reveal his awakening interest in De Chirico and Magritte; he may have been exposed to Ernst's new collages that were compiled into a *roman-collage* around that time. Still, *Un Chien andalou* had shown him the way of giving shape to a latent content, that remained hidden from view in the earlier work, without making it any less enigmatic or irrational. The discovery of these new vistas in his painting may have dulled the edge of his enthusiasm for film. It is also quite probable that by the time he participated in the shooting of *Un Chien andalou*, Dalí realized that it was Buñuel after all who was the true *cineaste;* and not wishing to play second fiddle to him, chose to pursue the new course opened to him in his painting. Dalí was on the whole more interested in ideas than in their realization, even with regard to painting. *L'Age d'or* proved to be an incentive again for a flow of ideas, many of which found their way to the final version of the script and to the film itself (many more than those grudgingly accounted for by some Buñuel scholars). In fact, Dalí did not have to be physically present on the shooting set of *L'Age d'or* for his presence to be felt. Dalí and Buñuel's collaboration on *Un Chien andalou* was too intense not to leave its mark on both.

Notes

1. The Spanish and Catalan magazines to which Dalí contributed essays and poetry in the late 1920s are often hard to obtain. A few of his articles in their original version are included in Paul Ilie, ed. *Documents of the Spanish Vanguard.* Others may be found in the second volume of the catalogue accompanying Dalí's 1984 exhibition in Madrid and in Barcelona, *400 Obras de Salvador Dalí (1914-1983).* The most easily accessible collection of Dalí's writing, to which I have made my references, is Salvador Dalí, *Oui 1. La révolution paranoïaque-critique,* which includes translations into French of almost all of his early writings. Some of these may also be found in the exhibition catalogue *Salvador Dalí, rétrospective 1920-1980* (18 Décembre 1979-14 Avril 1980, Centre Georges Pompidou, Musée National d'Art Moderne). I have checked the French version against the Spanish and Catalan original versions, and while my references are to the French edition I have felt free, in cases of discrepancy between the two, to retain the sense of the original version. Buñuel's writings present a more difficult case. The most complete collection of his writings to appear so far is, to the best of my knowledge, Luis Aranda's *Luis Buñuel: A Critical Biography,* which includes a few of his unpublished texts and poems together with most of his critical essays. My references are mostly to the English edition of this book. In the case of published poems, references are to the original publication. A few of his critical essays published in *Cahiers d'Art* in the late 1920s, as well as his "Letter to José Bello," appeared in Ado Kyrou, *Luis Buñuel* (1962). Two of his essays, "Una noche en el 'Studio des Ursulines'" and his theoretical essay concerning "découpage," are included in Paul Ilie, *Documents of the Spanish Vanguard.* Buñuel's writings still await their turn for a comprehensive critical edition.

2. The subject of Surrealist film aesthetics has been extensively dealt with in numerous publications such as the two issues of *Études cinématographiques (Surréalisme et cinéma* 38-39 and 40-42 [1965]) devoted to Surrealism and film; J. H. Matthews, *Surrealism and Film* (1971); Alain and Odette Virmaux, *Les surréalistes et le cinéma* (1976); Ado Kyrou, *Le surréalisme au cinéma* (Paris: Le terrain vague, 1963), etc.

3. For a comprehensive treatment of *Entr'acte*'s debt to the Sennett Chase see Noël Carroll, "Entr'acte, Paris and Dada," *Millenium Film Journal* 1.1 (1977-78):5-11.

4. "Lettre a Pépin," as it is entitled in its French version, appeared first in *Positif* 31 (1959) and later in Ado Kyrou, *Luis Buñuel,* 128-131.

Works Cited

Ades, Dawn. *Dalí and Surrealism.* New York: Harper & Row, 1982.

Aranda, Francisco. *Luis Buñuel: A Critical Biography.* Trans. and Ed. David Robinson. New York: De Capo Press, 1976.

Artaud, Antonin. *Oeuvres Complètes.* 10 vols. Paris: Editions Gallimard, 1970. Vol. 3.

Buñuel, Luis. *L'Age d'Or and Un Chien Andalou: Films by Luis Buñuel.* Trans. Marianne Alexandre. Classic Film Scripts. New York: Simon and Schuster, 1968.

Dalí, Salvador. *Babaouo: Scenario inédit précédé d'un abrégé d'une histoire critique du cinéma et suivi de Guillaume Tell Ballet Portugais.* Paris: Éditions des cahiers libres, 1932.

———, *Oui 1. La révolution paranoïaque-critique.* Paris: Denoël/Gonthier, 1971.

———, *The Secret Life of Salvador Dalí.* Trans. Haakon M. Chevalier. London: Vision Press, 1973.

Ilie, Paul, ed. *Documents of the Spanish Vanguard.* Studies in Romance Languages and Literatures 78. Chapel Hill: The University of North Carolina Press, 1969.

Kyrou, Ado. *Luis Buñuel.* Coll. Cinéma d'aujourd'hui. Paris: Seghers, 1962.

Matthews, J. H. *Surrealism and Film.* Ann Arbor: The University of Michigan Press, 1971.

Oswald, Laura. "Figure/Discourse: Configurations of Desire in *Un Chien andalou.*" *Semiotica* 33:1–2 (1981): 105–122.

Virmaux, Alain, and Odette Virmaux. *Les surréalistes et le cinéma.* Paris: Seghers, 1976.

Williams, Linda. "Dream Rhetoric and Film Rhetoric: Metaphor and Metonymy in *Un Chien andalou.*" *Semiotica* 33:1–2 (1981): 87–103.

Un Chien andalou: The Talking Cure
Stuart Liebman

Parler français comme une vache espagnole
French idiom

The eye should listen before it looks.
Jean-Luc Godard, *Le Gai Savoir*

Near the end of *Un Chien andalou,* there is a scene rarely discussed by critics in any detail. In it, the hitherto passive heroine "argues" with the brooding male protagonist and finally defies him by opening the door to leave the apartment they have shared since she rescued him from the gutter. As we will soon learn, the door does not lead to the stairway and street we had been led to believe was there. Rather, she will walk through it onto a dazzling beach where "in the Spring,"[1] after a brief rendezvous with another man, she will die a truly sordid death. Even in a film whose space has been extraordinarily unstable and "dream-like," this fantastic liaison of disparate spaces is so astonishing that it deflects attention from the gestures – actually, they are more like grotesque grimaces – she makes as she leaves. What happens is this: as the sea breeze blows through her hair, she pivots toward the seemingly catatonic hero off-screen and vigorously *sticks out her tongue.* She then walks out of the room, returns, and sticks out her tongue again, this time so directly into the camera (that is, toward *us*) that we can almost peer down her throat (Fig. 1). When she is finally out the door, moreover, she sticks out her tongue a last time back into the room before proceeding to the beach. However "natural" and spontaneous her petulant tongue-lashing is made to seem, the repetition and visual emphasis ought to alert us to the possibility that more may be at stake here than is immediately apparent. Her gesture *is* highly significant, and my purpose in this essay is to explore some of the new insights it offers into this perpetually perplexing film.

I believe we must read the exaggerated wagging of her tongue as a particularly vivid instance – indeed, a highly contrived emblem – of a formal process that generates much of the film's action, imagery and structure. That is to say, we must dispense with a number of myths about the film's creation spread by Dalí and Buñuel themselves during the years after *Un Chien andalou* was released, for the procedures they used to structure the film, while still not entirely known to us, were certainly no more spontaneous than the gesture I have been discussing.[2] The reluctance on the part of the young would-be Surrealists to admit they worked hard and

Figure 1

methodically in making their film is quite understandable given the vaunted irrationality and spontaneity that was so central to the Surrealist ethos. In a now well-known essay written eighteen years after the film was made, however, Buñuel was more candid and provided a clue about the method he and Dalí used. Significantly, he underscores the importance of psychoanalytic constructs as models for the film. *Un Chien andalou* "does not attempt to recount a dream, although it profits by a mechanism analogous to that of dreams," he wrote, and "the only method of investigation of the symbols would be, perhaps, psychoanalysis."[3] Unfortunately, his remarks are less helpful than they might be, for they are both vague and potentially misleading. Despite his general reference to dream "symbols," Buñuel does not seem to limit the potential range of dream "mechanisms" to the one Freud calls "the symbolic."[4] In fact, he and Dalí surely used several different mechanisms as models. It seems certain in any case that the two Spaniards were fascinated by the mechanism Freud himself called "the most psychologically interesting achievement of the dream-work," namely, the transformation of a latent verbal thought into manifest visual images.[5] According to Freud, the dream work must reformulate scandalous or morally repugnant thoughts in order to allow them to be represented in the dream. This reformulation can proceed in several ways. For example, words can be found whose concreteness or, alternatively, ambiguity, enable them to slip past the censorship and serve as the basis for both the odd and the innocuous dream images. This is the primary mechanism used by "verbal disguise" dreams.[6] The important point to note here is that the form of (if not the motive for) this kind of operation on language readily lends itself for conscious use in the making of a film.[7] If Dalí and Buñuel

144

were intrigued by the possibilities opened up by such an adaptation – and that is my claim – then one might expect to find instances in *Un Chien andalou* in which gestures, images, or indeed entire sequences were created by finding visual forms for verbal expressions.[8]

Such is the case with the tongue-wagging I have been describing. In French, the language in which the script was written,[9] "tirer la langue" means "to put (or stick) out one's tongue." Both noun and verb, however, have many other meanings regularly used by native speakers. "Tirer" also means to pull or stretch, and "la langue," of course, is also the word for language. Her gesture, therefore, may be said to incarnate a more abstract meaning, and as such is emblematic of a procedure Dalí and Buñuel exploit throughout the film. Just as she extends and contorts her tongue, they explore the outlying reaches of the French "tongue" – slang, idioms, figures of speech, etc. – and these expressions become a complex subtext underlying many of their most memorable images and sequences.

In other words, *Un Chien andalou* must be heard as well as seen. This may seem a rather paradoxical assertion because *language* seems to have been almost entirely eliminated from the film. Dialogue is only suggested at two points in the scenario and these "lines" are clearly meant to be conveyed through gestures rather than speech. In the film, actors rarely even appear to speak, and on the few occasions when they do, we are invariably forced to read their lips; no dialogue titles are inserted, contrary to what one might have expected in a film from this period. In fact, there are only five intertitles in the film, and their only apparent function is to thwart any attempt to construct a logical sequence of events as well as any motivation for them. And finally, of course, except for some musical accompaniment – alternately Wagner and a tango – the film is silent. Nevertheless, the film is a "talkie," albeit a unique one, and its imagery and structure are intimately tied to the French language, in particular to *argot* and popular figurative forms of speech. It is the way it "speaks" – and induces us to "hear" the murmuring speech beneath the evolving spectacle – that makes *Un Chien andalou* into a distinctly Surrealist work of art, at least as much as its imagery or narration.[10]

Some stills from what is usually referred to as the Prologue of the film will help to make what I have been saying more concrete. There is, of course, an opening title, "Il était une fois," which introduces the sequence and suggests that a narrative will unfold.[11] The space in which that narrative occurs, even as it is articulated in this first sequence, however, is curiously unstable, a feature of the film that will become more and more apparent as we continue to watch.[12] As I will show, some of the most perplexing events that occur "in" that space and that are a major cause of its instability are produced in whole or in part by the kind of linguistic play I have been describing.

For example, the first truly baffling shot in the prologue is the eleventh. A woman suddenly appears who is never clearly placed within the space of the diegesis (Fig. 2). Who is this staring woman? Where does she come from? Why is she staring so intently? A first clue can be derived from her position in this sequence. She appears immediately after the second shot of

Figure 2

the man who glances up at the moon. In sequences of this kind, which appear to represent the man's point of view, we might ordinarily expect a second shot of what the man is looking at, i.e. a second shot of the moon. The cinematic syntax thus suggests that we are to think of this woman as a substitute for the moon, or "la lune." If we accept this suggested metaphoric identity and if we focus on the metaphoric vehicle "la lune" as an initial starting point for our analysis, then a quite surprising rationale for her presence begins to emerge. In fact, the French language deploys a surprisingly large number of metaphoric or idiomatic expressions based on the word "la lune," and several seem astonishingly relevant to the events pictured in this sequence. For example, the French describe people staring as she does by using the idiom: "tomber de la lune," to look blank or moonstruck. What is more, the *literal* meaning of the words also seems to apply. Where has she come from? She seems to have come *from nowhere;* it is as if she has *fallen from the moon* onto this balcony. The convergence of these two familiar expressions so aptly describing her distinguishing attributes suggests that her mysterious presence may be a function of the phrases by which she can be figured.

This hypothesis gains support from the fact that another phrase revolving around "la lune" is also invoked by the sequence's other character, played, by the way, by Buñuel himself. In his case, the expression "être dans la lune" aptly describes his dreamy state as he glances up at the moon, surrounded by the clouds of his cigarette smoke (Fig. 3). These are not, however, the only expressions involving this word or commonplace associations that it calls up that figure in this sequence. As Freud reminds us, in France "la lune" is routinely associated with female buttocks.[13] If we read

146

Figure 3

her face – is it coincidental that we see it vertically split by shadow? – metaphorically as "la lune" or buttocks, then a somewhat perverse note enters into the linguistic nexus underlying the sequence.[14] For if her face is to be
read as an ass, then her eye would become its center, that is, the anus.
Though it might sound far-fetched, the reading is made possible by the existence of another French idiom. The polite French word for buttocks is "les
fesses." In slang, however, this part of the anatomy is more commonly
called "le cul" and its center, the anus, is consequently referred to as "the eye
of the ass": "l'oeil du cul." Introducing this expression is not as arbitrary as it
may seem, for it is not the first time that these words, or at least words
sounding very much like them, have figured in the sequence. Recall that
the man on the balcony glanced at the moon and that it was as a substitute
for the expected object of his glance that the woman appeared. In French,
one could describe him quite precisely as "un homme qui jette un coup
d'oeil." As should be apparent, the phrase "coup d'oeil" when inverted becomes "oeil de coup" which sounds almost identical to "oeil de cul." What is
more, although in their scenario Dalí and Buñuel use the word "sectionnant"
to describe the cutting of the eye, the verb "couper" also means "to cut," and
therefore the expression "coup d'oeil" could, given a certain perverse will to
misunderstand the language, generate the truly horrifying image of a cut
eye.[15]

The uncanny congregation of expressions continues to expand as we
"listen" to the events of the Prologue. We know that the woman's eye was
not really cut. Rather, a cow's eye was substituted (Fig. 4). The editing, however, has been so precisely calculated that spectators at least temporarily
are fooled into believing that this gruesome act really occurs. In French,

147

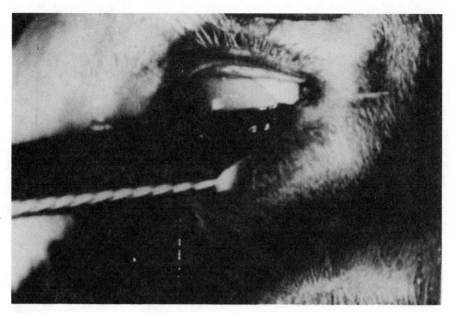

Figure 4

one might well use the idiom "faire voir la lune à quelqu'un," literally, to make someone – in this case, us – see the "moon." Or, given the pain that watching this horror causes, one could also say that Dalí and Buñuel have played a dirty trick, "un coup vache" on us. (Alternatively, one could also use the expression "faire une vacherie.") In short, "we've been had in the eye," as the French would put it, using the idiom "l'avoir dans l'oeil." And that is not all. Another pun, one that Marcel Duchamp, at least, would have heartily appreciated, is operative here. The word for cow in German is "Kuh." We have therefore witnessed the slashing of an "oeil de Kuh," that is "un oeil de vache."[16]

If what I have suggested so far is right on target – that is, if I have hit a bull's eye and have not just been slinging a lot of bull – then noting other important verbal connections will only strengthen my case. Recall that two objects are sliced in the sequence, a thumb as well as a "woman's" eye. Thumb in French is *"le pouce"* and it is pronounced only slightly differently from the slang word "la puce," which refers to a slut and which is also related to the adjective for virgin, "pucelle" (or "puceau" for men) and the word for hymen, "le pucelage." (In fact, the shift from the sound pattern "ou" to "u" is identical to the shift already observed from "coup" to "cul.") Just as the man puts the finishing touches to the sharpening of his razor ("donner le coup de pouce"), that razor, easily construed as a substitute phallus, puts the finishing touch to the hymen of a slut, or, "le pucelage d'une puce," or alternatively, a "vache," another word in *argot* for trollop or bitch. Significantly, one slang expression for penis is "la queue," which is linked to the series of similar-sounding words "cul-coup-Kuh" that runs through the sequence and which will eventually be related to two others we will meet later "cou-co*cu*" (respectively, in the major scene when the man pulls the

148

furniture by means of a rope around his *neck* and in the scene at the end during which he is *cuckolded*). Finally, it is interesting to note that a synonym for "couper" in French is "trancher," which also means "to have intercourse with" in slang.[17]

It would perhaps be wise now to step back from the film in order to clarify what I have uncovered and the method I have used to do so. I first identified an anomalous shot in the prologue that appeared in place of the expected shot of the moon. Using the French word for moon as a starting point, I explored its literal and a number of its figurative meanings as well as several idiomatic phrases in which it appeared. I then expanded my purview to examine the literal, metaphorical and idiomatic meanings of several other objects or actions that were shown prominently on screen, such as "l'oeil" and "le pouce," or with synonyms for the object seen or figured, paying particular attention to words or phrases composed of similar and often *identical* sound patterns. A primary example here would be "le cul," the synonym for "la lune" and the homonym of "le coup."

This investigation renders audible, as it were, a latent "babble" beneath the strange spectacle that is presented to us. This babble is composed of a set of words that overlap in sound or in sense to a degree that can hardly be coincidental. What is more, these words slide quickly back and forth from literal to figurative to sexual and even to scatological meanings, making each word and the object and actions connected to it ambiguous but suggestively resonant. We "hear" in our inner ear a series of words, phrases and implied sentence-fragments that circle around themes of violence, eroticism and perversity. We are listening to the murmuring of the French language as it ferments, or rather, since Dalí was involved, I ought to say, as it putrefies.

These sorts of rollicking shifts of sound and meaning that produce flashes of erotic and scatological sense amid a welter of apparent nonsense are certainly not unprecedented in Surrealist literature, and before it, in the verse of an impressive roster of French Dada poets whose work Dalí and Buñuel were closely following from Spain.[18] The prime mover was Marcel Duchamp, but many other Dada poets who later became Surrealists contributed major works in this idiom: Robert Desnos, Roger Vitrac, Jacques-André Boiffard, Michel Leiris, Leiris' revered uncle Raymond Roussel, Picabia, Tzara and André Breton.[19] These poets were second to none in their zealous attempts to dismantle the French language in order to reap the allegedly bountiful artistic and political dividends that its destruction would yield.[20]

The verse they produced is often ingenious and so closely tied to the French language as to be practically untranslatable. One simple example by Robert Desnos will have to suffice. "La solution d'un sage est-elle la pollution d'une page?" Literally: "Is the solution of a sage the pollution (in the sense of ejaculation on) of a page?" By merely changing the initial consonants while retaining the same endings, Desnos slyly undercuts any scholar's pretensions to knowledge by insinuating that writing an article is little more than a corrupt form of sexual behavior. This is a simple example; many others, particularly those by Marcel Duchamp whose texts were seminal, are far more demanding and outrageous. It is important to remember that these kinds of poems were highly esteemed at the time. Breton himself championed Duchamp's *"jeux de mots"* – and the scarce quotes he uses show how unwilling he was to deprecate Duchamp's achievement – as exemplary texts. More importantly, Breton was the first to provide an account of the strategies Duchamp used. He observed that merely by displacing a letter or two from the beginning to the interior of a word or vice versa, or by exchanging syllables between words, or by exploiting ambiguities between literal and figurative senses, Duchamp had enabled the words "to make love" and to evade "the persecutions of usage."[21] The erotic metaphor is apt because Duchamp and those like Desnos, Leiris and Vitrac who also exploited similar strategies almost invariably generated texts insinuating scandalously funny erotic meanings, results that were believed to reflect the transgressive impulses of the unconscious. This should not surprise us because perhaps the primary impetus behind this sort of poetic practice was Freud, in particular his *Psychopathology of Everyday Life,* that had been published in French translation in 1922. If one adds to these strategies the use of foreign or corrupt words (one of Duchamp's favorite tricks), the principal devices are all accounted for.[22]

Efforts were made, however, to link this sort of wordplay with visual images. Once again, Duchamp was the first. "Fresh Widow" (1920) gets its title from pronouncing the English name for the object we see in the way we would if we had a severe headcold. The joke, of course, also relies on the projection of the English phrase awkwardly denoting a recently widowed woman onto the framed window with its black panes. The result is a curiously erotic amalgam composed of image and language. Or, consider the famous "ready-made" with the enigmatic title "L.H.O.O.Q." (1919). Its vicious humor depends on pronouncing the letters inscribed at the bottom to yield a perverse meaning Da Vinci is unlikely to have had in mind: "elle a chaud au cul."

In 1926, Duchamp made a film entitled *Anémic Cinéma* which he signed with his punning pseudonym, Rrose Sélavy.[23] The film is composed of a series of rotating spirals Duchamp called "roto-reliefs" alternating with a series of his playful sentences, also arranged in spirals on the surfaces of disks. Language and image become palpably similar and profoundly interdependent. Both spiral into an illusory "depth" – in the case of the image, into the illusion of three dimensions, in the case of the rotating texts, into the illusion of meaning generated by grammatical structure – only with another half turn to be forced back to their respective "surfaces" of two-dimensional pattern and sound. And this kind of slow, deliberate pushing and pulling is explicitly linked to a familiar erotic movement, one that is taken up and figured by the texts themselves. The differences between language and image are collapsed as both are made to undulate with the same slyly erotic innuendo.

This admittedly schematic digression has enabled me to establish several relevant points. First, interest by Dada authors in manipulating language in ways Breton had described in 1923 was sustained during the transition to Surrealism and featured prominently in *La Revolution Surréaliste* at least

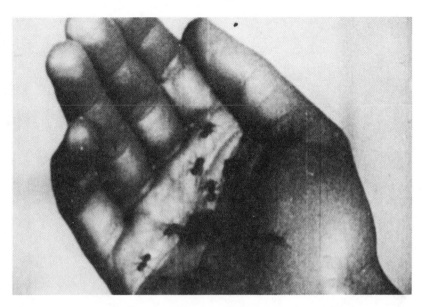

Figure 5

through 1926. Second, several significant examples of Surrealist visual practice – one of them a film – exist whose images are intimately bound up with
the sort of linguistic play characteristic of the poetic texts.[24] There are, in
other words, a number of precedents for the kinds of concerns that are evident in *Un Chien andalou*. I am not suggesting, of course, that the film invokes and uses language in the same way as these earlier texts, only that it
shares their interest in playing with language as such and that *Un Chien andalou*, like the poems and objects I have discussed, often draws on the vivid
metaphors and curiously twisted meanings employed in popular idiomatic
speech.[25]

The extent to which the Prologue draws upon phrases from *argot* is, indeed, one of its most striking features. This should not surprise us since the
Surrealists' favorite haunts were underworld and working-class cafes where
"la langue verte" was the *lingua franca*. Recourse to this kind of language explains the recurrence of expressions dealing with deception, boredom,
stupidity, and, of course, sexuality, especially in its most censored forms.[26]
During the rest of the film, variations on these themes (as well as some new
ones), some based on synonyms for words I have discussed, some based on
puns for sound patterns already established, will enter the text especially, as
one might expect, during those sequences marked by striking visual incongruities.[27]

I will confine myself to a few more observations about some of the best
known shots and sequences. The picture of the ants in the protagonist's
palm, for example, is certainly among the most famous in the film (Fig. 5).
This classic image of desire comically literalizes the expression "avoir four-
mis dans les jambes" meaning "to have ants in one's pants," to be itchy. The
noun "la fourmi" also ties together the spectacular digression that ensues. A

Figure 6

Figure 7

series of visual rhymes, subtly supported by a hinted repetition of the central vowel sounds *"our"* (in the shot of the "l'oursin") lead to the high angle shot of the crowd milling about the androgyne poking the severed hand, a scene the French can describe using a figurative sense of the verb "fourmiller," to mill about (Fig. 6).[28] "La fourmi" also has another meaning in

Figure 8

French that connects – albeit more tenuously because at longer range – with another puzzling image seen earlier. The French use the word for ant to describe individuals who work hard, generally at small tasks, and this phrase may in part explain the enigmatic presence of the image of Vermeer's lacemaker, since she is the only figure seen working in the film (Fig. 7). All the rest are conspicuous idlers.[29] I say in part because "La Dentellière," as she is known in French, is also connected with the *teeth* imagery ("les dents") that figures in several scenes, most prominently in the scene with the donkeys and in the scene where the protagonist erases his mouth.[30]

This example illustrates that words do not only tie together the sequences in which they initially appear or in which they are repeated several times. They are also distributed throughout the text, creating unsuspected connections between widely dispersed objects and events. As I noted earlier, the family of words "coup-cul-Kuh-queue" is woven into many different scenes. A word derived from "queue," for example, is invoked at precisely the moment when the hitherto passive protagonist, aroused by the sight of the androgyne's fatal accident, becomes a "queutard" or womanizer. A new word in the family, "le cou," is added in the famous piano-pulling sequence as part of the expression "se mettre la corde au cou" meaning to get married, which is interesting because it invites attention to the ambiguous and hence somewhat "naughty" marital status of the two principal characters (Fig. 8).[31] Moreover, the largest objects he pulls are two grand pianos, in French, "piano à queue." And finally, near the end, when the woman leaves the mysteriously bearded protagonist and runs off with another man, the French could say, mixing two idioms, "elle fait des queues à la barbe de son mari," that is, she is unfaithful to her husband right in front of his (bearded) face.[32]

And this, of course, makes him into a cuckold, a "co*cu.*"

These verbal connections – and there are many others – demonstrate that most of the images are overdetermined, tied together in countless obvious or elusive ways by a series of phrases and concepts. To use Freud's metaphor, each image is like a rebus. In order to pursue its meaning, the film analyst, like the psychoanalyst, must break apart each image into the words or syllables that compose it.[33] That is what I have tried to do with *Un Chien andalou,* undiscouraged by the inaccessibility of Dalí and Buñuel, because in "verbal disguise" dreams, which are the model for this film, "the keys are generally known and laid down by firmly established linguistic usage. If one has the right idea at one's disposal at the right moment, one can solve dreams of this kind wholly or in part, even independently of information from the dreamer."[34]

I do not mean to suggest that I have found *the* meaning of *Un Chien andalou* – or even that the film has *any* meaning. Indeed, the film's playful, tantalizing, but ultimately frustrating lack of an ultimate meaning may be the very basis of its surreality. Certainly it would be unwise to see in the film or in its method anything intimately revealing about its authors other than their knack for appropriating psychoanalytic concepts in a very sophisticated and amusing way. Nor do I want to suggest that the underlying verbal network I have uncovered supplants other sorts of psychoanalytic readings of other aspects of the film. Perhaps the existence of this latent verbal nexus, however, should make film critics who use psychoanalytic theories somewhat more cautious than they have been. What my analysis of *Un Chien andalou* shows is that analysis of the manifest visual content and its symbols may be insufficient. Critics must listen to as well as look at the film text, for, as Anna O. said, psychoanalysis is above all a "talking cure."[35]

Notes

1. Annette Michelson informs me that the script used for the intertitle as well as the phrase itself is part of the advertising for the famous Parisian department store chain. In a film in which the act of looking in its many different modes – staring, gaping, glancing and so forth – plays such a crucial role, the Printemps' advertising slogan, *"au Printemps, j'achète tout les yeux fermés,"* also seems to apply, especially since it is invoked as we observe the doomed lovers, "buried up to their chests in sand, blinded, in rags, being eaten alive by the sun and swarms of insects." Few examples of the black humor beloved by the Surrealists can match this one. I want to take this opportunity to thank Professor Michelson for thoughtfully reviewing an earlier draft of this essay.

2. These are the basic facts known about the making of the film. The script was written jointly by Dalí and Buñuel in Cadaques and Figueras, Spain during January and February, 1929. The script was filmed in six days in Paris and Le Havre during March, and the film was ready to be shown by April of that year. According to Buñuel, a kind of automatic writing was used to generate the film, a process he referred to as a "conscious psychic automatism," involving the probing of the two authors' dream images. The process is most fully described in Luis Buñuel, "Notes on the Making of *Un Chien andalou,"* in Frank Stauffacher, ed. *Art in Cinema* (San Francisco: San Francisco Museum of Art, 1947) 29–30.

154

3. Ibid.

4. "'The essence of this symbolic relation is that it is a comparison, though not a comparison of *any* sort . . . [W]e must admit, too, that the concept of a symbol cannot at present be sharply delimited: it shades off into such notions as those of a replacement or representation, and even approaches that of an allusion." S. Freud, "Lecture X" in *Introductory Lectures on Psychoanalysis* (New York: Norton, 1966) 152 and passim.

5. Ibid.: 175.

6. Sigmund Freud, *The Interpretation of Dreams* (New York: Basic Books, 1953) 342.

7. This is what Buñuel meant when he summarized the method as "CONSCIOUS psychic automatism." "Notes" 29.

8. Dalí and Buñuel developed arcane variants of "verbal images" which have been discussed in depth by Noel Carroll in "Language and Cinema: Preliminary Notes for a Theory of Verbal Images." *Millennium Film Journal* 7/8/9 (Fall/Winter 1980-81): 186–217. Although my discussion suggests that some of Professor Carroll's ideas may need to be reformulated somewhat, I would like to express my debt to this very stimulating essay.

9. Professor Michel Beaujour of New York University wryly reminded me at the outset of this project that my interpretation assumes that Dalí and Buñuel were speaking French and not Spanish. Indeed, I do. By 1929, the year in which the film was conceived and made, both Dalí and Buñuel were effectively fluent in French. Buñuel had begun studying French with French Jesuits when he was thirteen and had lived and worked in Paris for nearly four years. Both he and Dalí had also been actively following French avant-garde developments for many years. Their script was first published in French and, perhaps most important, the primary audiences for their film were the Surrealist groups they aspired to join. See Luis Buñuel, *My Last Sigh* (New York: Vintage Books, 1984), and Dawn Ades, *Dalí and Surrealism* (New York: Harper & Row, 1982). Incidentally, although Breton was the leader of the best-known Surrealist group in Paris, his was not the only one. Much more work needs to be done to define Dalí's and Buñuel's relationship with the very important dissident Surrealist group around Georges Bataille, who was one of the earliest champions of Dalí's work and of *Un Chien andalou*. See his texts "Oeil," *Documents* 4 (September 1929): 216, and "Le Jeu lugubre," *Documents* 7 (December 1929): 297–302.

10. As late as the publication of the *Second Manifesto,* at a moment when orthodox Surrealism's beachhead in the visual arts had long been established and its interest in politics had arguably reached its peak, Breton soberly reminded his readers that "whoever speaks of expression speaks of language first and foremost. It should therefore come as no surprise to anyone to see Surrealism almost exclusively concerned with the question of language at first, nor should it surprise anyone to see it return to language, after some foray into another area, as though for the pleasure of travelling in conquered territory." André Breton, *Manifestoes of Surrealism.* Trans. Richard Seaver and Helen R. Lane (Ann Arbor: University of Michigan Press, 1969): 151-2. Even in 1929, the date of the *Second Manifesto* and of the production of *Un Chien andalou,* therefore, the "magus" of Surrealist orthodoxy presented the "conquest" of *language* as the heart of the Surrealist project and the sure ground on which Surrealism's other achievements were based.

11. For the importance of such narrative markers in Surrealist texts, see Laurent Jenny, "La surréalité et ses signes narratifs." *Poétique* 16 (1973): 499–520.

12. Phillip Drummond, "Textual Space in *Un Chien andalou.*" *Screen,* 18, No. 3 (Autumn 1977): 55–119. One should also consult Linda Williams, *Figures of Desire* (Urbana: University of Illinois Press, 1981) 63ff.

13. Freud, *Interpretation* 400.

14. The cinematic syntax also permits a reading of the woman as a figment of his imagination, a reading that might be confirmed by the suddenness and inexplicability of her presence, the unexplained appearance of a tie in his costume, and the hyperbolic violence that erupts at the end. This interpretation would not significantly affect the underlying linguistic network.

15. "Trancher" is another synonym for "couper," used in such expressions as "tranche de vie" (slice of life) and "trancher (or couper) dans le vif" (to cut to the quick), which is, of course, exactly what we are fooled into believing happens to "her" eye. Could it be that this savage act is actually a kind of joke, the result of a linguistic condensation (in Freud's sense) of two phrases directly relevant to a description of what we watch? Is the "cancelling" of the eye a figure for the cancelling essential to the condensation process?

trancher ~~dans le vif~~

~~trompe~~   l'oeil

trancher   l'oeil

See Sigmund Freud, *Jokes and Their Relation to the Unconscious* (New York: Norton, 1963) 16–89.

16. The possibility of such an interlinguistic pun is supported by the possible existence of two others: the German word for donkey (French: "l'âne") is "Esel" which is pronounced by French speakers very much like the word "aisselle" (armpit) which is featured prominently in two other sequences I discuss below. Another suggested pun involves the cocktail shaker that functions as a doorbell. As I will show, one of the principal conceptual themes of the film involves the playing with words for the sexual and excretory organs such as "queue" and "cul," or as we say in English, cock and tail.

17. "Tranche" (or alternatively, "tronche") also means a jerk or lunkhead in *argot*, a fair description of the "hero" of the film. As such, it links up with a number of expressions with nearly identical connotations – âne-melon-andouille-boite-rasoir-barbe – which figure in the text.

18. Francisco Aranda, *Luis Buñuel* (New York: DaCapo, 1976) and Dawn Ades, *Dalí and Surrealism* (New York: Harper & Row, 1982).

19. Selected texts include: Jacques-André Boiffard, "Nomenclature," *La Revolution Surréaliste* (hereafter *LRS*) 4 (15 July 1925):22; André Breton, "Les Mots sans rides," *Littérature*, Nouvelle Serie 7 (December 1922): 12–14; Robert Desnos, Rrose Sélavy," *Littérature*, N.S. 7 (December 1922): 14–22; Michel Leiris, "Glossaire," in *LRS* 3 (1925): 6–7, 4 (15 July 1925): 20–21, and 6 (1 March 1926): 20–21; Raymond Roussel, *Comment j'ai écrit certains de mes livres* (Paris: Jean-Jacques Pauvert, 1963) 11–35; Roger Vitrac, "Peau-Asie," *Littérature*, N.S. 9 (February–March 1923): 18–20.

20. One can observe similarly aggressive attempted assassinations of language by poets all across Europe during the decade preceding and succeeding the First World War. For a recent account of this phenomenon within the Russian Futurist, Dutch and German Dada circles, see Annette Michelson, "De Stijl, Its Other Face: Abstraction and Cacaphony, or What Was the Matter with Hegel?" *October* 22 (Fall 1982): 5–26.

21. Breton, "Les Mots sans rides," passim.

22. Freud himself was always sensitive to foreign words whose sounds allowed them to be used by his patients to mask unconscious thoughts. Recall the patient's substitu-

tion of the German word "Glanz" (shine) for the English word "glance" in Freud's article "Fetishism" (1927) in Sigmund Freud, *Sexuality and the Psychology of Love,* ed. Philip Rieff (New York: Collier Books, 1972) 214–219.

23. Two highly illuminating essays about the film are: Katrina Martin, "Marcel Duchamp's *Anémic Cinéma,*" *Studio International* (January–February 1975): 53–60. See also Annette Michelson, "Anémic Cinéma, Reflections on an Emblematic Work," *Artforum* (October 1973): 64–69.

24. Rosalind Krauss has recently explored the relationship between language and vision in Surrealist theory in her essay, "The Photographic Conditions of Surrealism," *October* 19 (Winter 1981): 3–34. See also her "Photography in the Service of Surrealism" in Rosalind Krauss and Jane Livingston, eds., *L'Amour Fou* (New York: Abbeville, 1985) 15–54.

25. Analysts of the film must take seriously Buñuel's later comment that "the sources from which the film draws inspiration are those of poetry, freed from the ballast of reason and tradition," that is, the Dada and the Surrealist poetry he admired.

26. Joseph Marks reminds us that ". . . at the outset, slang was linked with the language of the underworld. The vocabulary of thieving and deception, of prostitution and sexual intercourse still figures among its richest elements. Argot . . . is linked not only with a particular *milieu,* but often with specific circumstances. Used out of 'situation' and so away from its normal context it can appear ludicrous if not offensive." See his Introduction to *Harraps French-English Dictionary of Slang and Colloquialisms* (London: George Harrap, 1970) 5. Cf. also Buñuel's memoir *My Last Sigh,* 106, for a brief description of one of their haunts, the "Cyrano" on Place Blanche. The Surrealists' enthusiasm for the underworld milieu is also clearly evident in Brassai's famous *Paris de Nuit* (1933), now available as *The Secret Paris of the 1930s.* (New York: Pantheon Books, 1976).

27. Incongruity per se is not a necessary but it is usually a sufficient sign for the existence of an underlying verbal expression. It is also important to point out that not all sequences are as densely supported by underlying linguistic networks.

28. Incidentally, in an earlier Catalan text entitled "Dues Proses," Dalí imagined an event that similarly links ants and sea urchins with the sensation of anesthesia: "One morning I painted with ripolin a new-born baby which I then left to dry on the tennis court. After two days I found it bristling with ants which made it move with the anesthetized and silent rhythm of sea-urchins. . . ." Quoted in Ades, *Dalí* 51. The pun on "la fourmi" and "fourmiller" also works in Spanish. The word for ant in Spanish is "hormiga," itching is "hormigueo," and "hormiguero" refers both to an anthill as well as to a swarm of people.

29. Many phrases associated with being unemployed, penniless, and at leisure, basic concerns in the "lower depths," also run throughout the text.

30. Teeth are very evident in the scene with the donkeys because Dalí cut back the animals' gums in order to expose them and then set them against the white piano keys. In this shot, visual redundancy helps to evoke the verbal image. Incidentally, Freud connects the image of scales on a keyboard and teeth with sexual fantasies, especially of masturbation, and this may also have a bearing on the moment in the film when the protagonist suddenly grips his mouth as if he were, in the words of the scenario, "quelqu'un qui perd ses dents." Freud, *Interpretation* 371–2, 385–6. It is also important to remember that Dalí remained obsessed for decades with "La Dentellière," which appears here for the first time in his work. See Salvador Dalí, "Aspects phénoménologiques de la methode paranoiaque-critique," in *Oui* (Paris: Gonthier, 1971) 39–52.

31. Buñuel mentions that when he arrived in Paris, he was fascinated by the unmarried couples who lived together. *My Last Sigh* 79. The actor Pierre Batcheff also thereby becomes a "vache."

32. Closely related to the word "barbe," of course, is the word "barbu" which means vulva or pussy, an association that the image clearly suggests, and one for which we have been prepared by the image of the razor sharpened for shaving. "Rasoir" and "barbe" are also both used to refer to people who are boring.

33. Freud, *Interpretation* 288.

34. Ibid. 342.

35. Her famous remark comes from the case history "Fräulein Anna O," in Sigmund Freud and Josef Breuer, *Studies on Hysteria* (New York: Discus Books, 1966) 64.

Between the Sign of the Scorpion and the Sign of the Cross:
L'Âge d'or
Allen S. Weiss

> It is because the Scorpion is infinity that it must, to the contrary, include all of the real; those who said the contrary derive from the possessive infinite spirit's hatred of me, the Real.
> — Antonin Artaud, *Cahiers de Rodez*

In the sixth volume of the Surrealist journal *Minotaure* (Winter 1935), an illumination is reproduced by Pol de Limbourg from the 15th-century manuscript *Les Très Riches Heures du Duc de Berry*, entitled "L'Homme anatomique." Ironically, what is represented is neither anatomical nor a man: it is a dual representation of the posterior of a woman partially eclipsed by the anterior of another woman, bordered by the signs of the zodiac. Marked upon the front of her body are the twelve astrological symbols, each situated upon the part of the body which it governs. Saliently located upon, and immodestly covering, the central position of her genitals is Scorpio, the scorpion. The scorpion, governing the genitals and the anus, is the symbol of sex, excrement and death, dweller in shadows and in hell.

Several years earlier, this symbol of anal-sadistic determinations was to serve as the prologue of the archetypical Surrealist film, *L'Âge d'or*, which opens with a quasi-documentary about scorpions, where we learn of their venomousness, aggressiveness, unsociability and hatred of the sun. As we shall see, the function of this prologue must not be understood simply in terms of a startling diegetic rupture within the film, but rather as a symbolic protasis in which is prefigured a Surrealist "theory" of culture where the established values of sublimation are consistently challenged by the disruptive effects of perversion.

> The demons and the Devil are justified in always leading me towards Evil and towards being for it is by dint of denying it and saying other than what is that God has completely fallen into the mud.
> — Antonin Artaud, *Cahiers de Rodez*

In 1930, the year in which *L'Âge d'or* was filmed and already a year after the great succès de scandale of *Un Chien andalou,* Salvador Dalí wrote an article entitled "L'Ane pourri," in which he defended the ideality of Surrealist imagery as a revolutionary praxis, according to the laws of his "paranoic-critical" method of pictorial production. His claims could have served as the program for the film *L'Âge d'or:*

And we don't know if the desired "land of treasures" is not hidden behind the three great simulacra: shit, blood and putrefaction. Connoisseurs of simulacra, we have long known how to recognize the image of desire behind the simulacra of terror, and even the awakening of the "ages of gold" (âges d'or) behind the ignominious scatological simulacra.[1]

Indeed, the first major diegetical section of *L'Âge d'or,* culminating in the "founding of Rome" cut, is structured according to two parallel but antithetical excremental simulacra. The material foundations of symbolism engender images according to two modes of symbolization: sublimation and perversion, which in turn generate two types of phantasms. Yet it is precisely the perverse manifestations of desire that disrupt the established exigencies of sublimation and, as Dalí claims, "contribute to the ruin of reality . . . lead us to the clear sources of masturbation, exhibitionism, crime, love."[2]

As is well documented in Bourke's *Scatologic Rites of All Nations,* excrement is often found as an ingredient in love potions.[3] This cultivated sign of a scatological erotism, a remnant of primal symbolizations where the potentially dangerous excreta is transformed into a magical good object,[4] restoring to its possessor long lost powers of potency and omnipotence, is but a symbol of the perverse erotic syndrome of coprophilia. Shit, that zero-degree of matter, is erotized by the body,[5] mixing horror and desire in its object as is the case in all fetishism.

Whence the first moment of excremental vision in *L'Âge d'or:* the ceremony of the founding of Rome is interrupted by the screams of a woman wrestling with a man in the mud, in the throes of passion and ecstasy. They are quickly separated, and as the woman is led away, the first phantasm arises for the man: he first fantasizes the woman sitting on a toilet; then simply a toilet with a roll of burning toilet-paper beside it; then the bubbling, steaming lava of a volcano, with the sound of a toilet flushing. The coprophilic event of making love in the mud is doubled in his fantasy of her sitting on a toilet, which is further symbolized by the cosmic hyperbole entailed in the condensation of images of the toilet and volcano (excrement/lava, burning toilet-paper/fiery eruption). As Georges Bataille claims in "L'Anus solaire": "The terrestrial globe is covered with volcanos which serve as the anus."[6] This cosmic/corporeal metaphor, equivalent to that of the scorpion, signifies a perverse modality of eroticism which is intricately bound to a position of rebellion against societal and natural norms. If society is founded upon murder and power, and if, as Canetti claims, excrement "is loaded with our whole blood guilt. By it we know what we have murdered. It is the compressed sum of all the evidence against us,"[7] then it is apparent why during the period of the infant's socialization the anus becomes the place of possession and exclusion. If the individual is to be socialized, what must be excluded is this first sign of our power (good object, gift, magical object, artwork). Such exclusion is the destruction of our own sovereignty, the process whereby the body becomes the topos of its own rejection, i.e. the very scene of sublimation. Death and aggression are organized by the cultural machine of production within the symbolic, and all non-productive expenditure is denigrated.

Excrement, as an image of death, as the formless, as pure heterogeneous matter, is excluded from the order of the symbolic. Excrement is a sign that is doubly threatening to cultural formations: first because it signifies a pure, wasteful expenditure, circumventing societal modes and organizations of production; secondly, because it is a sign of self-production, an autonomous, sovereign creativity which eludes the exigencies of the Oedipal situation, since the origin of the creation of excrement is the body, not the socius. Thus a non-sublimated return to anality in adult life (in art, dreams, delirium, or erotic perversion) breaks the significative chain of quotidian existence by inaugurating a return of the repressed. Yet while the scatological is a mode of ontological heterogeneity, an anti-metaphysical subject position, the pervert is not, unlike the psychotic, outside the symbolic Law. Perversion is the substitution of a personal law for the collective symbolic Law, and is thus a contestation of the Symbolic.

Surrealism attempted to constitute one such set of sovereign, revolutionary laws, and utilized a perverse iconography to express its rebellious critique of culture. L'Âge d'or is a love story which is organized according to such a transgressive mode of eroticism. It recognizes, as Yeats understood, that "Love has pitched his mansion in the place of excrement." This is not only a specific expression of the coprophilic perversion, but a general truth about the very origins of love and culture.

> And I don't engender beings like glossola-
> liating turds [crottes glossolaliantes],
> doubles [doublures] arising from what?
> — Antonin Artaud, *Cahiers de Rodez*

The second moment of the excremental vision in the film is the ceremony of the founding of Rome. This ceremony, which was interrupted by the scatological events previously described, continues with the diminutive master of ceremonies enunciating a speech composed of glossolalic babble (in decidedly adult intonations and timbre), amidst which the only words which may be discerned are, ". . . les matières primaires elles-mêmes" ("the primary matters themselves). In this ironic babbling within a highly civilized event, the highly encoded metalinguistic term "matières primaires" is substituted for the primal infantile term "caca." Consultation of a dictionary on this matter is instructive. *Le Petit Robert: Dictionnaire de la langue française* informs us that on the ontological level, "matière primaire" (primary matter) is that which is "not yet transformed by work," hence it is chaotic matter, pure potentiality. We also discover that by ellipsis, "matières fécales" becomes simply "matières," a euphemism (a subset of irony) synonymous with excrement, feces, stool.

The "matières primaires elles-même" to which the orator refers are none other than the cement in the form of a turd which is placed upon the cornerstone of the foundation of Rome. (And we might note the visual pun in French: the word "fondement" means both "foundation" and "fundament," "ass"). Excrement is indeed the primal matter, serving as gift, tool, weapon, and as the prototype of the artwork. Sublimation is thus a function of the sublation of anal erotism in all activity; coprophilic perversion is the enunciation, the revelation, of the displaced and repressed origins of culture, an objective euphemism.

The history of the Western onto-theological tradition is the history of the disavowal of chaos, matter, the formless, the body proper. Where matter could not be fully disavowed (as is usually the case), it was thoroughly denigrated, so that, for example, within Manicheanism, stemming from the Neo-Platonic tradition, matter was equated with Evil. Within the Scholastic, Aristotelian tradition, "prime matter" is considered to be the lowest grade of sensible existence. And within the history of Scholasticism occurs an ellipsis parallel to that of the etymological ellipsis from "matières fécales" to "matières." This shift is outlined in André Lalande's *Vocabulaire technique et critique de la philosophie* in the article on "Matière":

B. In expressions of Aristotelian and Scholastic origin (and, in this case, always opposed to form): 1. that which, in a being, constitutes the potential, indeterminate element, in opposition to what is actualized; 2. every already determined physical or mental given that an activity receives and ulteriorly elaborates.

Originally the terms "primary matter" and "secondary matter" were used to distinguish these two meanings, but the term "primary matter," passing into current use, has become the synonym of "secondary matter," which has fallen into disuse, in the same time that the Aristotelian idea of pure potentiality was effaced in the word "matter."[8]

As in the case of the substitution of "matière primaire" for "matière fécale," and the ellipsis of "matière" for "matière primaire," the original significance of the term is lexically suppressed, and the denotation of an originary lack of determination on the material level is suppressed. This is a function of cultural censorship, a mode of euphemism which emphasizes the transformative powers of sublimation: the cultural will to overcome and obfuscate its own material origins necessitates this transumption of terms, with all of its inherent ironies. Sublimation is a system of substitutions, deflections, deferrals and differences which function as a metamorphosis of desire. Within this systematic transfiguration of desire, this perpetual displacement of libido, all defenses are tropes which dissimulate the origins and aims of the libido. Eros is deflected from the body and the body's products onto cultural objects and formations, yet the meaning of these sublimated (sublime!) objects are always a function of the primary cathected objects. Thus culture provides a symbolic system which is nothing other than a system of symbols for the body. The civilized disavowal of these origins serves as guarantor of the collective Law of the Symbolic.

The orator's enunciation of the phrase "matières primaires" serves as a magical incantation, a Logos Spermatikos which effects an active reworking of the passive matter to which it refers: the excrement as the foundation of Rome. For, apparently inscribed on that foundation stone are the words: "In the Year of Our Lord, 1930, on the site of the last resting-place of the four Majorcans, this stone was laid as the first foundation for the city of . . ." and we see an aerial view of modern Rome, ". . . Imperial Rome." Within this vast historical ellipsis effected by one cinematic cut, we find that Rome was indeed built, not in a day, but in an instant. Rome, founded circa 600 B.C., was here instantaneously created in the year 1930 A.D.: an ellipsis of 2530 years! This cut produces a chronological ellipsis, a psychological prolepsis, and a narrative irony. Rome, Vatican City, St. Peter's, which are the highest points of Western civilization and the center of Christianity, are seen to be but a sublimation of the "matières primaires" of all creation, i.e. a trope for excrement. Yet this trope is the effect of a peculiarly Surrealist mode of creation, where the temporality inherent in work is abolished within the causality of desire, where creation is instantaneous upon volition. Thus the founding of Rome is here a collective phantasm, where both power as simulacrum and history as phantasmagoria are inaugurated. It is an allegory for the process of sublimation itself. Yet it is diametrically opposed to the individual, sovereign phantasm which preceded it, the perverse excremental vision of the film's hero.

Nineteen-thirty, the year of the "founding of Rome," is also the year in which André Breton wrote the *Second Manifesto of Surrealism,* where he reaffirmed the Surrealist desire to eliminate time and to transform reality according to the forms of our desire.[9] Perfectly in accordance with this project is Harold Bloom's recognition that eros is the will's revenge against time, which leads to the material transformations of all figuration.[10] This revenge, this desire to eliminate time, is made manifest in the instantaneity of the founding of Rome. Yet if the "origins" of Rome are traced back to the babble and excrement of the magical incantation, we find that irony is the central trope of sublimation. History is hysteresis, a trajectory of symptoms, where there are only stories of origins and no real eschatology. History is the grand syntagma of sublimation, where the corporeal, material origins of existence are dissimulated. Historical mimesis is dissimulated by the abstractions of a mathesis universalis which is none other than the program of the universal domination of rationality and the suppression of desire.

Psychoanalytic symptomatology teaches us that origins are the place of a loss: loss of truth, love object, even desire. Such loss necessitates a hermeneutic procedure to reinstate the lacking truth and desire. Yet if the central trope of sublimation is irony, then the central form of an appropriate hermeneutic, genealogical procedure must be parody. If ironic, carnivalesque reversals are the very trajectory of primary matter becoming cultural artefacts, then Bataille is correct in claiming, in "L'Anus solaire," that "the world is purely parodic,"[11] (in obvious contradistinction to Marx's claim that historical events occur twice, "the first time as tragedy, the second time as farce"), and Foucault rightly understands that "Genealogy is history in the form of a concerted carnival."[12]

Yet the founding of Rome entails a paradox about the formation of founding/founded relations, according to the rhetorical figure of fabulation. Rome, the collective phantasm, is not distinguished from perception: thus it becomes the scene of the diegesis which contains the very personages who founded the city. Such a visionary mise-en-scène is emblematic of the idealizing and sublimatory position of Surrealist creativity: origins are metaleptically dissimulated in their effects; culture becomes a symptom. This is the very structure of ideology, where material heterogeneity is dissimulated by present cultural forms. This mode of disavowal entails the fact, as Merleau-Ponty claims, that "every historical object is a fetish."[13] The originary, corporeal paradigm of such material heterogeneity is sexual differentiation, which is codified within the symbolic paternal Law. But it is the constitution of fetishism (the paradigm for all modes of perversion), that inaugurates a revulsive, contestatory set of "laws" outside the symbolic Law of sublimation. Fetishism is the disavowal of representations of sexual differentiation, the condensation of contradictions whereby the lacking female phallus is instituted by metaphor or metonymy as a fetish object. This simultaneous affirmation and denial entails a radical questioning of the very basis of Oedipal Law by the recognition that desire is the law. Such disavowal is a transgression of normative modes of sexual expression: within perversion, the enigma of sexual differentiation cannot be resolved by sexual union, but only by a series of substitutions. In a sense, the pervert cannot merely interpret the world, but must change it, since the very form of sexual difference is antithetical to the exigencies of desire. Thus, as a revolt against the Oedipal Law, perversion entails the revolutionary position of either the murder or forgetting of the idealized father of whom the Law is a symbolic tributary, or, failing that possibility, it entails the ascetic martyrdom of the pervert: one must either change the world or perish.[14]

Hence the radical role of the protagonists' passion in *L'Âge d'or*: the perverse is manifested not only in the coprophilia already discussed, but also by fetishism proper. After the protagonist is separated from his beloved, as he is led through the city he is aroused by the sight of an advertisement for a powder puff, which becomes animated as he phantasizes it as a woman's hand in the act of masturbation; then he is further aroused by the picture of a woman's stockinged legs on another advertisement; and immediately afterwards he sees a photograph of a woman's face in a bookshop window, which in his fantasy is transformed into his beloved lying on a couch, evidently just having masturbated, with a bandaged finger. This phantasm then becomes the next segment of the diegesis: as she arises from the couch, her mother asks her, "Tu as la main bandée?" (Have you got a bandaged hand?) — with the pun on the word "bandée: "bandaged" or "erection." Thus her masturbation takes on the perverse tones of fetishism, with the finger "bandée" as the substitute phallus. And later on, as she is buffing her fingernails (unbandaged), she senses the approach of her lover and, as she becomes aroused, the bandage appears — the substitute phallus is erect.

Thus the substitute gratifications and continual coitus interruptus which determine the course of the narrative must not simply be taken as a result of societal interference and disapproval: rather, it is an integral aspect of the logic of perversion.

> When the state of the world tires you, one draws new forces from sexuality; this is an opium formed by walking and sadness, which aids in ascending higher after a thundering impregnation of the toes and heels with shit, be this a revindicated torture.
>
> — Antonin Artaud, *Cahiers de Rodez*

Richard von Krafft-Ebing, in *Psychopathia Sexualis* (a book known both to the Surrealists and to Bataille), categorized foot fetishism and coprophilia under the same heading: "Disgusting Acts for the Purpose of Self-Humiliation and Sexual Gratification – Latent Masochism – Coprolagnia." We learn, for example, that, "The beatified Marie Alacoque licked up with her tongue the excrement of sick people to 'mortify' herself, and sucked their festering toes."[15]

Hence the appropriateness of the apparent foot fetishism in the culminating love scene of *L'Âge d'or*, where the protagonists attempt to consummate their love in the garden, only to be interrupted yet again. They begin by sucking on the fingers of each others' hands; he then caresses her face with a hand that is missing his fingers: this is no longer a hand "bandée," but now a hand "castrée." Immediately afterwards, the fetishistic substitution for this symbolic castration is indicated: he is distracted by the foot of a nearby statue, and as he is called away to the telephone, she (whether from perversion or sheer desperation) begins to erotically suck and kiss the toes of the statue. This is a substitution and sublimation of symbolic wounds, where apparently the perversions of fetishism and coprophilia are united.

In "Le gros orteil," Georges Bataille explains how the big toe is the most human part of the body: embarassing, ignoble, ignominious, filthy, cadaveresque, fetishistic, deformed, idiotic, and associated with the lowness of mud. For Bataille, human existence is a perpetual exchange between the spiritual and the material, between the high and the low, between garbage and the ideal: the foot, the big toe, is the sign par excellence of material baseness.

It is there that a seduction occurs which is radically opposed to that which is caused by beauty and the light. The two orders of seduction are often confused because we continually move between one and the other; being given this movement of coming-and-going with its termination in either one direction or the other, the more brutal the movement, all the more keen the seduction.[16]

It is precisely with the Surrealist aesthetic that this confusion is valorized: Breton claims in the *Second Manifesto of Surrealism*, following Hegelian metaphysics and Freudian metapsychology, that the goal of Surrealism is to reach the point in the mind where contradictions cease to exist.

We may be seduced by the high or the low or, in psychoanalytic terms, according to the formations of sublimation or perversion. While the act of kissing the statue's foot appears to be a combination of the scatological and fetishistic perversions which determine the protagonists' erotic activities, it is actually the culmination of ironic sublimation. What is kissed is not that lowest part of the human body, a filthy foot, but rather the cold, clean stone foot of a sculpture; the filthy fetish is replaced by an artwork, a cultural object of the highest order, symptomatic of the collective phantasm in which the protagonists find their erotic dissatisfaction. And this dissatisfaction is hyperbolically expressed in the reaction shot of the statue's unmoved, expressionless face: this is the ultimately ironic reaction shot, since there is no reaction at all.

Thus the statue's foot is not a fetish object, but the simulacrum of a fetish, a typically Surrealist conflation of the high and the low (foot as artwork; foot in stone). Indeed, Dalí himself, ceding to Breton's distaste for perversion, excused himself for a scatological image in his painting, *Le Jeu lugubre*, by claiming that, "It was necessary that I justify myself by saying that it was only a simulacrum of excrement."[17] Mutatis mutandis, this explains why the pseudo-fetishism/coprophilia of this event in *L'Âge d'or* is emblematic of the Surrealist ethic and aesthetic, and serves as an allegory of the Surrealist theory of sublimation. It illustrates N. O. Brown's observation that, "Sublimation is a mortification of the body and the sequestration of the life of the body into dead things."[18]

In view of such an aesthetics, with its ironic reversals and extremely idealized sublimations, it might be well to consider the provocation of Bataille's admonishment, "I defy any art lover to love a painting as much as a fetishist loves a shoe."[19] Yet, in turning to consider the epilogue of the film, it might be well to remember too that one also kisses the feet of Christ.

—Do you know anything more outrageously fecal than the history of God and of His being: SATAN?

The Holy Virgin will never rejoin the wife of the Scorpion, never.

The science of Satan is still only that of our surplus.

—Antonin Artaud,
Le Théâtre de la cruauté,
and *Cahiers de Rodez*

The film's epilogue occurs after the final interruption of their lovemaking. The protagonist, in a rage of frustration, defenestrates several symbolic objects: a bishop, a plow, a burning pine tree, a giraffe, and finally the feathers of a pillow that he has torn apart. In a beautiful metaphor, these feathers metamorphize into snow falling on an isolated chateau which the intertitles identify as the Chateau de Selliny (sic), the site where four godless libertines, lead by the Duke of Blangy, retired for 120 days to celebrate the most brutal of orgies. This is, of course, a synopsis of D. A. F. Sade's masterpiece, *120*

Days of Sodom,[20] which is an encyclopedic fictional compendium of the perverse manifestations of desire.

The dissolve from the feathers falling from the window of the Roman mansion (1930) to the snow falling on the Chateau de Selliny (early 18th century) takes place, as the intertitles inform us, at the same time. While the ellipsis responsible for the founding of Rome establishes a progressive temporal shift, indicating a sublimatory activity, the reverse ellipsis from Rome to Selliny establishes a regressive temporal shift, indicative of a desublimating activity.

The ironic reversals inherent in these temporal antitheses are paralleled by the differences in the symbolic topoi of the two scenarios: Rome, the site of the Vatican and St. Peter's, is the center of Christianity; the Chateau de Selliny is the site of the most horrendous atheistic orgies. This opposition is further inherent in the architectural structure of the chateau itself: as described in Sade's text, the tower of the chateau, which originally contained a chapel, was transformed into a privy.[21] This condensation of topoi, of high places and low, of theological and scatological, is yet one more comment on the relations between sublimated and material conditions of existence. Thus, given the fact that coprophagy, the extreme limit of coprophilia, has both a theological (high) and a pathological (low) value, it is not at all surprising that Sade's text goes so far in its radical indictment of culture as to establish a scatological gastronomy!

This reconciliation, or rather, fusion, of sacred and profane topoi is prefigured and mediated by an object that appears earlier in the film: the catholic reliquary which is placed at the feet of some people leaving a limousine as they arrive at the mansion. Such a reliquary contains a putrified waste part of some saint's body, a fetish object: it thus mediates between St. Peter's and Selliny, between the divine and the diabolic, insofar as this corporeal relic is a sign fo both the ideological foundation of the sacred, and the evil inherent in the production of tortured, dismembered bodies. Thus the reliquary serves as the symbolic articulation of the two phantasmatic topoi.

This conflation of the sacred and the blasphemous is also a sign of the most scandalous figure in the film – the Duke de Blangy, organizer of the events at the Chateau de Selliny, appears at the door of the chateau in the form of Jesus Christ. Beyond its apparent shock value, this figure has the same semiotic value as the privy in the chapel and the duplicity of meanings of the reliquary, of Rome and Selliny: according to the Surrealist desire for the reconciliation of opposites, we have a primal psycho-theological identification of God and the Devil, a typically ambivalent expression of love and hate, desire and detestation of the absolute figure of authority. Indeed, as Luther had realized, the worst torment is when "one does not know whether God is the devil or the devil God."[22] Within the phantasm of Rome, that of Judeo-Christian culture, God had been sublimated into a universal homogeneity, where He lost His terrifying, demoniacal character; in the perverse Sadean phantasm of Selliny (Silling), the demoniacal nature of God reappeared by means of a desublimation, as also occurs in our nightmares and in the temptations of the saints. The devil, as a sublimated manifestation of anality, signifies the repressed aspects of the deity. Within such a desublimated position, which manifests the base material origins of existence, there are basically two possible alternatives: one may accept, for example, the position of the Cathar heresy, which does not recognize the possibility of a material manifestation of divinity. As one pious Cathar mother explained to her daughter: "Do not believe, daughter, that a man of flesh, who produces excrement, can save souls."[23] Hence the desacralization of the figure of Christ. The alternative is that of the Stercoranist heresy, which attests to "The grossly sensual conception of the presence of the Lord's body in the sacrament, according to which that body is eaten, digested, and evacuated like ordinary food. . . ."[24] Hence the sacralization of excrement.

André Breton glorified Teresa de Avila's vision of her wooden cross transformed into a crucifix of precious stones.[25] This is hardly the image with which *L'Âge d'or* ends: we see here a Sadean cross, with several scalps hanging from it. Rather than bearing the body of Christ, it bears parts of the dismembered bodies of the victims of Blangy's orgies. Yet in both symbols, the notion of the expiatory suffering of the innocent is the rationalization of death: within Christian theology, Christ's sacrifice was necessary for the expiation of humankind's sins; within the Sadean universe, the sacrifice of the innocent was necessary for the realization of the libertine's perverse pleasures. (Hence the exultation with which our protagonist says, during the final love scene, "What joy! What joy to have murdered our children!").

This final symbol of the cross with the scalps hanging from it establishes the same signification as was figured by the symbol of the scorpions with which the film began: the anal realm of the devil governing perverse sexuality, excrement and death. (And we might remember that in Christian iconography, the scorpion appears on the shields of the Roman soldiers who assisted at Christ's crucifixion).[26]

Writing of Sade's *120 Days of Sodom,* Georges Bataille, in a marginal note to the manuscript of *Le petit,* provides a gloss which may serve as an epilogue to the film *L'Âge d'or*:

The age of gold is an infinite conflagration, but real eroticism leaves the age of gold to enter into chance . . .[27]

The problem is that the Sadean libertine cannot transform the entire world into a Sadean chateau. Thus, in relation to such erotic desires of mastery, an infinite conflagration would be nonsense. Hence the fall into a material heterology. And yet, isn't sublimated civilization itself the site of the loss of the "age of gold"? Isn't this precisely the reason of the film's tragedy and Sade's irony?

> The body is the first abstraction.
> Antonin Artaud, *Cahiers de Rodez*

Nineteen-thirty was the year of the "founding of Rome;" it was the year in which *L'Âge d'or* was made; and it was the year in which Breton wrote the *Second Manifesto of Surrealism,* which made definitive the rupture in the Surrealist movement, most notably the excommunication of Artaud and Bataille. In this manifesto, Breton criticizes Bataille insofar as, "M. Bataille pro-

168

fesses to wish to consider in the world 'that which is vilest, most discouraging, and most corrupted. . . ." Hence, "It is to be noted that M. Bataille misuses adjectives with a passion: befouled, senile, rank, sordid, lewd, doddering. . . ." Such monomania is explicated by a citation from Marx, which Breton presents in obvious reference to Bataille's "Le gros orteil": "Marx tells us how, in every age, there thus come into being hair-philosophers, fingernail-philosophers, toenail-philosophers, excrement-philosophers, etc." And in further reference to Bataille's article, "La figure humaine," Breton ridicules Bataille's supposed love of flies:

The only reason we are going on at such length about flies is that M. Bataille loves flies. Not we: we love the miters of old evocators, the miters of pure linen to whose front point was affixed a blade of gold and upon which flies did not settle, because they had been purified to keep them away. M. Bataille's misfortune is to reason: admittedly, he reasons like someone who "has a fly on his nose," which allies him more closely with the dead than with the living, but he does reason.[28]

Thus Bataille, according to Breton, wishes to share his obsessions, and in the communication of such obsessions he is already within the realm of ideology; since his obsessions form a de facto system, he cannot be logically opposed to all systems.

In Bataille's response to Breton, "La 'vieille taupe' et le préfixe sur dans les mots surhomme et surréaliste," Bataille counters with an epigram which is also from Marx: "In history as in nature, the rotten is the laboratory of life." Bataille accuses the Surrealists of "pretentious idealist aberrations" and utopianism, and elsewhere claims that they are "idealist nuisances" (emmerdeurs idéalistes).

More exactly even, since Surrealism is immediately distinguishable by a share of base values (the unconscious, sexuality, filthy language, etc.), it is concerned with giving these values an eminent character by associating them with the most immaterial values.[29]

Thus the grounds of the rupture within Surrealism are precisely the terms of the irony in L'Âge d'or, i.e. the relative position of the two phantasms. The question is whether revolutionary action is to be effected according to a sublimated or desublimated version of dialectical materialism.

Indeed, Bataille loves flies. In a parodic critique of the metaphysical tradition, Bataille writes in "La figure humaine":

It is impossible to reduce the apparition of a fly on an orator's nose to the supposedly logical contradiction between the self and the metaphysical totality (for Hegel this fortuitous apparition would simply be attributed to the "imperfections of nature.") But, if we lend a general value to the improbable nature of the scientific universe, it would be possible to proceed to an operation contrary to that of Hegel and to reduce the apparition of the self to that of the fly.[30]

We will remember that the condition of having a fly on the nose was depicted in L'Âge d'or, when during the party in the mansion the father is seen talking, quite nonchalantly, his face covered with flies. A typically Surrealist sardonic conciliation of opposites: the flies, associated with filth, excrement and garbage (base materiality), cover the face, which is the highest part of the human body, the mask that hides the human soul. This contradiction is obviously "corrected," desublimated, in the acephalic condition of the women in the Chateau de Selligny whose scalps are seen fluttering on the cross.

It is not in Surrealism but in neo-Dadaism that we find an unambiguous expression of this base materiality: Marcel Duchamp's *Torture morte* (1959), which is a plaster cast of a foot covered with flies. The foot, the flies, and death are all characteristics of the lowest level of materiality, of the unformed. Such a desublimatory iconography is at one of the centers of Duchamp's system of representations, and was already evident in his short film, *Anémic cinéma* (1925–26). The titles of the film may be read as the refusal to sublimate; the form of the film, spiraling titles alternating with visual spirals, without representational images or narrative connection, make this film the antithesis of the Surrealist project (as Dada in most cases was). Among the titles is: "L'enfant qui tète est un souffleur de chair chaude et n'aime pas le chou-fleur de serre chaude (The nursing infant is a lover of hot flesh and doesn't like hot-house cauliflowers). Here, the infant at the breast refuses a substitute breast, the cauliflower, and in doing so refuses the refined product of cultural creation – this condition is parodied in the visual spirals, some of which appear in the form of a breast. Sublimation is refused; the corporeal, material condition of erotic existence is valorized.

> I am an anarchist, a pariah, a fanatic [un enragé], a serf of the heart and the soul.
> – Antonin Artaud, *Cahiers de Rodez*

Artaud played a brief but central role in the development of the Surrealist movement. In 1925 he was made the director of Le Bureau des recherches surréalistes, and in the third issue of *La Révolution surréaliste* we find his report on the activities of the bureau. And yet, within that very report is a central theme of Artaud's work, a theme antithetical to the Surrealist ethic: "Surrealism registers a certain order of repulsions rather than beliefs." Just as was the case for Bataille, Artaud's excommunication from the Surrealist movement must be understood according to his basic desublimatory position. Breton first denounces Artaud in *Au grand jour,* a pamphlet published in 1927, where Artaud is characterized in terms of his "veritable bestiality," doubtlessly because of the vehemence, candor and baseness of Artaud's diatribes against established values and institutions. Artaud's response, much like Bataille's, revolved around the nature of the politicization of the Surrealist movement. In "À la grande nuit ou le bluff surréaliste," Artaud explains that "all of the exasperations of our quarrel turn around the word Revolution." Artaud didn't believe that a collective social revolution could change the nature of existence, which could only be changed by a "metamorphosis of the interior conditions of the soul." Thus the Surrealists were "revolutionaries who revolutionize nothing," and merely creators of "grotesque simulacra."[31] We must remember that by this time, Surrealism was already "au service de la révolution": while Artaud wished to inaugurate a psychical revolution, and Bataille wished, to the contrary, to recognize the material level of the revolution, they both opposed surrealist aestheticizations and idealizations.

While the vehemence and scatological vision did not reach its blasphemous limits until Artaud's *Cahiers de Rodez* which were written during his incarceration in 1945–46, his central concern with desublimation was already made manifest in his early Surrealist writings and especially in his theory of the theater of cruelty, an anti-dialectical art of difference, transgression and forgetting. Such a theater is a mode of artistic production, and not reproduction or representation: it is the scene in which enunciation is no longer ruled by a metaphysical Logos. This was also to be the condition of his madness at Rodez. And it was, no doubt, one of the preconditions of his expulsion from the Surrealist movement. A vision of sovereignty, perversion and madness could never be in accordance with a vision of collectivity, sublimation and joy.

> We must make reason shit.
> [Il faut faire chier la raison.]
> — Antonin Artaud, *Cahiers de Rodez*

The irony of the "age of gold" is apparent. Freud reminds us that, "We know how the money which the devil gives his paramours turns to excrement after his departure,"[32] and in a more general sense Bataille explains the antithetical condensation of these terms:

While in a dream a diamond has an excremental signification, this does not occur only through an association by contrast: in the unconscious, jewels as excrements are accursed matter which flow from a wound, from the parts of oneself destined to an ostensive sacrifice (they serve in fact as sumptuous gifts charged with sexual love.[33]

This gift, this stain of love, may originate in either sublimatory or desublimatory phantasms, may be either romantic or perverse. The symbolic wound, the sacrifice, may be a sign of either a Liebestod, or a totem. Two dreams may illustrate this difference.

In one dream a priest reached into the patient's rectum and pulled out an arabesque fecal piece to be used in a ceremony.[34]

This is an expression of a process of self-repair, of a cure, of the renewed self-realization of value. Hence the trajectory of the object in question: from worthless excrement to valuable, albeit perhaps still fetishistic, sacred object. This dream signifies the same phantasm as that of the "founding of Rome": it is an allegory of sublimation.

The second dream is recounted by Bourke in his *Scatological Rites of All Nations*:

... which represents Zador as making a compact with his satanic majesty whereby in exchange for Zador's soul the devil discloses a gold mine in a graveyard, from which the poor dupe extracts enough for his present needs, and then marks the locality by an ingenious method, only to be awakened by his angry wife to the mortifying consciousness that he has defiled his own bed . . .[35]

If the object of a ceremony is subsequently maintained as a relic, as is the case in fetishism and totemism, then it is particularly appropriate that this goldmine is to be found in a graveyard: the trajectory of devaluation of the object (from gold to excrement) is a sign of the recognition of the corporeal origin and limit of existence, as well as the teleological limit of limits: death. Whence the impossibility of living in the Age of Gold.

In the *Cahiers de Rodez* Artaud explains how he too was driven from Paradise, and that this was doubtlessly a result of the fact that, "my consciousness is not in my mouth but in my cunt."[36] Here, consciousness is not a function of human or Divine Logos, but rather of the corporeal place of sex and excrement. And that this place be his own female genitalia reveals that his rebellion, his quest for self-engenderment at Rodez, his madness, led him to discover the very secrets of sexual differentiation, and led him to live this difference. Within that psychiatric cloister, Artaud lived as man and woman, God and Devil, Christ and Anti-Christ. Rather than excluding the representations of sexual differentiation from consciousness, as is the case in fetishism, he lived this difference in seriality, in alternating subject positions which marked the multifarious possibilities of psychic delirium.

But what are we to make of Artaud's delirium, his solution; we, whose very presence here attests to the extent to which we value the objects, rituals and effects of sublimation? Bataille provides one possibility:

From the moment that the effort of rational comprehension ends in a contradiction, the practice of intellectual scatology requires the dejection of the inassimilable elements; this amounts to saying, crudely, that a burst of laughter is the only imaginable, definitely final, outcome, and not the means, of philosophical speculation.[37]

Such a laugh is a non-material excrement, an expulsion of the exigencies of reason, a valorization of the material heteronomy of existence. This is a Nietzschean laugh of affirmation and celebration, of parody and irony: it is meant to shatter the silence imposed by the theological and ontological infinity of the cosmic void which for Pascal was God. Such laughter is the sign of an atheological certainty, where we finally recover both language and the body, liberated from metaphysical closure. Eros is no longer a metaphysical supplement, but an originary disruption in existence. Yet such a laugh nevertheless remains vocal, and is always in danger of being appropriated by the cultural system of linguistic signifiers which it purports to disrupt. Hence one more contradiction; hence we must laugh again.

Notes

All translations from sources listed in French are my own. I wish to express my deep thanks to Annette Michelson, to whom I owe both the central theme and several specific observations of this article. I also wish to thank Jacob John Berger for a seminar presentation on Bourke and Dominique Laporte which was of great help.

1.   Salvador Dalí, "L'âne pourri," in *Oui* (Paris: Denoël/Gonthier, 1971) 2: 158–59.

2.   Idem.

3. John G. Bourke, *Scatologic Rites of All Nations* (New York: Johnson Reprint Co., 1981) 216.

4. Melanie Klein, "On the Relation Between Obsessional Neurosis and the Early Stages of the Super-ego," in her *The Psychoanalysis of Children* (New York: Delacorte Press, 1975) 165.

5. Marcel Hénaff, *L'Invention du corps libertin* (Paris: Presses Universitaires de France, 1978) 238.

6. Georges Bataille, "L'Anus solaire," in *Oeuvres complètes* (Paris: Gallimard, 1970) 1:85. Note that in *Story of the Eye* (New York: Urizen, 1977, p. 25) Bataille likens the cunt to a volcano: this establishes an inverse but equally cloacal and scatological equivalence to that of anus and volcano. Cf. Artaud's reference to the "solaire anus roulant" (*OC* 19:11). The symbolically transgressive roles of the volcano in Sade is also of interest.

7. Elias Canetti, *Crowds and Power* (New York: Continuum, 1981) 211.

8. André Lalande, *Vocabulaire technique et critique de la philosophie* (Paris: PUF, 1972) 595–596.

9. André Breton, *Second Manifesto of Surrealism* (1930), in *Manifestoes of Surrealism* (Ann Arbor: University of Michigan Press, 1969) 128.

10. Harold Bloom, "Freud's Concepts of Defense and the Poetic Will," in *Agon* (New York: Oxford University Press, 1982) 136. Cf. also my "The Other as Muse: On the Ontology and Aesthetics of Narcissism," forthcoming.

11. Georges Bataille, "L'Anus solaire" 81.

12. Michel Foucault, "Nietzsche, Genealogy, History," in *Language, Counter-Memory, Practice* (Ithaca: Cornell University Press, 1977) 161. Cf. also my "The Body Dionysian: Nietzsche, Freud, Merleau-Ponty," in *The Great Year of Zarathustra*, ed. D. Goicoechea, (Lanham MD: University Press of America, 1983) passim.

13. Maurice Merleau-Ponty, *The Visible and the Invisible* (Evanston: Northwestern University Press, 1968) 275. Cf. Artaud's question: "What is being? A totem. . . ." (*OC* 19:80).

14. Guy Rosolato, "Étude des perversions sexuelles à partir du fetichisme," in *Le désir et la perversion.* (Paris: Seuil, 1967) passim.

15. Richard von Krafft-Ebing, *Psychopathia Sexualis* (New York: Bell, 1965) 123ff. Such foot fetishism is also noted by Bataille, op. cit., 204. The dual meaning of the fetish as symbolic object and displaced non-existent body part, is made evident in René Magritte's painting *Philosophy in the Bedroom* (a reference to Sade's novel of the same name) where a shoe is partially metamorphized into a foot.

16. Georges Bataille, 204; cf. Artaud's similar assertion that "the toes are sexual" (*OC* 19:149).

17. Salvador Dalí, *La vie secrète de Salvador Dalí* 202. The polemic between Breton (especially in the *Second Manifesto of Surrealism*) and Bataille (especially in "Dossier de la polémique avec André Breton, *OC* II) is of special interest here. As a humorous example of intertextuality, in Water's film *Pink Flamingos,* Divine (!), while desecrating the house of an enemy by licking everything in it, briefly licks a small model of a foot.

Such ironic reversals of high and low are elsewhere apparent in this scene: during the internal dialogue (!) between the two lovers, one asks the other, "where is the light switch?," and the response is, "At the foot of the bed;" hence through a gross catachresis that which controls the light (pure, high) is to be found at the *foot* of the bed (low, base, fetishistic). Furthermore, when the Minister of the Interior commits suicide as a result of the protagonist's political incompetence, we see a blood stain, a revolver, and his shoes (!) on the floor, and the camera pans up to show that his body has hit the ceiling: this reverses the prevailing belief that after death the soul ascends and the body becomes part of the earth. Here it is the body that rises.

The interplay of spirituality and materiality, sexual and sublime, is doubled by the signification of the music played during this scene, from *Tristan und Isolde.* We should note that this opera is a tale of passion being worked and diverted through substitution and interruption. While the kissing of the statue's foot serves as an allegory of Surrealist iconography, the diegetic background music serves as an allegory of Surrealist narratology, and of sublimation in general.

18. Norman O. Brown, *Life Against Death* (Middletown: Wesleyan University Press, 1959) 298.

19. Georges Bataille, "L'esprit moderne et le jeu des transpositions," in *OC* 1:273.

20. It should be noted that Sade was taken to be one of the precursors of Surrealism, as noted by Breton in the *First Manifesto of Surrealism.* Sade is also central to Bataille's atheological project, as is made evident in his "Dalí hurle avec Sade" (*OC* II), and "La Valeur d'usage de D. A. F. Sade" (which is part of his polemic with Breton), "Sade et Platon," as well as sections of his major works *Death and Sensuality* and *Literature and Evil.* Sade was also included in Breton's later *Anthologie de l'humour noir.*

21. N. O. Brown, 203. Brown also informs us that as for Luther's recognition that one's life must be justified by faith, Luther says that, "This knowledge the Holy Spirit gave me on the privy in the tower."

22. Ibid. 217. It might be remembered that just as the figures of Christ and Blangy are conflated in this film, Nietzsche, as he entered into madness, identified himself in his last letters variously as Dionysus and The Crucified; Artaud, during his incarceration at Rodez, identified himself variously as Christ and Anti-Christ, God and Devil.

23. Emmanuel Le Roy Ladurie, *Montaillou* (New York: Vintage, 1979) 299.

24. Bourke, 54. Bakhtin, throughout *Rabelais and His World,* discusses the scatological aspects of the carnivalesque reversals of power and symbols. In particular, consider that during the medieval festival of fools, the elected bishops used to utilize dung instead of incense.

25. Ferdinand Alquié, *The Philosophy of Surrealism* (Ann Arbor: University of Michigan Press, 1969) 130.

26. In a 14th-century gradual, illuminated by Silvestro dei Gherarducci, (in the collection of the Morgan Library), there is an illuminated letter "C" which contains a scene of the Last Supper, where Judas is distinguished by a black halo with scorpions inscribed on it.

27. Georges Bataille, "Notes to *Le Petit,*" *OC* 3:498.

28. Breton, *Second Manifesto* 181–185.

29. Georges Bataille, "La 'vieille taupe' et le préfixe *sur* dans les mots *surhomme* et *surréaliste,*" *OC* 2:103.

30. Georges Bataille, "La figure humaine," *OC* 1:184. This view was also expressed in Nietzsche in "On Truth and Lie in an Extra-Moral Sense," where he writes: "But if we could communicate with the mosquito, then we would learn that it floats through the air with the same self-importance, feeling within itself the flying center of the world."

31. Antonin Artaud, "A la grande nuit ou le bluff surréaliste," *OC* 1:363ff.

32. Sigmund Freud, "Character and Anal Erotism," in *Character and Culture* (New York: Collier, 1972) 31.

33. Georges Bataille, "La notion de dépense," in *La part maudite* précédé de La notion de dépense (Paris: Minuit, 1967) 29.

34. Michael Eigen, "Musings on Freud and Schreber: Breakthrough and Failure" (Unpublished manuscript, presented at the conference *Schreber and Contemporary Thought,* held at SUNY Stony Brook, April 1984; p. 14).

35. Bourke, 401.

36. Antonin Artaud, *Cahiers de Rodez,* in *OC* 17:74.

37. Georges Bataille, "La valeur d'usage de D. A. F. Sade," in *OC* 2:64.

Documentary Surrealism:
On *Land without Bread*

Tom Conley

In a certain fashion the cinema of Surrealism conditioned the great narrative styles that dominated film of the 1930s. Today it can offer ways of theorizing narrative in fictional or feature film. Its legacy is important for the study of the history and technique of documentary cinema, where truth generally takes precedence over the rhetoric articulating its realism. The violence of "facts" in documentaries overwhelms spectators by blinding the critical power of the eye to the esthetics that constitute the very basis of its veracity. Analysis of surreal cinema, it seems, re-establishes that power. In this respect, the legacy of Surrealism seems to be perpetually active; it cannot merely be studied as a moment in an evolution of cinema because it persistently questions the order of any history that would pigeonhole it in the European milieu of the 1920s.

The relationship between Surrealism and documentary cinema is exceptionally productive. Surrealism did not actively pursue the documentary or ethnographic cinema to further its manifesto of 1924. Yet with *Land without Bread* (1932, also titled as *Las Hurdes, Terre sans pain, Tierra sin pan, Unpromised Land*), Buñuel, a signatory of the second *Manifeste du surréalisme*, appears to be one of its most important proponents. *Land without Bread* is absolutely crucial to documentary realism and stands, we shall argue, as a model that tests all *cinéma-vérité*. The paragraphs which follow shall examine the junctures, rifts or punctuations by which its filmic style appears to be fashioned. Attention will be directed away from the subject of the film – a forlorn corner of Spain in the early 1930s – in order to dwell on some modes that convey the disquiet of its documentary. Five aspects will be taken up: 1) the compositional ensemble and its overall visual effects; 2) the very cursive use of the lap-dissolve; 3) the uncanny framing that both conceals and manifests a cinema of sacrifice (as we shall see, "scapegoating" in a quite literal sense); 4) the breakdown of illusory space through the presence of writing or scripture in the cinematic frame, and 5) the nagging presence of a latently Spanish painterly tradition foregrounding the representation of the Hurdano population.

The Compositional Ensemble

As the appended shot sequence evinces, *Land without Bread* consists of 238 shots over a duration of twenty-seven minutes (or about 865 meters of film).

Even if averaged to a mean of seven seconds per shot, the total number would be inordinately high for a documentary. The film abounds with varied shots; its sheer number would lead a viewer to believe that the film is inspired by Eisensteinian montage instead of poetic realism. Cursory viewing proves otherwise, since the impression is one of redundancy, inertia, and unchanging, unmediated portraits of life on the verge of death. It may be that the thematic orientation of *Land without Bread,* dealing unremittingly with a moribund culture that refuses to die in the midst of the "hostile forces" surrounding it, produces an effect of stasis contrary to the liveliness of the *découpage.* Or else, the contradiction between the dizzying ensemble of shots and sequences entirely betrays the deathly interpretation the sound track imposes upon the array of images.

Unlike the tradition of montage, the shots rarely depend on each other for their resonance or continuity of meaning. Generally, each is composed as a unified segment carrying rich paradox within itself, as well as in relation to shots both in the immediate context (three to six shots before and after) and in the scope of the entire film (a shot near the end will modulate or rhyme with a scene in the early moments of the exposition). Thus the viewer's eye is asked to extend its field of perception beyond the scope of narrative and montage. Only one sequence shows signs of cross-cutting, and this is in the final seconds (shots 222–236), where the Hurdano household, finishing its evening meal and preparing for slumber, is punctuated by the arrival of an old lady knelling death in an adjacent street. Yet even this hardly appears contrived enough to hasten the viewer to associate the end of the film with a cherished Iberian topos of sleep bringing on dreams of death or monsters. The closeups of the old hag are too deliciously creatural and the bedtime is too staged to allow us to fall into a commonplace. We wonder how the lighting is achieved so well in *contrejour;* how the locals can mime sleep under the glare of light shed upon them; how the extreme closeup of the old soothsayer's wrinkled face has been shot in the illusion of night. Cinematic issues of composition break the sense of movement inherent to cross-cutting, to the point that the spectator can wonder if the bell of death and slumber is apposed to the real death and sleep of the film – that is, its own end. In the mechanism of transfer common to surreal cinema, the contiguity of this sequence in respect to the end of the film suggests that *we* are being chimed to sleep, that we are seeing ourselves die when the film ends.

Such an obviously loose or open montage could suggest that the director is crafting a double-edged film. On one side, *Land without Bread* is shot in a style that conveys "reality" by virtue of deep-focus photography, where everything in the field of view is focused and subject to documentary report, and where the shot itself has content ample enough to be deciphered patiently. In this latter sense the view of the Hurdano world would depend on the building block of poetic realism, the long take, which is also associated with Renoir, Flaherty, Wyler, or other champions of reality. But the shooting sequence tells us it does not: with the 238 shots in twenty-nine minutes, there is (seemingly) hardly any sign of the long take, or even a shot of teasingly extended duration – from ten to forty seconds – that we would align with the realistic tradition. Hence, the other side: Buñuel forces the viewer

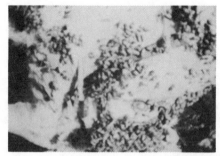

Shot 11   Shot 136

to compress the effects of the long take into disgruntling rapidity. Most of the
shots suggest careful (as we shall note, painterly) composition, but the
editing either does not allow the viewer to comprehend them in rational
cinematic terms, or else it radicalizes the realistic style, defining and distorting its principles simultaneously, somewhat before the style gains historical
currency.

The latter might be due to the surreal backdrop informing the film. Evidently many visual compositions reiterate scenes from *Un Chien andalou*
(shots 11, 102, 136, etc.) and *L'Age d'or* (the bull exiting into the street in shot
11 recalling the plow Gaston Modot tosses from the apartment window, or
the rocky landscape in the mountain goat sequence reiterating the seaside of
rocks and bishops' bones), but they are executed in a context of veracity. By
reducing the future trademark of realism to a minimum, the film adduces
how the oneiric camera, seen in the immense field of unmediated contradictions, yields documentary reality. All the more astonishing – and this point is
advanced to insist on the pertinence of *Land without Bread* in the tradition of
documentary cinema, which criticism does not emphasize enough – is that
truth is always identified with equilibrium.

The shots have pictural austerity in their tensions of form. All the drastic
shifts from closeups or medium shots to extreme long shots (in 46–47, 51–52,
88–89, 152–58, 177–78, 236–37, etc.) are contextualized or softened with
fade-outs or infrequent dissolves. Countrysides are intermediate scenes
separating the sequences depicting the different activities of everyday life.
The balance in the compositions is so striking that every shift can only be
smooth, no matter how extreme the gaps are from one sequence to another.
Most of the cinematography reflects the intensely unremitting glare of the
Spanish sun. High contrasts of light and shade would generally produce a
jagged tempo of hard edges in succession; yet the equilibrium of the whole is
enhanced by the emphasis on absence of penumbra. Humans are portrayed
under a bright sky and are deprived of shadows or soft forms that might
modify – or humanize – their depiction. The film disallows any visual redemption of mankind in settings that might offer comfort, relief, or any empathy to be shared among viewers and subjects (especially in shots 4, 13, 21,
40, 62, 81, 87, 95, 126, 156, 158, 211–13, 217, and so forth).

178

The voice-off establishes the documentary continuity. It tends to freeze the images by directing the viewer's eyes to only several of many elements (generally the human as opposed to the natural or organic or seasonal ones) in frame. Betraying, trivializing, or, better, repressing many of the visuals, it marks a difference of consciousness. When the voice reflects the view of a focused, "Western" or industrial view of continuity, history, culture, humankind, or missionary reason, the visuals provide a rich flow of images exceeding – in pleasure, disgust, wonder, Eros, marvel – what the voice or Brahms's accompaniment cannot express about them. A psychoanalytic process emerges from that difference, but in such a manner that, like the synchronous production of *Civilization and Its Discontents* (also issued in 1932), the film implies that the voice cannot be dissociated from repression of optical splendor. The pictogrammatical element avers to be the film's unconscious; it is evident, clear, and immediately accessible. When disaster or plight is reported (in the British accent of the colonizer), oblivious to what is being said of them, children smile at the camera. They contradict the anthropological project of redemption (most evident in shots 21, 61, 71 or in the dwarf sequence). It would be oversimple to observe that the film scaffolds a double bind in the contradiction between voice and image, as *Land without Bread* does not merely question the viewer's right to see the sacred – hence invisible – side of Hurdano culture. It articulates a highly varied tempo of shifts that modulate repulsion and attraction within a unified narrative.

Lap Dissolves and Extended Perspectives

Not only a basic unit of perspective in Surrealist cinema, the dissolve provides transitions essential for narrative. It also, paradoxically, allows the greatest initial access to the "other" or obverse side of the composition of *Land without Bread.* The dissolve "opens" the obsessions of the film and places all stages of consciousness, history, and documentary on the same surface. In these transitions the stable relation of a figure to a ground is lost; the image becomes of a texture, but also, like a manifest dream, a rebus. In these instants the process of displacement and condensation conditions the rhetoric of the film. The dissolve is clearly a modus vivendi of Surrealism, but less so of documentary. In narrative cinema, it mediates conscious and unconscious realities to the degree it produces the very ideology of the unconscious.[1]

Five dissolves punctuate *Land without Bread.* Each marks the film at a moment seemingly unrelated in time and space to the others. As in the overall impressions lent by the montage, a classical, somewhat restrained use of the transition would also underscore the same documentary motives at the heart of the film. The dissolve never dominates enough to project an oneiric dimension onto the content, as had been the practice in *Un Chien andalou* only four years before. In that film the dissolve is so frequent that distinctions between shots are hard to draw; at least forty mark the duration of twenty-four minutes. In contrast, in the light of realism in this film, the dissolve gives credence to the director's effort to associate each shot with

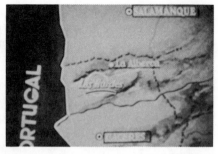

Shot 1   Shot 3

raw, unmediated truth. When the dissolve is used, it would appear "natural" or simply part of a deliberately controlled style.

The first dissolve elides the credits (shots 1–2) into the clouds over which they are written. The second, immediately following (three collages make up shot 3), superimposes a relief map of Europe, Iberia, and Western Spain over one another. In effect, the eye is dissolved into the film before it can witness the ensuing truth which would be located through or beyond the screen. The style in the initial shots virtually slides the viewer from a dreamy, cottony, nebulous condition to the hard edges of the world. Clouds and a protean mass of geographic relief give way to shots of archaic streets in crisp deep focus.

One minute later (in shot 34), in a transition moving from city to country, the fourth dissolve registers a passage from a long shot to a closeup of the Western tower of a Baroque church nestled in a valley. Begun from above, a long track flows from the altitudes into the darker depths of trees growing around the church. Next, in countertilt (from the ground), an attractive, sturdy peasant woman is portrayed. Only near the end of the film do other dissolves recur: one (shot 150), in closeup, moves from a shot of running water at the edge of a river to a man-made embankment of soil held up by rock walls; another, in medium depth (adjacently, in a brief volley in shots 146–49), depicts peasants who are cutting brush. The voice-off explains that these men provide fertilizer for the terraced soil along the edge of the river. The two transitions evoke a culture of gatherers, the passage of agrarian time, and, like the initial dissolves, have nothing particularly striking about them.

Unless the surreal mode of the dissolve is kept in view as a highly charged graphic form, the transition appears only to punctuate the film with balance and restraint. Upon closer view, the dissolves telescope passage of seasons and labors. Shorter, contingent rhythms of change are erased in favor of a temporal oblivion, or a medieval naturalism. Cycles of growth and regeneration mark the image-track exactly when the voice-off reports of endless erosion and futility. Betraying the voice, the transitions effectively disallow the narration from acceding to the status of document. Despite its restrained style, *Land without Bread* is never far in time, space, or history from the ex-

Shot 147   Shot 149

perience of *Un Chien andalou* or *L'Age d'or;* their style often depends upon the fugacious emergence of one dissolve from many others. Boundaries between objects and planes of depth are melted in reality as well as in dream; for a moment, forms swim indiscriminately and without apparent contradiction. The dissolve would embody film as automatic writing, where a primary process could be glimpsed, lost, and then retrieved through subsequent viewings.

There is no reason to see why the same device does not advance the principles of cinematic realism. By suggesting that an undeniable flow of force and endless, timeless energy is inaccessible to the eye but ubiquitously visible, surreal cinema could make the unconscious manifest. *Land without Bread* suggests that realism accomplishes the task no less effectively than vanguard experiment.

The fourth dissolve is most obvious; for the great tower of the church is identified with the heroic stature of the peasant woman. Dissolving *into* her, the shot implies that she is a timeless bedrock of the universe. The tower penetrates the female from below at the same time it is identical to her. The vacuity of shadow cast from the rounded arch of the entry to the narthex of the church is situated by her belly, in such a way that the play of the erection, penetration, and containment are absolutely unified within the space of the dissolve. The female is fornicated by the spire, its extension traveling up through her body; yet it also is the cavernous area defining her belly. Thus any "subliminal" effect of this penetration is immediately reversed. The dynamic of the transition disallows any symbolic association of one form with a masculine iconography that would be opposed to a female figure, or vice-versa, according to a binary reason. The two are at once mixed, undifferentiated and self-contained within the unit of the dissolve. The ambiguity is all the more trenchant insofar as the high medieval tradition that eroticized luminosity now figures in the cinematic rendering of the edifice and the female. The church has been likened to the Virgin Mary, a wall of stone penetrated by light passing into her body without rupturing her hymen. Here, the same: the photographic equipment in the Spanish hills maculates the female without destroying her, enacting a violence of a sacred order, producing from the dissolve of the steeple and the physical form the

Shot 33

Shot 34

very illumination of the film itself. Here tradition, the erotic, and sacred orders establish and sacralize the documentary.

Perspective embodies the same ambivalences. In the establishing shots describing the plights of the Hurdanos in one of their villages (shots of 99–102), the camera looks down a city street that opens onto the mountainous landscape in the background. A staggered row of whitewashed dwellings give way to the vista of hills which descend from the right, behind a wall in shadow, covered by lush tufts of leaves and branches. Almost imperceptible – a second or third viewing reveals the figure – in the street is a tiny, genuflected human form. Within the lapse of the dissolve which moves to a medium closeup of the figure bent over a rock, the eye glimpses the figure simultaneously from far and near. Both are lost in the landscape and merge together from a play of shadows and light. For an instant the camera extends perspective by putting the subject in two places at once. Perceived from near and far, the figure broadens the image. Both lost in the landscape and central to it, the child is the mediating mark of a transition connoting a broad and active process analogy animating the physical and human world. The effect of the dissolve counters the depiction of barrenness when the voice-off on the soundtrack decries the scene: the child, it reports, suffers from malnutrition and dysentery. Where death is reported, the cinema expands the visual range of the frame.

After the dissolve, for the first and only time in the film, the camera records the presence of the filmmaker. A human, dressed in slacks and a short-sleeved shirt, enters the frame from the left, in the foreground near the camera, and proceeds to inspect the child, who wakes from its slumber, raises her left arm to shield her eyes from the light (or too, possibly from the sight of the cameraman or anthropologist). The voice-off declares that nothing could be done to save the child. After an inspection, seen as a closeup of the child's open mouth, the sound-track reports that she died three days later. The moral implications of the shooting sequence are obvious: the recording crew did no more than film a calamitous social condition as if it were tourism. It invested money in cinema rather than welfare. Even worse, the viewers are rendered culpable for witnessing what they should have remedied, not filmed. The double bind of the human predicament is seen as

Shot 99   Shot 100

an esthetic spectacle. Once a relation of voyeurism is established in the relation of the film to the spectator, the unassailable distance held between
viewers and subjects disallows any relation of enraged empathy, in this instance, that would have marked the collective perception of the child in its
plight.

The sequence overtly specifies the nature of the anthropologist's research
and his apparatus. The sight of a sleepy child also identifies a very standard
scene, that of the *dormeuse,* that had been a topic of Symbolist painting and
lyric from Rimbaud to Valéry. An unabated, favored, intimate view of a dormant beauty allows a voyeur's fantasy to flourish. Here, the sequence begins
in the same fashion, with the sight of a subject in profile, who does not look
back at the spectator.[2] The sequence ends by carrying the commonplace to
what its unconscious dimension never articulated in the eroticized distance
kept between the viewer and the figure. The *dormeuse* plays a role in the network of analogies operating elsewhere in the film. The child is likened to a
dummy, a doll,[3] or a mannequin that establishes a perspectival field. It also
repeats the other scenes of sleeping children who counterpoint the diurnal
world to their own of imperceptible dream. The shots in the dissolve-
sequence hark back to scenes in Alberca where, in shot 13, local women pre-
pare for Sunday festivities. The foreground captures an old lady knotting the
locks of a young girl, while in the background another infant sleeps in exactly the same pose as the child in the Hurdano's street in shot 100. Not unlike the lap-dissolve that perspectivized the relation of the human to the
landscape, the film now casts its play of identical forms across the horizontal, narrative geography of the documentary. The infant tends to reflect the
view of the spectator. In a state of hazy, dreamy consciousness, it represents
the very regress necessary for a view of the film as a field of undifferentiated
form, of a manifest surface that a child can apprehend. In one shot (90) of
what the voice-off describes as the "turtle-like back" of the rooftops of a Hurdano village, a female holding a child – looking back at the camera – sets a
median ground between the animistic texture of the agglomeration and the
camera's viewpoint. The infant allows the metaphor to take visual hold and
have credibility in the imaginary surface of the film.

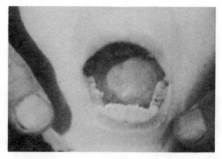

Shot 101   Shot 102

The same function marks the procession of the child's funeral just prior to the end of the film (shots 202–21). In that sequence an infant – seen both as a doll and a corpse – is transported across a river to a graveyard overgrown with weeds. Ostensibly portrayed to bring a resonant closure of death to a film about an already dead culture, the penultimate sequence establishes the *other* end of a perspectival topography that uses the sleepy infant as one key to the multiple intersections of dream and document. Once more, what the lap dissolve embodied in a vertical fashion – in the interpenetration of forms up and through landscapes – the presence of the child analogously reiterates the crisscrossing of narrative lines leading from the city to the province and from the diurnal world of culture (work, play, festival, everyday life) to nocturnal scenes of sleep and death (the beginning of the film bathed in intense Mediterranean light, and the end in deep chiaroscuro).

Framings: A Cinema of Sacrifice

Scenes appear framed according to a great tradition of portraiture reaching back to the seventeenth century, yet the context denies the presence of such heroic sources. No shot fails to articulate a tension between the subjects in view, depth of field, and the borders of the image. The documentary is most effective when it makes these tensions the topic of its montage, when the harsh reality depicted on screen is put into question by the study of the unconscious will or tradition – of modeling a painted world – that lends veracity to an image. Hence the reality is produced by its relation to paintings.

The dynamics of the relation between a classical style of framing and the cinematic recording of brutal reality (we are seeing an archaic world, it is reported, for the very first time) are most visible in the way that one pictural tradition effectively murders and sacralizes the other. The sequence reporting the culinary habits of the Hurdanos is emblematic. We are told that the natives indulge in meat only when, on a rare occasion, "this happens" (shots 108–16). "This" is the sight of a goat suddenly falling from its perch on a ledge on the side of a mountain. To heighten the pathos and improbability of the event, the camera shoots a closeup of the carcass just as it begins to roll and plummet into the valley. The animal recedes from the immediate foreground and is quickly lost from view. The sequence indicates a careful montage. A first shot of the mountainside precedes a medium closeup, shot from

Shot 108   Shot 109

a telephoto lens, of two goats on rocky pinnacles. The third depicts them in a medium view on the mountainside, while the fourth reframes the same scene from afar, registering the goat's fall. The fifth shot begins as a closeup of the animal's carcass as it drops away from the camera.

Even a passive viewer would not hesitate to note a puff of smoke (in the fourth shot) capturing the goat's fall from its perch. We are baited to ask, upon observing that the animal is sacrificed to precipitate the accident, if the camera is guilty of poor framing: a more carefully positioned lens would have concealed the real cause of the goat's death in order to preserve the illusion necessary for the truth of realism. As such, the sequence seems either patently "sloppy" or uncannily genial. The frame reveals that the crew has murdered the beast in order to produce an outlandishly *documentary effect.* The shot would have been innocuous if it were not underscored by the narrative jump when the camera is placed next to the carcass of the beast in the following shot, recording the fall down the mountainside. The murder becomes a photographic ritual and an exemplary sacrifice.

What seems so far from the world of credibility is cast as a visible form of religious tension. In filmic terms, the two shots of the fall caused by the gunblast and the closeup of the goat's descent underscore the presence of the ritualized murder.[4] The fifth shot virtually explains the other and allows the eye to discern the violence of the edge, where a rift between absence – dream, or primary process – and the world is respected and dissolved. The sequence has analogues everywhere else in the film which also undermine the realism. In the Alberca sequence (shots 13–29), the ritual murder of the cock in the street was depicted identically. A rooster was shot hanging from a cord stretched across the frame, then immediately decapitated by a blow of a razor entering from the right in the closeup. Several shots follow in which men are seen drinking the blood (as wine) of the beast and eating wafers of unleavened bread. A secular Eucharist, clearly mixed within the ritual process of a pagan culture in this initial sequence, counterpoints the spectacle of the goats "scaped" on the Hurdano mountainside. The images betray the narrator's report, or at best they show that the murder is staged by the camera in order to be displaced from the world of archaic life in provincial Spain. The shots of the Albercan youth in regalia on horseback, lighting and smoking cigarettes; their ride through the streets; the long, establishing view of the crowd with the cord stretched across the street with the cock hanging in the center; the closeup of the bird and the sudden entry of the hand; all offer a very logical plan homologous to the mountain goat's astonishing fall from the ledge in the Hurdano mountains. A stage is set, a ritual murder is performed on two levels (both in the field of view and in the cinematic dynamic), and a community is produced in the residue of the collective, somatic absorption of the death.

No images confirm the presence of a community, no doubt because they would work against the process of division at the basis of the framing style. A body is rendered integral when it is cut off; any cohering image of a group would undermine the filmic ritual that produces a community of views in total invisibility and in places far removed from the geography of the film. The framing therefore must not convey delimited or self-contained images of the culture it puts into view; instead, it must render the viewing as something generating confusions of culpability and redemption.

Writings

Few documentaries about illiterate, archaic, or post-neolithic cultures are infused with so much *writing* in the field of view. The map of Europe details all the primitive communities in majuscule in circular form (Tchecoslovaquie, Hongrie, Savoie, Italie, Espagne—all other nations or regions are unnamed). Place-names are carefully written in the last dissolve of the closeup of Southwestern Spain (shot 3). The camera records inscriptions on stone adjacent to skulls in alcoves on the façade of the church in La Alberca (shot 8 or also shot 36). But most important, in the sequence (shots 68–88) in the regional school on one side of the mountains separating the Hurdanos from contemporary civilization, we are led to believe that we have reached the limitrophe regions of Scripture. The shots taken in the classroom mark the last, ultimate line of the Western world. Great care is taken to show a child tracing the Golden Rule in shots 85 and 87). A boy has just walked toward the blackboard washed out by the bright light cast upon it; he raises his right arm to begin drawing the sentences in cursive characters, *Respectad los bienes ajenos.*

The sequence seems bizarre for at least two reasons. As writing always mediates visibility and alterity in the field of an image, wherever script appears in frame, the recognizable world becomes, as it were, a paginal surface. Writing forces the eye to move from illusory apprehension of a simulated three-dimensional volume to one of solely horizontal and vertical extension. In cinema it encourages the spectator to view the images as a pictorial surface that is only real in a compositional sense. Here the long shot of the child writing on the blackboard signals that the reported observations must be viewed as tension rather than the groundings of an apparent reality. The film reveals *its own rules* by breaking down the perspective of illusion. In the dynamic of scripture and anthropology, what the first intertitle scripted as "human geography," the writing paradoxically embodies the double bind of the missionary project it constructs elsewhere. The film ostensively depicts the world of these others, but its presence in their milieu is seen as an element that hardly respects their objects: the daily life in school is

186

disrupted by a camera that catches the children smiling at the lens, or squinting in the mirrored light artificially illuminating the interior. Writing in the image-field bounces onto the spectator a statement that reads, analyzes, or even impugns the camera in the act of filming. The ultimate anthropological lesson being taught in the class is directed at the viewer: stay away, do not shoot a world that ought to be kept foreign; please do not aestheticize the Hurdanos, respect the objects of others.

Respectad los bienes ajenos can also subscribe the film in the manner of an emblem, producing alterity in the image. In this way, an unconscious can be glimpsed in the utter difference between scripture and cinema highlighted throughout the film. One of the many figures of death (and civilization) is the scene of the schoolboy's "writing lesson," which indicates where the relations of power are invested in the ethnographer's optical apparatus. The generics of *Land without Bread* are another case in point: the title is less important than its relation to the image on which it is superimposed. In the English version, UNPROMISED LAND is placed over cumulus clouds. Where the writing indicates land or earth (*Las Hurdes, Tierra sin pan, Land without bread, Pays sans pain* making the same point), the image offers an absence of grounding. The forlorn land is in the sky, in oblivion, absolution or absence; or, too, the unpromised earth is the product of the almost spontaneous generation of scripture over and from an image. Culture is defined by orders of difference and superimposition. These can be coded as repression, stratification, or by other metaphors, but in every event they are conveyed by the absolute alterity offered by scripture in its relation to the palpable world.

Paintings

Despite its portrayal of conditions far from our own, *Land without Bread* flashes many familiar figures before our eyes. The scenes are all recognizable, even agonizingly so. Use of the long shot and extended depth of field throws the film into the great painterly traditions of the Spanish Renaissance and Baroque found in the Prado. The flat, foreshortened view of the country idiots harks back to Velasquez's portraits of four dwarfs in the court of Philip. And, in a shot taken in a village en route from La Alberca (shot 57), a Spanish peasant in the lower right hand corner mimes the frontal stare of one of the Dionysian drunkards in the same painter's rustic scene of "Los Borrachos." Rural streets recall David Teniers. Courbet's "Stonebreakers" marks an obvious visual and conceptual presence (see shot 151). In a different vein, the stark mountainscapes contrasting a dark, jagged outline against bright skies seem reminiscent of the surreal tradition or the broken line of Goya's drawings. The possibility of myriad references points to the fact that most documentary evidence is always filtered through a common cultural conscience formed by esthetic models. These are part of the unconscious "rhetoric" of images that produce the meaning of realism. Akin to an "other" writing with which the filmmaker must work, they mediate the unknown in offering a fragmentary familiarity that aligns the museum with the anthropological tradition. In effect, the more the realistic genre appeals to an esthetic heritage, the more objective – and documentary – the film becomes. In the context of Spain, presence of the treasure from the collection of Philip the Fourth also exacerbates the political dimension of the aesthetic vision. That *Land without Bread* was banned by Republican Spain can be explained by the relation it holds between the presence of a Royalist heritage and the archaic, timeless, equally royal world of the Hurdano culture. Allusive presence of paintings establishes a broad perspectival range, within which the lowest order of the universe is seen in terms of the highest, and vice-versa.

Perspectives serve to reproduce the effect of a loss of grounding where, in many of the shots, the viewer cannot ascertain the vantage point of the camera. Sometimes a closeup of the earth will appear to be an aerial view until a snake or a toad enters the frame in the same or a subsequent shot (see shot 40). Or, in the scenes of street life, the camera often spirals from an extreme closeup of the waterbed to a view from afar (shot 63). The camera marries the low, close perspective to the lofty, omniscient long shot. One modulates the other, just as the presence of art treasures questions the cultural scope of ethnography in the camera's shooting style.

Such appear to be some of the salient traits of the camera in *Land without Bread*. All operate in similarly disjunctive fashions. Further study would probably show how the image and sound tracks persist in betraying one another, how the presence of Brahms deifies the subjects in the film, or how the montage articulates a network of obsessions and allusions to arcana going back to *Un Chien andalou* and *L'Age d'or* and forward to *El Bruto, Los Olvidados*, and *Robinson Crusoe*. At this point it is clear that *Land without Bread* determines much of the ground of the documentary and anthropological enterprise in cinema. Its combinations of theology and montage model a critique of grounding of filmic truth. Its construction offers an acuitous reading of realistic cinema in which objects, figures, voices, or mises-en-scène are seen through the art of montage. Most prominently, the film produces an extended perspective within its own styles in the junctures of shots, the composition of individual sequences, the contradictory relation of image and voice, the tensions established through the rapport of the edge to the center of the frame, the redundancy of the scenarios and their abruptness of exposition within a classical frame. For the first time a film sets forth a sacrificial function which both murders and revivifies both viewers and inhabitants of a land without bread.

Notes

1.   On this point, see Francesc Llinas and Javier Maqua's rich discussion of collage in *El Cadaver del tiempo: el collage como transmision narrative/ideologica* (Valencia: Fernando Torres, 1976).

2.   The relation of the subject filmed to the spectator is multifarious in the tradition of Surrealism, film and painting. In his *Words and Pictures* (The Hague; Mouton, 1973), Meyer Schapiro notes that humans facing the spectator are generally given a role of power – such as the Pantocrator in the hemicycles of Byzantine churches – while those seen in profile convey a relation of inferiority. They do not look back or offer a view that would disquiet the viewer. The same holds for Degas's early paintings, which never allow the female to gaze upon the spectator; the artist imagines a

voyeuristic relation with women who comb their hair without heeding the presence of the painter or viewer. The same relation marks the tradition of invisible editing in the tradition of Hollywood, in which actors are trained never to look directly at the camera or, if they do, to brush their look by the camera en route to fixing upon another subject or object in frame. The tradition of the *dormeuse* in shots 99–102 and elsewhere makes the political, visual, and erotic dimensions of the relation of spectator to subject entirely visible. It is essential for the theory of viewing (and violence) subtending *Land without Bread*.

3. It is both a compositional form that provides visual perspective *and* a pictographic marker allowing the viewer to engage in a heightened, almost irritable sensibility. The doll-baby will figure similarly in Renoir's work (*Toni,* 1934) and in Italian neorealism (e.g., Puiran).

4. Ritualized murder and cinema are part of a tradition shared with Renoir. We think of the sudden, almost morbid effect that a closeup of a rabbit has when shot during the hunt sequence of *The Rules of the Game*. The camera holds for almost three seconds on the animal as its body clenches into death, when the surrounding shots are more rapid. All of a sudden, the viewer either seizes the baneful gratuity of murder or, closer to Buñuel, the fact that the director has positioned the camera adjacent to a hunter who shoots the freed beast to produce the effect as such. Here the camera murders in order to engage a sense of collective sacrifice with the collectivity of viewers. It is at once deeply religious and cinematographic.

Appendix

Land without Bread (1932): Shot Sequence

KEY

ECU = extreme closeup	MS = medium shot	ELS = extreme long shot
CU = closeup	LS = long shot	

Credits

1. First credits: Title over clouds dissolves to credits a) of director dissolving to b) of photographer and assistants. Fade-out in black to second credits.

2. Intertitle, still over clouds ("The Hurdanos were unknown, even in Spain, until a road was built for the first time in 1922. Nowhere does man need to wage a more desperate fight against the hostile forces of nature") dissolves to next intertitle: "In light of this, the film may be considered as a study of 'human geography.'" Fade-out in black.

3. Relief map of Europe in dark tones with primitive regions circled and named; dissolve to map of Spain; dissolve to CU of Southwestern Spain in same rugged relief. Fade-out in black.

La Alberca

4. LS in deep focus of street of La Alberca seen in deep, frontal view.

5. MS of street with man on mule penetrating space in moving away from perspective of camera. Fade to (6).

6. Reverse shot of street with mule seen in deep focus at end of street; tilt up to space between buildings under a bright sky.

7. Church in LS, shot from side and bottom of street, revealing porch and tower under a limpid sky.

8. MCU of alcove on church with a Latin cross at crown of border; two skulls are visible in adjacent openings to left and right.

9. MLS of street.

10. LS of street with tilt up (redoing scene of shot 6).

11. Cut to MS of doorway in street seen from one side: a bull exits from doorway, next to which a youth stands; a dog then exits right from a smaller doorway on the right.

12. MS of Christian inscription over a doorway in street.

13. MS of old woman combing the hair of a festively dressed girl in right foreground; a doll-like form, a girl, is being attended to similarly in the background.

14. LS in slight tilt down (taken from a second story of a building) of a small crowd milling in a local square.

15. LS of six youths in formal attire on horseback.

16. MS of three of the youths lighting and smoking cigarettes while on horseback.

17. MCU of a cock hanging upside-down, its head immediately cut and its carcass raised, upside-down, on a cord stretching left and right (the cutting is of an abrupt violence reminiscent of the laceration of the eye in *Un Chien andalou*).

18. LS of cord and cock seen, reframed, from view over street (as in shot 14).

19. MLS from below (with telephoto lens) of youth riding toward and by the camera in the street.

20. MS reframing shot 19 with youths galloping by.

21. Frontally taken MCU of peasant woman looking up and over camera; a vacant stare marks her face as two children are also in frame; one looks up and another smiles at camera.

22. LS of street once again.

23. LS of festive group on side of street. Two of the handsomely bedecked youths pour wine from large jugs.

24. MS of same scene.

25. MCU of one of the youths pouring wine.

26. MS of townsmen drinking (man at left standing before a semi-circle of four others at the right).

27. MCU of one of the townsmen eating and chewing a wafer.

28. Cut back to MS of shot 26.

29. MCU of man of shot 27, now drinking wine.

30. CU of baby with white garb and trinkets; a hand enters left and fondles the jeweled necklace. Camera tilts down along body layered with clothes and pendant jewels with forms of animals decorating the necklace.

31. Extreme LS, from above, of square and people below. Three-story houses of town are now seen against greater landscape. Fade-out in black.

The Countryside and Abandoned Churches

32. Fade-in, pan left in extreme LS of silhouette of a jagged mountain range on a bright horizon.

33. Long pan in extreme LS alongside of a wooded valley that stops in LS on abandoned shell of a chapel seen from the west end.

34. Dissolve into tilt-up in MS of front tower of chapel with woman standing adjacent to the Southwest corner. Dissolve of church in shot 33 and woman in shot 34 blend for an instant.

35. MCU of woman seen frontally, with white kerchief over her head.

36. MCU, tilt-up, of tabernacle of church with Christian sculpture of a saint emerging from shadowed alcove. Rapid tilt-down and left to catch an eroded placard (Santiago de las Bathegas).

37. Tracking shot into the space below the rounded arch of the same church.

38. Track left before a row of trees through which, deep in background, the church is framed as the dark shadows punctuate the nervous, jostled movement of the camera.

39. Tilt-up into MLS of façade of an abandoned church from the arcade and rounded arch below to the bell tower and Latin cross on the pinnacle above.

40. MS of a fountainhead spurting water. A wall is in background; tilt-down to fountain amid overgrowth and rocks at its base and to the sight of a toad crawling right.

41. ECU of a toad entering from right on the same rocky surface of shot 40.

42. LS of a grove of blossoming trees with wall and cloister of church in background.

43. CU of reptant snake on rocks moving from lower right corner of frame to upper left corner.

44. LS from above of trees blowing in the wind.

45. MLS of trees along a shore of a river with whitewater rapids.

46. MLS of river from above. Tilt downward to record flow of river. Cut to (47).

Approaching the Hurdano Region

47. ELS of mountain silhouetted in background over dead branches of a tree, in very soft focus, in foreground.

48. LS of rocky landscape and slow pan left that goes by another abandoned chapel.

49. LS reframing chapel in lower right corner of frame. Pan and tilt down and up from left and right of landscape and buildings.

50. LS of two high trees dwarfing chapel below.

51. MS of chapel reframed.

52. ELS of mountainous horizon (crags, jagged surface silhouetted under bright light).

53. LS of undulating hills and desert-like surface of scrubby vegetation.

54. LS of village nestled in valley of the same décor.

The First Hurdano Village Scenes

55. MS of street with woman limping, following a child up the street in a direction away from the camera.

56. MS of child following a pig up the same street; he hits the beast with a stick.

57. MS of man on mule carrying a fagot entering the street from the right background; one peasant looks frontally at the camera as he smokes a cigarette; three men repose in medium background on left side of frame.

58. MS looking down the street with women washing in the central rivulet trickling down the middle.

59. MCU of child washing lettuce in the water.

60. MCU of pig drinking water from the rivulet.

61. MCU of girl holding a baby; the two shove each other and drink water.

62. CU in profile of boy kneeling over and drinking water from the rivulet with his mouth.

63. Cut to LS of rivulet, spiraling in a 360-degree turn overhead to give a sense of extension to the river, ending with the sight of two women arched over the river, washing clothing.

64. MLS of one of the two women, arched right, rinsing a pot in the water.

65. MCU of woman arched left, bathing (anointing) a child's head with water.

66. MCU of three girls soaking bread in the rivulet.

67. CU of two of the girls tasting the wet bread.

School and Writing

68. MLS, from below, of a boy ringing a bell from the second-story window of a school designated by a flag waving from a pole erected below the sill.

69. MLS, from above, of woman wearing a skirt and a scarf over her head, fetching the same children; pan left in street following the woman scurrying the children off along the street.

70. MS over desks seen in lower part of screen, of children entering into schoolroom through a door in back to the left of the room.

71. MCU of little urchins smiling and snickering, passing through the door.

72. MCU of children filing to their desks from right side front of schoolroom.

73. Continuation of shot 70.

74. MCU of a boy seated at his desk, his eyes squinting in bright light and looking left.

75. CU and slow pan right of three girls seated at their desks, directly facing camera.

76. MLS of children in school as teacher (in formal attire) opens books on their desks as he moves down aisle from front to back of classroom.

77. CU and pan right of children's bare feet dangling below the desks.

78. MCU of girl seated at her desk (seen diagonally, as in shot 74).

79. MCU of a girl in class, now seen frontally. She walks toward camera.

80. Cut to diametrically reframed reverse shot of the child walking away, toward the blackboard of the classroom.

81. Cutaway to child in shot 74, who now walks to the blackboard.

82. MCU, shot from above, of a boy seated at his desk. Tilt and pan up to a drawing of an *infanta*.

83. Cut to MLS of children circled around instructor seated by the blackboard.

84. Shot of classroom with children seated at their desks. Slow pan right reframing the pictures just seen on the walls that are now visible in the background.

85. MLS of child tracing the Golden Rule on the blackboard; the teacher is seen seated at the right.

86. Cutaway to children, in MCU, writing at their desks, looking up and ostensibly copying the writing on the blackboard.

87. MCU of long duration recording the child tracing the Rule in cursive script; reflection of light on blackboard almost washes out the contrasts.

88. Cut back to children gazing upward (seemingly at the blackboard), as depicted in shot 86.

The Lower Depths: Extreme Hurdano Town and Country

89. Pan right following a rugged mountainscape in extreme LS.

90. LS of town nestled in the landscape (voice-off compares the tiled roofs to the back of a giant turtle).

91. MS of village rooftops with a woman, in median ground, facing the scene and holding a child over her shoulder; it looks back at the point of view of the camera.

92. MS of street with pigs in the foreground and children with a woman (identified by a tattered dress) slowly limping toward the camera.

93. MCU of child in rags walking toward the camera, visibly holding a doll in her left hand.

94. MCU of pig in intense light seen from above; insects buzz in soft focus between the pig and the camera.

95. MCU of a man, staring directly at the camera, as he holds an infant in his arms.

96. MCU of three children and mother facing the camera; pan left to mother who has visible swell of goiter on her neck (as identified by the voice-off).

97. MCU of a child slowly walking toward the camera as she holds the hand of an adult who enters frame from above and left.

98. MCU of aged woman giving her breast to an infant (in pose not dissimilar to later medieval topical scene of the *mère allaitante*). Fade-out in black.

99. Fade-in to LS of child slumped over a rock in open street in medium field below the mountains in background; walls of buildings are visible on left, and vegetation on right.

100. Dissolve to MCU of same child; a man (reported as part of the film crew and who wears more contemporary clothing definitely out of place in the Hurdano context) enters from front and left and awakens the child, who looks up and just beyond the camera. She shields her eyes from the light with her right hand.

101. CU of the same child facing camera; she opens her mouth.

102. ECU of open mouth with man's hands around it (relation of hands and ocular pose of mouth is reminiscent of relation of eye and hands in the famous laceration scene in *Un Chien andalou*); fade-out in black.

103. Fade-in to MS of woman in doorway seated next to a pig.

104. MCU of woman and girl peeling potatoes.

105. CU of feet of both women; the peels fall onto a plate arranged between their bare feet.

106. LS of olive trees in a grove; their leaves flutter in the wind.

107. MCU of olive blossoms and branches.

Scaped Goats

108. MCU in telephoto of two goats perched on a peak; they clamber down to a ledge.

109. ELS of mountainside; tiny silhouettes of goats on the crest can be seen – with difficulty – in the far distance.

110. Return to movement of animals as in shot 108.

111. Cut back to establishing shot 109 in ELS.

112. MLS of goat walking on ledges against an escarpment of rocks.

113. Same shot, slightly reframed.

114. MCU of goat entering left.

115. LS of goat beginning to fall from ledge (an alert viewer notices a tuft of smoke entering from the right edge of frame)

116. CU of goat's carcass which falls and rolls earthward (or upward) from the immediate proximity of the camera into the distance. Fade-out in black.

Daily Economy and Tribulation: Beehives

117. Fade-in to CU of cylindrically shaped beehives seen below blossoming flowers. Shots 117–37 are all of very short duration.

118. MS of same reframed.

119. MS of longitudinal row of hives.

120. CU of buzzing bees in intense light.

121. MCU of bees swarming around the hives.

122. CU of the same scene.

123. MS of hives.

124. Same scene as shot 120.

125. Shot 118 reframed.

126. MLS, tilted down, of two men accompanying a small white mule carrying hives stacked on its back; a river and lush landscape are visible far below.

127. LS of mountainside reminiscent of scene of goats in shot 109.

128. Return to the scene of shot 126.

129. MS of same white mule, seen in profile, now being swarmed by bees.

130. CU of bees swarming by the mule's legs which kick the air with futility.

131. CU of goat shaking its head to ward off the bees swarming around it.

132. MCU of mule's body shaking.

133. ECU of its head shaking.

134. MCU of body in swarm, its leg kicking.

135. CU of body writhing amidst the swarm.

136. CU of dead body, with one visible eye in the (de)composition, the carcass covered by bees (the scene recalls the pose of the mule's head and eye in the piano sequence of *Un Chien andalou*).

137. MLS of fox pulling at the carcass now framed against the landscape.

Cultivation and Gathering of Food

138. MS of woman (right) and boy (left) fondling and picking cherries from a branch they hold in their hands.

139. CU of their fingers touching the cherries (reminiscent of shot 30).

140. LS of men gathering in street and walking directly toward the camera.

141. MS of a man descending from a house seen above; at upward end of street to the left a door displays a cross near the upper left side of the frame.

142. Return to LS of shot 135 (shot lasts almost 8 seconds).

143. MS of men, their heads sagging, walking toward the camera with entire concavity of the landscape below, mountains visible in background.

144. MCU of same scene, men now walking by the camera on left and right sides.

145. MLS of men walking away from camera in diametrically reframed position. Fade-out in black.

146. Fade-in to MS of landscape of earth and bushes. Tilt-up and dissolve to (147).

147. Several men seen from behind in same landscape, chopping brush; dissolve to (148).

148. Same two men, seen from behind, in MCU, chopping, and dissolve to (149).

149. One man, chopping, and dissolve to (150).

150. Tilt-down of landscape leading to the flow of water of a stream in CU; dissolve to (151).

151. MCU of a ledge and wall. Pan right to two men working – somewhat as portrayed in Courbet's "Stonebreakers" – at the wall to the right.

152. MS of man shoveling dirt into a burlap sack held by another man in profile on the left.

153. LS of two men descending a mountainside; they bear heavy sacks on their shoulders.

154. MCU of man emptying sack of earth by a ledge crafted with layered stone.

155. CU of water flowing right. Pan up to MS of a cutaway view of an earthen terrace; the shot ends on a man's lower torso in upper right frame, seen hoeing the earth.

156. LS of cultivated field by the riverside shot from above. Long, slow pan along the meander of the cultivated strip that follows the contour of the river's edge.

157. ELS of river and strip in the same fluid pan now shot from a more remote are above. Fade-out in black.

158. Fade-in to tracking shot following a man in tatters who walks erectly toward the left of frame on a steep hillside; the track hastens and catches four other persons walking in the same direction before it overtakes them.

159. LS of barren hillside in distance with back of a man's head (under a black hat) in the foreground. Continuity is held as the four persons walk past the frame from right.

160. MS of same group now moving directly toward the camera.

161. MCU of woman in tatters, sickle in hand, passing over a rocky surface below, followed by another person's bare feet that step firmly on the same path.

162. MLS of the group moving away from the camera and into the landscape.

163. MCU of a woman in frontal view, arched over the shrubs around her, cutting and gathering branches with her sickle.

164. MS of the woman bending over, filling the sack held by a young man who stands in profile as he contemplates the landscape to the right.

165. MCU of boy showing his bandaged right arm to the camera (voice-off reports that he is suffering from a viper's bite).

166. CU of boy's bandaged arm in tatters.

167. CU of boy's face evincing his plight and pain.

168. MCU of boy that reframes shot 120.

169. Cut to back of woman in MS clambering up the mountainside.

170. MS of man carrying a sack in a street. Camera pans left to follow him as he walks into a small doorway in extreme shade.

171. Reverse MS in contrejour, from the interior, of the man opening a door, emptying a sack and spreading leaves around the threshold of the entry; the view diametrically reframes the end of shot 170.

172. MS in chiaroscuro of entry and the darkness. A small human figure enters into light seen across the darkness of the doorway in the background.

173. Reverse shot from outside, in MS, of a man entering the door directly along the camera's sightline. He goes into the background in the interior darkness.

174. MS of interior with a woman posed next to a girl, left, holding a baby in her arms (composition is reminiscent of Le Nain's or Teniers's rustic interiors).

175. Outdoor scene in MLS of smoke emanating from rooftops of village.

176. MCU of same, reframed.

177. CU of same, reframed.

Mosquitoes and Death

178. LS of mountains and parched riverbed below, with olive trees growing near shore to the right.

179. MLS of man in river, his pants rolled up, holding a staff as he walks barefoot over its rocky bed.

180. MCU of same man, shot from above, who examines larvae in dish attached to the end of the staff.

181. ECU of larvae in dish.

182. ECU of a picture of two types of mosquito larvae illustrated in a scientific book.

183. ECU of fully grown mosquitoes in same encyclopaedia (under names in boldface characters: ANOPHELES and CULEX).

184. MS of man seated on a ledge, his body occasionally shaking (reports the voice-off) from malaria.

185. MS of woman dormant in street; pan right down the opening of the street.

186. MS of woman sleeping on a terrace above the street.

187. CU of same dormant figure (insects are visibly buzzing in foreground of frame); fade-out in black.

Dwarfs

188. Fade-in to LS of three dwarfs walking upward toward camera in front of a mountainside. Shot ends in MS of three dwarfs sitting near the camera.

189. MS of one child, smiling, his legs crossed, facing the camera; his feet project in with feet in foreground as the foot of another dwarf pierces the frame from the lower right.

190. MS from behind, repeating the end of shot 188, recording a second dwarf moving about.

191. MCU of smiling dwarf turning his head.

192. MS of two dwarfs smiling and looking at each other.

193. CU of their bare feet.

194. Pan left of dwarfs playing, beginning with MS of shot 192 and ending on the smiling dwarf of shot 189; his bare feet are visible in the foreground.

195. Reframed scene of kneeling dwarfs looking left.

196. MLS of landscape (ostensibly seen from their viewpoint) with a fourth, ugly dwarf suddenly jumping into view, out of the landscape in MS; he walks forward.

197. Same scene of shot 195. One dwarf beckons the other, who is out of frame.

198. CU of the miserable, wart-ridden (fourth) dwarf.

199. MS of same dwarf walking toward camera into MCU

200. Cutaway shot to a human figure reclining against a wall (seemingly out of all context established by the preceding and following shots).

201. Over-the-shoulder shot of smiling dwarf of shot 189.

Death: A Child's Funeral

202. Fade-in to MLS of a home seen from outside; the doorway in the center with a group of six figures gathered around.

203. MCU of a doll-like baby dressed in finery (reported as dead).

204. MCU of an interior with seated female (identified as the infant's mother) staring blankly at the camera. A child comes into view in lower right of frame.

205. Cut back to scene of shot 202 with one man, holding a child in his arms, advancing toward camera.

206. MLS of funeral procession moving left and up by the camera.

207. MS from above of a man carrying the baby in a wooden manger over his right shoulder, moving right, through the brush, following another man who frays his way through the vegetation.

208. MS from above of the two men walking over a scrubby earth, from right to left.

209. LS of river and vegetation to the right.

210. Dissolve to MS of two men, seated, facing each other, rolling up their trousers and exposing their naked calves and feet in front of the river in the background.

211. MS of man before the manger who lifts its veil.

212. CU of sleeping (or dead) child seen from viewpoint of man seen in preceding shot.

213. Cut back to shot 211, now with man lowering its veil.

214. MS of men passing the manger across the river.

215. Pan left to CU of manger floating left on limpid water flowing over a rocky riverbed below.

216. Pan left to MS of man picking up the manger and passing it left. Slight track left as the camera follows them from its position on the shoreline.

217. LS of adjacent mountains. Tilt and pan down to cemetery with cross at right and stone building with open passageway in the middle. A man, seen in LS, is crouched in the shadows inside.

218. MS, pan left of wall and grassy growth in the foreground; the shot passes by the same wooden cross of shot 217.

219. CU of grass with entry of hands separating grass in order to reveal small stakes in the soil. Hands move like the arms and legs of the toad seen earlier.

220. MS of choir sculpture under a baldaquin displaying finely carved wood in high gothic style.

221. CU of same baldaquins and tabernacles. Fade-out in black.

Home Life: Interior Scenes and the Death Knell

222. Fade-in to MCU of an interior with a family around a pot; the scene evokes the night in high contrast of light and dark tones.

223. MCU of the central figure, a man, stirring the pot over the fire.

224. MS of interior seen through doorway. Pan downward to record pots and pans hanging on the wall.

225. MCU of scene in shot 222, reframed; the female to the left picks up a child.

226. LS of street seen in chiaroscuro; an old lady enters from its darkness in the center.

227. Reverse shot of the old lady, ringing a bell, lumbering up the street (toward spot that camera held in shot 226).

228. MCU of scene in shot 225; the man stands up, picking up a child, as the camera pans left to catch a woman following him exiting frame to the left.

229. MS of the doorway, with man and child entering.

230. Back to scene of shot 225; in illuminated space, the last man in right of frame exits left.

231. Cut to doorway of shot 229 with activity (family going to bed) in background.

232. Cut to street with old hag moving upward as in shot 226.

233. CU of heads of bodies clothed in pajamas. They sleep with their faces turned away from or oblivious to the camera and the light illuminating them. Camera pans slowly left and right to register the six recumbent bodies.

234. MCU of old woman moving her lips; darkness of street is in the background.

235. ECU of her wrinkled face as she utters words in silence.

236. MLS of same dark street with old woman reframed in distance.

The End

237. ELS of mountains under a bright sky.

238. Final credits with FIN cut in angular art-deco style, dropping into view and then disappearing.

The Critical Grasp:
Buñuelian Cinema and Its Critics
Linda Williams

"Thank God, I'm still an atheist!"[1] – Luis Buñuel's playful riposte to the critics who would pin down the belief system behind so remarkable a body of films is emblematic of the challenge those films pose to critical discourse. Like these films, the statement refuses to commit itself to a a univocal meaning. Also like the films, it posits an opposition – the belief/non-belief in God – one term of which it appears to choose. At the same time, however, it subverts this choice (of atheism) by thanking God for it. Thus, among other things, Buñuel demonstrates that the very form of the critical question – "Do you believe in God?" – prejudges the existence of God even if the answer to the question is no. Even a non-existent God structures the atheist's non-belief in Him.

Both this question, and its answer, exemplify in microcosm the wary dance between filmmaker and critic. What is interesting, however, is the very different nature this dance can assume depending upon the different nature of the intellectual terrain on which it takes place. In what follows I would like to examine the different steps of this dance in four major phases of Buñuel criticism. My goal is to demonstrate how each of these critical discourses has constructed a different "Buñuel" and how each has failed, in its own peculiar way, to grasp the meaning of this most elusive oeuvre. The point is not the obvious and pessimistic one that all critical discourse is doomed to fail in this task, but rather the (I hope) more interesting one of the particular nature of the Surrealist film text's encounter with different critical schools.

Each of these schools has constructed a very different Buñuel. They are, in rough order of their first appearance on the critical scene: 1) the "Surrealist Buñuel," originally constructed by the members of the Surrealist movement and then later by the next generation of Surrealist sympathizers; 2) an opposed "realist Buñuel," constructed primarily by politically left critics, whether Marxists, Humanists or Christians; 3) a resolution to the above opposition that emerges in the individualist approach of auteurism; and, finally, 4) a reaction to all of the above in what I term the "revenge of Formalism" that constructs a Semiotic and Lacanian Buñuel. These categories are not intended as a comprehensive typology of Buñuel criticism but, rather, as representatives of major trends. At least two very important recent critical approaches – Feminism and Deconstruction – have been excluded because they have not yet been developed in any sustained way with respect to Buñuel's films.

Buñuel and Dalí's first two films received their initial readings in the late twenties and early thirties in the form of official endorsements of their surreality from the members of the Surrealist group. A radical refusal of all analysis or explanation, these readings extravagantly praise the revolutionary power of a given film by practicing a kind of second order Surrealist response to it. An extended example of this form of criticism is the famous "Manifesto Concerning *L'Age D'or*."[2] The work is a group text that uses the film as a point of departure for an amusing, passionate and often incoherent diatribe against capitalism, the clergy and the police, and in favor of *amour fou*, revolutionary violence and the "Divine" Marquis. The film is implicitly understood as an attack on all the rational complacencies of bourgeois existence. Proof of this understanding is offered in the continuation of the attack in the manifesto itself.

A primary goal of this form of criticism is to avert the recuperation of the Surrealist text by "mere" avant-garde aestheticism. The tactic is to emphasize the film's violent assault on all received ideas of beauty and its call to direct, violent action. It is the same tactic employed by Buñuel himself in his famous pronouncement that *Un Chien andalou* was nothing more than a "passionate call for murder."[3] This form of what might be called second order Surrealist response derives from Louis Aragon's practice of "synthetic literary criticism."[4] In film, it had already been practiced by Robert Desnos on works that were not themselves Surrealist but which could be made to seem so by a Surrealist commentary.[5]

In the 1950s a younger generation of Surrealists – or at least Surrealist sympathizers and nostalgicists – began to tackle the writing of film history, including its various movements and modes. In the process, they also began to formulate a canon of the Surrealist and the surrealis*tic* film at the center of which were *Un Chien andalou* and *L'Age d'or*. These two films were viewed as the crowning achievements of a pure Surrealism that could now be seen to extend back through the more grotesque moments of Von Stroheim, the more dreamlike passages of Keaton, Chaplin and Feuillade, and finally, back to the original Surrealist essence of cinema in Méliès. At the periphery of this canon were the many films with occasional moments of accidental or involuntary Surrealism.

These critics – Georges Sadoul, Ado Kyrou, Jacques Brunius and, more recently, Paul Hammond and Michael Gould – continued to take their inspiration from the celebratory manifesto style of the first generation of Surrealist critics. Like them, they saw their first task as promoting the surreal in a medium that is inherently dreamlike and thus destined to Surrealist use. Unlike them, they were willing to risk a certain degree of ordinary discursive explanation and analysis.

But explanation and analysis were ultimately inhibited by the belief that discussions of form and technique were anathema to the spontaneity and free association of the Surrealist enterprise. This disdain for form was inherited from the first generation's eagerness to distinguish itself from the formal aesthetics of an avant-garde of so-called "pure" cinema. Following this line, the second generation of Surrealist critics disavowed any concern with form and threw their emphasis upon the shockingly revolutionary content of the Surrealist film images. The effect was to make it nearly impossible for any of these critics to acknowledge the formal complexities of Buñuel's most surreal films. Armed with this simplified thematic, and with no formal approach at all, there was no way for a critic like Ado Kyrou, for example, to deal with the complex episodic structure of a film like *L'Age d'or*. We can see his discomfort as he struggles to absorb the final narrative gesture of the film – the emergence of the survivors from the "Chateau de Selliny" that provides a grisly comic conclusion to Sade's unfinished *120 Journées de Sodome* – into what he takes to be the unified theme of a liberatory love story. Kyrou writes:

This final sequence is most enigmatic when considered in relation to the love story of Lya Lys and Modot. I believe that Buñuel wished to acknowledge the importance of de Sade's work in which love must find renewed strength if it is to triumph over itself, that is, over its inhibitions. Only then will it become the great liberator.[6]

Kyrou achieves thematic consistency between the two narratives at the cost of grossly distorting both Sade and the film into mere celebrations of a liberatory love. Thus the latter day Surrealist critics began to ignore the most obvious Freudian lessons of the dynamic structure of the unconscious, and came to believe that free association modeled on the dream meant a freedom from form altogether. In the end, with Kyrou, they came to embrace a paradoxically content-oriented criticism that left them with no method or inclination for extended analysis. It is worth noting that the first generation of Surrealist critics had avoided such an impasse by devising a method of discourse that at least paid hommage to the Surrealist form of the film.

Buñuel the Realist

Although not blind to the dreamlike, surrealistic qualities of Buñuel's films, Socialist, Marxist and even left-Christian approaches to this work have tended to seize upon its more realistic, socially satirical and anti-bourgeois elements. This approach emerged originally in the 1950s in France under the enthusiasm for neo-realism presided over by André Bazin at *Cahiers du Cinéma*. It continues today in journals and monographs committed to the cinema as a weapon in class struggle and as a significant revelation of social and economic reality.

Where the Surrealist critic aims at defining the films' radical departures from mere reality, the left-realist critic tends to identify Buñuel's uncompromisingly "truthful" representation of the violence and cruelty of life. Thus Bazin, remarking on Buñuel's "perverse taste for cruelty" in *Los Olvidados*, qualifies this observation with the following:

The cruelty is not Buñuel's. He is only revealing the cruelty that exists in the world. . . . He proves the cruelty of creation itself. This theme was already evident in *Land without Bread*. It makes little difference whether the miserable Hurdanos were truly representative of the Spanish peasant. They undoubtedly were. But they represent, first of all, the misery of all mankind.[7]

At the limit, this re-reading of Buñuel's earlier films through the greater so-cial realism of *Los Olvidados* amounts to the recuperation of Surrealism by tragedy. Bazin writes again:

Buñuel's surrealism reaches to the bottom of reality. We feel it. It knocks the breath out of us. . . . But it would be a mistake to accord it too great a place in his work. His surrealism is a part of the rich and fortunate influence of a totally Spanish tradition. His taste for the horrible, his sense of brutality, his tendency to delve into the utmost extremes of humanity – these are all the heritage of Goya, Zurbaran, Ribera. And above all, it reflects a tragic sense of life which these painters expressed through the ultimate human degradations: war, sickness, misery and decay.[8]

Thus Surrealism gives way to a purely Spanish naturalism that in turn be-comes an emblem of a universally tragic sense of life. For Bazin this tragic sense of life becomes, tautologically, nothing more than reality pure and simple.

Even when a critic in this tradition attempts to come to terms with the ob-vious Surrealism of Buñuel's films, the tendency is to have recourse to tragic analogues. Randal Conrad, an American critic writing an extended article on the politics of Buñuel's films in a 1977 issue of *Cineaste*, characterizes his work as having "a firm surrealist basis that is overlaid with a deliberate Marx-ist slant." Conrad attempts to deal with these two ideologies through the con-cept of a "permanent dialectic" between them. But in the end he too echoes Bazin. Writing about *Los Olvidados*, he claims that "every character is a play-thing of destructive forces as inescapable as destiny in ancient tragedy."[9]

Neither Bazin nor Conrad can get beyond the familiar either/or of much politically oriented criticism: either Buñuel's films reflect optimism about the possibilities for radical change, or their social critiques are so dev-astating that they are pessimistic about these possibilities. Either human de-sire can lead the way to effective political change, or it selfishly impedes it. The dialectic is strangely static and the critic, uncomfortable with indeci-sion, consults the oracle for confirmation. Buñuel obliges: "Surrealism taught me that man is never free yet fights for what he can never be, that is tragic."[10]

Buñuel the Auteur

Given the overwhelming dominance of auteurism within international film study, it is not surprising that the most frequently invoked critical school should be auteurism. By any common understanding of the term, it must be granted that Buñuel is an *auteur* of the first order. And yet once the obvious sense of the term is granted as indicating recognizable and consis-tent thematic and stylistic qualities, it becomes apparent that there are also ways in which he resists the designation.

On the one hand, Buñuel's avant-garde Surrealist origins have meant that his work begins with the kind of anti-commercial independence that most *auteurs* achieve, if at all, late in their careers. To some extent then, and in contrast with the major *auteurs* of his generation, Buñuel is too much a gen-uine author, in control of all aspects of his work, to be treated as an *auteur*. His work begins and ends in nearly total directorial freedom. This remarkable creative freedom gives rise to an interesting reversal of the usual terms of the *auteur* approach. Instead of observing a steady evolution towards maturity, many *auteur* studies read the late works of maturity in terms of the early avant-garde works of commercial independence. Thus Raymond Durgnat writes that Buñuel is an artist who "evolved very little, maturing early and continuing to work in the same vein."[11] In fact, Buñuel's whole career, with its unusual gap in the middle, is typically read by auteurist critics as a long struggle to get back to its Surrealist beginnings in what, even for auteurism, is a remarkably static, ahistorical approach.

There is also a characteristic selflessness and impersonality to the Buñuelian cinema that resists auteurism: the rather unremarkable "look" of many of the films; their lack of elegance, beauty or any other marked style; the disciplined adherence to the tenets and goals of Surrealism long after the movement itself had ceased to be a major avant-garde force. (Here we might imagine the likely comparisons: a René Clair continuing to adhere to the anti-aesthetic of Dada, or a Fritz Lang continuing to work according to the principles of German Expressionism.) It would seem that there is something in the very modesty and discipline of the commitment to a collective movement that goes against the individualist values of auteurism.

Finally, it is a dubious tribute to the recuperative power of the *auteur* approach that, in the end, the very absence of a personal style gets to be read, late in Buñuel's career, as the most significant mark of the *auteur* — in, for example, the many critical references to the "effortlessness" of Buñuel's late films.[12] In contrast, the repeated presence of certain themes — whether *amour fou,* foot fetishes or the foibles of the bourgeoisie — are read as static symbols, the marks of constancy of the old Surrealist and Freudian.[13]

Thus, even more than Surrealist criticism, auteurism seems to be the critical method that most mystifies and mythifies the Buñuelian *oeuvre.* Like Surrealist criticism, though for very different reasons, auteurism is content to identify and label the absence of form and the presence of certain familiar contents. Both critical approaches have ceased to actively read the relation between the two.

The Revenge of Formalism: Semiotic and Lacanian Approaches

All of the above forms of criticism lack a way of treating either cinematic textuality or the specific form of the film work. Although the Surrealist critics were fascinated by the dreamlike nature of the visual image with only a few exceptions, they willfully merged their discussion of film, dream and the images of Surrealist poems. Leftist political critics applauded the political and social content of Buñuel's films but had no concept of a genuinely political form and so fell back upon humanistic notions of tragedy and Bazin's problematic equation of film and reality. Finally, the auteurists tended to conflate recurring themes into a master thematic, ignoring, or committing outright distortions of, textual details along the way.

In reaction, the primary rule of the new formalist and semiotically-influenced textual analyses was first and foremost to eschew any impressionistic naming of either theme or form until close textual scrutiny had taken place. The first such careful, cinema-specific, extended scrutiny was offered by

Phillip Drummond's 1977 article in *Screen*, "Textual Space in *Un Chien Andalou*."[14] Drummond resists what no previous critic since the first generation of Surrealists had been able to: the impulse to name what the film's dreamlike structure of erotic ritual behavior seems to mean. Confining himself to a meticulous description of its unique spatial relations, Drummond goes a long way towards defining the film's mixture of only partial, mock classical continuities and equally partial avant-garde disruptions. Thus Drummond reads the textual system of the film as specific kinds of disruptions of both the classic representational and the avant-garde, "pure cinema" texts.[15]

Another approach to textual specificity is that of semiotics and its extension, via the work of Roman Jakobson, into the study of rhetoric. With these methods it became possible to analyze both the diegetic and the rhetorical planes of the Buñuelian text. Susan Suleiman's extended analysis of *The Phantom of Liberty*, for example, demonstrates the structural principle of metonymic displacement underlying the apparent chaos of a film narrative that tells no story.[16] My own analysis of the prologue of *Un Chien andalou* does the same for metaphor.[17]

The above analyses were all limited to identifying the formal features of the Buñuelian and Surrealist film text. Nevertheless, the question of meaning remained irresistible even if it was now re-phrased through what seemed a more properly structural method of examining their latent content. And for me, Jacques Lacan's re-interpretation of Freud in the light of both semiotics and Jakobsonian rhetoric seemed to offer the best hope of uncovering both the dynamics of the film text's similarity to unconscious processes and the latent contents of these same processes.

In my book on Buñuel's Surrealist cinema I argued that Lacan's theory of the splitting of the subject and the subsequent quest for "obscure objects of desire," motivated by the subject's fundamental "lack-in-being," provided a handy account of both the content and the form of many of Buñuel's most intriguing, and most surreal, films. Lacan's theory also provided another way of stating the difference between the Surrealist cinema and that of the classical narrative film. Where most fictional film uses the lure of the imaginary identification with the image to draw the spectator into a belief in the diegetic world of the film, Buñuel's Surrealist films disrupt and expose this imaginary lure by foregrounding the work of the signifier and its production of desire in the subject.[18]

Lacan's theory thus made possible the statement of meaning in the face of texts that have seemed to successfully resist such statement. But in answer to the stubborn question of meaning the Lacanian film theorist constructs a critical net that fails to catch the films in its fabric just as surely as the other methods have failed. For in answer to the question what do Buñuel's films finally mean? the Lacanian response is that they mean exactly what Lacan means: they are about the human subject's entrance into a symbolic that governs the loss of the final signified and the regressive lure of the mirror-dream-film-imaginary as the impossible promise of its restoration.

The reductive nature of such a statement of meaning is camouflaged (or at least was camouflaged for me) by its self-reflective quality: the textual practice of the films acts out the psychoanalytic process of desire through the dominance of its surrealistic rhetorical figures which then act out the Lacanian nature of desire.

One example should suffice: Near the end of Buñuel's last film, *That Obscure Object of Desire,* an unknown woman in a store window removes a torn and bloodied dress from a burlap sack and begins to sew it up. The sack has been a running gag throughout the film; here, finally, its mysterious contents are revealed in an object and an activity that resonate with the fetishes, wounds, and lace imagery of so much Buñuelian cinema. In my reading it becomes a master metaphor attempting to sew up, in a sense, what *Un Chien andalou's* eye-cutting so brutally opened up almost fifty years earlier. That original cut opened up a literal wound that it then became the figurative work of cinematic signifiers to suture. For me, then, this final metaphor of sewing a torn and bloodied garment represents the perpetual but incomplete attempt to reconnect the two edges of a wound. The metaphor of suture comes to signify an original lack-in-being that can never be joined.

In Lacanian theory, however, suture is a process of provisional connections and lack-in-being is the effect of the work of signifiers alone. Neither stands for a signified in any static way. The problem with my reading, I am now aware, is that it posits an ultimately static statement of meaning that it has been the work of the Buñuelian cinema to perpetually evade. It tries to pin down – or sew up – that meaning in a critical statement that only sees its own theoretical reflection in images that may be most remarkable for their moments of genuine undecidability.

Undecidability – the word evokes another, as yet undeveloped, direction of Buñuelian criticism: that of deconstruction. If deconstruction is the critical method that identifies the oppositions upon which meaning are based, and if it also situates itself in the space between humanistic significance and anarchistic destruction of all meaning, then such a method would appear to be well equipped to tease out the structure of the Buñuelian cinema's similar oppositions. Like the statement, "thank God, I'm still an atheist!," which can neither be read as an assertion nor a denial of belief, but which instead demands to be read as a revelation of the theistic significance hidden behind atheistic denial, the most elusive, Surrealist elements of the Buñuelian cinema would seem to lend themselves to deconstruction. But if this "deconstructed Buñuel" is to be the next item on the critical agenda, we can be sure that it will only remain so until the films again wiggle out of even this tenuous grasp and force us, once again, to question our critical methods.

Notes

1. Over the years this statement has been repeatedly attributed to Buñuel by various interviewer-critics. The phrase's most recent manifestation is as a chapter title in Buñuel's autobiography, *My Last Sigh* (New York: Knopf, 1983) 171.

2. Reprinted in *The Shadow and Its Shadow: Surrealist Writings on Cinema,* edited by Paul Hammond (London: British Film Institute, 1978) 115–123.

3. From the published Preface to *Un Chien andalou. La Révolution surréaliste* 12 (15 Dec. 1920).

4. Paul Hammond defines this form of criticism as a tangential reading: "Instead of criticizing a film from an objective position . . . the surrealist spectator decomposed it as he saw fit" and then re-synthesized them in the critical text. Hammond, p. 5.

5. Robert Desnos, *Cinéma,* ed. André Tchernia (Paris: Gallimard, 1966).

6. Reprinted from *Buñuel: An Introduction* (New York: Simon and Schuster, 1955) in Joan Mellen ed., *The World of Luis Buñuel: Essays in Criticism* (New York: Oxford University Press, 1978) 160.

7. From Vol. III of *Qu'est-ce le Cinéma?* Reprinted in Mellen, p. 198.

8. Mellen, 198, 200.

9. Originally published in *Cineaste,* Vol. VII, No. 4 (1977). In Mellen, p. 353.

10. Mellen, p. 351.

11. Durgnat, *Luis Buñuel* (Berkeley: University of California Press, 1968) 8.

12. See, for example, Pauline Kael's review of *That Obscure Object of Desire,*"The Cutting Light," *The New Yorker,* December 19, 1977, pp. 128–130.

13. See, for example, Freddy Buache's discussion of *Belle de Jour* in *The Cinema of Luis Buñuel,* trans. Peter Graham (London: Tantivy Press, 1973), 173–175.

14. *Screen* 18 (Autumn 1977):55.

15. Drummond, pp. 55–119.

16. "Freedom and Necessity: Narrative Structure in *The Phantom of Liberty.*" *Quarterly Review of Film Studies* 3 (Summer 1978) :277–295.

17. "The Prologue to *Un Chien Andalou:* A Surrealist Film Metaphor," *Screen* 17 (Winter 1976–77) 24–33.

18. *Figures of Desire: A Theory and Analysis of Surrealist Film* (Urbana: University of Illinois Press, 1981) 229pp.

Robert Desnos's and Man Ray's Manuscript Scenario for *L'Etoile de mer*

The manuscript for the scenario of *L'Etoile de mer* has been in the collection of the Museum of Modern Art since 1972, and was believed until very recently to be in the hand of Man Ray. However, it has been possible to establish definitively that it is mainly in Desnos's hand by comparing it with a manuscript by Robert Desnos dating from 1928–29 for *The Night of Loveless Nights,* which is also part of the Museum's collection.

In the second manuscript, Desnos omits many accents, as he does in the scenario manuscript. Both manuscripts appear to have been written with a similar quill pen. The following transcription restores the accents left out by Desnos. Notations in pencil, red and blue crayon, which are in the hand of Man Ray, are marked in boldface. Musical notations, which have been authenticated by Francis Naumann to be in the hand of Man Ray, are supplied at the end. Other notations by Man Ray include changes in the order of images after VIII, XVIII, XXI, XXII, and XXVIII (these are noted in red pencil; the implication of these changes is discussed in my essay), underlining (subtitle 1, in blue pencil, and "une rue déserte, XV, in blue pencil), and the crossing out of some musical notations (in pencil). In addition, there are question marks in red pencil in section VIII and in pencil in section XVII, and arrows between sections XI, XII, and XIV.

The manuscript is written on the back of seven sheets, each consisting of two glued sheets of a mimeoed letter dated March 26, 1927, providing additional proof, if any were needed, that the text was written by Robert Desnos. The letterhead is that of *Paris Matin,* and we know that in May of 1927 Desnos left his job with *Le Soir* to join the short-lived *Paris Matin* founded by his friend Eugène Merle.[1] The letter itself is transcribed below:

Monsieur,

Paris Matin, grand quotidien d'information républicain qui paraîtra prochainement, avec plusieures éditions, fera dans ses colonnes une large part aux nouvelles de votre région. Pour l'oeuvre d'interêt général qu'il se propose de poursuivre, il désire être entouré de conseillers éprouvés et de guides sûrs. Aussi serions-nous très heureux si vous acceptiez de nous donner votre concours comme correspondant de *Paris Matin* dans votre commune. Dès lors que nous aurions votre acceptation de ce principe, votre carte de presse vous sera attribuée et nous vous ferons parvenir quelques directions pour le choix et la transmission des nouvelles.

Si, pour une raison quelconque, vous ne pouviez assurer cette correspondance, nous vous serions très obligés de nous indiquer une personne sérieuse et active qui pourrait s'en charger. Mais rien ne nous serait plus agréable que votre acceptation.

Dans cet espoir, veuillez agréer, Monsieur, l'assurance de nos sentiments très distingués.

Chef du Service Régional[2]

What makes the discovery of the Desnos manuscript so exciting is that it sheds new light on the nature of Desnos's and Man Ray's collaboration. It is illuminating, in this respect, to compare their two versions of how the film came to be.

MAN RAY:

Desnos eked out a precarious living as a newspaperman; dramatic, literary and art critic. One evening he announced he was being sent to the West Indies on a reporting mission and would be away for a couple of months. We had a farewell dinner together, including Kiki and a friend of hers with whom Robert was in love. At the end of the meal he . . . produced a crumpled sheet from his pocket; it was a poem he'd written that day . . . Desnos's poem was like a scenario for a film, consisting of fifteen or twenty lines, each line presenting a clear, detached image of a place or of a man and woman. There was no dramatic action, yet all the elements for a possible action. The title of the poem was "L'Etoile de Mer," Star of the Sea . . . the poem moved me very much, I saw it clearly as a film – a Surrealist film, and told Desnos that when he returned I'd have made a film with his poem . . . Not being able to sleep, I made some notes dealing with the more practical aspects of the realization . . . The next day, I made my preparations quickly, deciding to shoot the last scene with the woman and the two men before Robert's departure on his press assignment. Then I could plan and work more leisurely on the production. . . . After a few weeks of shooting, I had all my sequences in hand. I had enough for a film of about a half-hour's running time, but cut and rejected ruthlessly . . . until the film lasted only half as long.[3]

ROBERT DESNOS:

I own a sea-star (born in which ocean?) that I bought from a Jewish second-hand dealer of the rue des Rosiers and which is the very embodiment of a lost love, a love well lost – without this sea-star I would not have kept its moving memory. It is under its influence that I have written, in a form propitious to the apparitions and to the ghosts of a scenario, what Man Ray and I saw as a poem simple like love, simple like good morning, simple and terrible like goodbye. Man Ray is the only one who could conceive the spectres that, rising from the paper and from the film, could embody, under the features of my dear André de la Rivière and the moving Kiki, the spontaneous and tragic action of an adventure born in reality and pursued in dreams. I gave the manuscript to Man and left for a journey. When I came back the film was finished. Thanks to the dark operations with which he has constituted an alchemy of appearances, and with the help of inventions that owe less to science than to inspiration, Man Ray has constructed a domain that no longer belonged to me and was not totally his . . . Man Ray deliberately triumphing over technique has granted me the most flattering and moving image of myself and my dreams.[4]

In the light of these two statements, the manuscript we now have is still something of a mystery. Since it is subtitled "tel que l'a vu Man Ray," it evidences a stage of collaborative work that Man Ray fails to mention and Desnos only hints at ("It is under its influence that I have written . . . what Man Ray and I saw . . ."). Secondly, at what point were the additional texts (discussed in my article) added? Both men say that the film was already finished upon Desnos's return, yet many of the subtitles seem related to the poetry of Desnos. It seems clear, however, that Desnos made a much larger contribution to the film than Man Ray claimed, and than has hitherto been supposed. The scenario for *L'Etoile de mer* deserves to be included among his other cinematic writings, which were collected and published by Gallimard in 1966.

One final, surrealistic note: Janis Ekdahl, Special Collections Curator of the Museum of Modern Art Library and I established the identity of the *Etoile de mer* manuscript on July 14, 1986, exactly sixty-five years after Man Ray's arrival in Paris.

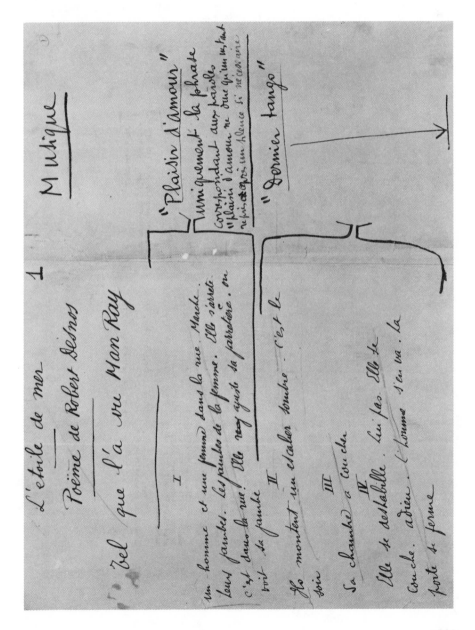

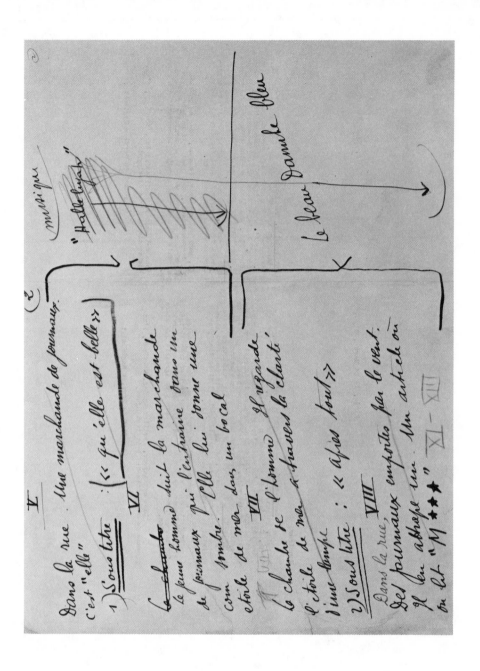

V

Dans la rue . Une marchande de journaux.
c'est "elle"

1) Sous titre :(« qu'elle est belle »)

VI

La chanté Le jeune homme suit la marchande dans un
de journaux qui l'entraine dans un Elle lui donne une
com sombre. Elle lui donne un bocal
étoile de mer dans un bocal

VII

Il regarde
le chante de l'homme à travers la clarté
l'étoile de mer à travers la clarté
d'une temps : « Après tout »

2) Sous titre

VIII

Dans la rue. Les journaux emportés par le vent.
Il les attrape un Un autre où
on lit "M ★★★" XI – XII

musique

"Halleluiah"

La peur Danube bleu

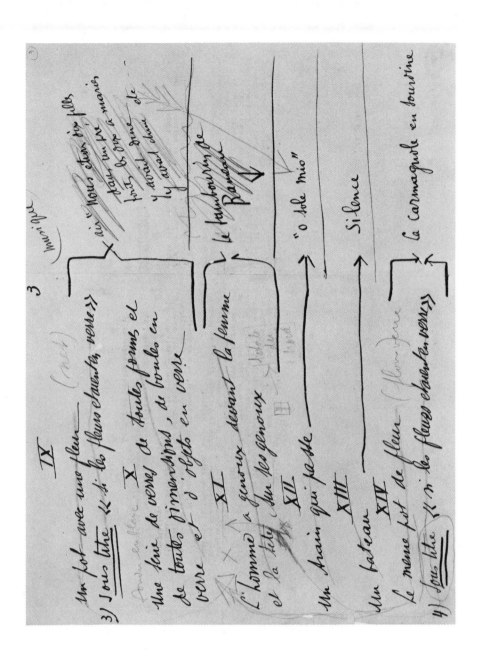

211

(musique)

XV

La femme et jeu de loto

La femme en bonnet phrygien, de la fumée, du feu, dans une rue déserte.

peinte à travers fleu

La Carmagnole très fort puis lente et en sourdine "O sole mio"

XVI

La femme frotique se habille. Un pied sur un chaise. L'étoile de mer dans un coin

"O Sole Mio"

XVII – XXVII

La femme propre se habille. Des bouteilles brisées autour d'elle d'or. L'étoile

se closse du vin rouge... l'étoile un coin la XIX XX XXI

de mer fem. XVIII

la femme toute seule XXII

L'aria de Bach

une route

5   sous titre «Belle, belle comme l'étoile une fleur de verre »>

de mer vient en murmurant.

212

l'avion
de chasse

5

XIX

Le jeune homme qui regarde ses mains.
l'école de md dans un coin

XX

les mains de l'homme. les lignes
de ses mains marquées en
noir

XXI XXIV

Un escalier éclairé. La femme
monte un long couteau à
la main. l'étole de ses ...
une manche

XXII une XIX

le jeune homme. La femme

le jeune homme devant lui.

XXIII

mas quê bon masque c'est elle.
Elle retire un masque c'est elle.
G... «Belle comme une fleur de chair»

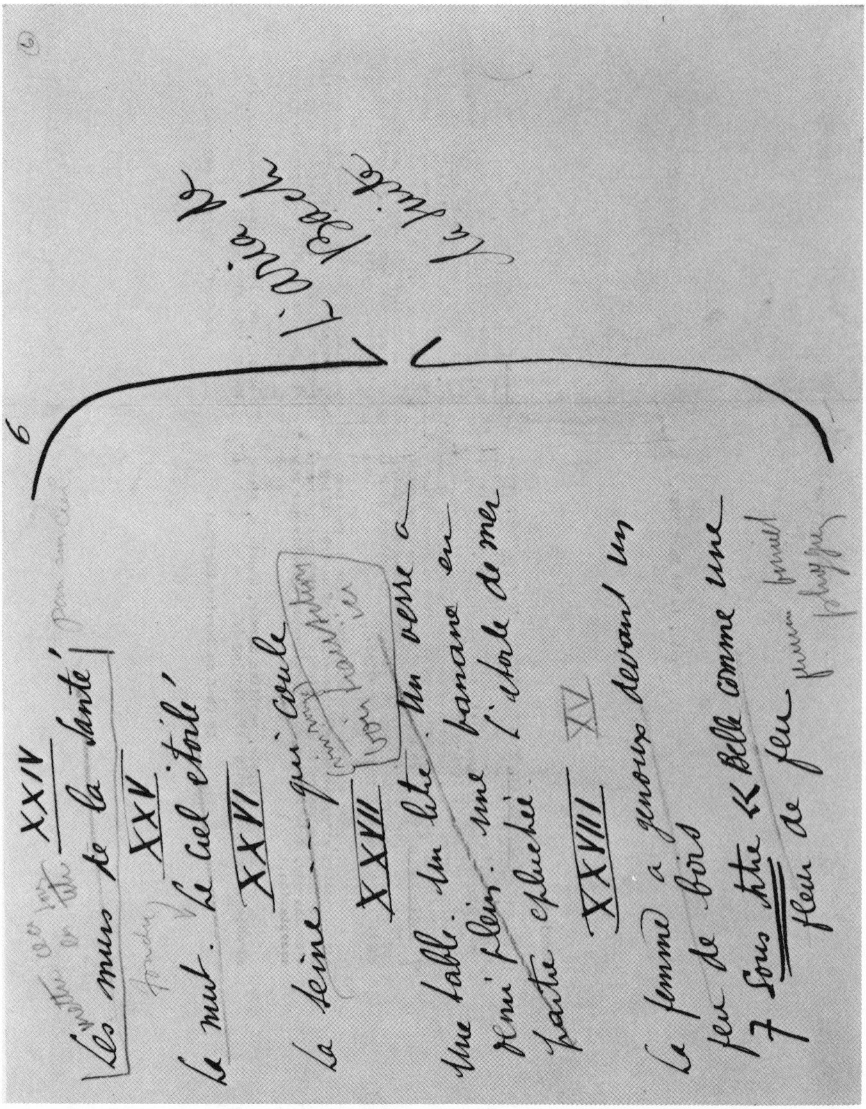

6

XXIV

Les murs de la Santé

XXV

le nuit. Le ciel étoilé

XXVI

La Seine qui coule

XXVII

Une table. Un lit. Un verre à
demi plein, une banane en
pâte épluchée

XXVIII   XV

La femme à genoux devant un
feu de bois
Sous titre « Belle comme une
fleur de feu »

XXIX (amour home)

Le femme endormie dans son lit 7

XXX
<< tous ne vivez pas >> 77

la vie.

XXXI

La femme et l'homme arrive par
deux directions et se rencontrent

XXXII

arrive un deuxième homme.

La femme part avec lui

8) << qu'elle "était belle >>
sous titre (en italique)

XXXIII

Le jeune homme devant
l'étoile de mer

9) sous titre << qu'elle est "belle" >>

L'aria Bach
de Just
la

"Plaisir d'amour"

J'ai correspondant à ces pacols
"chagrin d'amour dure toute
la vie"
au besoin faire un blanc au
relut-pour que la musique finisse
avec le sous titre.

TRANSCRIPTION

L'Etoile de mer / Poëme de Robert Desnos / tel que l'a vu Man Ray [in the hand of Robert Desnos with annotations by Man Ray in boldface]

I.   Un homme et une femme dans la rue. Marche. Leurs jambes. Les jambes de la femme. Elle s'arrête. c'est dans la rue. Elle ajuste sa jarretière. on voit sa jambe

II.   Ils montent un escalier sombre. c'est le soir

III.   Sa chambre à coucher

IV.   Elle se déshabille. Lui pas. Elle se couche. adieu. L'homme s'en va. La porte se ferme

V.   Dans la rue. Une marchande de journaux. c'est "elle."
         1) *Sous-titre* ("qu'elle est belle")

VI.   Le jeune homme suit la marchande de journaux qui l'entraîne dans un coin sombre. Elle lui donne une étoile de mer dans un bocal

VII.   La chambre de l'homme. Il regarde l'étoile de mer à travers la clarté d'une lampe
         2) *Sous-titre:* "Après tout"

VIII.   Dans la rue, Des journaux emportés par le vent. Il en attrape un. Un article où on lit "M***" **XI-XIII**

IX.   Un pot avec une fleur
         3) *Sous-titre* "si les fleurs étaient en verre" **net**

X.   Une série de verres de toutes formes et de toutes dimensions, de boules en verre et d'objets en verre **fondu en blanc**

XI.   L'homme à genoux devant la femme et la tête sur ses genoux

XII.   Un train qui passe **L'étoile du nord** (with square drawing)

XIII.   Un bâteau

XIV.   La [sic] même pot de fleur
         4) *Sous-titre* "si les fleurs étaient en verre" **(flou) verre**

XV.   La femme en bonnet phrygien, de la fumée, du feu, une rue déserte **voir femme et feu de bois; fenêtre à travers le feu**

XVI.   La femme presque déshabillée. Un pied sur un livre L'étoile de mer dans un coin

XVII.   La femme presque déshabillée. Des bouteilles brisées autour d'elle d'où s'échappe du vin rouge. L'étoile de mer dans un coin **XVII ici XIX et XX**

XVIII.   Une route. La femme toute seule
         5) *Sous titre* "Belle, belle comme une fleur de verre" L'étoile de mer vient en surimpression **mettre avant XXII**

XIX.   Le jeune homme regarde ses mains. L'étoile de mer dans un coin

XX.   Les mains de l'homme. Les lignes de ses mains marqués [sic] en noir

XXI.   Un escalier éclairé. La femme monte un long couteau à la main. L'étoile de mer sur une marche **XXIV**

XXII.   Le jeune homme. Une femme masquée devant lui **XIX**

XXIII.   Elle retire son masque. C'est elle
         6) *Sous titre* "Belle comme une fleur de chair" **toutes expressions** (with grid drawing)

216

XXIV.   Les murs de la Santé **pan sur ciel; mettre ceci en sous-titre**
XXV.   La nuit. Le ciel étoilé
XXVI.   La Seine . . . qui coule
XXVII.   Une table. Un litre. Un verre à demi plein. une banane en partie épluchée. L'étoile de mer **vin rouge; voir transition ici**
XXVIII. La femme à genoux devant un feu de bois **XV**
         7) *Sous titre* "Belle comme une fleur de feu" **bonnet phrygien**
XXIX.   La femme endormie dans son lit **amorce noire**
XXX.   La rue **sous-titre: "vous ne révez [sic] pas"**
XXXI.   La femme et l'homme arrive [sic] par deux directions et se rencontrent
XXXII.   Arrive un deuxième homme. La femme part avec lui
         8) *Sous titre* "qu'elle 'était' belle" (en italique)
XXXIII. Le jeune homme devant l'étoile de mer
         9) *Sous titre* "qu'elle 'est' belle" (*en italique*)
         L'étoile de mer en surimpression **explosion**

TRANSLATION:

I.   A man and a woman in the street. Walk. Their legs. The woman's legs. She stops. It's in the street. She adjusts her garter. You can see her leg
II.   They go up a dark staircase. It's evening
III.   Her bedroom
IV.   She gets undressed. He doesn't. She lies down. goodbye. The man leaves. The door closes
V.   In the street. A woman selling newspapers. It's "she"
         1) *Subtitle:* ("how beautiful she is")
VI.   The young man follows the woman selling newspapers who entices him into a dark place. She gives him a starfish in a jar
VII.   The man's room. He looks at the starfish by the light of a lamp
         2) *Subtitle:* ("after all")
VIII.   In the street, newspapers blown around by the wind. He catches one. You can read "Mr. ***" **XI-XII**
IX.   A pot containing a flower
         3) *Subtitle:* "If flowers were made of glass" **focused**
X.   A series of glass containers, glass spheres and glass objects of all shapes and sizes **fade to white**
XI.   The man kneeling down before the woman with his head on her knees
XII.   A passing train **the North star** (with square drawing)
XIII.   A ship
XIV.   The same flower pot
         4) *Subtitle:* "If flowers were made of glass" **unfocused**
XV.   The woman in a Phrygian bonnet, smoke, fire, a deserted street **see woman and wood fire; window through the fire**

XVI.   The woman almost nude. One foot on a book. The starfish in a corner

XVII.   The woman almost nude. Broken bottles around her from which red wine oozes. The starfish in a corner **XVII; here XIX and XX**

XVIII. A road. The woman all by herself
        5) *Subtitle:* "Beautiful, beautiful as a glass flower"
        The starfish superimposed **put this before XXII**

XIX.   The young man looks at his hands. The starfish in a corner

XX.   The man's hands. The lines of his hands outlined in black

XXI.   A lit staircase. The woman goes up the stairs holding a long knife. The starfish on a step **XXIV**

XXII.   The young man. In front of him, a masked woman **XIX**

XXIII. She removes her mask. It is she
        6) *Subtitle:* "Beautiful as a flower of flesh" **all expressions** (with grid drawing)

XXIV.   The walls of La Santé **pan to the sky; put this in a subtitle**

XXV.   Night. The starry sky

XVI.   The Seine . . . flowing

XXVII. A table. A wine bottle. A half-filled glass. A partly peeled banana. The starfish **red wine; see transition here**

XXVIII. The woman kneeling before a wood fire
        7) *Subtitle:* "Beautiful as a flower of fire" **Phrygian bonnet; XV**

XXIX.   The woman asleep in her bed **begin with black**

XXX.   The street **subtitle: "you are not dreaming"**

XXXI.   The woman and the man arrive from two directions and meet

XXXII. A second man arrives. The woman leaves with him
        8) *Subtitle:* "how beautiful she 'was'" (in italics)

XXXIII. The young man before the starfish
        9) *Subtitle:* "how beautiful she 'is'" (in italics)
        the starfish superimposed **explosion**

Musical Notations (in the hand of Man Ray)

I.   "Plaisir d'amour" (uniquement la phrase correspondant aux paroles "plaisir d'amour ne dure qu'un instant" repris après un silence si nécessaire)

II–V.   "Dernier tango"

V–VIII.   Le beau Danube bleu (V–VI, "Hallelujah," scratched out)

IX–XII.   "O sole mio" (IX–X, "Nous étions dix filles dans un pré toutes les dix à marier y avait Dine y avait Anne etc." scratched out; XI, le tambourin de Rameau, scratched out)

XII.   Silence

XIV.   La carmagnole en sourdine

XV.   La carmagnole très fort puis silence et en sourdine; "O sole mio"

XVI.   "O sole mio"

XVII–XXXII. L'aria de Bach

XXXIII.   "Plaisir d'amour" (l'air correspondant à ces paroles "chagrin d'amour dure toute la vie") au besoin faire un silence au début pour que la musique finisse avec le sous titre.

(Translation: "Love's Pleasure" (only the phrase corresponding to the words "love's pleasure lasts but a moment" repeated after a silence if necessary); "Last Tango"; "The Beautiful Blue Danube"; "O sole mio"; "We were ten girls in a field all getting married there was Dine there was Anne, etc."; Rameau's Tambourine; Silence; The Carmagnole, muffled; The Carmagnole, very loud, then silence, then muffled; "O sole mio"; Bach aria)

Inez Hedges

Notes

1. Robert Desnos, *Cinéma*, ed. André Tchernia (Paris: Gallimard, 1966) 12.

2. Translation: Dear Sir, *Paris Matin,* a large republican daily newspaper which will be published soon in several editions, will devote several columns to news from your region. We wish to be surrounded by experienced advisors and knowledgeable guides in order to pursue the work that we propose, which is of great public interest. Therefore we would be very happy if you would assist us as a correspondent of *Paris Matin* in your district. As soon as we have received your acceptance, you will be sent a press card and instructions concerning the selection and transmission of news items. If, for any reason, you are unable to become our correspondent, we would be very grateful if you would give us the name of a serious and active person who could do it. But nothing would please us more than your acceptance. In the hope of an affirmative response, please be assured of our sincere good wishes. Chief, Regional Branch.

3. Man Ray, *Self Portrait* (Boston: Little, Brown and Co., 1963) 275-77.

4. Robert Desnos to Pierre Migennes, "Les Photographies de Man Ray" (1928), p. 160; quoted in Arturo Schwarz, *Man Ray: The Rigour of Imagination* (New York: Rizzoli, 1977) 297.

III. BIBLIOGRAPHY: DADA AND SURREALIST FILM

The following selective bibliography is divided into two parts. The first section consists of monographs, dissertations, parts of books, and articles on general aspects of Dada and Surrealist film. The scope of this part is thematically and chronologically broad. Selected writings on film by Dadaists and Surrealists, who did not collaborate on film productions, are also included in this section.

The second part consists of selective bibliographies on the film-related work of eighteen individuals, who were involved in the making of Dada and Surrealist films in the period between 1920 and 1933. Primary and secondary sources in this section are limited to their activities in film.

Filmographies are not included, since they are readily available in monographs on individual filmmakers (e.g. F. Aranda, *Luis Buñuel: A Critical Biography*), or in the following general presentations: Paul Hammond, ed., *The Shadow and Its Shadow: Surrealist Writings on Cinema* (Appendix, pp. 131–33); Alan Sayag, ed., *Cinéma dadaiste et surréaliste* (pp. 61–62); *Film as Film: Formal Experiment in Film 1910–1975* ("Filmographies 1910–40," pp. 72–89).

I would like to thank my assistant Robert Gladstein for his valuable help in compiling this bibliography, and June Fischer for her superb typing.

Rudolf E. Kuenzli

I. Books and Articles on General Aspects of Dada and Surrealist Film

1. BOOKS, DISSERTATIONS, AND THESES

Abel, Richard. *French Cinema: The First Wave, 1915–1929.* Princeton: Princeton University Press, 1984.

Bagier, Guido. *Der kommende Film. Eine Abrechnung und eine Hoffnung. Was war? Was ist? Was wird?* Stuttgart, Berlin and Leipzig: Deutsche Verlags-Anstalt, 1928.

Balázs, Béla. *Der sichtbare Mensch oder die Kultur des Films.* Vienna and Leipzig: Deutsch-Österreichischer Verlag, 1924.

Ballo, Francesco. *Aspetti del cinema non commerciale di alcuni artisti delle avanguardie storiche.* Milan: Silvana, 1979.

Brunius, Jacques B. *En Marge du cinéma français.* Paris: Arcanes, 1954.

Buache, F. *Le Cinema indépendant et d'avant-garde à la fin du muet.* Lausanne: Documents Cinémathique Suisse, 1979.

Carter, Huntley. *The New Spirit in Cinema.* Rpt. New York: Arno Press, 1970.

Chesler, Judd. "Toward a Surrealist Film Aesthetic with an Investigation into the Elements of Surrealism in the Marx Brothers and Jean Vigo." Diss. Northwestern University, 1976.

Curtis, David. *Experimental Cinema*. New York: Universe Books, 1971.

Dwoskin, Stephen. *Film Is: The International Free Cinema*. Woodstock, N.Y.: Overlook, 1975.

Fauré, Elie. *The Art of Cineplastics*. Boston: Four Seas Press, 1923.

Film as Film: Formal Experiment in Film, 1910–1975. London: Arts Council of Great Britain, 1979 [Exhibition catalog].

Fokine, M., Rolf de Mare, Haquinus, Remon Tansman, and Tugal. *Les ballets suédois dans l'art contemporain*. Paris: Trianon, 1931.

Foorsterling, Erwin. "Surrealism and the Cinema." M.F.A. Thesis, University of Iowa, 1954.

Gordon, Bette. "Surrealism in Film." M.A. Thesis, University of Wisconsin, 1975.

Gould, Michael. *Surrealism and the Cinema*. Cranbury, N.J.: A. S. Barnes, 1976.

Haas, Patrick de. *Cinéma Intégral. De la peinture au cinéma dans les années 20*. Brussels: Transédition, 1986.

———. *Le Corps traversé par des films vites. L'Art comme utopie*. Le Havre: Maison de la Culture du Havre, 1979 [Exhibition catalog].

Hammond, Paul, ed. *The Shadow and Its Shadow: Surrealist Writings on Cinema*. London: British Film Institute, 1978.

Hedges, Inez. *Languages of Revolt: Dada and Surrealist Literature and Film*. Durham, N.C.: Duke University Press, 1983.

Hein, Birgit, and Wulf Herzogenrath, eds. *Film als Film: 1910 bis heute*. Cologne: Kölnischer Kunstverein, 1977.

Kaes, Anton, ed. *Kino-Debatte. Literatur und Film 1909–1929*. Tübingen: Niemeyer, 1978.

Kovács, Steven. *From Enchantment to Rage: The Story of Surrealist Cinema*. Rutherford, N.J.: Fairleigh Dickinson University Press, 1980.

Kovacs, Yves, ed. *Surréalisme et cinéma (I)*. Special issue of *Études Cinématographiques*. 38–39, Spring, 1965.

———, ed. *Surréalisme et cinéma (II)*. Special issue of *Études Cinématographiques* 40–42, Summer 1965.

Kurtz, Rudolf. *Expressionismus und Film*. Berlin: Verlag der Lichtbühne, 1926.

Kyrou, Ado. *Amour-Erotisme et cinéma*. Rev. Ed. Paris: Losfeld, 1966.

Kyrou, Ado. *Le Surréalisme au cinéma*. Paris: Editions Arcanes, 1953.

Lawder, Standish D. *The Cubist Cinema*. New York: New York University Press, 1975.

———. "Structuralism and Movement in Experimental Film and Modern Art." Diss. Yale University, 1967.

Le Grice, Malcom. *Abstract Film and Beyond*. Cambridge: MIT Press, 1977.

Leonard, Arthur Byron. "Poetry and Film: Aspects of the Avant-Garde in France (1918–1932)." Diss. Stanford University, 1975.

Levy, Julien. *Surrealism*. New York: The Black Sun Press, 1936 [contains scenario for *Un Chien andalou*, synopsis of *L'Age d'or*, text of *Monsieur Phot* (Joseph Cornell), and a fragment of *Baboauo* (Dali)].

Lindemann, Bernhard. *Experimentalfilm als Metafilm*. Hildesheim: Olms, 1977.

Loevgren, Hakan. "Cine-Montage in Development: Symbolist, Futurist, and Dadaist Influences in Sergei Eisenstein's Early Works." M.S. Thesis, Boston University, 1975.

Manvell, Roger, ed. *Experiment in the Film*. London: Grey Walls Press, 1949.

Matthews, J. H. *Languages of Surrealism*. Columbia: University of Missouri Press, 1986.

———. *Surrealism and American Feature Films*. Boston: Twayne, 1979.

———. *Surrealism and Film*. Ann Arbor: University of Michigan Press, 1971.

Mitry, Jean. *Le Cinéma experimental: histoire et perspectives*. Paris: Seghers, 1974.

Moholy-Nagy, Laszlo. *Painting, Photography, Film*. Trans. J. Seligman. Cambridge: MIT Press. 1969.

Moussinac, Léon. *Panoramique du cinéma*. Paris: Au Sans Pareil, 1929.

Polan, Dana Bart. *The Political Language of Film and the Avant-Garde*. Ann Arbor: UMI Research Press, 1985.

Rondolino, Gianni, ed. *L'Occhio tagliato: documenti del cinema dadaista e surrealista*. Turin: Martano, 1972.

Sayag, Alain. *Cinéma dadaiste et surréaliste*. Paris: Centre Georges Pompidou, 1976 [Exhibition catalog].

Schamoni, Victor. *Das Lichtspiel, Möglichkeiten des absoluten Films*. Hamburg: Reimann, 1936.

Schneede, Uwe. *Surrealistische Filme: Das Prinzip der Schockmontage*. Darmstadt: Wissenschaftliche Buchgesellschaft, 1982.

Sitney, P. Adams, ed. *The Avant-Garde Film*. New York: New York University Press, 1978.

———. *Visionary Film: The American Avant-Garde*. New York: Oxford University Press, 1974.

Stauffacher, Frank, ed. *Art in Cinema. A Symposium on the Avantgarde Film*. San Francisco: San Francisco Museum of Art, 1947.

Stern, Seymour, and Lewis Jacobs, eds. *Experimental Cinema, 1930–34: Nos. 1– 5*. Rpt. New York: Arno, n.d.

Taylor, John Russel. *Cinema Eye, Cinema Ear*. London: Methuen, 1964.

Turim, Maureen. *Abstraction in Avant-Garde Films*. Ann Arbor: UMI Research Press, 1985.

Tyler, Parker. *The Underground Film: A Critical History*. New York: Grove, 1969.

Verdone, M. *Le Avanguardie storiche del cinema*. Turin: Società Editrice Internazionale, 1977.

Virmaux, Alain and Odette. *Les Surréalistes et le cinéma*. Paris: Seghers, 1976.

Vogel, Amos. *Film as a Subversive Art*. New York: Random, 1974.

Weiss, Peter. *Avantgardefilm*. Stockholm: Wahlström and Widstrand, 1956.

Williams, Linda. *Figures of Desire: A Theory and Analysis of Surrealist Film*. Urbana: University of Illinois Press, 1981.

2. ARTICLES AND PARTS OF BOOKS

Abel, Richard. "The Contribution of the French Literary Avant-Garde to Film Theory and Criticism (1907–1924)." *Cinema Journal* 14.3 (Spring 1975): 18–40.

————. "American Film and the French Literary Avant-Garde." *Contemporary Literature* 17.1 (Winter 1976): 84–109.

Aiken, Edward. "Reflections on Dada and the Cinema." *Post Script* 3.2 (Winter 1984): 5–19.

Albersheimer, Franz-Josef. "Kinematographischer versus literarischer 'Esprit nouveau': zur Antinomie von kinematographischer und literarischer Avantgarde in Frankreich (1895–1930)." In *Absolut modern sein: Zwischen Fahrrad und Fliessband: Culture technique in Frankreich 1889–1937*. Berlin: Elefanten Press, 1986. 203–10.

Amberg, G. "Documentary of Another Realm: Surrealism from Cocteau to Polanski." *University Film Study Newsletter* 6.3 (Supplement 1976): 1–4.

Amengual, B. "Le Cinéma d'animation, expression privilégiée du surréalisme à l'écran." In *Surréalisme et cinéma II*, ed. Yves Kovacs. Special issue of *Études cinématographiques* 40–42 (Summer 1965): 209–45.

Aragon, Louis. "Charlot Sentimental [poem]." *Le Film* 1 March 1918.

————. "Du Décor." *Le Film* September 1918; in English in *The Shadow and Its Shadow*, ed. Paul Hammond. London: British Film Institute, 1978. 28–31.

————. "Louis Delluc: *Cinéma et Cie*." *Littérature* 4 (June 1919): 15–16.

————, and Sergei Eisenstein. "Le Potemkine à 50 ans." *Écran* 42 (December 1975): 8–11.

————. "Réponse à un 'Appel à la curiosité.' " *Les Cahiers de la cinémathèque* 30–31 (1980): 85.

Aranda, J. F. "Cinema experimental e de vanguarda." *Celuloide* 28.348 (May 1983):126– 29.

Astre, Georges-Albert. "Surréalisme et cinéma." In *Surréalisme et cinéma I*, ed. Yves Kovacs. Special issue of *Études cinématographiques* 38–39 (Spring 1965): 3–5.

Bassan, R. "L'Avantgarde à l'est." *Image et Son* 349 (April 1980): 134–35.

————. "1929: Entre le voile et la chrysalide." *Écran* 86 (December 1979): 12–19.

————. "Ultime Tabou: le discours sur l'avantgarde." *Écran* 57 (April 1977): 10–11.

Beaujour, Michel. "Surréalisme ou cinéma." In *Surréalisme et cinéma I*, ed. Yves Kovacs. Special issue of *Études cinématographiques* 38–39 (Spring 1965): 57–63.

Becker, Rolf. "Film, Montage, Magie, Dada." *Magnum* 22 (February 1959): 37.

Behne, Adolf. "Der Film als Kunstwerk." *Sozialistische Monatshefte* 57 (1921): 1116–18.

Belz, Carl. "The Terror of the Surreal." In *Focus on the Horror Film*, ed. R. Huss and T. J. Ross. Englewood Cliffs, N.J.: Prentice-Hall, 1972.

Benjamin, Walter. "Rückblick auf Chaplin [1929]." In *Kino-Debatte*, ed. Anton Kaes. Tübingen: Niemeyer, 1978. 173–75.

————. "The Work of Art in the Age of Mechanical Reproduction." In *Illuminations*, ed. Hannah Arendt. New York: Schocken, 1969. 217–252.

Bertetto, P. "L'Avanguardia cinematografica: technologia e dialettica del valore." *Filmcritica* 26 (January-February 1975): 23–36.

Bertrand, Marc. "Image cinématographique et image surréaliste." *Les Cahiers de la Cinémathèque* 30–31 (1980): 41–47.

Blanchot, Maurice. "Reflexions sur le surréalisme." In his *La Part du feu*. Paris: Gallimard, 1949.

Blot, C. and A. Labarrère. "Dimension sociale du cinéma surréaliste." In *Surréalisme et cinéma II*, ed. Yves Kovacs. Special issue of *Études cinématographiques* 40–42 (Summer 1965): 261–66.

Bonnet, Marguerite. "L'Aube du surréalisme et le cinéma: attente et rencontres." In *Surréalisme et cinéma I*, ed. Yves Kovacs. Special issue of *Études cinématographiques* 38–39 (Spring 1965): 83–101.

Borde, R., et al. "Le Cinéma des surréalistes." *Les Cahiers de la cinémathèque* (1979): 1–43.

Breton, André. "Comme dans un bois." *L'Age du cinéma* 4–5 (1951): 26–30; in English in *The Shadow and Its Shadow*, ed. Paul Hammond. London: British Film Institute, 1978. 42–45.

Brunius, Jacques. "Crossing the Bridge [Translator's title]." In *The Shadow and Its Shadow*, ed. Paul Hammond. London: British Film Institute, 1978. 60–62.

———. "Experimental Film in France." In *Experiment in the Film*, ed. Roger Manvell. London: Grey Walls Press, 1949. 60–112.

———. "The Lights Go Up [Translator's title]." In *The Shadow and Its Shadow*. London: British Film Institute, 1978. 48.

———. "The Screen's Prestige." In *The Shadow and Its Shadow*, ed. Paul Hammond. London: British Film Institute, 1978. 65.

Brzekowski, Jan. "Pour le film abstrait." *Cercle et Carré* 3:30 (June 1930).

Burch, N. "Avant-Garde or Vanguard?" *Afterimage* 6 (Summer 1976): 52–63.

Capdenac, M. "Confrontation XV: le surréalisme." *Écran* 81 (June 1979): 13–14.

Carroll, Noel. "Avant-Guarde Film and Film Theory." *Millennium* 4–5 (1979): 135–43.

Chevallier, J. "Le Cinéma des surréalistes." *Revue du cinéma* 359 (March 1981): 139.

Christie, Ian. "French Avant-garde Film in the Twenties: from 'Specificity' to Surrealism." In *Film as Film*. London: Arts Council, 1979. 37–45.

———. "Le Cinéma des surréalistes à Perpignan." *Revue du cinéma* 340 (June 1979): 17–19.

———. "Les Surréalistes devant l'écran." *Revue du cinéma* 346 (January 1980): 93–106.

Cook, P. "Teaching Avant-Garde Film: Notes Towards Practice." *Screen Education* 32–33 (1979–80): 83–97.

Courant, G. "Le Cinéma des surréalistes: après les rencontres de Perpignan: 'cette belle chose qu'un film vu par la foule.'" *Cinéma 80* 253 (January 1980): 44–46.

———. "Notes sur quelques films anciens et/ou peu connus mais qui méritent de l'être." *Cinéma 80* 253 (January 1980): 47–51.

Curtis, David. "The European Avant-Garde." In his *Experimental Cinema*. New York: Universe Books, 1971. 9–37.

Dal Co, F. "Cinema città avanguardia 1919–1939." *Bianco e Nero* 35 (1974): 294–320.

Décaudin, Michel. "Les Poètes découvrent le cinéma (1914–1918)." In *Surréalisme et cinéma I*, ed. Yves Kovacs. Special issue of *Études cinématographiques* 38–39 (Spring 1965): 75–82.

Decaux, E. "Le Cinéma des surréalistes." *Cinématographie* 69 (July 1981): 67.

De la Bretèque, François. " 'À l'echelle animale' (Notes pour un bestiaire dans le cinéma des surréalistes)." *Les Cahiers de la cinémathèque* 30–31 (1980): 58–67.

Delteil, Joseph. "Le Cinéma." *La Revue européenne* 1 March 1925.

Deslaw, Eugen. "Cinéma abstrait." *Cercle et Carré* 3 (June 1980).

Despax, J.-C., et al. "Claude Autant-Lara dans l'avant-garde française." *Cahiers de la cinémathèque* 9 (Spring 1973): 9–15.

Devaux, F. "Approaching Letterist Cinema." *Visible Language* 17.3 (1983): 48–56.

Devilliers, M. "Dossier: le rêve à l'écran. Rêves informulés." *Cinématographe* 35 (February 1978): 2–5.

Diebold, Bernhard. "Expressionismus und Kino." *Neue Zürcher Zeitung*, 14, 15, and 16 September, 1916.

———. "Film und Kunst. Ein Memento an die Filmkulturträger." *Frankfurter Zeitung*, 7 September 1920: 1–2.

Doesburg, Theo van. "Abstracte Filmbeelding." *De Stijl* 4.5 (1921): 71–75.

———. "Film as Pure Form." Trans. Standish Lawder. *Form* 1 (Summer 1966): 5–11.

———. "Licht – en Tijdbeelding." *De Stijl* 6.5 (1923): 58–62.

"Documents on German Abstract Film." In *Film as Film.* London: Arts Council, 1979.

Drummond, Phillip. "Notions of Avant-garde Cinema." In *Film as Film.* London: Arts Council, 1979. 9–16.

Ducros, Franc. "Le Surréalisme excédé." *Les Cahiers de la cinémathèque* 30–31 (1980): 68–75.

Dusinberre, Deke. "The Other Avant-gardes." In *Film as Film.* London: Arts Council, 1979. 53–58.

Dyer, Peter John. "Some Personal Visions." *Films and Filming* 5.2 (1958): 13–15, 30–31.

Earle, W. "Cinema Banality and Surrealism." *Quarterly Review of Film Studies* 2.2 (1977): 179–84.

Edwards, Tudor. "Film and Unreality." *Sight and Sound* 58 (Summer 1946): 59–61.

Fauré, Elie. "The Art of Cinéplastics [Excerpt]." In *Art in Cinema,* ed. F. Stauffacher. San Francisco: San Francisco Museum of Art, 1947. 22–24.

Ferry, Jean. "Concerning *King Kong.*" *Minotaure* 3 (1934); trans. in *The Shadow and Its Shadow,* ed. Paul Hammond. London: British Film Institute, 1978. 105

Field, S. "Re-Viewing the Avant-Garde." *Monthly Film Bulletin* 50 (August 1983): 204–6.

———. "Underground 2: Reviewing the Avant-Garde." *Monthly Film Bulletin* 50 (September 1983): 234–36.

Frank, André. "Éclatement du spectacle, naissance d'une dramaturgie . . . ." In *Surréalisme et cinéma II,* ed. Yves Kovacs. Special issue of *Études cinématographiques* 40–42 (Summer 1965): 267–71.

French Surrealist Group. "Data towards the Irrational Enlargement of a Film: *Shanghai Gesture.*" *L'Age du cinéma* 4–5 (1951); transl. in *The Shadow and Its Shadow,* ed. Paul Hammond. London: British Film Institute, 1978. 74–80.

———. "Manifesto of the Surrealists Concerning *L'Age d'or.*" In *The Shadow and Its Shadow,* ed. Paul Hammond. London: British Film Institute, 1978. 115–21.

———. "Some Surrealist Advice." *L'Age du cinéma* 4–5 (1951); trans. in *The Shadow and Its Shadow,* ed. Paul Hammond. London: British Film Institute, 1978. 25–26.

Frenkel, Lise. "Un Balcon en forêt." *Les Cahiers de la cinémathèque* 30–31 (l980): 140–48.

————. "'Je' sur le Pont Neuf." *Les Cahiers de la cinémathèque* 30–31 (1980): 135–36.

————. "Rencontre avec Julien Gracq." *Les Cahiers de la cinémathèque* 30–31 (1980): 149.

Garriba, Mario. "I sogni che non si possono comprare." *Filmcritica* 34. 335–36 (1983): 278–82.

Garroni, E. "Esiste e cos' è un' 'avanguardia cinematografica'?" *Filmcritica* 25. 241 (January 1974): 3–16.

Goudal, Jean. "Surrealism and Cinema." *La Revue hebdomadaire* (Feb. 1925); transl. in *The Shadow and Its Shadow*, ed. Paul Hammond. London: British Film Institute. 1978. 49–56.

Greene, Naomi. "Godard and Surrealism." *Dada/Surrealism* 3 (1973): 23–28.

Grossman, Manuel. "Jean Vigo and the Development of Surrealist Cinema." *Symposium* (June 1973).

————. "Surrealism in *Dog Star Man*." *Dada/Surrealism* 2 (1972): 71–77.

Gubern, Roman. "L'Avant-garde cinématographique en Espagne (1926–1930)." *Les Cahiers de la cinémathèque* 30–31 (1980): 155–62.

Haas, Patrick de. "Cinema: The Manipulation of Materials." In *Dada-Constructivism*. London: Annely Juda Gallery, 1984. 53–71.

————. "Constructivisme et avant-garde polonaise dans les années 20 et 30." *L'Avant-Scène: Cinema* 317–318 (December 1983): 15–18.

Hammond, Paul. "Off at a Tangent." In his *The Shadow and Its Shadow*. London: British Film Institute, 1978. 1–22.

Hausmann, Raoul. "De L'enregistrement cinématographique à la vision filmée." *L'Age du cinéma* 6 (1952): 43–45.

————. "Filmdämmerung." *A bis Z* 7 (April 1930): 26–27; in French in *Cercle et Carré* 3 (June) 1930.

————. "Vom sprechenden Film zur Optophonetik." *G* 1 (July 1923): 2–3.

Hein, Birgit. "The Futurist Film." In *Film as Film*. London: Arts Council, 1979. 19–21.

Henderson, B. "Film Theory and the Avant-Garde." *Australian Journal of Screen Theory* 9–10 (1981): 155–65.

Hennebelle, G. "L'Avant-garde en question: la blanche ou la rouge?" *Écran* 55 (Feb. 1977): 13–22; 56 (March 1977): 27–38.

Herzogenrath, Wulf. "Light-Play and Kinetic Theatre as Parallels to Absolute Film." In *Film as Film*. London: Arts Council, 1979. 22–26.

Hilbersheimer, Ludwig. "Filmmöglichkeiten." *Sozialistische Monatshefte* 59 (1922): 741–43.

Hoberman, J. "Three Myths of Avant-Garde Film." *Film Comment* 17 (May-June 1981): 34–35.

Horak, J.-C. "Discovering Pure Cinema: Avant-Garde Film in the '20s." *After-Image* 8 (Summer 1980): 4–7.

Ilie, Paul. "Surrealism and Cinema." *Diacritics* (Winter 1972): 54–59.

Jouvet, P. "Dossier: le rêve à l'écran. Le rêve tomato ketchup." *Cinématographe* 35 (Feb. 1978): 11–13.

Kaes, Anton. "The Expressionist Vision in Theater and Cinema." In *Expressionism Reconsidered. Affinities and Relationships*. ed. Gertrud B. Pickar and Karl E. Webb. Munich: Fink, 1979. 89–98.

————. "Verfremdung als Verfahren: Film und Dada." In *Sinn aus Unsinn: Dada International*, ed. Wolfgang Paulsen. Bern: Francke, 1982. 71–83.

Kállai, Ernst. "Filmrhythmus." *Sozialistische Monatshefte* 72 (1930): 942–44.

————. "Malerei und Film." *Sozialistische Monatshefte* 63 (1926): 164–68.

Kaplan, Nelly. "At the Warriors' Table." In *The Shadow and Its Shadow*, ed. Paul Hammond. London: British Film Institute, 1978. 127.

Kawan, B. G. "Abstrakte Filmkunst." *Film-Kurier* 276:3 (Supplement) 22 November 1924.

Kleinhans, C. "Reading and Thinking about the Avant-Garde." *Jump-Cut* 6 (March–April 1975): 21–25.

Kovacs, Yves. "L'Esprit et la lettre." In his *Surréalisme et cinéma II*. Special issue of *Études cinématographiques* 40–42 (Summer 1965): 183–98.

————, ed. "Témoignages." In his *Surréalisme et cinéma I*. Special issue of *Études cinématographiques* 38–39 (Spring 1965): 35–56.

————, ed. "Témoignages." In his *Surréalisme et cinéma II*. Special issue of *Études cinématographiques* 40–42 (Summer 1965): 153–76.

Král, Petr. "Larry Semon's Message." In *The Shadow and Its Shadow*, ed. Paul Hammond. London: British Film Institute, 1978. 109–14.

Krauss, Rosalind. "The Photographic Conditions of Surrealism" *October* 19 (Winter 1981): 3–34.

————. "Photography in the Service of Surrealism." In *L'Amour Fou*, ed. Rosalind Krauss and Jane Livingston. New York: Abbeville, 1985. 15–54.

Kurtz, Rudolf. "Absolute Kunst." In his *Expressionismus und Film*. Berlin: Verlag der Lichtbühne, 1926. 68–108.

Kyrou, Ado. "The Fantastic – the Marvellous." In *The Shadow and Its Shadow*, ed. Paul Hammond. London: British Film Institute, 1978. 102–4.

————. "The Film and I." In *The Shadow and Its Shadow*, ed. Paul Hammond. London: British Film Institute, 1978. 81–83.

————. "The Marvellous Is Popular." In *The Shadow and Its Shadow*, ed. Paul Hammond. London: British Film Institute, 1978. 39–41.

————. "Romantisme et cinéma." *L'Age du cinéma* 1 (1951): 3–6.

Larouche, Michel. "Surréalisme cinématographique au Québec." In *Surréalisme périphérique*, ed. Luis de Moura Sobral. Montréal: Université de Montréal, 1984. 147–58.

Lauher, T. "Filmmaker's Scrapbook: Surrealism, circa 1920." *Filmmaker* 3.1 (1973): 28–30.

Lawder, Standish. "A Chronology of Abstract Film, 1892–1930." *Image* (October 1965): 23.

Legrand, Gérard. "Elixir of Potboiler and Unlabelled Love Potions." In *The Shadow and Its Shadow*, ed. Paul Hammond. London: British Film Institute, 1978. 98–101.

Le Grice, Malcom. "German Abstract Film in the Twenties." In *Film as Film*. London: Arts Council, 1979. 31–35.

Lehman, Peter. "The Avant-Garde: Power, Change, and the Power to Change." In *Cinema Histories, Cinema Practices*, ed. Patricia Mellencamp and Philip Rosen. Los Angeles: American Film Institute, 1984. 120–31.

Linden, G. W. "Film, Fantasy, and the Extension of Reality." *Journal of Aesthetic Education* 18.3 (1984): 37–54.

Logette, L. "Note sur le cinéma des surréalistes." *Jeune Cinéma* 134 (1981): 10–11.

———. "Surréalisme et cinéma." *Jeune Cinéma* 134 (1981): 1–5.

Lukács, Georg. "Gedanken zu einer Aesthetik des Kinos [1913]." Rpt. in *Kino-Debatte,* ed. Anton Kaes. Tübingen: Niemeyer, 1978. 112–117.

Lynch, Joan D. "Music Videos: From Performance to Dada-Surrealism." *Journal of Popular Culture* 18 (Summer 1984): 28–37.

Magny, Joel. "Le Cinéma des surréalistes." *Cinéma 81* 270 (June 1981): 152–53.

———. "Des Marx Brothers . . . à Luis Buñuel." *Cinéma 81* 269 (May 1981): 1967.

Manvell, Roger. "Experiment in the Film." In *Experiment in the Film,* ed. Roger Manvell. London: Grey Walls Press, 1949. 13–59.

Mariën, Marcel. "Another Kind of Cinema." *Film Comment* 1.3 (1962): 14–19.

Matthews, J. H. "Du Cinéma comme langage surréaliste." In *Surréalisme et cinéma I,* ed. Yves Kovacs. Special issue of Études cinématographiques 38–39 (Spring 1965): 65–74.

———. "Sound in Surrealist Cinema." In his *Languages of Surrealism.* Columbia: University of Missouri Press, 1986. 217–37.

———. "Surrealism and the Cinema." *Criticism* 4.2 (Spring 1962): 120–33.

———. "The Visual Language of Film." In his *Languages of Surrealism.* Columbia: University of Missouri Press, 1986. 195–216.

Mazars, Pierre. "Surréalisme et cinéma contemporain: prolongements et convergences." In *Surréalisme et cinéma II.* Special issue of *Études cinématographiques* 40–42 (Summer 1965): 177–82.

Metz, Christian. "Third Degree Cinéma?" *Wide Angle* 7.1–2 (1985): 30–32.

Milne, Tom. "The Real Avant-Garde." *Sight and Sound* 32.3 (Summer 1963): 148–52.

Mitjaville, Alain. "La Clepsydre. Une Liturgie du père." *Les Cahiers de la cinémathèque* 30–31 (1980): 150–54.

———. "Un étrange rendez-vous, ou le corridor des mirroirs." *Les Cahiers de la cinémathèque* 30–31 (1980): 129–31.

Mitrani, Michel. "'Je' sur le Pont Neuf [Scenario]." *Les Cahiers de la cinémathèque* 30–31 (1980): 137–42.

Mitrani, Nora. "Intention and Surprise." In *The Shadow and Its Shadow,* ed. Paul Hammond. London: British Film Institute, 1978. 96–97.

Mitry, Jean. "Témoignage: deux manifestations peu connues." *Les Cahiers de la cinémathèque* 30–31 (1980): 115–16.

Mizrachi, François. "Thèmes surréalistes dans l'oeuvre d'Alain Resnais." In *Surréalisme et cinéma II,* ed. Yves Kovacs. Special issue of Études cinématographiques 40–42 (Summer 1965): 199–207.

Moussinac, Léon. "Du Rythme cinégraphique." *Le Crapouillot* (March 1923).

Müller, Dorothee. "Film und Foto der Zwanziger Jahre." *Kunstforum International* 34.4 (1979): 140–45.

Mussman, Toby. "Early Surrealist Expression in the Film." *Film Culture* 41 (Summer 1966): 8–17.

———. "The Surrealist Film." *Artforum* 5.1 (September 1966): 26–31.

Noguez, D. "Dal Futurismo all 'underground.'" *Filmcritica* 241 (January 1974): 22–30.

Oblowitz, M. "Two Avant-Gardes: Privileged Signs, Empty Signs." *Framework* 20 (1983): 17–19.

Oms, Marcel. "Légitime défense." *Les Cahiers de la cinémathèque* 30–31 (1980): 9.

———. "La Terre de la mort sans yeux." *Positif* 42 (November 1961): 4–18.

Ostaijen, Paul van. "Bankruptcy Jazz." *Drama Review* 14.3 (1970): 145–62.

Penley, Constance, and Janet Bergstrom. "The Avant-Garde Histories and Theories." *Screen* 19.3 (Autumn 1978): 113–127.

Péret, Benjamin. "Contre le cinéma commercial." *L'Age du cinéma* 1 (1951); rpt. in *Les Surréalistes et le cinéma,* ed. Alain and Odette Virmaux. Paris: Seghers, 1976. 283–84.

———. "La Semaine dernière. Actualités de Benjamin Péret presentées par Jindrich Heisler [Scenario]." *L'Age du Cinéma* 4–5 (1951): 31–33.

———. "L'Escalier aux cent marches [poem entirely composed of film titles]." *L'Age du Cinéma* 4–5 (1951): 16.

———. "Pulchérie veut une auto [Scenario]." *Littérature* 10 (May 1923): 17–23.

Perlmutter, Ruth. "Dada Sine-ma Dada." *Dada/Surrealism* 3 (1973): 7–16.

Petat, Jacques. "L'Avant-garde française des années vingt." *Cinéma* 217 (January 1977): 19–31.

Philippe, C.-J. "La Comédie burlesque et le surréalisme." In *Surréalisme et cinéma II,* ed. Yves Kovacs. Special issue of *Études cinématographiques* 40–42 (Summer 1965): 247–51.

Prawer, Siegbert. "A New Muse Climbs Parnassus: German Debates about Literature and the Cinema 1909–1929." *German Life and Letters,* 32.3 (April 1979): 196–205.

Rabourdin, D. "Le Cinéma des surréalistes: après les Rencontres de Perpignan: pour en finir avec les définitions." *Cinema 80* 253 (January 1980): 39–43.

Rapisarda, Giusi. "Dada al cinema." In *Il Dadaismo.* Ed. Silvia Danesi. Milan: Fratelli Fabri, 1977. 88–89.

Reef, Betty. "Avant-Garde Artists Make a Surrealist-Abstract Movie." *Vogue* 107 (15 April 1946): 156–57, 174–80.

Reverdy, Pierre. "Cinématographe." *Nord-Sud* (October 1918).

Ribemont-Dessaignes, Georges. "Le Banquier ou La Fortune aveugle [Scenario]." *Les Cahiers jaunes* (1933): 37–42.

———. "Le Huitième Jour de la semaine [Scenario]." *Revue du cinéma* (February 1930); rpt. in *Les Surréalistes et le cinéma,* ed. Alain and Odette Virmaux. Paris: Seghers, 1976. 235–51.

———. "Printemps, surréalisme et cinéma." *L'Écran français* 45 (May 1946); rpt in *Les Surréalistes et le cinéma,* ed. Alain and Odette Virmaux. Paris: Seghers, 1976. 294–97.

Rigaut, Jacques. "Mae Murray." *Littérature* N.S. 1 (March 1922): 18.

Roelens, Maurice. "Sur quelques figures de l'imaginaire." *Les Cahiers de la cinémathèque* 30–31 (1980): 49–57.

Rondolino, Gianni. "L'Occhio tagliato." In his *L'Occhio tagliato.* Turin: Martano, 1972. 267–86.

Roquefort, Georges. "Situation du cinéma dans l'économie psychique du groupe surréaliste." *Les Cahiers de la cinémathèque* 30–31 (1980): 37–40.

———, with Franc Ducros, Alain Mitjaville, Jo Marty, Marcel Oms, Maurice Roelens, Adrien Dax, Georges Goldfayn, Dionys Mascolo, Jean Schuster. "Table ronde sur le cinéma des surréalistes." *Les Cahiers de la cinémathèque* 30–31 (1980): 95–114.

Rosenbaum, J. "Course File: Experimental Film: From 'Un Chien andalou' to Chantal Akerman." *AFI Education Newsletter* 5 (Jan.-Feb. 1982): 4-7.

Rumanian Surrealist Group. "Malombra, Dark Ring of Absolute Love." In *The Shadow and Its Shadow,* ed. Paul Hammond. London: British Film Institute, 1978. 71-73.

Sadoul, Georges. "Souvenirs d'un témoin." In *Surréalisme et Cinéma I,* ed. Yves Kovacs. Special issue of *Études cinématographiques* 38-39 (Spring 1965): 9-28.

Sayag, Alain. "Der abstrakte Film im Frankreich der Zwanziger Jahre." In *Film als Film: 1910 bis heute,* ed. Hein and Herzogenrath. Cologne: Kölnischer Kunstverein, 1977. 115-18.

Schneider, Rudolf. "Formspiel durch Kino." *Frankfurter Zeitung* 511, 12 July 1926: 1.

Schuhl, Pierre-Maxime. "Pour un cinéma abstrait." *Revue Internationale de Filmologie* (Sept.-Oct. 1947): 183-85.

Serner, Walter. "Kino und Schaulust." *Die Schaubühne* 9 (1913): 807-11; rpt. in *Kino-Debatte,* ed. Anton Kaes. Tübingen: Niemeyer. 1978, 53-58.

Seuphor, Michel. "Petit scénario pour amateurs." *Cercle et Carré* 3 (June 1930).

Shi, D. E. "Transatlantic Visions: The Impact of American Cinema upon the French Avant-Garde." *Journal of Popular Culture* 14.4 (1980): 583-96.

Sitney, P. Adams. "The Idea of Morphology." *Film Culture* 53.4-5 (Spring 1972): 1-24.

Starr, C. "Programming Early Avant-Garde Films." *Sightlines* 13.2 (1979-80): 19-21.

Stern, Lisbeth. "Film." *Sozialistische Monatshefte* 63 (1926): 501-5.

Stoneman, R. "Perspective Correction: Early Film to the Avant-Garde." *Afterimage* 8-9 (Spring 1981): 50-63.

Szittya, Emil. "Paris am Anfang der neuen Kunst." *Das Kunstblatt* 9 (1925): 115-19.

Teige, Karl. "Zur Aesthetik des Filmes." *Das Kunstblatt* 9 (1925): 332-39.

Tena, Jean. "Panique hispanique. (Une nouvelle Pandora? Le surréalisme dans le film.)" *Les Cahiers de la Cinémathèque* 30-31 (1980): 196-98.

Vaché, Jacques. "War Letter [14 November 1918]." In *The Shadow and Its Shadow,* ed. Paul Hammond. London: British Film Institute, 1978. 27.

Valentin, Albert. "Introduction to Black and White Magic." In *The Shadow and Its Shadow,* ed. Paul Hammond. London: British Film Institute, 1978. 57-59.

Vanoye, Francis. "Ciné-cubisme." *Europe* 638-39 (June-July 1982): 81-87.

Velguth, Paul. "Accompaniment to the Silent Films." In *Art in Cinema,* ed. Frank Stauffacher. San Francisco: San Francisco Museum of Art, 1947. 91-95.

Verdone, Mario. "Scenarii surrealisti cinematografici non realizzati o 'irrealizzabili.'" *Terzoocchio* 32 (September 1984): 36-38.

Virmaux, Alain. "La Bréhatine et le cinéma: Apollinaire en quête d'un langage neuf." *Archives des lettres modernes* 7 (1971).

———. "Une Promesse mal tenue: le film surréaliste (1924-1932)." In *Surréalisme et cinéma I,* ed. Yves Kovacs. Special issue of *Études cinématographiques* 38-39 (Spring 1965): 103-33.

———, and Odette. "Compléments à une anthologie." *Les Cahiers de la cinémathèque* 30-31 (1980): 77-88.

Wapshott, N. "The World on Its Head: The National Film Theatre Opens Its Dada and Surrealism Season." *Times Educational Supplement* 3269, 3 February 1978: 22.

Wills, David. "Langage surréaliste, langage cinématographique." *Le Siècle éclaté* 3 (1985): 67-84.

Wollen, Peter. "The Two Avant-Gardes." *Studio International* 190 (Nov.–Dec. 1975): 171–75.

———. "The Avant-Gardes: Europe and America." *Framework* 14 (Spring 1981): 9–10.

II. Books and Articles by and on Individual Dadaists and Surrealists Who Were Involved in Making Films. In the bibliographies on individuals, the following subdivisions are followed:
A. Books by the individuals.
B. Articles, scenarios by individuals.
C. Books and dissertations on individuals.
D. Articles and parts of books on individuals.

ANTONIN ARTAUD

A. Artaud, Antonin. *Antonin Artaud: Selected Writings,* ed. Susan Sontag. New York: Farrar and Giroux, 1976.

———. *Oeuvres complètes.* Vol. 3. Paris: Gallimard, 1978.

B. Antonin Artaud. "À Jean Paulhan [letter of January 1932 concerning *Le Sang d'un poète*]." *Oeuvres complètes.* 3: 261–76.

———. "Antonin Artaud [interview]." *Cinémonde* 1 August 1929. Rpt. *Oeuvres complètes.* 3: 107–111.

———. "Antonin Artaud nous parle du cinéma allemand [interview]." *Oeuvres complètes.* 3: 112–14.

———. "L'Avion solaire." In his *Oeuvres complètes.* 3: 44–45.

———. "Le Cinéma et l'abstraction." *Oeuvres complètes.* 3: 68–69.

———. "Cinéma et réalité. *La Nouvelle Revue Française* 170 (1 November 1927).

———. "La Coquille et le clergyman." *Oeuvres complètes.* 3: 71–72.

———. "La Coquille et le clergyman [Scenario]." *Oeuvres complètes.* 3: 18–25.

———. "Deux nations sur les confins de la Mongolie [Scenario]." *Oeuvres complètes.* 3: 14–17.

———. "Distinction entre avant-garde de fond et de forme." *Oeuvres complètes.* 3: 70.

———. "Les Dix-huit secondes [Scenario]." *Oeuvres complètes.* 3: 9–13.

———. "Les Frères Marx." *La Nouvelle Revue française* 220 (Jan. 1932).

———. "Le Juif polonais à l'Olympia." *Oeuvres complètes.* 3: 78–80.

———. "Interview, *Paris-Journal* 27 April 1923." Rpt. in *Cinématographe* 107 (Feb. 1985): 38.

———. "Le Maître de Ballantrae [Scenario]." *Oeuvres complètes.* 3: 46–53.

———. "Projet de constitution d'une firme destinée à produire des films de court métrage, d'un amortissement rapide et sûr." *Oeuvres complètes.* 3: 73–78.

———. "Réponse à une enquête." *Oeuvres complètes.* 3: 63–64.

———. "La Revolte du boucher [Scenario]." *Oeuvres complètes.* 3: 54–59.

———. "Selections from Artaud's Writings." *Tulane Drama Review* 11.1 (1966): 166–85.

──────. "Sorcellerie et cinéma." *Oeuvres complètes*. 3: 65–67; transl. into English in *The Shadow and Its Shadow*, ed. Paul Hammond. London: British Film Institute, 1978. 63–64.

──────. "Les Souffrances du 'Dubbing.'" *Oeuvres complètes*. 3: 85–87.

──────. "Les 32 [Scenario]." *Oeuvres complètes*. 3: 31–43.

──────. "La Vieillesse précoce du cinéma." *Oeuvres complètes*. 3: 81–84.

──────. "Vols [Scenario]." *Oeuvres complètes*. 3: 26–30.

──────, and Salvador Dali. "Animal Crackers." *Les Cahiers de la cinémathèque* 25 (1979).

C. Knapp, Bettina. *Antonin Artaud, Man of Vision*. New York: David Lewis, 1969.

Rose, Mark V. "The Actor and His Double: Antonin Artaud's Theory and Practice of Movement." Diss. U. of California at Davis, 1983.

Virmaux, Alain and Odette. *Artaud vivant*. Paris: Nouvelles Editions Oswald, 1980.

D. Amengual, B. "Un Disciple inattendu d'Eisenstein: Antonin Artaud." *Écran* 18 (1973): 45–53.

Dozoretz, W. "Dulac versus Artaud." *Wide Angle* 3.1 (1979): 46–53.

Flitterman, Sandy. "Theorizing 'the Feminine': Woman as the Figure of Desire in *The Seashell and the Clergyman*." *Wide Angle* 6.3 (1984): 32–39.

Greene, Naomi. "Artaud and Film: A Reconsideration." *Cinema Journal* 23.4 (1984): 28–40.

Kestner, Joseph. "Stevenson and Artaud: 'The Master of Ballantrae.'" *Film Heritage* 7.4 (1972): 19–28.

Knapp, Bettina. "Antonin Artaud: Cinéma. Bouleversement de l'optique, de la perspective, de la logique." *Kentucky Romance Quarterly* 23.3 (1981): 229–36.

──────. "Artaud: A New Type of Magic." *Yale French Studies* 31 (1964): 95–97.

Termine, L. "La poetica della crudelta nel cinema di Artaud." *Cinema Nuovo* 275 (1982): 59–60.

Virmaux, Alain. "Artaud and Film." *Tulane Drama Review* 11.1 (1966): 155–65.

──────, and Odette. "Lettre d'Alain et Odette Virmaux." *Cinématographe* 58 (1980): 70.

──────, ──────. "Rendre justice à Artaud." In their *Les Surréalistes et le cinéma*. Paris: Seghers, 1976. 42–49.

LUIS BUÑUEL

A. Buñuel, Luis, and Salvador Dali. *L'Age d'or and Un Chien andalou: Films by Luis Buñuel*. New York: Simon and Schuster, 1968.

──────. *My Last Sigh*. New York: Vintage Books, 1984.

──────. *Scritti letterari e cinematografici*. Venice: Marsilio Editori, 1984.

B. Buñuel, Luis. "'L'Age d'or.'" *L'Avant-Scène: Cinéma* 315–316 (1983): 7–9.

──────. "L'Age d'or [Scenario]." In *L'Occhio tagliato*, ed. Gianni Rondolino. Turin: Martano, 1972. 222–51.

──────. "'L'Age d'or': Plans 302 à 633." *L'Avant-Scène: Cinéma* 315–316 (1983): 10–32.

————. "Buster Keaton's College." In Francisco Aranda, *Luis Buñuel: A Critical Biography.* New York: Da Capo, 1976. 272–73.

————. "Carl Dreyer's *Jeanne d'Arc.*" In Aranda, *Luis Buñuel: A Critical Biography.* 268–69.

————. "Cinema, Instrument of Poetry." In Aranda, *Luis Buñuel: A Critical Biography.* 273–75.

————. "Le Comique dans le cinéma." *Positif* 272 (1983): 14.

————. "La Duchesse d'Aloe et Goya" [Scenario]. *Positif* 272 (1983): 15.

————. "Film und Poesie." *Film und Fernsehen* 12.1 (1984): 36.

————. "A Giraffe." In Aranda, *Luis Buñuel: A Critical Biography.* 262–64.

————. "Hallucinations autour d'une main morte." *Positif* 272 (1983): 15.

————. "Hamlet (Tragédie comique)." *Positif* 272 (1983): 6–13.

————. "Las Hurdes (Terre sans pain) [Scenario]." In *L'Occhio tagliato,* ed. Gianni Rondolino. Turin: Martano, 1972. 251–60.

————. "Ilegible, Son of Flauta [Scenario]." In Aranda, *Luis Buñuel: A Critical Biography.* 285–87.

————. "Instrumentation (pour Adolfo Salazar)." *L'Avant-Scène: Cinéma* 315–316 (1983): 92–93.

————, and J.-L. Carrière. "'La-bas': Extrait d'un scenario inédit et non tourné d'après J. K. Huysmans." *Positif* 200–202 (December 1977–January 1978): 11–20.

————. "Lettre à Marcel Oms." *Les Cahiers de la cinémathèque* 30–31 (1980): 200.

————. "Life among the Americans." *American Film* 8 (1983): 18+.

————. "Luis Buñuel hace la anatomía del churro cinematografico [interview]." *Cine Cubano* 78–80 (1973): 112–13.

————. "Metropolis." In Aranda, *Luis Buñuel: A Critical Biography.* 266–68.

————. "Napoleon Bonaparte by Abel Gance." In Aranda, *Luis Buñuel: A Critical Biography.* 271–72.

————. "A Night at the 'Studio des Ursulines.'" In Aranda, *Luis Buñuel: A Critical Biography.* 265–66.

————. "Notes on the Making of *Un Chien andalou.*" In *The World of Luis Buñuel. Essays in Criticism,* ed. Joan Mellen. New York: Oxford University Press, 1978. 151–53.

————. "Poetry and Cinema." In *The World of Luis Buñuel: Essays in Criticism,* ed. Joan Mellen. 105–110.

————. "Se o filme ficar curto, en ponho um sonho." *Film Cultura* 43 (1984): 16–17.

————. "Sportif par amour de Buster Keaton." In Ado Kyrou, *Luis Buñuel.* Paris: Seghers, 1970. 91–93.

————. "A Statement." *Film Culture* 21 (1960): 41–42.

————. "Un Chien andalou [Scenario]." *La Révolution surréaliste* 12 (1929): 34–37; rpt. in *L'Occhio tagliato,* ed. Gianni Rondolino. Turin: Martano, 1972. 210–22; rpt. in *Ça* 2.5-6 (1975): 3–8.

————. "Variations sur la moustache de Menjou." *Cinématographe* 92 (1983): 3–4.

————. "The Way of All Flesh, Directed by Victor Fleming." In Aranda, *Luis Buñuel: A Critical Biography.* 272.

C. Alcalá, Manuel. *Buñuel (Cine e ideología).* Madrid: Cuadernos para el diálogo, 1973.

Aranda, Francisco. *Luis Buñuel: A Critical Biography.* Trans. David Robinson. New York: Da Capo Press, 1976.

Bazin, André. *Le Cinéma de la cruauté: de Buñuel à Hitchcock.* Paris: Flammarion, 1975.

Bernardi, Auro. *L'Arte dello scandalo: "L'Age d'or" di Luis Buñuel.* Bari: Dedalco, 1984.

Buache, Freddy. *The Cinema of Luis Buñuel.* Trans. Peter Graham. New York: Barnes, 1973.

————. *Luis Buñuel.* Lausanne: La Cité, 1970.

Cameron, I. A. *Luis Buñuel.* Berkeley: Univ. of California Press, 1979.

Cesarman, Fernando. *El Ojo de Buñuel; psicoanalysis desde una butaca.* Barcelona: Editorial Anagrama, 1976.

Drouzy, M. *Luis Buñuel, architecte du rêve.* Paris: L'Herminier, 1978.

Durgnat, Raymond. *Luis Buñuel.* Berkeley: Univ. of California Press, 1968.

Fernández, Henri Cecilio. "The Influence of Galdós on the Films of Luis Buñuel." Thesis, Indiana University, 1976.

Goetz, Alice and Helmut W. Banz, eds. *Luis Buñuel, eine Dokumentation.* Bad Ems: Verband des deutschen Filmclubs, 1975.

Higginbotham, Virginia. *Luis Buñuel.* Boston: Twayne, 1979.

Kyrou, Adou. *Luis Buñuel.* Paris: Seghers, 1970.

————. *Luis Buñuel: An Introduction.* Trans. Adrienne Foulke. New York: Simon and Schuster, 1963.

Lovell, Alan. *Anarchist Cinema.* London: Peace News, 1962.

Mellen, Joan, ed. *The World of Luis Buñuel: Essays in Criticism.* New York: Oxford University Press, 1978.

Oms, Marcel. *Don Luis Buñuel.* Paris: Le Cerf, 1985.

Ramsey, Cynthia. "The Problem of Dual Consciousness: The Structures of Dream and Reality in the Films of Luis Buñuel." Diss. Florida State Univ., 1981.

Rejda, Roger. "Surrealism and Buñuel's *The Discreet Charm of the Bourgeoisie.*" Diss. Univ. of Nebraska, 1981.

Sandro, Paul. "Assault and Disruption in the Cinema: Four Films by Luis Buñuel." Diss. Cornell Univ., 1974.

Williams, Linda. *Figures of Desire. A Theory and Analysis of Surrealist Film.* Urbana: University of Illinois Press, 1981.

D. Ahrens, J. "Getting What You Need: Changing Surrealist Vision in Luis Buñuel's *Un Chien andalou, Discreet Charm of the Bourgeoisie,* and *That Obscure Object of Desire.*" *Movietone News* 58–59 (1978): 17–21.

Almendros, N. "Buñuel cinéaste hispanique." *Cinématographe* 30 (1977): 28–29.

Aranda, J. F. "Una entrevista essencial e desconhecida de Luis Buñuel [interview]." *Celuloide* 318–319 (1981): 1–3.

————. "Out of Innocence." In *The World of Luis Buñuel,* ed. Joan Mellen. New York: Oxford Univ. Press, 1978. 31–50.

————. "Surrealist and Spanish Giant." *Films and Filming* 8.1 (1961): 17–18; 8.2 (1961): 29–30.

Aubry, Daniel, and J. M. Lacor. "Luis Buñuel." *Film Quarterly* 12.2 (1958): 7-9.

Bachmann, Gideon. "The Films of Luis Buñuel." *Cinemage* 1 (1955): 10-17.

Barnes, Peter. "The Rebel Who Grew Up." *Films and Filming* 1.12 (1955): 9.

Benigni, P. "Quei pallidi oggetti del desiderio." *Bianco e Nero* 45 (1984): 35-50.

Beylie, C. "Post-scriptum sur 'L'Age d'or.'" *Cinématographe* 73 (Dec. 1981): 83.

De Bongnie, J. "À propos du 'Prix de L'Age d'Or': Buñuel, Dali, le Christ et . . . Godard." *Amis du film et de la télévision* 292 (Sept. 1980): 13.

Bonitzer, P. "Un Documentaire anamorphique." *Cahiers du cinéma* 327 (Sept. 1981): 56-58.

Bonnet, J.-C. "L'Age d'or." *Cinématographe* 69 (July 1981): 52-53.

Brunius, J. B. "Sur 'L'Age d'or' et 'Le Sang d'un poète.'" *Les Cahiers de la cinémathèque* 30-31 (1980): 88.

Buache, F. "Dialogue avec Luis Buñuel." *L'Avant-Scène: Cinéma* 315-316 (1983): 4-6.

Carbonnier, A. "Luis Buñuel [interview]." *Cinéma 83* 297 (Sept. 1983): 13-19.

Carrassou, Michel. "Artaud, Fondane, même combat!" *Europe* 667-68 (Nov.-Dec. 1984): 84-86.

Carrière, J.-C. "The Buñuel Mystery." In *The World of Luis Buñuel,* ed. Joan Mellen. New York: Oxford University Press, 1978. 90-102.

———. "Luis Buñuel." *Cinéma* 297 (Sept. 1983): 13-19.

Casaus, Victor. "Las Hurdes: Land Without Bread." In *The World of Luis Buñuel,* ed. Joan Mellen. 180-85.

Cohn, Bernard. "Les Aventures de Don Luis de Calanda." *Positif* 103 (1969): 6-17.

De la Colina, J., and T. Perez-Turrent. "Entretien avec Luis Buñuel." *Positif* 238 (1981): 2-14.

Conrad, R. "The Minister of the Interior Is on the Telephone: The Early Films of Luis Buñuel." *Cinéaste* 7.3 (1976): 2-14.

Cosendey, Roland. "L'Age d'or. Analyse du récit." *Les Cahiers de la cinémathèque* 30-31 (1980): 184-90.

Dale, R. C. Un Chien andalou, L'Age d'or, Las Hurdes, Los Olvidados." *Movietone News* 39 (Feb. 1975): 3-8.

Decaux, Emmanuel. "L'Age d'or des mécènes." *Cinématographe* 100 (May 1984): 117-120.

Demeure, Jacques. "Luis Buñuel – poète de la cruauté." *Positif* 2.10 (1954): 41-44.

Desnos, Robert. "Un Chien andalou." *Les Cahiers de la cinémathèque* 30-31 (1980): 86.

Detassis, P. "Gli anagrammi del corpo in Luis Buñuel." *Bianco e Nero* 45 (1984): 6-34.

Doniol-Valcroze, Jacques, and André Bazin. "Conversation with Luis Buñuel." *Sight and Sound* 24.4 (Spring 1955): 181-85.

Drummond, Phillip. "Textual Space in 'Un Chien andalou.'" *Screen* 18.3 (1977): 55-119.

Durgnat, Raymond. "Style and Anti-Style." In *The World of Luis Buñuel,* ed. Joan Mellen. 116-24.

Fuentes, Carlos. "Buñuel Scenes." *Movietone News* 39 (Feb. 1975): 1-2.

———. "The Discreet Charm of Luis Buñuel." In *The World of Luis Buñuel,* ed. Joan Mellen. 51-71.

Goldmann, A., and L. "Structures of Absence in the Films of Godard, Buñuel, and Pasolini." *Australian Journal of Screen Theory* 1 (1976): 67–80.

Harcourt, Peter. "Luis Buñuel: Spaniard and Surrealist." *Film Quarterly* 20.3 (1967): 2–19.

Král, Petr. "'L'Age d'or' aujourd'hui." *Positif* 247 (Oct. 1981): 44–50.

Kyrou, Ado. "L'Age d'or." In *The World of Luis Buñuel*, ed. Joan Mellen, 154–65.

———. "La Grande Tendresse de Luis Buñuel." *Positif* 2.10 (1954): 39–40.

Logette, L. "Un Film irrécuperable: 'L'Age d'or.'" *Jeune Cinéma* 137 (1981): 20–22.

———. "Sur le tournage de 'L'Age d'or,' entretien avec Claude Heymann." *Jeune Cinéma* 134 (1981): 6–10.

Lyon, Elizabeth. "Luis Buñuel: The Process of Dissociation in Three Films." *Cinema Journal* 13.1 (1973): 45–48.

Mellen, Joan. "An Overview of Buñuel's Career." In *The World of Luis Buñuel*, ed. Joan Mellen. 3–27.

Miller, Henry. "The Golden Age." In his *The Cosmological Eye*. Norfolk, Conn.: New Directions, 1939. 47–62.

Mourier, Maurice. "El Dorado: tentative d'évaluation (subjective) de L'Age d'or aujourd'hui." *Mélusine* 7 (1985): 135–152.

Muñoz-Suay, Ricardo. "Buñuel et quelques-uns de ses apports surréalistes." *Les Cahiers de la cinémathèque* 30–31 (1980): 173–76.

———. "Correspondance avec Luis Buñuel." *Les Cahiers de la cinémathèque* 30–31 (1980): 192–95.

———. "Nell' amicizia con Lorca il surrealismo di Buñuel." *Cinema Nuovo* 278–279 (1982): 42–47.

Oms, Marcel. "Notes de lecture." *Les Cahiers de la Cinémathèque* 38–39 (1984): 203–6.

Oswald, L. "Figure/Discourse: Configurations of Desire in 'Un Chien andalou.'" *Semiotica* 33.1–2 (1981): 105–22.

Paz, Octavio. "Le Poète Buñuel." *L'Age du cinéma* 3 (1951): 26–29.

Renaud, Pierre. "Symbolisme au second degré: *Un Chien andalou.*" *Études cinématographiques* 20–23 (1963): 147–57.

Richardson, Tony. "The Films of Luis Buñuel." In *The World of Luis Buñuel*, ed. Joan Mellen. 111–15.

Richie, Donald. "The Moral Code of Luis Buñuel." In *The World of Luis Buñuel*, ed. Joan Mellen. 111–15.

Rubinstein, E. "Visit to a Familiar Planet: Buñuel Among the Hurdanos." *Cinema Journal* 22.4 (1983): 3–17.

Saint-Jean, R. "Entretien avec Luis Buñuel." *Positif* 162 (1974): 9–13.

Thiher, A. "Surrealism's Enduring Bite: 'Un Chien andalou.'" *Literature Film Quarterly* 5.1 (1977): 38–49.

Virmaux, Alain, and Odette. "Le Règne de 'L'Age d'or.'" In their *Les Surréalistes et le cinéma*. Paris: Seghers, 1976. 49–54.

Weiss, P. "Luis Buñuel." *Filmkritik* 25 (1981): 273–82.

Williams, Linda. "Dream Rhetoric and Film Rhetoric: Metaphor and Metonomy in 'Un Chien andalou.'" *Semiotica* 33.1–2 (1981): 86–103.

———. "The Prologue to *Un Chien andalou:* A Surrealist Film Metaphor." *Screen* 17.4 (Winter 1976–77): 24–33.

BLAISE CENDRARS

A. Cendrars, Blaise. *L'ABC du cinéma.* Paris: Grasset, 1926. Rpt. in *Oeuvres complètes.* Paris: Denoël, 1961, vol. VI.

———. *Films sans images.* Paris: Denoël, 1959.

———. *La Fin du monde filmée par l'ange Notre-Dame* [film scenario]. Paris: Editions de la Sirène, 1919. Rpt. in *Oeuvres complètes.* Paris: Denoël, 1961. II, 11–50.

———. *La Perle fiévreuse* [film script]. In *Signaux de France et de Belgique* 7, 9, 10, 11–12 (1921–22). Rpt. in *Oeuvres complètes.* Paris: Denoël, 1961. IV, 10–61.

C. Bochner, Jay. *Blaise Cendrars, Discovery and Re-Creation.* Toronto: University of Toronto Press, 1978.

Chefdor, Monique. *Blaise Cendrars.* Boston: Twayne, 1980.

D. Bochner, Jay. "Writing a Cinema: Blaise Cendrars and the Documentary Idea." *Feuille de routes* 9 (April 1983): 36.

Caws, Mary Ann. "Blaise Cendrars: A Cinema of Poetry." In her *The Inner Theater of Recent French Poetry.* Princeton: Princeton Univ. Press, 1972. 25–51.

Kellman, Steven. "Cendrars, *L'Or,* and the Cinematic Novel." *Feuille de routes* 9 (April 1983): 23–35.

Mourier, Maurice. "Cendrars: une écriture travaillée par le cinéma." *Feuille de route* 9 (April 1983): 49–57.

RENÉ CLAIR

A. Clair, René. *Cinema Yesterday and Today.* Trans. Stanley Appelbaum. Ed. R. C. Dale. New York: Dover, 1972. Trans. of his *Cinéma d'hier, cinéma d'aujourd'hui.* Paris: Gallimard, 1970.

———. *Comédies et commentaires.* Paris: Gallimard, 1959.

———. *Entr'acte.* Ed. Glauco Viazzi. Milan: Poligono, 1945.

———. *"À Nous La Liberté," and "Entr'acte": Films by René Clair.* Trans. Richard Jacques and Nicola Hayden. New York: Simon and Schuster, 1970.

Clair, René. *Reflections on Cinema.* Trans. Vera Traill. London: Kimber, 1953. Trans. of *Réflexion faite.* Paris: Éditions N.R.F.: 1951.

B. Clair, René. "Cinéma et surréalisme." *Les Cahiers du mois* 16–17 (1925): 90–91; rpt. in Alain and Odette Virmaux, *Les Surréalistes et le cinéma.* Paris: Seghers, 1976. 318.

———. "Cinéma pur et cinéma commercial." *Les Cahiers du mois* 16–17 (1925): 89.

———. "Entr'acte [Scenario]." In *L'Occhio tagliato,* ed. Gianni Rondolino. Turin: Martano, 1972. 167–74.

———. "Et demain?" *Le Crapouillot* (March 1927); rpt. in *Le Crapouillot.* Special Film Issue (Nov. 1932): 26–28.

———. "Picabia, Satie and the First Night of *Entr'acte.*" In *'A Nous La Liberté' and 'Entr'acte.'* New York: Simon and Schuster, 1970. 108–112. Trans. of "La Première d'Entr'acte." *Le Figaro Littéraire* 26 June–2 July 1967: 38–39.

———. "Rythme." *Les Cahiers du mois* 16–17 (1925): 13–16.

C. Amengual. B. *René Clair*. Paris: Seghers, 1969.

Barrot, Olivier. *René Clair ou le temps mesuré*. Paris: Hatier, 1985.

Charensol, Georges, and Roger Régent. *Cinquante ans de cinéma avec René Clair*. Paris: La Table Ronde, 1979.

————, ————. *Un Maître du cinéma: René Clair*. Paris: La Table Ronde, 1952.

Cvenca, C. Fernandez. *René Clair*. Madrid, 1951.

De la Roche, Catherine. *René Clair: An Index*. London: British Film Institute, 1958.

Greene, Naomi. *René Clair: A Guide to References and Resources*. Boston: G. K. Hall, 1985.

McGerr, Celia. *René Clair*. Boston: Twayne, 1980.

Mitry, Jean. *René Clair*. Paris: Éditions Universitaires, 1960.

D. Adair, G. "Utopia Ltd.: The Cinema of René Clair." *Sight and Sound* 50.3 (1981): 188–91.

Amengual, B. "'Entr'acte' et ses mystères." *L'Avant-Scène: Cinéma* 281 (1982): 19–25.

Baxter, J., and J. Gillette. "A Conversation with René Clair." *Focus on Film* 12 (1972): 38–42.

Beylie, Claude. "*Entr'acte:* Le Film sans maître." *Cinema 69* 133 (February 1969): 115–17.

Brunius, Jacques B. "Entr'acte." In his *En Marge du cinéma français*. Paris: Arcanes, 1954.

Bruno, Edoardo. "La simplicità delle forme." *Filmcritica* 337 (1983): 371–82.

Carroll, Noel. "Entr'acte, Paris and Dada." *Millenium Film Journal* 1.1 (1977): 5–11.

Dale, R. C. "René Clair's *Entr'acte* or Motion Victorious." *Wide Angle* 2.2 (1977): 38–43.

Desnos, Robert. "*Entr'acte.*" In his *Cinéma*. Paris: Gallimard, 1966. 121.

D'Hughes, Philippe. "Gli anni della formazione." *Filmcritica* 342 (1984): 112–16.

"*Entr'acte.*" [a shot-by-shot breakdown of the film by the editors of *L'Avant-Scène: Cinéma*]. *L'Avant-Scène: Cinéma* 86 (Nov. 1968): 9–18.

Fondane, Benjamin. "Entr'acte ou le cinéma autonôme." *Intégral* 1.1 (March 1925).

Gallez, Douglas. "Satie's *Entr'acte:* A Model of Film Music." *Cinema Journal* 16.1 (Fall 1976): 36–50.

Kovacs, Steven. "Dada Comes In at Intermission: Picabia and René Clair on *Entr'acte.*" In his *From Enchantment to Rage. The Story of Surrealist Cinema*. London and Toronto: Associated University Presses, 1980. 64–114.

Kracauer, Siegfried. "Entr'acte." In his *Nature of Film*. London: Dobson, 1961. 182–83.

Mason, G. "René Clair at 80." *Literature Film Quarterly* 10.2 (1982): 85–99.

McGilligan, P., and D. Weiner. "René Clair [interview]." *Take One* 4 (1973): 8–12.

Michelson, Annette. "Dr. Crase and Mr. Clair." *October* 11 (Winter 1979): 30–53.

Mitry, Jean. "Film abstrait et musique visuelle." In his *Le Cinéma expérimental*. Paris: Seghers, 1974. 74–98.

Mueller, J. "Films: 'Relâche' and 'Entr'acte.'" *Dance Magazine* 51 (July 1977): 102–3.

Oms, Marcel, and J. Baldizzone. "Entretien avec René Clair." *Les Cahiers de la cinémathèque* 35–36 (1982): 209–16.

Picabia, Francis. "(Sur René Clair)." In his *Écrits*. Paris: Belfond, 1978. 2:167.

Potamkin, Harry Alan. "René Clair and Film Humour." *Hound and Horn* 6.1 (Oct.-Dec. 1932): 114-23.

Sandro, Paul. "Parodic Narration in 'Entr'acte.'" *Film Criticism* 4.1 (1979): 44-55.

Souday, Paul, Benjamin Péret, and Robert Desnos. "Entr'acte: Trois opinions de 1924." *L'Avant-Scène: Cinéma* 86 (November 1968): 7.

Thiher, Allen. "From *Entr'acte* to *A nous la liberté:* René Clair and the Order of Farce." In his *The Cinematic Muse.* Columbia: University of Missouri Press, 1979. 64-77.

Verdone, Mario. "Entr'acte." In his *Le avanguardie storiche del cinema.* Turin: Società Editrice Internazionale, 1977. 96-99.

White, Mimi. "Two French Dada Films: *Entr'acte* and *Emak Bakia.*" *Dada/Surrealism* 13 (1984): 37-47.

JEAN COCTEAU

A. Cocteau, Jean. *La Belle et la bête: Journal d'un Film.* Paris: J. B. Janin, 1946.

———. *The Blood of a Poet.* New York: Bodley Press, 1949.

———. *Cocteau on Film.* New York: Dover, 1972.

———. *Cocteau on the Film: A Conversation.* Ed. André Fraigneau. New York: Roy, 1954.

———. *Journals of Jean Cocteau.* Magnolia, Mass.: Peter Smith, n.d.

———. *Professional Secrets: An Autobiography of Jean Cocteau, Drawn from His Lifetime Writings by Robert Phelps.* New York: Farrar, Straus and Giroux, 1970.

———. *Two Screenplays: The Blood of a Poet; The Testament of Orpheus.* New York: Orion Press, 1968.

B. Cocteau, Jean. "Aphorismes cinématographiques." *L'Avant-Scène: Cinéma* 138-139 (1973): 55.

———. "Cocteau inconnu." *Cinéma 83* 298 (1983): 69-70.

———. "Cocteau retrouvés." *Lumière du cinéma* 7 (1977): 48-55; 82.

———. "Conversations." *Sight and Sound* 22.1 (1952): 6-8.

———. "Four Letters by Jean Cocteau to Leni Riefensthal." *Film Culture* 56-57 (1973): 90-93.

C. Brown, Frederick. *Impersonation of Angels: A Biography of Jean Cocteau.* New York: Viking, 1968.

Crosland, Margaret. *Jean Cocteau.* New York: Crown, 1955.

Fowlie, Wallace. *Jean Cocteau: The History of a Poet's Age.* Bloomington: Indiana University Press, 1966.

Fraigneau, André. *Cocteau.* Trans. Donald Lehmkuhl. New York: Grove, 1961.

Gilson, René. *Jean Cocteau.* Trans. Ciba Vaughan. New York: Crown, 1970.

Keller, Marjorie E. "The Theme of Childhood in the Films of Jean Cocteau, Joseph Cornell, and Stan Brakhage." Diss. New York University, 1982.

Oxenhandler, Neal. *Scandal and Parade: The Theater of Jean Cocteau.* New Brunswick, N.J.: Rutgers Univ. Press, 1957.

Popkin, Michael C. "The Orpheus Story and the Films of Jean Cocteau." Diss. Columbia University, 1980.

Sprigge, Elizabeth, and Jean-Jacques Kihm. *Jean Cocteau: The Man and the Mirror.* New York: Coward-McCann, 1968.

Steegmuller, Francis. *Cocteau.* Boston: Little, Brown, 1970.

Tomek, James J. "Relationship of Literature and Film in Cocteau." Diss. Duke University, 1974.

Zwickey, Jon. "The Influence of Drugs on the Films of Jean Cocteau." Thesis, Univ. of Wisconsin, 1965.

D. Amberg, G. "The Testament of Jean Cocteau." *Film Comment* 7.4 (1971–72): 23–27.

Artaud, Antonin. "À Jean Paulhan [letter of 22 January 1932 concerning Cocteau's *The Blood of a Poet*]." In *Oeuvres complètes d'Antonin Artaud.* Vol. 3. Paris: Gallimard, 1978. 261–76.

Brunius, Jacques B. "Sur 'L'Age d'or' et 'Le Sang d'un poète.' " *Les Cahiers de la cinémathèque* 30–31 (1980): 88.

Campigli, M. "La vita del poeta." *L'Italia Letteraria* 27 Dec. 1931; rpt. in *Bianco e Nero* 34 (1973): 105–7.

Durgnat, Raymond. "Images of the Mind – Part Thirteen: Time and Timelessness." *Films and Filming* 15.10 (1969): 62–67.

Gow, G. "Astonishments: Magic Film from Jean Cocteau." *Films and Filming* 24 (1978): 20–25.

———. "The Mirrors of Life: The Myth and Magic of Jean Cocteau." *Films and Filming* 24 (1978): 28–33.

Jouhet, S. " 'Le Sang d'un poète' et les surréalistes." *L'Avant-Scène: Cinéma* 307–308 (1983): 11–13.

Koval, Francis. "Interview with Cocteau." *Sight and Sound* 19.6 (1950): 229–31.

Milani, Raffaele. "Cocteau dell'immaginario." *Filmcritica* 35.345 (1984): 251–64.

Oxenhandler, Neal. "Poetry in Three Films of Jean Cocteau." *Yale French Studies* 17 (Summer 1956): 14–20.

Philippon, A. "La Magie des origines." *L'Avant-Scène: Cinéma* 307–308 (May 1983): 4–10.

Rayns, T. "Sang d'un poète (The Blood of a Poet)." *Monthly Film Bulletin* 44.520 (May 1977): 112.

Renaud, T. "Jean Cocteau: un cinéaste? Peut-être un auteur? Certainement." *Cinéma* 182 (Dec. 1973): 24–26.

Steegmuller, Francis. "New York Celebrates the Genius of Jean Cocteau." *New York Times* 133, 13 May 1984: Sec. 2, 17–18.

Weiss, P. "Cocteau: 'Le Sang d'un poète.'" *Filmkritik* 25 (June 1981): 283–85.

JOSEPH CORNELL

B. Cornell, Joseph. " 'Enchanted Wanderer.' Excerpt from a Journey Album for Hedy Lamarr." *View* (Dec. 1941–Jan. 1942): 3. Rpt. in *The Shadow and Its Shadow,* ed. Paul Hammond. London: British Film Institute, 1978. 129–30.

———. "M. Phot [Scenario]." In Julien Levy, *Surrealism.* New York: Black Sun Press, 1936. 77–88.

————. "Theatre of Hans Christian Andersen [Scenario]." *Dance Index* 4.9 (1945): 155–59.

C. Keller, Marjorie E. "The Theme of Childhood in the Films of Jean Cocteau, Joseph Cornell, and Stan Brakhage." Diss. New York University, 1982.

D. Lawson, T. "Silently, by Means of a Flashing Light." *October* 15 (Winter 1980): 49–60.

Mekas, Jonas. "The Invisible Cathedrals of Joseph Cornell." In his *Movie Journal.* New York: Macmillan, 1972. 407–10.

————. "Notes on Films of Joseph Cornell." In *Joseph Cornell Portfolio.* New York: Leo Castelly Gallery, 1976.

Michelson, Annette. "Rose Hobart and Monsieur Phot: Early Films from Utopia Parkway." *Artforum* 11 (June 1973): 47–57.

Sitney, P. Adams. "The Cinematic Gaze of Joseph Cornell." In *Joseph Cornell,* ed. Kynaston McShine. New York: The Museum of Modern Art, 1980. 69–89.

————. "Recovered Innocence." In his *Visionary Film. The American Avant-Garde.* 2nd Ed. New York: Oxford U. Press, 1979. 330–68.

SALVADOR DALI

A. *L'Age d'Or and Un Chien Andalou.* Trans. Marianne Alexandre. Classic Film Scripts. New York: Simon and Schuster, 1968.

Dali, Salvador. *Babaouo, sénario inédit précédé d'un abrégé d'une histoire critique du cinéma et suivi de Guillaume Tell, ballet portugais.* Paris: Ed. des Cahiers Libres, 1932.

————. *Oui 1. La Révolution paranoïaque-critique.* Paris: Denoël/Gonthier, 1971.

Dali, Salvador. *The Secret Life of Salvador Dali.* Trans. H. M. Chevalier. London: Vision Press, 1973.

B. Dali, Salvador, and Antonin Artaud. "Animal Crackers." *Les Cahiers de la cinémathèque* 25 (1979).

————. "Babaouo [Scenario]." *Cinémage* 9 (1958): 19–28.

————, et al. "Manifesto of the Surrealists Concerning *L'Age d'or.*" In *The Shadow and Its Shadow,* ed. Paul Hammond. London: British Film Institute, 1978. 115–21.

————. "Unpublished Film Scenario by Salvador Dali." *Studio International* 195 (March 1982): 63–77.

C. Ades, Dawn. *Dali and Surrealism.* New York: Harper & Row, 1982.

Bosquet, Alain. *Entretiens avec Salvador Dali.* Paris: Belfond, 1983.

D. Ades, Dawn. "Dali and the Cinema." In her *Dali and Surrealism.* New York: Harper & Row, 1982. 192–206.

————. "Introduction to Dali's Unpublished Film Scenario." *Studio International* 195 (March 1982): 62.

Bigwood, J. "Salvador Dali: Reluctant Filmmaker." *American Film* 5 (Nov. 1979): 62–63.

De Bongnie, J. "À propos du 'Prix de l'Age d'Or': Buñuel, Dali, le Christ et . . . Godard." *Amis du film et de la Télévision* 292 (Sept. 1980): 13.

Lipton, Lenny. "The Surrealistic Shooting of 'Le Pink Grapefruit.'" *American Cinematographer* 58 (March 1977): 306–7.

Reyzabel, M.V. "El cine de Dalí." *Cinema 2002* 59 (Jan. 1980): 39.

ROBERT DESNOS

A. Desnos, Robert. *Cinéma.* Ed. André Tchernia. Paris: Gallimard, 1966 [scenarios and texts on cinema].

———. *Nouvelles Hébrides et autres textes 1922–1930,* ed. Marie-Claire Dumas. Paris: Gallimard, 1978.

B. Desnos, Robert. "Avant-Garde Cinema." In *The Shadow and Its Shadow,* ed. Paul Hammond. London: British Film Institute, 1978. 36–38.

———. "Un Chien andalou." *Les Cahiers de la cinémathèque* 30–31 (1980): 86.

———. "Eroticism." In *The Shadow and Its Shadow,* ed. Paul Hammond. London: British Film Institute, 1978.

———. "Excerpt from *L'Homme de la Pampa.*" *Cinématographe* 107 (Feb. 1985): 39–40.

———. "Midnight to Fourteen Hundred Hours – Writing a Modern Marvel [scenario]." *Film Culture* 67–69 (1979): 229–34.

———. "La Part des lionnes [scenario]." *Les Cahiers de la cinémathèque* 30–31 (1980): 88–90.

———. "Picture Palaces." In *The Shadow and Its Shadow,* ed. Paul Hammond. London: British Film Institute, 1978. 46–47.

———. "On Cinema." *Film Culture* 67–69 (1979): 235.

———. "The Work of Man Ray." *Transition* 15 (Feb. 1929): 264–66.

C. Caws, Mary Ann. *The Surrealist Voice of Robert Desnos.* Amherst: Univ. of Massachusetts Press, 1977.

Dumas, Marie-Claire. *Robert Desnos ou l'exploration des limites.* Paris: Klincksieck, 1980.

D. De la Breteque, François. "L'Etoile de mer de Robert Desnos et Man Ray (1928) vu par des lycéens d'aujourd'hui." *Les Cahiers de la cinémathèque* 33–34 (1981): 200–3.

Dumas, Marie-Claire. "Un Scénario exemplaire de Robert Desnos." In *Surréalisme et cinéma I,* ed. Yves Kovacs. Special issue of Etudes cinématographiques 38–39 (1965): 135–39.

Proia, François. "Robert Desnos: poesia e cinema." *Berenice* 5.10 (1984): 321–31.

MARCEL DUCHAMP

A. Duchamp, Marcel. *Duchamp du signe. Ecrits.* Ed. Michel Sanouillet and Elmer Peterson. Paris: Flammarion, 1975.

———. *Salt Seller: The Writings of Marcel Duchamp.* Ed. Michel Sanouillet and Elmer Peterson. New York: Oxford Univ. Press, 1973.

C. Duchamp, Marcel, and Pierre Cabanne. *Dialogues with Marcel Duchamp.* Trans. Ron Padgett. New York: Viking, 1971.

Clair, Jean. *Duchamp et la photographie.* Paris: Editions du Chêne, 1977.

D'Harnoncourt, Anne, and Kynaston McShine, eds. *Marcel Duchamp.* New York: Museum of Modern Art, 1973.

Lebel, Robert. *Marcel Duchamp.* Trans. George Heard Hamilton. New York: Paragraphic Books, 1959.

Masheck, Joseph, comp. *Marcel Duchamp in Perspective.* Englewood Cliffs, N.J.: Prentice-Hall, 1974.

Paz, Octavio. *Marcel Duchamp: Appearance Stripped Bare.* Trans. R. Phillips and D. Gardner. New York: Viking, 1978.

Schwarz, Arturo. *The Complete Works of Marcel Duchamp.* New York: Abrams, 1970.

———. *Marcel Duchamp. Ready-mades, etc. (1913-1964).* Paris: Le Terrain Vague, 1964.

D. Amberg, George. "The Rationale of the Irrationale." *Minnesota Review* 3.3 (Spring 1963): 323-47.

Coenen, J. P. "Marcel Duchamp: Anémic Cinéma." *Jaarboek van het Koninklijk Museum voor schone Kunsten Antwerpen.* (1975): 279-88.

Imponente, A. "Vecchiali invisibe." *Filmcritica* 32.312 (Feb. 1981): 79-81.

Levesque, Jacques-Henri, and Jean Van Heeckeren. "Anémic cinéma." *Orbes* Series 2.2 (Summer 1933): n. pag.

Martin, Katrina. "Marcel Duchamp's *Anémic Cinéma.*" *Studio International* 189/973 (Jan.-Feb. 1975): 53-60.

Michelson, Annette. "Anémic cinéma." *Segnocinema* 13 (May 1984): 17-22.

———. "'Anemic Cinema.' Reflections on an Emblematic Work." *Artforum* 12.2 (Oct. 1973): 64-69.

Mussman, Toby. "Anémic cinéma." *Art and Artists* 1.4 (July 1966): 48-51.

———. "Marcel Duchamp's 'Anémic cinéma.'" In *The New American Cinema. A Critical Anthology.* Ed. Gregory Battock. New York, 1967. 147-55.

Ray, Man. "Bilingual Biography, I and Marcel." *Opus International* 49 (March 1974): 31-33.

———. "[Tribute to Duchamp]." *Art in America* 57.4 (1969): 43.

Richter, Hans. "A propos de Marcel Duchamp, des 'disques' et du 'Nu descendant un escalier.' " *Style* (Special issue on film. Paris, 1946).

Roché, Henri-Pierre. "Diskoptics de Marcel." *Phases* 1 (Jan. 1954): 14.

Sayag, Alain. "Marcel Duchamp." In *Film als Film: 1910 bis heute.* Ed. Hein and Herzogenrath. Cologne: Kölnischer Kunstverein, 1977. 120-21.

GERMAINE DULAC

A. Dulac, Germaine. *Germaine Dulac présente: Schémas.* Paris: Gutenberg, 1927.

B. Dulac, Germaine. "The Aesthetics, the Obstacles. Integral Cinegraphie." *Framework* 19 (1982): 6-9.

———. "The Avant-Garde Cinema." In *The Avant-Garde Film.* Ed. P. Adams Sitney. New York: New York Univ. Press, 1978. 43-48.

————. "Le Cinéma d'avant-garde. Les oeuvres d'avant-garde cinématographique. Leur destin devant le public et l'industrie du film." In *Le Cinéma des origines à nos jours*. Ed. Henri Frescourt. Paris: Eds. du Cygne, 1932. 357–64.

————. "The Essence of the Cinema: The Visual Idea." In *The Avant-Garde Cinema*. Ed. P. Adams Sitney. New York: New York University Press, 1978. 36–42.

————. "La Musique du silence." *Cinégraphie* 5 (Jan. 15, 1928).

————. "Visual and Anti-Visual Films." In *The Avant-Garde Film*. Ed. P. Adams Sitney. New York: New York Univ. Press, 1978. 31–35.

C. Dozoretz, Wendy Harriet. "Germaine Dulac: Filmmaker, Polemicist, Theoretician." Diss. New York University, 1982.

D. Cornwell, Regina. "Maya Deren and Germaine Dulac: Activists of the Avant-Garde." *Film Library Quarterly* 5.1 (Winter 1971–72): 29–38.

Dozoretz, Wendy. "Dulac versus Artaud." *Wide Angle* 3.1 (1979): 46–53.

Flitterman, Sandy. "Germaine Dulac's *The Smiling Madame Beudet*." *Wide Angle* 4 (1981).

————. "Heart of the Avant-Garde: Some Biographical Notes on Germaine Dulac." *Women and Film* 1.5–6 (1974): 58–61.

————. "Theorizing 'the Feminine': Woman as the Figure of Desire in *The Seashell and the Clergyman*." *Wide Angle* 6.3 (1984): 32–39.

Lawder, Standish D. "Dulac and Seeber." In his *The Cubist Cinema*. New York: New York Univ. Press, 1975. 169–81.

Liebman, Stuart. "Archeology of Film Theory: 5: Germaine Dulac: Integral Cinegraphie." *Framework* 19 (1982): 4–5.

Van Wert, William. "Germaine Dulac: First Feminist Filmmaker." *Women and Film* 1.5–6 (1974): 55–57.

Virmaux, Alain and Odette, eds. "Trois récits du scandale des Ursulines." In their *Les Surréalistes et le cinéma*. Paris: Seghers, 1976. 171–75.

VIKING EGGELING

B. Eggeling, Viking. "Aus dem Nachlass von Viking Eggeling." *G* 5–6 (1924).

C. Hultén, Karl G., ed. *Apropa Eggeling*. Stockholm: Moderna Museet, 1958.

O'Konor, Louise. *Viking Eggeling, 1880–1925: Artist and Film-maker, Life and Work*. Stockholm: Almqvist and Wiksell, 1971.

Viking Eggeling. Copenhagen: Galerie Tokanten, 1951 [exhibition catalog].

Viking Eggeling 1880–1925. Tecknare och Filmkonstnär. Stockholm: Nationalmuseum, 1950 [exhibition catalog].

D. Arp, Hans. "[In Commemoration of Viking Eggeling]." In *Viking Eggeling, 1880–1925*. Stockholm: Nationalmuseum, 1950. 10–11.

Bandi, Miklos N. [Nicolas Baudy]. "La Symphonie diagonale de Vicking [sic] Eggeling." *Schémas* 1 (1927): 9–19.

Hausmann, Raoul. "Viking Eggeling." *A bis Z* 9 (July 1930): 33.

Hultén, Karl G. "Viking Eggeling." *Art d'aujourd'hui*. 7 (1953): 3.

Kurtz, Rudolf. "Viking Eggeling." In his *Expressionismus und Film*. Berlin: Verlag der Lichtbildbühne, 1926. 94–98.

Lawder, Standish D. "The Abstract Film: Richter, Eggeling, and Ruttmann." In his *The Cubist Cinema*. New York: New York Univ. Press, 1975. 35–64.

McLaren, Norman. "Animation Is Not the Art of Drawings-That-Move, but the Art of Movements-That-Are-Drawn . . ." In *Apropa Eggeling*. Ed. K. G. Hultén. Stockholm: Moderna Museet, 1958. 25.

Mies van der Rohe, Ludwig. "[In Commemoration of Viking Eggeling]." In *Viking Eggeling, 1880–1925*. Stockholm: Nationalmuseum, 1950. 11.

Nordenfalk, Carl. "Viking Eggeling, Malere och Filmpionjär." *Dagens Nyheter* 13 Aug. 1950: 2.

O'Konor, Louise. "The Film Experiments of Viking Eggeling." *Cinema Studies* 2.2 (June 1966): 26–31.

———. "Tva Filmpionjärer." *Dagens Nyheter* 5 April 1969: 3.

Richter, Hans. "[In Commemoration of Viking Eggeling]." In *Viking Eggeling, 1880–1925*. Stockholm: Nationalmuseum, 1950. 9–10.

———. "Om Viking Eggeling." In *Apropa Eggeling*. Ed. K. G. Hultén. Stockholm: Moderna Museet, 1958. 15–17.

Schmidt, Georg. "[In Commemoration of Viking Eggeling]." In *Viking Eggeling, 1880–1925*. Stockholm: Nationalmuseum, 1950. 12–15.

———. "Viking Eggeling." *Konstrevy*. 26.4–5 (1950): 234–37.

Schmidt, Paul. "Eggelings Kunstfilm." *Das Kunstblatt*. 8 (1924): 381.

Türck, Walter C. "Den förste abstrakta filmen." In *Apropa Eggeling*. Ed. K. G. Hultén. Stockholm: Moderna Museet, 1958: 27.

Tzara, Tristan. "[In Commemoration of Viking Eggeling]." In *Viking Eggeling, 1880–1925*. Stockholm: Nationalmuseum, 1950. 11.

Weibel, Peter. "Kino klipp und klar. Viking Eggeling." *Film* (Velber bei Hannover) 7.2 (1969): 13.

Wolfradt, Willi. "Der absolute Film." *Das Kunstblatt* 9 (1925): 187–88.

Zurhake, Monika. "Diagonal-Symphonie von Viking Eggeling." In her *Filmische Realitätsaneignung*. Heidelberg: Winter, 1982, pp. 93–126.

BENJAMIN FONDANE

A. Fondane, Benjamin. *Ecrits pour le cinéma*. Ed. Michel Carassou. Paris: Plasma, 1984.

———. *Faux Traité d'ésthétique: essai sur la crise de réalité*. Paris: Plasma, 1980.

———. *Trois scenarii "cinépoèmes."* Paris: Documents Internationaux de l'Esprit Nouveau, 1928.

B. Fondane, Benjamin. "Du muet au parlant: grandeur et décadence du cinéma." *Bifur* 5 (1930): 137–50.

———. "Entr'acte ou le cinéma autonôme." *Intégral* 1.1 (March 1925).

———. "Lettre ouverte à Antonin Artaud sur le Théâtre Alfred-Jarry." *Europe* 667–68 (Nov.–Dec. 1984): 87–93.

──────. "Paupières mûres (ciné-poème)." In Alain and Odette Virmaux, *Les Surréalistes et le cinéma.* Paris: Seghers, 1976. 221-27.

──────. "Réflexions sur le spectacle." *Cahiers de l'Etoile* 2 (1929): 256-67.

C. Hyde, John K. *Benjamin Fondane: A Presentation of His Life and Work.* Geneva: Droz, 1971.

D. Carassou, Michel. "Artaud, Fondane, même combat!" *Europe* 667-68 (Nov.-Dec. 1984): 84-86.

──────. "Benjamin Fondane, du surréalisme à l'existentialisme." In *Des Années trente.* Ed. Anne Roche and Christian Tarting. Paris: Editions du CNRS, 1986. 247-58.

──────. "Benjamin Fondane et la conscience honteuse du surréalisme." *Mélusine* (1982): 181-190.

FERNAND LÉGER

A. Léger, Fernand. *Functions of Painting.* Trans. Alexandra Anderson. New York: Viking, 1973.

B. Léger, Fernand. "A propos du cinéma." *Cahiers d'art* 8.3-4 (1933): 135.

──────. "Ballet mécanique." In his *Functions of Painting.* Trans. A. Anderson. New York: Viking, 1973. 48-51.

──────. "Ballet mécanique [film]." In *Internationale Ausstellung neuer Theatertechnik.* Vienna, 1924 [exhibition catalog].

──────. "A Critical Essay on the Plastic Quality of Abel Gance's Film *The Wheel* (1922)." In his *Functions of Painting.* New York: Viking, 1973 [originally published in *Comoedia* 1922].

──────. "The New Realism." In his *Functions of Painting.* New York: Viking, 1973. 109-13.

──────. "Les Réalisations picturales actuelles. Conférence faite à l'Académie Wassilieff." *Les Soirées de Paris* 3.25 (15 June 1914): 349-56.

──────. "Speaking of Cinema." In his *Functions of Painting.* New York: Viking, 1973. 100-4.

──────. "Le Spectacle: lumière, couleur, image mobile, objet-spectacle." Rpt. in *L'Occhio tagliato.* Ed. Gianni Rondolino. Turin: Martano, 1972. 117-24.

C. Cooper, D. *Fernand Léger.* Paris: Editions Trois Collines, 1949.

De Francia, Peter. *Fernand Léger.* New Haven: Yale Univ. Press, 1983.

Delevoy, Robert L. *Léger: Biographical and Critical Study.* Trans. Stuart Gilbert. Geneva: Skira, 1962.

Green, Christopher. *Léger and the Avant-Garde.* New Haven: Yale Univ. Press, 1976.

Laugier, Claude. *Oeuvres de Fernand Léger.* Paris: Centre Georges Pompidou, 1981 [exhibition catalog].

Léger et l'esprit moderne. Paris: Musée d'Art moderne de la ville de Paris, 1982 [exhibition catalog].

D. Antheil, George. "My Ballet mécanique." *De Stijl* 6.12 (1924-25): 141-44.

Brender, Richard. "Functions of Film: Léger's Cinema on Paper and on Cellulose." *Cinema Journal* 24.1 (Fall 1984): 41-64.

Brown, G. "Ballet mécanique." *Monthly Film Bulletin* 44 (April 1977): 84-85.

Jackiewicz, A. "Epizod filmowy w dziele Fernanda Leger." *Kino* 9 (March 1974): 28-33.

Lawder, Standish D. "Ballet mécanique." In his *The Cubist Cinema*. New York: New York Univ. Press, 1975. 117-167.

———. "Fernand Léger and 'Ballet mécanique.' " *Image* (Oct. 1965): 13-15.

Rondolino, Gianni. "Pittori e uomini di cinema: Francis Picabia e Ferdinand [sic] Léger." *D'Ars* (Milan) 14 (Nov.-Dec. 1973): 68-81.

Sayag, Alain. "Fernand Léger." In *Film als Film: 1910 bis heute*. Ed. Hein and Herzogenrath. Cologne: Kölnischer Kunstverein, 1977. 119.

Serenellini, Mario. "I contrasti delle forme in 'Ballet mécanique.' " *Cinema Nuovo* 33.6 (Dec 1984): 15-16.

LASZLO MOHOLY-NAGY

A. Moholy-Nagy, Laszlo. *Painting, Photography, Film*. Trans. Janet Seligman. Cambridge, MA: MIT Press, 1969.

———. *Vision in Motion*. Chicago: Theobald, 1956.

B. Moholy-Nagy, Laszlo. "Cinéma simultané ou polycinéma." *Cahiers du cinéma* 294 (Nov. 1978): 51.

———. "Dynamique de la grande ville." *Cahiers du cinéma* 294 (Nov. 1978): 52-53.

———. "Dynamique d'une métropole" [scenario]. *MA* 1924. Rpt. in *Action Poétique* 49 (1972): 50-55.

———. "Problèmes du nouveau film." *Cahiers d'art* 7.6-7 (1932): 277-80.

C. Caton, Joseph Harris. "The Utopian Vision of Moholy-Nagy: Technology, Society, and the Avant-Garde. An Analysis of the Writings of Moholy-Nagy on the Visual Arts." Diss. Princeton University, 1980.

Kostelanetz, Richard, ed. *Moholy-Nagy*. New York: Praeger, 1970.

Moholy-Nagy, Sibyl. *Moholy-Nagy: Experiment in Totality*. New York: Harper, 1950.

D. Biro, Y. "Laszlo Moholy-Nagy." *Travelling* 55 (Summer 1979): 45-47.

———. "Laszlo Moholy-Nagy: Présentation." *Cahiers du cinéma* 294 (Nov. 1978): 44-53.

Horak, J.-C. "The Films of Moholy-Nagy." *Afterimage* 13 (Summer 1985): 20-23.

Lippert, K. "Bauhaus et cinématographie." *Travelling* 56-57 (Spring 1980): 42-52.

Rose, Barbara. "The Films of Man Ray and Moholy-Nagy." *Artforum* 10.1 (Sept. 1971): 68-73.

FRANCIS PICABIA

A. Picabia, Francis. *Ecrits.* Ed. Olivier Revault d'Allonnes. 2 volumes. Paris: Belfond, 1975–1978.

B. Picabia, Francis. "A propos d'Entr'acte." *Films* 28 (1 Nov. 1924).

———. "A propos de 'Relâche' ballet instantanéiste." *Comoedia* 27 Nov. 1924. Rpt. in *Ecrits II* 163–64.

———. "Les Ballets suédois." *Montparnasse* 1 Dec. 1924. Rpt. in *Ecrits II* 169.

———. "Cinéma." *Cinéa* (May 1922). Rpt. in *Ecrits II* 69–71.

———. "'Entr'acte.'" *This Quarter* 1.3 (Spring 1927): 301–2. Rpt. in *Ecrits II* 190.

———. "'Entr'acte.'" *Orbes* (Spring 1932). Rpt. in *Ecrits II* 222–23.

———. "'Entr'acte' un peu de Picabia au Star." *Le Journal des Hivernants* (Jan. 1927): 19. Rpt. in *Ecrits II* 181.

———. "Erik Satie." *Paris-Journal* 27 June 1924. Rpt. *Ecrits II* 145–47.

———. "Instantanéisme." *Comoedia* 21 Nov. 1924:4. Rpt. in *Ecrits II* 159–60.

———. "Interview sur 'Entr'acte.'" *Comoedia* 31 Oct. 1924:4. Rpt. in *Ecrits II* 156.

———. "Lettre de Francis Picabia à propos d' 'Entr'acte.'" *L'Avant-scène cinéma* 86 (Nov. 1968): 2.

———. "La Loi d'accommodation chez les Borgnes" [scenario, 1928]. Rpt. in *Ecrits II* 193–206.

———. "Pourquoi j'ai écrit 'Relâche.'" *Le Siècle* 27 Nov. 1924. Rpt. in *Ecrits II* 162–63.

———. "Pourquoi 'Relâche' a fait relâche." *Comoedia* 2 Dec. 1924. Rpt. in *Ecrits II* 169–70.

———. "Programme de 'Relâche.'" *La Danse* (Nov. 1924). Rpt. *Ecrits II* 165–68.

———. "Relâche." In *Ecrits II* 155–56.

———. "Réponse au 'Figaro.' " *Le Figaro* 15 Oct. 1946:4. Rpt. in *Ecrits II* 264.

———. "Scénario d'Entr'acte.'" *L'Avant-scène du cinéma* (Nov. 1968). Rpt. in *Ecrits II* 154.

C. Camfield, William A. *Francis Picabia: His Art, Life, and Times.* Princeton: Princeton Univ. Press. 1979.

D. Amengual, B. "'Entr'acte' et ses mystères." *L'Avant-scène cinéma* 281 (Feb. 1982): 19–25.

Beylie, Claude. "Entr'acte: le film sans maître." *Cinéma 69* 133 (Feb. 1969): 115–17.

Brunius, Jacques B. "Entr'acte." In his *En marge du cinéma français.* Paris: Arcanes, 1954.

Carroll, Noel. "*Entr'acte*, Paris and Dada." *Millenium Film Journal* 1.1 (Winter 1977): 5–11.

Clair, René. "Picabia, Satie, and the First Night of *Entr'acte*." In *A Nous la Liberté and Entr'acte.* Classic Film Scripts. New York: Simon and Schuster, 1970. 108–12.

Dale, R. C. "René Clair's 'Entr'acte,' or Motion Victorious." *Wide Angle* 2.2 (1978): 38–43.

Desnos, Robert. "Entr'acte." In his *Cinéma.* Paris: Gallimard, 1966. 121.

"*Entr'acte*" [shot analysis] *L'Avant-scène: Cinéma* 86 (Nov. 1968): 9–18.

Fondane, Benjamin. "Entr'acte ou le cinéma autonôme." *Intégral* 1.1 (March 1925).

Kovacs, Steven. "Dada comes in at Intermission: Picabia and René Clair on *Entr'acte.*" In his *From Enchantment to Rage.* London and Toronto; Associated University Presses, 1980. 64-114.

Kracauer, Siegfried. "*Entr'acte.*" In his *Nature of Film.* London: Dobson, 1961. 182-83.

Kurtz, Rudolf. "Francis Picabia." In his *Expressionismus und Film.* Berlin: Verlag der Lichtbildbühne, 1926. 106-8.

Mitry, Jean. "Film abstrait et musique visuelle." In his *Le Cinéma experimental.* Paris: Seghers, 1974. 74-98.

Mueller, J. "Films: 'Relâche' and 'Entr'acte.' " *Dance Magazine* 51 (July 1977): 102-3.

Puccini, Gianni. "*Entr'acte.*" *Cinema* (Rome) 60 (1938): 385-86.

Rondolino, Gianni. "Pittori e uomini di cinema: Francis Picabia e Fernand Léger." *D'Ars* (Milan) 14 (Nov.-Dec. 1973): 68-81.

Sandro, Paul. "Parodic Narration in 'Entr'acte.' " *Film Criticism* 4.1 (1979): 44-55.

Verdone, Mario. "Entr'acte." In his *Le avanguardie storiche del cinema.* Turin: Società Editrice Internationale, 1977. 96-99.

White, Mimi. "Two French Dada Films: *Entr'acte* and *Emak Bakia.*" *Dada/Surrealism* 13 (1984): 37-47.

MAN RAY

A. Ray, Man, and Pierre Bourgeade. *Bonsoir, Man Ray.* [interview]. Paris: Belfond, 1972.

―――. *Man Ray: Photographs.* Introduction Jean-Hubert Martin. London: Thames and Hudson, 1982.

―――. *Man Ray: 60 anni di libertà.* Ed. Arturo Schwarz. Paris: Losfeld, 1971.

―――. *Self Portrait.* Boston: Little, Brown, 1963.

B. Ray, Man. "The Age of Light." *Panderma* 1 (1957): 25. Trans. of "L'Age de lumière." *Minotaure* 3-4 (1933):1.

―――. "Art et cinéma." *L'Age du cinema* 2 (May 1951): 15-16.

―――. "Aurore des objets." *Minotaure* 10 (Winter 1937): 41-44.

―――. "Bilingual Biography, I and Marcel." *Opus International* 49 (March 1974): 31-33.

―――. "Cinémage." *L'Age du cinéma.* 4-5 (Aug.-Nov. 1951): 24-25. English transl. in *The Shadow and Its Shadow.* Ed. Paul Hammond. London: British Film Institute, 1978. 84-85.

―――. "[Excerpt on Film from His *Autoportrait*]." *Cinématographe* 107 (Feb. 1985): 40.

―――. "Films Dada et surréalisme" [from *Autoportrait*]. In *L'Occhio tagliato.* Ed. Gianni Rondolino. Turin: Martano, 1972. 69-86.

―――, and Arturo Schwarz. "An Interview with Man Ray: 'This Is Not for America.'" *Arts Magazine* 51.9 (May 1977): 116-21.

―――. "It Has Never Been My Object to Record My Dreams." In *Man Ray: 60 anni di libertà.* Ed. Arturo Schwarz. Paris: Losfeld, 1971. 48.

―――. "Lettera a voce a Hans Richter." *Filmcritica* 27 (May-June 1976): 176-77.

————. "Photography Is Not Art." *View* 3.1 (April 1943): 23; 3.3 (Oct. 1943): 77–78, 97.

————. "A Talk by Man Ray at a Film Screening Oct. 15, 1943." In *Art in Cinema*. Ed. Frank Stauffacher. San Francisco: San Francisco Museum of Art, 1947.

————. "[Tribute to Duchamp]." *Art in America* 57.4 (1969): 43.

————. "[Tous les films que j'ai réalisés . . .]." In *Surréalisme et cinéma I*. Ed. Yves Kovacs. Special issue of *Études cinématographiques* 38–39 (Spring 1965): 43–46.

C. Alexandrian, Sarane. *Man Ray*. Paris: Filipacchi, 1973.

Belz, Carl. "The Role of Man Ray in the Dada and Surrealist Movements." Diss. Princeton University, 1963.

Bramley, Serge. *Man Ray*. Paris: Belfond, 1980.

Penrose, Sir Roland. *Man Ray*. Boston: New York Graphic Society, 1975.

Schwarz, Arturo. *Man Ray: The Rigour of Imagination*. New York: Rizzoli, 1977.

Teres, Michael. "Man Ray, Painter and Photographer." Thesis, U. of Iowa, 1965.

D. Amberg, George. "The Rationale of the Irrationale." *Minnesota Review* 3.3 (1963): 323–47.

Belz, Carl. "The Film Poetry of Man Ray." *Criticism* 7.2 (1965): 117–30.

————. "A Man Ray Retrospective in Los Angeles." *Artforum* 5.4 (Dec. 1966): 22–26.

Biard, Ida. "An Interview with Man Ray." *Flash Art* 56–57 (1975): 14–15.

Coleman, A. D. "The Practical Dreamer: Man Ray." *Camera 35* 26 (July 1981): 54–57.

De la Breteque, François. "L'Etoile de mer de Robert Desnos et Man Ray (1928) vu par des lycéens d'aujourd'hui." *Les Cahiers de la cinémathèque* 33–34 (1981): 200–3.

Desnos, Robert. "The Work of Man Ray." *Transition* 15 (Feb. 1929): 264–66.

Fuller, John. "Atget and Man Ray in the Context of Surrealism." *Art Journal* 36.2 (Winter 1976–77): 130–38.

Hill, Paul, and Thomas Cooper. "Camera-Interview." *Camera* 54 (Feb. 1975): 37–40.

Kovács, Steven. "An American in Paris: Man Ray as Filmmaker." In his *From Enchantment to Rage: The Story of Surrealist Cinema*. London and Toronto: Associated University Presses, 1980. 114–154.

————. "Man Ray as Filmmaker." *Artforum* (Nov. 1972): 77–82; (Dec. 1972): 62–66.

Kramer, Arthur. "Man Ray: Always Avant-Garde." *Modern Photography* 38 (Sept. 1974): 84–89.

Kramer, Hilton. "His Heart Belongs to Dada." *Reporter* 28 (May 1963): 43–46.

Rabinovitz, Lauren. "Independent Journeyman: Man Ray, Dada and Surrealist Filmmaker." *Southwest Review* 64 (1979): 355–76.

Richter, Hans. "[Note on Man Ray]." *G* 3 (June 1924): 32.

Rose, Barbara. "The Films of Man Ray and Moholy-Nagy." *Artforum* 10.1 (Sept. 1971): 68–73.

Sayag, Alain. "Man Ray." In *Film als Film: 1910 bis heute*. Ed. Hein and Herzogenrath. Cologne: Kölnischer Kunstverein, 1977. 122–25.

Thiher, Allen. "The Surrealist Film: Man Ray and the Limits of Metaphor." *Dada/Surrealism* 6 (1976): 18–26.

Waldberg, Patrick. "Man Ray avant Man Ray." *XXe Siècle* 45 (Dec. 1975): 12–19.

————. "Les objets de Man Ray." *XXe Siècle* 31 (Dec. 1968): 65–80.

White, Mimi. "Two French Dada Films: *Entr'acte* and *Emak Bakia.*" *Dada/Surrealism* 13 (1984): 37–47.

HANS RICHTER

A. Richter, Hans. *Begegnungen von Dada bis heute.* Cologne: DuMont, 1973.

————. *Dada Art and Anti-Art.* London: Thames and Hudson, 1965.

————. *Filmgegner von heute – Filmfreunde von morgen.* Berlin: Reckendorf, 1929. Rpt. Frankfurt: Fischer, 1981.

————. *Hans Richter by Hans Richter.* Ed. Cleve Gray. New York: Holt, Rinehart and Winston, 1971.

————. *Der Kampf um den Film.* Ed. Jürgen Römhild. Munich: Hanser, 1976.

————. *Köpfe und Hinterköpfe.* Zürich: Arche, 1967.

B. Richter, Hans. "Der absolute Film braucht die Industrie." *Film-Kurier* 10.6 (January 1929).

————. "Anatomie de l'avant-garde." *L'Age du cinéma* 3 (1951): 3–6.

————. "Avant-Garde Film in Germany." In *Experiment in the Film.* Ed. Roger Manvell. London: Grey Walls Press, 1949. 219–33.

————. "The Avant-Garde Film Seen from Within." *Hollywood Quarterly* 4.1 (1949): 34–41.

————. "Avantgarde im Bereich des Möglichen." *Film-Kurier* (June 1929).

————. "Bemerkungen zu meinen Arbeiten." *Hamburger Filmgespräche* 3 (1967): 19–24.

————. "Cinéma américain d'avant-garde." *Style en France* 4 (1946): 96–97.

————. "Dada and the Film." In *Dada. Monograph of a Movement.* Ed. W. Verkauf. Teufen: Niggli, 1957. 64–71.

————. "Easel – Scroll – Film." *Magazine of Art* 45 (Feb. 1952): 78–86.

————. "Die eigentliche Sphäre des Films." *G* 5–6 (1926): 18.

————. "Eight Free Improvisations on the Game of Chess." *Film Culture* 1.1 (1955): 36–38.

————. "8 x 8. Hans Richter's Latest Experimental Film." *Film Culture* 1.5–6 (1955): 17–19.

————. "Erklärung vor dem Kongress der Internationale Fortschrittlicher Künstler Düsseldorf." *De Stijl* 5.4 (1922): 57–59.

————. "Film." *De Stijl* 5.6 (1922): 91–92.

————. "Film." *De Stijl* 6.5 (1923): 55–56.

Richter, Hans. "The Film as an Original Art Form." *College Art Journal* 10.2 (1951), 157–61.

————. "Film as Original Art." In *Film Culture Reader.* Ed. P. Adams Sitney. New York: Praeger, 1970. 15–20.

————. "Il film di avanguardia, il film astratto e il futurismo." *Cinema Italiano* 12 (Dec. 1953): 39–44.

————. "Filmen son konstform." In *Apropa Eggeling.* Ed. K. G. Hulten. Stockholm: Moderna Museet, 1958. 8–14.

————. "Filmmanifest." *G* 5-6 (1926): 1-2.

————. "Film von morgen." *Das Werk* (Zürich) 16.9 (1929): 278-84.

————. "From Interviews with Hans Richter during the Last Ten Years." *Film Culture* 31 (Winter 1963-64): 26-35.

————. "A History of the Avant-Garde." In *Art in Cinema*. Ed. Frank Stauffacher. San Francisco: San Francisco Museum of Art, 1947. 6-24.

————. "[In Commemoration of Viking Eggeling]." In *Viking Eggeling 1880-1925*. Stockholm: Nationalmuseum, 1950. 9-10.

————. "Je ne suis pas un cinéaste." *Positif* 40 (July 1961): 1-3.

————. "Learning from Film History." *Filmmaker's Newsletter* 7 (1973): 26-27.

————. "My Experience with Movement in Painting and Film." In *The Nature and Art of Motion*. New York, 1965.

————. "Neue Mittel der Filmgestaltung." *Die Form—Zeitschrift für gestaltende Arbeit*. 4.3 (1929): 53-56.

————. "[Note on Man Ray]." *G* 3 (1924): 32.

————. "L'Objet en mouvement." *Cercle et Carré* 3 (June 1930).

————. "Om Viking Eggeling." In *Apropa Eggeling*. Ed. K. G. Hulten. Stockholm: Moderna Museet, 1958. 15-17.

————. "Peinture et Film." *XXe Siècle* 21.12 (1959): 25-28.

————. "Publikum und Film." In his *Köpfe und Hinterköpfe*. Zürich: Arche, 1967. 145-53.

————. "Step by Step. An Account of the Transition from Painting to the First Abstract Films, 1919-1921." *Studies in the Twentieth Century* 2 (1968): 7-20.

————. "Témoignage." In *Surréalisme et cinéma I*. Ed. Yves Kovacs. Special issue of *Etudes cinématographiques* 38-39 (1965): 55-56.

————. "Der unabhängige Film in einer abhängigen Zeit." In his *Köpfe und Hinterköpfe*. Zürich: Arche, 1967. 193-95.

————. "Ur-Kino." *Neue Zürcher Zeitung* 25 February 1940: 6.

————. "Viking Eggeling." *G* 4 (1926): 14-16.

————. "Von der statischen zur dynamischen Form." *Plastique* 2 (1937): 12-18. Rpt. in *Dada—Eine literarische Dokumentation*. Ed. Richard Huelsenbeck. Reinbek: Rowohlt, 1964. 250-52.

C. Brissoni, A. *Imagine strutturate sul linguaggio cinematografico dei ritmi 21, 23, 25 e Filmstudie 1926 di Hans Richter*. Padua: Liviana, 1968.

Hans Richter, 1888-1976. Berlin: Akademie der Künste, 1982 [exhibition catalog].

Hans Richter. Ein Leben für Bild und Film. Berlin: Akademie der Künste, 1958 [exhibition catalog].

Weinberg, Herman G. *An Index to the Creative Work of Two Pioneers: I. Robert J. Flaherty, II. Hans Richter*. London: British Film Institute, 1946 [pamphlet].

Zurhake, Monika. *Filmische Realitätsaneignung. Ein Beitrag zur Filmtheorie, mit Analysen von Filmen Viking Eggelings und Hans Richters*. Heidelberg: Winter, 1982.

D. Arthur, P. "Look Back: Notes on the Graphic Cinema." *Millimeter* 3 (1975): 53.

Bassan, R., and M. Roudevitch. "Se souvenir de Hans Richter." *Ecran* 58 (May 1977): 6-10.

Codroico, R., and L. Pezzolato. "Richter e l'uomo visibile." *Cinema nuovo* 21.218 (1972): 254-55.

Courant, G. "Rêves à vendre." *Cinéma 80* 253 (Jan. 1980): 51.

Dumont, Boris. "Pourquoi le Minotaure?" *L'Age du cinéma* 4-5 (1951): 63-64.

"Filmographie de Hans Richter." *L'Age du cinéma* 1 (1951): 39-40.

Hart, Henry. "Acht mal acht." *Films in Review* 8.2 (Feb. 1957): 84-85.

Hossmann, Gisela. "Hans Richter." In *Film als Film: 1910 bis heute.* Ed. Hein and Herzogenrath. Cologne: Kölnischer Kunstverein, 1977. 48-55.

Kurtz, Rudolf. "Hans Richter." In his *Expressionismus und Film* Berlin: Verlag der Lichtbildbühne, 1926. 98-100.

Lawder, Standish D. "The Abstract Film: Richter, Eggeling, and Ruttmann." In his *The Cubist Cinema.* New York: New York Univ. Press, 1975. 35-64.

Leiser, Erwin. "Hans Richter – Maler als Filmpionier." In *Hans Richter, 1888-1976.* Berlin: Akademie der Künste, 1982. 37-41.

Mekas, Jonas. "Acht mal Acht." *Village Voice* 6.21 (16 March 1961): 11.

———. "Dadascope." *Village Voice* 13.36 (20 June 1968): 44, 46.

———. "Hans Richter on the Nature of Film Poetry." *Film Culture* 3.1 (1957): 5-8.

Ray, Man. "Lettera a voce a Hans Richter." *Filmcritica* 27 (May-June 1976): 176-77.

Römhild, Jürgen. "Hans Richter-Bibliographie." In Hans Richter, *Der Kampf um den Film.* Munich: Hanser, 1976. 173-80.

———. "Hans Richter-Filmographie." In Hans Richter, *Der Kampf um den Film.* Munich: Hanser, 1976. 169-72.

Rondolino, Gianni. "Appunti sul cinema e sulla teoria di Hans Richter." *Bianco e Nero* 39 (1978): 6-61.

Sherlock, M., and J. Goldsworthy. "Cinema's Free Spirit: Hans Richter, 1888-1976." *Film Criticism* 1.1 (1976): 39-42.

Simon, E. P. "Dada on Film: Richter's 'Rhythmus.' " *Thousand Eyes* 2 (Feb. 1977): 2.

Starr, C. "From the Abstract to the Concrete." *Film Library Quarterly* 7.1 (1974): 13-16.

Tallmer, Jerry. "Acht mal Acht." *Village Voice* 2.19 (6 March 1957): 6, 9.

Weinberg, H. G. "Besuch bei Hans Richter." *Filmkunst* 74 (1976): 7-8.

———. "30 Years of Experimental Films." *Films in Review* 2.10 (Dec. 1951): 22-27.

Young, Vernon. "Painter and Cinematographer." *Arts* 33 (Sept. 1959): 48-55.

Zurhake, Monika. "*Inflation* von Hans Richter." In her *Filmische Realitätsaneignung.* Heidelberg: Winter, 1982. 200-53.

———. "*Rhythmus 21* von Hans Richter." In her *Filmische Realitätsaneignung.* Heidelberg: Winter, 1982. 127-199.

WALTHER RUTTMANN

B. Ruttmann, Walther. "Letter to Oskar Fischinger [17 July 1922]." In *Film als Film: 1910 bis heute.* Ed. Hein and Herzogenrath. Cologne: Kölnischer Kunstverein, 1977. 22.

———. "Malerei mit Zeit [1919]." In *Film als Film,* 63-64.

———. "Patentschrift: Verfahren und Vorrichtung zum Herstellen kinematographischer Bilder [1920]." Rpt. in *Film als Film,* 14-15.

──────. "Technik und Film" In *Kunst und Technik*. Ed. Leo Kestenberg. Berlin: Wegweiser-Verlag, 1930. Rpt. in *Film als Film*, 65.

C. Fulks, Barry Alan. "Film Culture and 'Kulturfilm': Walther Ruttmann, the Avant-Garde Film, and the 'Kulturfilm' in Weimar Germany and the Third Reich." Diss. University of Wisconsin at Madison, 1982.

Lawder, Standish D. "The Abstract Film: Richter, Eggeling, and Ruttmann." In his *The Cubist Cinema*. New York: New York Univ. Press, 1975. 35–64.

Le Grice, Malcom. "The First Abstract Films" In his *Abstract Film and Beyond*. Cambridge: MIT Press, 1977. 17–31.

Diebold, Bernhard. "Eine neue Kunst: Die Augenmusik des Films." *Frankfurter Zeitung* 2 April 1921. Rpt. in *Film als Film*, 16–17.

O'Konor, Louise. "Tva Filmpionjärer." *Dagens Nyheter* 5 April 1969: 3.

Steike, Heinz. "Walther Ruttmann." In *Film als Film*. Ed. Hein and Herzogenrath. Cologne: Kölnischer Kunstverein, 1977. 61–67.

Zglinicki, Friedrich von. "Ruttmann-Aufführung 1919." In his *Der Weg des Films* (Berlin, 1956). 597. Rpt. in *Film als Film*, 13.

PHILIPPE SOUPAULT

A. Soupault, Philippe. *Ecrits de cinéma 1918–1931*. Ed. Alain and Odette Virmaux. Paris: Editions Plon, 1979.

──────. *Vingt mille et un jours: Entretiens avec Serge Fauchereau*. Paris: Belfond, 1980.

B. Soupault, Philippe. "Cinema U.S.A. [1924]." In *The Shadow and Its Shadow*. Ed. Paul Hammond. London: British Film Institute, 1978. 32–33.

──────, et al. "Enquête." *Les Cahiers de la cinémathèque* 30–31 (1980): 17–35.

──────. "Five Cinema Poems." Trans. Serge Gavronsky. *Film Culture* 67–69 (1979): 236–37.

──────. "'Rage' and 'Glory' [cinematic poems, 1925]." In *The Shadow and Its Shadow*. Ed. Paul Hammond. London: British Film Institute, 1978. 70.

D. Mabire, Jean-Marie. "Entretien avec Philippe Soupault." In *Surréalisme et cinéma I*. Ed. Yves Kovacs. Special issue of *Etudes cinématographiques* 38–39 (1965): 29–33.

Monnier, I. and C. Nerguy. "Philippe Soupault nous parle de Chaplin." *Ecran* 67 (March 1978): 38–39.

NOTES ON CONTRIBUTORS

RICHARD ABEL teaches in the English Department at Drake University. He is the author of *French Cinema: The First Wave, 1915–1929* (1984), and the editor of the forthcoming two-volume *French Film Theory and Criticism, 1907–1939* (1987).

PETER CHRISTENSEN teaches Comparative Literature at SUNY Binghamton. He is the author of numerous essays on Godard, Cocteau, Nizan, Yourcenar, among others.

TOM CONLEY teaches French at the University of Minnesota. He is the author of *Caesures: ensayos sobre cine* (1986) and a forthcoming collection of his essays.

THOMAS ELSAESSER teaches film and English literature at the University of East Anglia (England). He has contributed numerous essays to *Screen, October, Discourse, New German Critique, Sight and Sound,* and *American Film.*

HAIM FINKELSTEIN is Senior Lecturer in the Department of Foreign Languages and Director of the Art Program at Ben-Gurion University of the Negev (Israel). He is currently working on a book on Dalí's art and writing.

SANDY FLITTERMAN-LEWIS teaches literature and film in the English Department at Rutgers University. She has written numerous articles on feminism and film theory, and is the author of a forthcoming book, *To Desire Differently: Feminism and French Cinema.*

JUDI FREEMAN is associate curator of 20th-century art at the Los Angeles County Museum of Art. Her dissertation is devoted to Fernand Léger's collaborative projects and their relations to his painting from 1918–28.

INEZ HEDGES teaches French and is the coordinator of Film Studies at Northeastern University. She is the author of *Languages of Revolt: Dada and Surrealist Literature and Film,* and is currently working on a book on Queneau.

DALIA JUDOVITZ teaches French literature at UC-Berkeley. She has published essays on philosophy and literature, psychoanalysis, aesthetics, and she is the author of the forthcoming book on *Subjectivity and Representation: The Origins of Modern Thought in Descartes* (1987).

RUDOLF E. KUENZLI teaches English and Comparative Literature, and directs the International Dada Archive at the University of Iowa. He is the coauthor of *Dada Artifacts* (1978), coeditor of *Dada Spectrum: The Dialectics of Revolt* (1979), editor of *New York Dada* (1986), and coeditor of the journal *Dada/Surrealism.*

STUART LIEBMAN teaches film at Queens College. His essays have been published in *October, Framework, Cinema, Take One, Millenium Film Journal,* and *Film Comment.* He is currently preparing a retrospective of the films of Alexander Kluge.

ALLEN S. WEISS wrote his first doctoral thesis in philosophy on Merleau-Ponty's aesthetics, and is now writing a second doctoral thesis on the theorization of avant-garde cinema. He is currently preparing anthologies on Daniel Paul Schreber, D. A. F. Sade, and Nietzsche.

LINDA WILLIAMS teaches literature and film in the English Department at the University of Illinois at Chicago. She is the author of *Figures of Desire: A Theory and Analysis of Surrealist Film,* and is currently working on a book on the pornographic film entitled *Hard Core: Power, Pleasure, and the Female Film Body.*

DAVID WILLS teaches French and Film at Louisiana State University. He is the author of *Self De(con)struct: Writing and the Surrealist Text* (1985), and is the coauthor of a forthcoming book on Derrida and Film.